REGIONAL PRIVATE LAWS
AND CODIFICATION
IN EUROPE

Edited by
HECTOR L. MacQUEEN
ANTONI VAQUER
SANTIAGO ESPIAU ESPIAU

CAMBRIDGE
UNIVERSITY PRESS

PUBLISHED BY THE PRESS SYNDICATE OF THE UNIVERSITY OF CAMBRIDGE
The Pitt Building, Trumpington Street, Cambridge, United Kingdom

CAMBRIDGE UNIVERSITY PRESS
The Edinburgh Building, Cambridge, CB2 2RU, UK
40 West 20th Street, New York, NY 10011–4211, USA
477 Williamstown Road, Port Melbourne, VIC 3207, Australia
Ruiz de Alarcón 13, 28014 Madrid, Spain
Dock House, The Waterfront, Cape Town 8001, South Africa

http://www.cambridge.org

First published 2003

Printed in the United Kingdom at the University Press, Cambridge

Typeface Adobe Minion 10.5/13.5 pt.   *System* LaTeX 2$_\varepsilon$ [TB]

A catalogue record for this book is available from the British Library

Library of Congress Cataloguing-in-Publication Data
Regional private laws and codification in Europe / edited by Hector L. MacQueen,
Antoni Vaquer, Santiago Espiau Espiau.
p.   cm.
Includes index.
ISBN 0-521-82836-8
1. Civil law – Europe.   2. Civil law – Europe – Codification.   I. MacQueen, Hector L.
II. Vaquer i Aloy, Antoni.   III. Espiau Espiau, Santiago.
KJC985.R44   2003
346.4 – dc21   2003043809

ISBN 0 521 82836 8 hardback

CONTENTS

v

CONTRIBUTORS

Esther Arroyo i Amayuelas, Department of Civil Law, Universitat de Barcelona, Catalonia, Spain.

Ferran Badosa Coll, Professor of Civil Law, Universitat de Barcelona, Catalonia, Spain.

David L. Carey Miller, Professor of Private Law, University of Aberdeen, Scotland.

Eric Clive, Professor of Law, University of Edinburgh, Scotland.

Eugenia Dacoronia, Lecturer in Civil Law, University of Athens.

Santiago Espiau Espiau, Professor of Civil Law, Universitat de Lleida, Catalonia, Spain.

Núria de Gispert i Català, *Consellera* (Minister) of Justice of the Government of Catalonia.

Shael Herman, Judge John Minor Wisdom Professor of Civil Law, Tulane Law School, New Orleans, Louisiana; Associate Professor, University of Paris I (Pantheon-Sorbonne).

Martin Käerdi, Adviser to the Ministry of Justice, Republic of Estonia.

Hector L. MacQueen, Professor of Private Law, University of Edinburgh, Scotland.

Claude Masse, Professor of Law, Université du Québec à Montréal, Quebec.

Antoni Vaquer, Professor of Civil Law, Universitat de Lleida, Catalonia, Spain.

Niall R. Whitty, Professor of Law, University of Edinburgh, Scotland.

Reinhard Zimmermann, Director of the Max Planck Institute, Hamburg, Germany.

ACKNOWLEDGEMENTS

The conference and the translation into English of some of the papers has been supported by the government of Catalonia (Departments of Justice and Research and Universities), the Diputació de Lleida, the City Hall of Lleida, the University of Lleida, Caixaterrassa, the College of Advocates of Lleida and the Centre d'Estudis Canadencs. The editors wish to express their gratitude to all of them.

ABBREVIATIONS

ABGB   Allgemeinen bürgerlichen Gesetzbuch (Austrian General
           Civil Code)
AC   Appeal Cases (House of Lords, England)
AcP   *Archiv für die civilistische Praxis*
ADC   *Anuario de Derecho Civil*
AJCL   *American Journal of Comparative Law*
All ER   All England Law Reports
AnfG   Anfechtungsgesetz (Germany)
AnfO   Anfechtungsordnung (Austria)
BCC   Baltic Civil Code
BGB   Bürgerliches Gesetzbuch (German Civil Code)
BNA   British Nationality Act 1981
BOE   *Boletín Oficial del Estado*
BW   Burgerlijk Wetboek (Dutch Civil Code)
C.   Code of Justinian
CC   code civil (French Civil Code)
CCQ   code civil Quebec
C. de D.   *Cahiers de droit*
CDCC   Compilació del dret civil de Catalunya
CE   Spanish constitution
CEELI   Committee on East European Legal Initiatives
CISG   Vienna Convention on the International Sales of
           Goods (1980)
CJEL   *Columbia Journal of European Law*
CLJ   *Cambridge Law Journal*
CP du N   *Cours de perfectionnement du Notariat*
CYADC   Constitutions y Altres Drets de Catalunya
D.   Digest of Justinian
DLR   Dominion Law Reports (Canada)

ECR	European Court Reports
EEN	*Ephimeris Ellinon Nomikon*
ELR	*Edinburgh Law Review*
ERPL	*European Review of Private Law*
GCC	Greek Civil Code
ICLQ	*International and Comparative Law Quarterly*
Inst.	Institutes
IO	Insolvenzordnung (Germany)
JBl	*Juristische Blätter*
JhJb	*Jherings Jahrbücher für die Dogmatik des bürgerlichen Rechts*
JLH	*Journal of Legal History*
JLSS	*Journal of the Law Society of Scotland*
Jur. Rev.	*Juridical Review*
JuS	*Juristische Schulung*
JZ	*Juristenzeitung*
KO	Konkursordnung (Germany)
KritE	*Kritiki Epitheorissi*
LHR	*Law and History Review*
LQR	*Law Quarterly Review*
LTIT	Llei de la Tutela Institucions Tutelats (Catalan Act on Guardianship, abrogated)
NAFTA	North American Free Trade Agreement
NBW	Nieuw Burgerlijk Wetboek (New Dutch Civil Code)
NoV	*Nomiko Vima*
OJ	Official Journal of the European Communities
OJLS	*Oxford Journal of Legal Studies*
OR	Obligationenrecht (Swiss Code of Obligations)
PECL	Principles of European Contract Law
PrALR	Prussian Allgemeiner Landrecht
QB	Queen's Bench Law Reports (England)
RabelsZ	*Rabels Zeitschrift für ausländisches und internationales Privatrecht*
R. du B.	*Revue du barreau*
RDC	*Rivista di Diritto Civile*
RDP	*Revista de Derecho Privado*
RGD	*Revue générale due droit, de la législation et de jurisprudence en France et à l'étranger*
RGLJ	Revista General de Legislación y Jurisprudencia

RHDI	*Revue hellénique de droit international*
RIDA	*Revue internationale de droit d'antiquité*
RIDC	*Revue internationale de droit comparé*
RJC	*Revista Jurídica de Catalunya*
RJPIC	*Revue juridique et politique de l'indépendance et de la coopération*
RTDC	*Revue trimestrielle de droit civil*
SALJ	*South African Law Journal*
SALR	*South African Law Reports*
SC	Session Cases (Scotland)
SCCR	Scottish Criminal Case Reports
SC (HL)	Session Cases (House of Lords section) (Scotland)
SCLR	Scottish Civil Law Reports
SCR	Supreme Court Reports (Canada)
SLPQ	*Scottish Law and Practice Quarterly*
SLT	Scots Law Times
SME	*Stair Memorial Encyclopaedia*
SSL	*Scandinavian Studies in Law*
THRHR	*Tydskrif vir Hedendaagse Romeins-Hollandse Reg*
TR	*Tijdschrift voor Rechtsgeschiednis*
TSAR	*Tydskrif fir die Suid-Afrikaanse Reg*
Unidroit	International Institute for the Unification of Private Law
UPLR	*University of Pennsylvania Law Review*
WLR	Weekly Law Reports (England)
ZEUP	*Zeitschrift für Europäisches Privatrecht*
ZNR	*Zeitschrift für neuere Rechtsgeschichte*
ZSS	*Zeitschrift der Savigny-Stiftung für Rechtsgeschichte, Germanistische/Romanistische Abteilung*
ZvglRWiss	*Zeitschrift für vergleichende Rechtswissenschaft*

Introduction

HECTOR L. MacQUEEN, ANTONI VAQUER AND
SANTIAGO ESPIAU ESPIAU

This book consists of revised versions of the papers presented at a conference
held in the Universitat de Lleida, Catalonia, on 27–29 April 2000. Scholars
from all over the world came together to discuss a seemingly diverse range
of topics linked by three key concepts: (1) European private law; (2) regional
private law; and (3) codification of law. The purpose of this introduction
is to show how these concepts draw together, and why their interaction
is important at this juncture in the development of Europe as a cultural,
political and juridical entity.

European private law: the new *ius commune*

The idea of European private law has been central to much legal scholarship
at the end of the twentieth and the beginning of the twenty-first centuries.
It has been driven by at least three distinct engines: (1) the European Union;
(2) the findings of comparative law; (3) the history of law in Europe, in particular the medieval and early modern concept of a European *ius commune*,
based upon the learned Roman Civil Law and the Canon Law of the Roman
Church.

In practical terms, the most important of these engines for the idea
of a European private law has been the development of what is now the
European Union, linking together for political, economic and social purposes an increasing number of the states of western Europe, and doing so
by means, among other things, of law and legal instruments. The bitterly
contested modern arguments about the nature and future development of
the Union should not obscure its birth in the literally smouldering ruins in
which Europe was left by the experiences of the First and, in particular, the
Second World Wars, and the deeply rooted desire of all civilised Europeans

1

that further recurrence of such horrors should be prevented by the creation of indissoluble bonds working initially through the mechanisms of trade and extending later in other directions.

From the start, the project of European union has used laws as a means towards its ends, whether through the creation of its own legal structures and rules or by way of the harmonisation of the laws of the member states. Increasingly (and inevitably) that activity in law has entered upon the sphere of private and commercial legal relations. As a result, in some fields (an example might be intellectual property) it has become less and less the case within member states that the law is seen as domestic other than in form (i.e. it continues to be based upon national legislation albeit following upon a European directive or other instrument) or in enforcement (i.e. litigation takes place rather more in national than in European courts).

Thus it is already possible to observe as a matter of fact (and law) the growth of European private law;[1] but the growth is neither universal nor systematic. Rather it has been haphazard and piecemeal, dependent upon the identification of areas crucial to the project of union and upon which the political agreement of member states is achievable within the relatively short time-frames provided by political and economic agenda. Typical examples to which reference is often made in this book are the Product Liability Directive,[2] affecting part of the law of delict or tort, and, in the field of contract, the Unfair Terms and Consumer Guarantees Directives.[3] All of these are linked by policies favouring consumer protection, and they have been enacted, by and large, without consideration of how they might fit into a larger whole of even the national laws of delict and contract, never mind any possible or actual Europe-wide principles and rules.[4] Some of these difficulties were however recognised by the European Commission in July 2001 when it issued a Communication to the Council and the European Parliament on European contract law,[5] seeking views on whether problems

---

[1] See e.g. N. Lipari, *Diritto Privato Europeo* (Padua, 1997); C. Quigley, *European Community Contract Law* (London, 1997).

[2] Council Directive 85/374/EEC, OJ 1985 L210/29.

[3] Council Directive 93/13/EEC, OJ 1993 L95/29; Parliament and Council Directive 99/44/EC, OJ 1999 L171/12.

[4] A convenient collection of the legislative texts affecting the development of European private law may be found in U. Magnus (ed.), *European Law of Obligations: Regulations and Directives* (Munich, 2002) (texts in German, English and French).

[5] COM(2001) 398 final. See further the website http://europa.eu.int/comm/off/green/index_en. htm.

result from divergences in contract law between member states; and whether the proper functioning of the internal market might be hindered by problems in relation to the conclusion, interpretation and application of cross-border contracts. The Commission was also interested in whether different national contract laws discourage or increase the costs of cross-border transactions. If concrete problems were identified, the Commission also wanted views on possible solutions, such as

- leaving it to the market;
- promotion of the development of non-binding contract law principles such as the Principles of European Contract Law;[6]
- review and improvement of existing EC legislation in the area to make it more coherent and/or adaptable;
- adoption of a European contract code at EC level.

A further factor pointing in the direction of a European private law and closely linked to the development of the European Union is profound political and social change – revolution, indeed – in eastern Europe. The collapse of the Iron Curtain in 1989 and of the Soviet Union in 1991 brought to an end another division of Europe that was the product of its century of wars. The end of Communist economic systems in the east entailed the introduction of legal regimes there to provide the framework and support required for the establishment and maintenance of market economies, and also pointed to the expansion of the hitherto entirely western European Union. Moreover, it was not enough for the eastern European countries simply to adopt the Union's legislative framework and to follow that as it developed; the whole structure of private and commercial law, which the west had been able to take as essentially a given, needed to be absorbed in both form and substance. A necessary preliminary was, of course, the identification and formulation of that substance.

The second engine driving the idea of a European private law has been comparative law. Comparison of legal systems one with another has long been justified by pursuit of the unification of law and a search for the 'best' or the 'ideal' rules to prevail in any such unified law. As long ago as the 1920s the establishment of Unidroit, shorthand for the International Institute for the Unification of Private Law, gave formal backing to these goals, and it has manifested itself also in the achievements of numerous

---

[6] See further below, text at nn. 11–15.

international conventions embodying substantive rules bearing upon private and commercial relations, in particular where these necessarily involve cross-border transactions or persons from different national jurisdictions. For the purposes of this collection the most important recent example of such an instrument is the 1980 Vienna Convention on the International Sale of Goods (the Vienna Convention or CISG), which establishes a system of rules to govern such transactions that has now been adopted by over fifty countries (although not yet the UK). Unidroit has also been responsible for such informal documents as the Principles of International Commercial Contracts, published in 1994 as an elaboration of the general contractual rules contained in the CISG and available as 'soft law' for use particularly in international arbitrations.

That the results of comparative law might go further than transnational situations perhaps began to emerge from the view that the true basis of comparison between legal systems did not lie in their concepts and structures but rather in the functions performed and the social needs met by these concepts and structures. From such an approach there could emerge hitherto underlying unities in the seemingly diverse laws and legal systems of the modern world.[7] In the European context, the importance of this lay in opening up possibilities of reconciliation between the two major legal traditions in Europe: the Continental Civil Law and the English Common Law, whose contrasts in substance and method appeared to be otherwise unbridgeable, and so to present a major obstacle to any progress in the harmonisation and unification of private law in Europe.

Such divergence, to say nothing of any underlying unities, might also be explained by legal history, the third engine in the idea of European private law. Comparative study showed the historical connections between systems, much of which lay ultimately in the learned laws of Rome and the Church as expounded from the Middle Ages on in the universities of Europe. History also suggested that such supranational, essentially academic law – the *ius commune* – could exist in fruitful if variable interaction with the more restricted *iura propria* of specific territories, even in England.[8] As a law

---

[7] See generally K. Zweigert and H. Kötz, *Introduction to Comparative Law*, trans. T. Weir, 3rd edn (Oxford, 1998), chs. 1–4.

[8] Classic studies now available in English include F. Wieacker, *A History of Private Law in Europe*, trans. T. Weir (Oxford, 1995); O. F. Robinson, T. D. Fergus and W. M. Gordon, *Introduction to European Legal History*, 3rd edn (London, Edinburgh, Dublin, 1999); R. C. van Caenegem, *An Historical Introduction to Private Law* (Cambridge, 1992); M. Bellomo (trans. L. G. Cochrane),

created and sustained by scholarly study and publication, it also provided a model by which a modern renewal of the *ius commune* might be achieved.[9] So there have emerged over the last twenty years a number of academic projects with the goal of contribution, in various ways, to the creation and recognition of a new *ius commune*, or a European private law.[10] It is important to note that many of these projects involved or involve the substantial participation of all the European legal traditions, including those of the Common Law and of Scotland.

Perhaps the longest sustained and furthest advanced is the Principles of European Contract Law produced by the Commission for European Contract Law, a private group of mainly academic lawyers headed by Professor Ole Lando. Each jurisdiction within the European Union, including Scotland, was represented on the group.[11] The Lando Commission began work in the early 1980s, with the objective of producing a code or restatement of contract law for use within what was then the European Community. The Commission took a comparative approach, seeking to identify the goals of contract law and to find rules that would best express the results of this work. The American restatement model was important for the Lando Principles, involving the production, not only of a text of rules, but also of a commentary thereupon alongside notes of the state laws from which the text has been derived.[12] The goals of the project have now been largely achieved, with the publication of part I in 1995[13] and part II in 1999;[14] the third and final part appeared in 2003.[15]

The Common Legal Past of Europe 1100–1800 (Washington, D.C., 1995). Note also the series of publications, Comparative Studies in Continental and Anglo-American Legal History, sponsored by the Gerda Henkel Stiftung, in which a comparative approach to legal history has produced some interesting results.

[9] See most recently R. Zimmermann, *Roman Law, Contemporary Law, European Law: The Civilian Tradition Today* (Oxford, 2001), ch. 3.

[10] In addition to the specific projects discussed below, note the establishment in the 1990s of at least two journals dedicated to the development of European private law: *European Review of Private Law* and *Zeitschrift für Europäisches Privatrecht*.

[11] One of the authors became the Scottish representative on the group in 1995.

[12] See the interesting discussion by M. Hesselink in M. Hesselink and G. J. P. de Vries, *Principles of European Contract Law* (Dordrecht, 2001), pp. 12–32.

[13] O. Lando and H. Beale (eds.), *Principles of European Contract Law Part I: Performance and Non-Performance* (Dordrecht, 1995).

[14] O. Lando and H. Beale (eds.), *Principles of European Contract Law Parts I and II* (Dordrecht, 1999).

[15] O. Lando, E. Clive, A. Prum and R. Zimmermann (eds.), *Principles of European Contract Law Part III* (Dordrecht, 2003). The final meeting of the Lando group was held in Copenhagen

While the end product of the Lando Commission is unquestionably academic in nature, it is intended to influence law reform at national and European Union levels and also to be available as a potential legal basis for international contracts and arbitrations in commercial disputes.[16] A rival product on contract law is the work of a group headed by Professor Giuseppe Gandolfi of Pavia, which was published in 2000[17] and is based upon the Italian Civil Code and the Code of Contract Law drafted in the late 1960s by Harvey McGregor QC for the English and Scottish Law Commissions.[18] We will return to the significance of the latter document for European private law later in this introduction. But it should be noted that the existence of these privately produced Principles of the Lando and Gandolfi groups was a powerful factor underlying the European Commission's Green Paper of 2001 on European contract law.[19]

The codal or restatement method of the Lando and Gandolfi groups has had its followers in other areas of private law, most notably, perhaps, in the law of trusts,[20] although none have so fully worked out their results. But as the work of the Lando Commission has drawn to a close, it has given birth to an even larger new project, the Study Group towards a European Civil Code, which began work in 1999.[21] Following methods in essence the same as those of the Lando project, but involving several groups based in various European centres, the project incorporates work upon delict (tort), unjustified enrichment, *negotiorum gestio*, securities, sale of goods and contracts for services. It may go on to include projects on transfer of property, trusts and insurance. So far as contract is concerned, the results

---

in February 2001. The project has a website: http://www.cbs.dk/departments/law/staff/ ol/commission_on_ecl/index.html. The Principles are referred to by the House of Lords when searching for the meaning of good faith in the Unfair Terms Directive in *Director General of Fair Trading* v. *First National Bank plc* [2002] 1 AC 481.

[16] Compare in this regard the Unidroit *Principles of International Commercial Contracts* (Rome, 1994), another set of rules created by an essentially academic group working collaboratively and comparatively over a period of years and starting on the basis of the CISG. Further work is now taking place to extend the Unidroit Principles.

[17] G. Gandolfi (ed.), *Code européen des contrats: livre premier* (Pavia, 2001).

[18] H. McGregor, *Contract Code Drawn up on Behalf of the English Law Commission* (Milan, 1993).

[19] See above, text at n. 5.

[20] See D. J. Hayton, S. C. J. J. Kortmann and H. L. E. Verhagen (eds.), *Principles of European Trust Law* (The Hague, 1999); discussed in (2000) 8(3) *European Review of Private Law* (a special issue entitled 'Trusts in Mixed Legal Systems: A Challenge to Comparative Law') and reprinted as J. M. Milo and J. M. Smits (eds.), *Trusts in Mixed Legal Systems* (Nijmegen, 2001).

[21] See the Study Group's website, http://www.sgecc.net.

of the Lando Commission are a given, albeit subject to such modification as the realisation of the new overall project may require. The ambitions of the civil code groups are high: ultimately, coverage of most of the core areas of private law and, probably in the very long term, enactment as positive law in the European Union or the basis for such an enactment should the political will exist to go that far with European unification. Heart has been taken from the repeated call of the European Parliament for the production of a European civil code,[22] and from the Commission Green Paper on a European contract law, published in 2001.[23]

Rather different in method and output from the work of the Lando, Gandolfi and European civil code groups is the treatise on European contract law being produced by the German scholars Hein Kötz and Axel Flessner.[24] They argue that all that is needed to constitute European private law is its recognition and to teach it to the lawyers of the future, rather in the manner of the medieval universities and the original *ius commune*. Their text on European contract law, which is to be the basis for such teaching, proceeds by identifying principles and institutions common to the European legal systems and expounding them as a system in the manner of an introductory (although by no means elementary) textbook.

Even more ambitious is Christian von Bar's *Gemeineuropäisches Deliktsrecht*,[25] in which each national law of tort in Europe is seen as 'merely a national manifestation of a single discipline...it is therefore possible to condense different national laws to a *common* European law of torts, or delict'. 'To think in a European fashion', continues von Bar, 'means first to stress the common characteristics, secondly to understand national laws as reactions to developments in neighbouring countries, and thirdly, to tackle historical coincidences and rough edges, which, in view of the process of

---

[22] Resolution of 26 May 1989, OJ 1989 C158/401; repeated 6 May 1994, OJ 1994 C205/518. See also A. Hartkamp et al. (eds.), *Towards a European Civil Code*, 1st edn (Nijmegen, 1994), 2nd edn (Nijmegen, 1998); a 3rd edn is forthcoming; note further G. Barrett and L. Bernardeau (eds.), *Towards a European Civil Code: Reflections on the Codification of Civil Law in Europe* (Trier, 2002).

[23] See above, n. 5.

[24] H. Kötz, *Europäisches Vertragsrecht I* (Tübingen, 1996), trans. T. Weir as *European Contract Law Volume One: Formation, Validity, and Content of Contracts; Contract and Third Parties* (Oxford, 1997). Flessner is writing the second part dealing with the remainder of contract law.

[25] 2 vols. (Munich, 1996); published in English translation as *The Common European Law of Torts*, vol. I (Oxford, 1998) and vol. II (Oxford, 2000), trans. Christian von Bar. References below are to the latter version. The book is referred to by the House of Lords on issues of causation in *Fairchild v. Glenhaven Funeral Services Ltd* [2003] 1 AC 32.

European unification, can be ground down without substantial loss.'[26]
Where Kötz and Flessner focus mainly on the major legal systems of western
Europe – Germany, France and England – von Bar draws upon all sixteen
jurisdictions in the European Union, and his work goes well beyond the
scope of a textbook, being at the very least a major comparative analysis
and work of research and scholarship.

Other projects have also gone forward on the basis that European private
law will emerge and develop through university instruction and research,
picking up that characteristic product of the case method of the law schools
of the United States of America, the casebook. The year 2000 saw the publication of the first output of the Common Law of Europe Casebook series,
*Cases, Materials and Text on National, Supranational and International Tort
Law*, edited by Walter van Gerven, Jeremy Lever and Pierre Larouche. Like
von Bar, the editors aim 'to uncover common roots, notwithstanding differences in approach, of the European legal systems with a view to strengthening the common legal heritage of Europe'. They 'hope that the book will be
used as teaching material in universities and other institutions throughout
Europe and elsewhere in order to familiarize future generations of lawyers
with each other's legal systems and to assess and facilitate the impact of
European supranational legal systems on the development of national laws,
and *vice versa*'. But they deny an intention 'to unify the existing laws of
tort . . . that would not be possible, nor would it be desirable'.[27] This is echoed
by the editors of the second volume in the series to appear, *Cases, Materials
and Text on Contract Law*, which was published in 2002,[28] but they do make
use of the Principles of European Contract Law and the Unidroit Principles
of International Commercial Contracts as a basis for what is covered and
as a point of comparison with the national material surveyed (itself limited
to England, France and Germany). Further casebooks in preparation for
the series include one on unjustified enrichment,[29] and it will also move
into the domain of public law with a collection about judicial review of
administrative action.[30]

---

[26] Both quotations von Bar, *Common European Law of Torts*, vol. I, p. xxiii.
[27] (Oxford, 2000). Both quotations at introduction, p. v.
[28] H. Beale, A. Hartkamp, H. Kötz and D. Tallon (eds.), *Cases, Materials and Text on Contract Law* (Oxford, 2002), p. v.
[29] To be edited by E. J. H. Schrage (Amsterdam) and J. Beatson (Cambridge).
[30] The project website is http://www.rechten.unimaas.nl/casebook. The tort casebook is referred to by the House of Lords on issues of causation in *Fairchild* v. *Glenhaven Funeral Services Ltd* [2003] 1 AC 32. An earlier partial release of the tort casebook, published in 1998, is also referred to in *McFarlane* v. *Tayside Health Board* 2000 SC (HL) 1 (damages for birth of a child).

Finally, yet another grand project towards a European private law, the Common Core of European Private Law, led by Mauro Bassani of Trento and Ugo Mattei of Torino and Hastings, combines the approaches of searching for the common ground between systems and considering particular cases. In this instance, however, the cases are hypothetical ones, not actual decisions of the courts, and the methodology is to consider how they would be resolved in each national system (again including England and Scotland).[31] It might be called an inductive, Common Law, method of approaching European legal unity, as distinct from the more deductive codal or scholastic methods of the other projects mentioned above. The first publication, *Good Faith in European Contract Law*, edited by Reinhard Zimmermann and Simon Whittaker,[32] exemplifies the approach and shows two-thirds of the cases producing at least some harmony of result if not of analysis or technique, since several of the legal systems studied do not give overt or extensive recognition to a general and active concept of good faith. The book thus reasserts the classic comparative law notion of the functional unity of law, although it contains no prescription as to what a European law of good faith might look like or do. The second publication in the series is *The Enforceability of Promises in European Contract Law*, edited by James Gordley, which appeared in 2001. This examines a number of specific cases and argues that 'the results that different legal systems reach...can most often be explained as responses to common underlying problems'.[33] The book concludes by asking 'what is the most straightforward way to address the problems', meaning by this the solution 'that comes the closest to giving the right result – the one that resolves the problem – in the largest number of cases'.[34] So it comes rather closer to offering a prescriptive model of the ideal rule, but notes that this may not give rise to the most practical rule: 'One might be better off with a rule that gives the wrong answer more of the time but is clearer and simpler.'[35] The ideal rule may, however, provide a benchmark for how often the clearer, simpler rule goes wrong.

It would be wrong to conclude this discussion of European private law without observing that the whole idea has been the subject of profound criticism, most vigorously maintained by Professor Pierre Legrand.[36] In particular, Professor Legrand has attacked the whole idea of unifying, harmonising

---

[31] The project has a website: http://www.jus.unitn.it/dsg/common-core.
[32] (Cambridge, 2000).   [33] (Cambridge, 2001), p. 378.   [34] Ibid., p. 379.   [35] Ibid.
[36] See, e.g., his 'European Legal Systems are not Converging', (1996) 45 *International and Comparative Law Quarterly* 52; 'Against a European Civil Code', (1997) 60 *Modern Law Review* 45; 'Are Civilians Educable?' (1998) 18 *Legal Studies* 216.

or converging law in Europe, the deep flaw in such projects being their failure to take account of the deeper cultural and social reasons why laws are
different from each other. As he has put it with characteristic understate-
ment in a book review, 'these epitomes all desert serious thought for earnest
prostration before the instrumentalist sabotage of cognition'.[37] The division between the Common Law and the Civil Law *mentalités* is much more
profoundly rooted than mere technical distinctions of black-letter law, and
these intellectual differences far outweigh any functional unities that may
be perceived. The true general picture of law in Europe remains one of diversity and 'plurijurality'[38] which cannot be overcome by either bureaucratic
or academic means, and all attempts to do so are doomed to failure. Such
arguments appear to be of particular relevance to this work, concerned as it
is to analyse the links, possible and actual, between European and regional
developments in private law.

A Scots lawyer might begin a response to Legrand's arguments by asking
whether the existence of 'mixed' systems of law such as those of Scotland
does not at least raise questions about the supposed incompatibility of the
Civil Law and the Common Law. It might also be asked whether the proliferation of European projects does not suggest the existence of an increasingly
powerful third *mentalité* in Europe, strongly supported, consciously or not,
by the growth of European and, indeed, global legal practice impatient of
national and merely doctrinal differences. The differences and divisions
which Legrand sees as apparently unalterably fixed are essentially historical; but examination of what is happening now suggests that for some at
least change is under way and needs to be taken further.

The most interesting response to Legrand is by Jan Smits of Maastricht.[39]
He too is concerned by the loss of diversity involved in the Europeanisation of law, but is nonetheless in favour of this as an ultimate objective.
But it must be a natural development, one which responds to the growth
and actual needs of the single market as determined from and by experience in the market-place. Smits does not think, therefore, that the high
road to European legal unity will be best achieved by legislative or restatement vehicles, but will be better traversed by what he calls 'non-centralist'

---

[37] [1999] *Cambridge Law Journal* 439 at 441 (reviewing a release of part of the van Gerven tort
casebook referred to above, n. 27).
[38] For this coinage, see [1999] *CLJ* 442.
[39] See J. Smits, *The Making of European Private Law: Towards a Ius Commune Europaeum as a
Mixed Legal System*, trans. N. Kornet (Antwerp, 2002).

means, principally the willingness of national courts to borrow rules and solutions from other legal systems. He sees mixed legal systems as already embodying this approach, and argues that the increasing use by the highest English courts of insights from comparative law is another illustration of its merits. Further, this is an approach which never ends: unification is more of an ideal always just beyond reach, allowing for continuous further evolution and flexibility of response to changing social and economic conditions.

Smits' arguments are interesting and attractive in many ways. But it may be argued that there is room for the legislative/restatement approach of the Lando Commission and similar bodies as well as the gradualist evolutionary one. For many involved in such projects, it is rather important that the principles being developed are currently 'soft law', coming into effect only when chosen by contracting parties or when invoked in international commercial arbitrations. Their success is thus dependent upon acceptability in the market-place. They add to, rather than detract from, diversity; at the same time, where that diversity is an impediment to cross-border activity in particular, they point the way forward to solutions.

The point about cross-border activity can be taken further. National law is seldom at its happiest in dealing with such matters unless it can pretend that the whole transaction is an entirely domestic one. This is becoming less and less possible. It is commonplace, but nonetheless true, that we live increasingly in a European, a global economy, and that we transact, both commercially and privately, across national frontiers. The Internet is extending the possibility of such transactions dramatically. The E-Commerce Directive of 2000[40] seems to show the need for a common contract law to deal with this. Its artt. 9–11 tell us a great deal about procedures to be followed by those supplying goods and services across the Internet, but the consumer will know nothing from these texts about when she is entitled to hold the supplier to obligations of delivery.[41] It will not please her to be told that it depends on which law of contract applies to the transaction, or

[40] Parliament and Council Directive 2000/31/EC, OJ 2000 L178/1.

[41] There have been at least two recent cases in the UK where this was an issue. In September 1999 the Argos webpage mistakenly advertised at a price of £3 TVs normally selling at £399 and received a rush of orders. Argos refused to deliver and at least one customer was said to be willing to sue for breach of contract. This however seems to have come to nothing. In January 2002 Kodak's UK website advertised at £100 a digital camera normally retailing at £330. Over 5,000 orders were placed and after a dispute Kodak finally agreed to deliver the cameras.

that she will have to wait and see which of the various solutions offered by the national courts of Europe is deemed to be the best by the court in which her case is brought. How much better if there was a clear answer now, or at any rate a set of clearly stated principles by the application of which an answer could be reached.

Regional private law

Against a background of the European Union and a European private law, regional private law could easily be taken to mean simply the laws of the member states of the Union; but, at least for the purposes of this volume, what we have had principally in mind is regions within member states, as exemplified in particular by Catalonia in Spain and Scotland in the United Kingdom. There are, of course, other regions within both states, notably England in the case of the United Kingdom; but in that particular case, the region in question in fact provides the dominant legal culture within the member state, since in a sense it is true to say that there is no UK or British law, and English law is by far the largest system within the state. In Spain, by contrast, there is a general Spanish law coexisting with the laws of the autonomous regions such as Catalonia, Navarre, the Balearic islands, the Basque country, Aragon and Galicia.

We have extended the idea of regional private law somewhat for comparative purposes, by bringing also into consideration the private laws of states that exist within larger federal states, namely Louisiana in the United States and Quebec in Canada. Finally we have gone even further by adding in the position of small states within the European Union, the capacity of which to influence the content of any European private law may be relatively slight (Greece), as well as new eastern European states from without the Union, which seek admission in the future and are in the process of creating or re-creating their own private law (Estonia).

There are other, comparative law, reasons for bringing Louisiana and Quebec within the scope of our discussion: both have strong legal–cultural links with Europe which are somewhat out of tune with the general legal culture of the federations to which they belong; and in both can be found the combination of a basically Civil Law code of private law coupled with a Common Law judicial system and approach to commercial law in particular. Louisiana and Quebec are thus both examples of what comparative lawyers call 'mixed' legal systems, drawing together the supposedly incompatible Civil and Common Laws,[42] and they can be appropriately considered alongside Europe's only mixed system, Scotland, as possible models for the inevitably mixed system of European private law.[43] Indeed, they may be more comfortable models from a Continental perspective than Scotland, because they are more readily accessible and comparable codified systems, unlike Scots law, the Common Law characteristics of which for much of private law include, rather than a code, reliance upon a wealth of judicial decisions, the analysis of which is frequently contestable and as a result often contested. We will return to this point below in the discussion of codification. But in the meantime it may be noted that one of the reasons why the McGregor Contract Code was taken up in the 1990s by the Gandolfi contract project briefly described earlier on in this introduction was simply because its codal form made it accessible as well as because it was a mixed system drawing upon Scots and English law.

But there are more fundamental reasons still for highlighting the position of Catalonia and Scotland in relation to the European Union and European private law. As already mentioned, both are parts of a member state of the European Union, an organisation that works towards an ever closer union of its members, as well as increasing power and significance for its institutions in relation to those of the member states. Yet within Spain even before she became a member state, and within the United Kingdom since the election of the Labour government in 1997, processes have been under way for the devolution of legislative and political power away from the centre of the state to the regions which go to make it up. Indeed, Spain's variable and 'rolling' devolution has provided a model, at least in general terms, for what is happening in the United Kingdom.

Despite the European Union's recognition since the Treaty of Maastricht in 1991 of the principle of 'subsidiarity' (under which decisions are to be taken as closely to the citizen as possible, while in areas outside the Union's exclusive competence it will act only if the objectives in question

---

[42] On this concept, see further E. Örücü, E. Attwooll and S. Coyle (eds.), *Studies in Legal Systems: Mixed and Mixing* (The Hague, 1996); V. Palmer (ed.), *Mixed Jurisdictions Worldwide: The Third Legal Family* (Cambridge, 2001); Smits, *Making of European Private Law*, pp. 107–50; Zimmermann, *Roman Law, Contemporary Law, European Law*, pp. 126 ff. Note also a special issue of the *Juridical Review* in 2002, entitled 'Mixed Systems: Patterns of Development', 2002 Jur. Rev. 61–142.

[43] See H. L. MacQueen, *Scots Law and the Road to the New Ius Commune*, Ius Commune Lectures No. 1 (Amsterdam, 2000); Milo and Smits (eds.), *Trusts in Mixed Legal Systems*; Zimmermann, *Roman Law, Contemporary Law, European Law*, pp. 126–63.

cannot be sufficiently achieved by the member states themselves), there is an inevitable tension between its ideals and the proliferation and localisation of legislative bodies within member states, especially where, as in the cases of Catalonia and Scotland, the process is coloured politically by a history of distinctiveness and independence, not least in law. Quebec, which has already held referendums on the issue of its independence from Canada, is in a similar position, if indeed not already further down the road.

On the other hand, local legislative power is also an opportunity to develop the local law in accordance with modern standards and thinking, and it is not generally the case that devolution is being seen only as a way of preserving or restoring legal distinctiveness or peculiarity for its own sake. Indeed, in Scotland the separatist Scottish National Party has long had as one of its central slogans 'Scotland in Europe', and its goal of independence from the United Kingdom would not mean withdrawal from the European Union in any sense, even if that were possible.[44] Thus work on European private law remains highly relevant in the regional context, as at least a contribution to the processes of development and modernisation that devolution is designed to facilitate and encourage. Much the same can be said of the new states such as Estonia, in which the findings of European private law scholarship may be put into effect as positive law.

A further point following on from the creation of test beds for the operation of European private law models in practice is that, as the findings are tested at local levels, the results can feed back into the further development of the grand scheme. As previously noted, Scots law has already had the opportunity to participate in several of the projects related to European private law, but the same cannot be said of Catalan law or of the laws emerging in the other autonomous regions of Spain. The greater the awareness of European models in these regional developments, whether for or against, the more likely it is that work on European private law will take them into account in return, each strengthening the development of the other.

Finally, as already observed, the existence and proliferation of regional private laws certainly connects with Legrand's arguments about the diversity and plurality of laws existing in Europe (and, indeed, in other parts of the

---

[44] The position of a newly independent Scotland within the European Union is a matter of some debate: R. C. Lane, ' "Scotland in Europe": An Independent Scotland and the European Community', in W. Finnie et al. (eds.), *Edinburgh Essays in Public Law* (Edinburgh, 1991); M. Happold, 'Independence: in or out of Europe? An Independent Scotland and the European Union?' (2000) 49 *International and Comparative Law Quarterly* 15; A. Foyle, 'Scottish Independence and EU Membership: A Foregone Conclusion', 2001 *Jur. Rev.* 177.

world); but their attitude to and relationship with the European private
law projects may tell us something about the *mentalités* which are currently
informing their development in the wider context provided by Europe.
Further, as already noted, the existence of 'mixed' systems of law in Europe
and elsewhere at least raises questions about the supposed incompatibility
of the Civil Law and the Common Law, the answers to which may have
much to contribute to the development of a genuinely flourishing European
private law.[45]

Codification

Until recent times it was commonly said that the era of codification of
law had passed in Europe. Although the most recent of the great European codes, the new Dutch Civil Code, was only finally completed in 1992,
it represented the labour of nearly half a century; and the experience of
other codes suggested a tendency towards ossification or breakdown. But
perspectives have shifted, not least as a result of the fundamental changes
in the political and economic structures of eastern Europe. A change to
the law needed to support a market economy could not be effected by the
inductive, empirical methods of the Common Law, especially where the
judges had no relevant experience or background upon which to draw.
The only way in which a comprehensive and reasonably systematic law
could be established was through the vehicle of a code, reinforced by legal
education and comparative study.[46]

It is doubtful whether the same holds good for either European or regional private law, however, since both cases are building around some
kind of settled tradition and consensus as to what the function and role
of law are. As we have seen, although a central part of European private
law scholarship has involved work towards systems that can be presented in
codal form, other research has focused on alternative ways of identifying a
European private law through what can be seen as in essence Common Law

---

[45] For other critical responses to Legrand's arguments see e.g. J. Smits, 'How to Take the Road
Untravelled? European Private Law in the Making: A Review Essay', (1999) 6 *Maastricht Journal
of European and Comparative Law* 25; V. Zeno-Zencovich, 'The "European Civil Code", European
legal traditions and neo-positivism', (1998) 4 *European Review of Private Law* 349; A. Watson,
Legal Transplants and European Private Law, Ius Commune Lectures No. 2 (Amsterdam, 2000).

[46] See R. Zimmermann, 'Codification: History and Present Significance of an Idea: *A propos* the
Recodification of Private Law in the Czech Republic', (1995) 3 *European Review of Private Law*
95–120.

methods: building up from cases and specific situations, and identifying common principles empirically and inductively rather than from *a priori* concepts. Yet if European private law is ever to become positive law within the European Union, it seems inevitable that it will do so in legislative, and therefore in codal form; and this whether it coexists with or supplants national and regional laws.

So far as regional private law is concerned, codes are a long-established feature of the law of both Louisiana and Quebec: in the case of the former, since 1808, while there has been a code in Quebec since 1866. It is not surprising to find that the development of Catalan law is proceeding largely through the establishment of codes in particular areas such as family law and succession, and that this is seen as an important way of distinguishing Catalan from Spanish law and the código civil of 1889. In Scotland, however, the strength of the Common Law side of legal tradition has ensured that, despite much legislation across the whole of private and, especially, commercial law, codification has not often even arisen as a possibility. But the presence of a Scottish Parliament with legislative competence over the whole of private law creates an opportunity for action, should the political will exist or be created. Moreover, codification would be the principal route by which the mixed Scots law could draw upon, and make a contribution to, the development of European private law.

Thus the process of codification creates an opportunity for fruitful interaction between regional laws and the European private law initiatives discussed earlier in this introduction. Codifying the law in Europe without paying attention to the Lando or the Unidroit Principles makes little sense today.[47] These Principles are not, and will not be in the immediate future, part of any legal system. But the incorporation in new regional civil codes of some of the solutions contained in these restatements will allow their provisions to be tested by the courts and the legal profession. Then regional private laws would find themselves in a really advantageous position on the road to a new European *ius commune*.

---

[47] In Scotland the Scottish Law Commission has paid considerable attention to CISG and to the Lando and Unidroit Principles when bringing forward proposals for the reform of contract law: see Report on Formation of Contract: Scottish Law and the United Nations Convention on Contracts for the International Sale of Goods (Scot. Law Com. No. 144, 1993); Report on Interpretation in Private Law (Scot. Law Com. No. 160, 1997); Report on Penalty Clauses (Scot. Law Com. No 171, 1999); Report on Remedies for Breach of Contract (Scot. Law Com. No. 174, 1999).

Conclusion

This short introduction has sought to show why the material discussed in this wide-ranging collection has importance for the legal future of Europe. It demonstrates that the diversity of law in Europe extends much further than the classical Civil Law–Common Law divide and indeed goes beyond the level of the member states of the European Union. On the other hand, the example of Scotland, along with those of the other 'mixed' legal systems of the world (which include not only Louisiana and Quebec but also South Africa, Israel and Sri Lanka), shows that the great divide of comparative law is perhaps not so wide and unbridgeable as has often been supposed. All the legal systems of Europe are being affected by the harmonisation measures of the European Union, and as a result today their laws are in a state of constant flux and change. Ambitious projects for a more systematic European private law thus trigger local and regional responses, whether in adoption of the results as models, or in providing critical input towards further refinement, development or, perhaps, even rejection. Such interactions, it is suggested, will increasingly inform the development of private law in Europe, and so help to define and elaborate the complex relationship between unity and diversity which the future seems sure to see.

Postscript

After this introduction was completed, the European Commission issued a Communication to the European Parliament and Council entitled 'A More Coherent European Contract Law: An Action Plan', COM(2003) 68 final, 12.2.2003, OJ 2003/C63/01, accessible at http://europa.eu.int/comm/consumers/cons_int/safe_shop/fair_bus_pract/cont_law/index_en.htm. The Communication suggests a mix of non-regulatory and regulatory measures in order to solve the problems identified by its previous work on contract law (see text above accompanying n. 5), including: (1) increasing the coherence of the Community *acquis* in contract law; (2) promoting the elaboration of EU-wide general contract terms; and (3) examining further whether problems in European contract law may require non-sector-specific solutions such as an optional instrument on the subject.

1

The civil law in European codes

REINHARD ZIMMERMANN

The European codes: background and significance

I have been asked to discuss the civil law in European codes. This is not as straightforward a task as it may appear at first glance. We should, at the outset, therefore reflect on the background, scope and significance of the terms used in the title of my chapter. A code, or codification, in the modern technical sense of the word, is a peculiar kind of statute. Like all other statutes, it is enacted by a legislature, and its application is therefore backed by the authority of the state for which that legislature is competent to make laws. Its characteristic features are, firstly, that a codification must aim at being comprehensive. It has to provide a regulation not only for a number of specific issues but has to cover a field of law in its entirety. Secondly, a codification constitutes an attempt to present its subject matter as a logically consistent whole of legal rules and institutions. It provides both the conceptual framework and intellectual fulcrum for any further doctrinal refinement and judicial or legislative development of the law.

Codification, as outlined in these few sentences,[1] is a specific historical phenomenon that originated in late seventeenth- and eighteenth-century

---

An earlier version of this chapter has appeared in David L. Carey Miller and Reinhard Zimmermann (eds.), *The Civilian Tradition and Scots Law: Aberdeen Quincentenary Essays* (Munich and Berlin, 1997), pp. 259 ff.

[1] For a more detailed analysis, see Reinhard Zimmermann, 'Codification: History and Present Significance of an Idea', (1995) 3 *ERPL* 95 ff.; for other assessments, see Pierre Legrand, 'Strange Power of Words: Codification Situated', (1994) 9 *Tulane European and Civil Law Forum* 1 ff.; Pio Caroni, *Lecciones Catalanas sobre la historia de la codificación* (Madrid, 1996); Pio Caroni, *Saggi sulla storia della codificazione* (Milan, 1998); Karel V. Malý and Pio Caroni (eds.), *Kodifikation und Dekodifikation des Privatrechts in der heutigen Rechtsentwicklung* (Prague, 1998); Fábio Siebeneichler de Andrade, *Da codificação* (Porto Alegre, 1997).

legal science.[2] It was an enormously influential idea, that managed, within hardly more than 150 years, to recast the entire legal tradition on the European continent. It was much less successful in England.[3] Hence, for the modern legal mind, European private law and codification have become inseparably linked to each other. In reality, however, there is nothing intrinsically self-evident about that connection. Before the age of codification European private law flourished, for many centuries, as a 'common law'.[4] Moreover, it was ultimately based on Roman law, and Roman law itself was never codified. On the contrary, it was characterised by many features which a modern observer would associate with the English common law rather than the (modern) continental private law.[5]

The two oldest codifications still in force today are the French code civil of 1804 and the Austrian General Civil Code of 1811. They were preceded by the Prussian Code of 1794.[6] All three are usually referred to as the 'natural law codes': their purpose was to put the entire law into systematic order in pursuance of a general plan for society.[7] During the nineteenth century, the idea of codification became intimately linked to the emergence of the modern nation-states.[8] This is particularly obvious in

[2] Cf., e.g., J. H. A. Lokin and W. J. Zwalve, *Hoofdstukken uit de Europese Codificatiegeschiedenis* (Deventer, 1990); Helmut Coing, *Europäisches Privatrecht*, vol. I (Munich, 1985), pp. 67 ff.; Helmut Coing, *Europäisches Privatrecht*, vol. II (Munich, 1989), pp. 7 ff.

[3] Cf., e.g., J. H. Baker, *An Introduction to English Legal History*, 3rd edn (London, 1990), pp. 249 ff.

[4] Cf. Coing, *Europäisches Privatrecht*, vol. I, pp. 34 ff., 124 ff.; Manlio Bellomo, *The Common Legal Past of Europe, 1000–1800* (Washington, D.C., 1995); Antonio Padoa-Schioppa, *Il Diritto nella Storia d'Europa*, vol. I (Padua, 1995); Harold J. Berman and Charles Reid, 'Römisches Recht in Europa und das ius commune', (1995) 3 *ZEUP* 3 ff.; Peter Stein, *Roman Law in European History* (Cambridge, 1999), pp. 38 ff.; Reinhard Zimmermann, 'Roman Law and European Legal Unity', in A. S. Hartkamp, M. W. Hesselink et al. (eds.), *Towards a European Civil Code*, 2nd edn (Nijmegen, The Hague and Boston, 1998), pp. 21 ff.; Raoul van Caenegem, 'The Modernity of Medieval Law', (2000) 8 *European LR* 37 ff.

[5] See Peter Stein, 'Roman Law, Common Law, and Civil Law', (1992) 66 *Tulane LR* 1591 ff.

[6] For an important new assessment, see Andreas Schwennicke, *Die Entstehung der Einleitung des Preußischen Allgemeinen Landrechts von 1794* (Frankfurt am Main, 1993). Cf. also the evaluation by Gerhard Dilcher, 'Die janusköpfige Kodifikation – das Preußische Allgemeine Landrecht (1794) und die europäische Rechtsgeschichte', (1994) 2 *ZEUP* 446 ff.

[7] For a detailed discussion, now available in English, see Franz Wieacker, *A History of Private Law in Europe*, trans. Tony Weir (Oxford, 1995), pp. 257 ff.

[8] Cf., e.g., Franz Wieacker, 'Der Kampf des 19. Jahrhunderts um die Nationalgesetzbücher', in Franz Wieacker, *Industriegesellschaft und Privatrechtsordnung* (Frankfurt am Main, 1974), pp. 79 ff.; Reiner Schulze, 'Vom ius commune zum Gemeinschaftsrecht', in Reiner Schulze (ed.), *Europäische Rechts- und Verfassungsgeschichte* (Berlin, 1991), pp. 18 ff.

Germany,[9] where the preparation of a German civil code immediately became a matter of great – practical as well as symbolic – significance in the
years after the creation of the German Reich. By the time the German Civil
Code (Bürgerliches Gesetzbuch) came into effect (1 January 1900), just
about all the other states of central, southern and eastern Europe had codified their private law.[10] In most instances, the French code civil provided the
main source of inspiration. It continued to apply in Belgium and became
the basis of the Dutch Burgerlijk Wetboek of 1838. It provided the point of
departure for the Italian codice civile of 1865 (which could thus be enacted
a mere four years after the kingdom of Italy had come into being), for the
Portuguese código civil of 1867, the Spanish código civil of 1888/9 and the
Romanian Civil Code of 1865. The Serbian Civil Code of 1844, on the other
hand, was influenced mainly by the Austrian codification.

The enactment of the German Civil Code, in turn, stimulated a revision
of the Austrian Code (which took effect in three stages during the years of the
First World War[11]) and it prompted the Greeks to codify their law; the Greek
Civil Code, promulgated in 1940 but effective only from 1946, is generally
considered to be part of the German legal family. Another member of that
family is Switzerland, although both its Civil Code of 1907 and its revised
Code concerning the law of obligations of 1911 are in certain respects highly
original and cannot be said to be modelled on the German Code.[12] The
Swiss experiences influenced the draftsmen of the new Italian Civil Code of
1942 without, however, inducing them to break radically with the French
tradition.[13] A wholesale reception of the Swiss Codes occurred in Turkey.

[9] See Wieacker, *A History of Private Law*, pp. 363 ff.; Michael John, *Politics and Law in Late Nineteenth-Century Germany* (Oxford, 1989); and see the contributions to the special volume of Staudinger's *Kommentar zum Bürgerlichen Gesetzbuch* entitled *100 Jahre BGB: 100 Jahre Staudinger*, ed. Michael Martinek and Patrick L. Sellier (Munich and Berlin, 1999).

[10] For a general overview, see Carlos Bollen and Gerard-René de Groot, 'The Sources and Back-grounds of European Legal Systems', in Hartkamp et al. (eds.), *Towards a European Civil Code*, pp. 97 ff.

[11] Cf. Barbara Dölemeyer, 'Die Teilnovellen zum ABGB', in Herbert Hofmeister (ed.), *Kodifikation als Mittel der Politik* (Vienna, Graz and Cologne, 1986), pp. 49 ff.

[12] Wieacker, *A History of Private Law*, pp. 387 ff. More specifically on the relationship between the Swiss and German codes, see Rudolf Gmür, *Das Schweizerische Zivilgesetzbuch verglichen mit dem Deutschen Bürgerlichen Gesetzbuch* (Berne, 1965). On the influence of pandectist legal learning in nineteenth-century Switzerland, cf. Pio Caroni, 'Die Schweizer Romanistik im 19. Jahrhundert', (1994) 16 *ZNR* 243 ff.

[13] For a recent evaluation, see Giorgio Cian, 'Fünfzig Jahre italienischer codice civile', (1993) 1 *ZEUP* 120 ff.; cf. also the contributions in *I Cinquant'Anni del Codice Civile*, 2 vols. (Milan, 1993), and, on the more general topic of the relationship between German and Italian legal

Indeed, the idea of codification has shaped the civil law in many countries outside Europe, including regions as diverse as East Asia and Latin America;[14] it managed to gain a foothold even in British India and the United States of America;[15] and it asserted itself under radically different social and political conditions such as those prevailing in the former socialist states.[16]

Even today, and in spite of gloomy visions usually associated with the term *decodificazione*,[17] codification is not a spent force. More than fifty states have codified their private law since 1945.[18] The most recent example in western Europe is the Netherlands. Core parts of the Dutch Civil Code came into force on 1 January 1992; other parts had already been enacted in 1970, 1976 and 1991.[19] Many of the states of eastern Europe have, since the fall of the Iron Curtain, embarked on ambitious recodification schemes.[20] On an international level we have the Convention on Contracts for the International Sale of Goods, concluded in Vienna in 1980, which provides a codification of a particularly important area of international trade law. It has, to date, been adopted by more than fifty states.[21] And as far as the

---

cultures in the nineteenth century, Aldo Mazzacane and Reiner Schulze (eds.), *Die deutsche und die italienische Rechtskultur im 'Zeitalter der Vergleichung'* (Berlin, 1995). See also, concerning the development of Italian law of breach of contract, Christian Resch, *Das italienische Privatrecht im Spannungsfeld von code civil und BGB am Beispiel der Entwicklung des Leistungsstörungsrechts* (Berlin, 2000).

[14] For Latin America see, e.g., Thilo Scholl, *Die Rezeption kontinental-europäischen Privatrechts in Lateinamerika* (Berlin, 1999).

[15] For British India, see Bijay Kisor Acharyya, *Codification in British India*, Tagore Law Lectures (Calcutta, 1914); for the United States see Shael Herman, 'Schicksal und Zukunft der Kodifikationsidee in Amerika', in Reinhard Zimmermann (ed.), *Amerikanische Rechtskultur und europäisches Privatrecht: Impressionen aus der Neuen Welt* (Tübingen, 1995), pp. 45 ff.

[16] For an overview, see Konrad Zweigert and Hein Kötz, *Einführung in die Rechtsvergleichung auf dem Gebiete des Privatrechts*, vol. I, 2nd edn (Tübingen, 1984), pp. 355 ff.

[17] Natalino Irti, *L'età della decodificazione*, 3rd edn (Milan, 1989).

[18] Cf. Rodolfo Sacco, 'Codificare: modo superato di legiferare?', (1983) *RDC* 117 ff.; Konrad Zweigert and Hans-Jürgen Puttfarken, 'Allgemeines und Besonderes zur Kodifikation', in *Festschrift für Imre Zajtay* (Tübingen, 1982), pp. 569 ff.; and see the contributions to the symposium Codification in the Twenty-First Century, (1998) 31 *University of California Davis Law Review* 655 ff.

[19] Cf. the contributions in Franz Bydlinski, Theo Mayer-Maly and Johannes W. Pichler (eds.), *Renaissance der Idee der Kodifikation* (Vienna, Cologne and Weimar, 1991); A. S. Hartkamp, 'Das neue niederländische bürgerliche Gesetzbuch aus europäischer Sicht', (1993) 57 *RabelsZ* 664 ff.

[20] Cf., e.g., the report by Miroslav Libuda in (1995) 3 *ZEUP* 672 ff. (focusing on Czech law).

[21] See Ulrich Magnus, 'Aktuelle Fragen des UN-Kaufrechts', (1993) 1 *ZEUP* 97 ff.; Ulrich Magnus, 'Stand und Entwicklung des UN-Kaufrechts', (1995) 3 *ZEUP* 202 ff.; Ulrich Magnus, 'Das UN

'approximation' of the laws of the member states of the European Union in terms of the EC Treaty is concerned, the European Parliament has called for the preparation of a code for the entire European private law.[22] Code-like Principles of International Commercial Contracts have been published by the International Institute for the Unification of Private Law in 1994,[23] and in 2000 the first and second parts of the Principles of European Contract Law, prepared by a Commission on European Contract Law, have appeared in print.[24] An express purpose of the latter initiative is to provide a basis for a future European Code of Contracts.

Kaufrecht: Fragen und Probleme seiner praktischen Bewährung', (1997) 5 *ZEUP* 823 ff.; Ulrich Magnus, 'Wesentliche Fragen des UN-Kaufrechts', (1999) 7 *ZEUP* 642 ff.; Michael R. Will, *Twenty Years of International Sales Law under the CISG* (The Hague and Boston, 2000); and see the list of states in Reiner Schulze and Reinhard Zimmermann, *Basistexte zum Europäischen Privatrecht* (Baden-Baden, 2000), II.5.

[22] For a discussion, see Winfried Tilmann, 'Eine Privatrechtskodifikation für die Europäische Gemeinschaft?', in Peter-Christian Müller-Graff (ed.), *Gemeinsames Privatrecht in der Europäischen Gemeinschaft* (Baden-Baden, 1993), pp. 485 ff.; Winfried Tilmann, 'Zweiter Kodifikationsbeschluß des Europäischen Parlaments', (1995) 3 *ZEUP* 534 ff.; Winfried Tilmann, 'Artikel 100 a EGV als Grundlage für ein Europäisches Zivilgesetzbuch', in *Festskrift til Ole Lando* (Copenhagen, 1997), pp. 351 ff.; Jürgen Basedow, 'Über Privatrechtsvereinheitlichung und Marktintegration', in *Festschrift für Ernst-Joachim Mestmäker* (Baden-Baden, 1996), pp. 347 ff.; and see the contributions to Dieter Martiny and Normann Witzleb (eds.), *Auf dem Wege zu einem Europäischen Zivilgesetzbuch* (Berlin, Heidelberg and New York, 1999); Pierre Legrand, 'Against a European Civil Code', (1997) 60 *Modern LR* 44 ff. The question was discussed at a symposium in The Hague on 28 February 1997; cf. Winfried Tilmann, 'Towards a European Civil Code', (1997) 5 *ZEUP* 595 ff. and the contributions in (1997) 5 *ERPL* 455 ff. The concept of a 'creeping codification' is propagated by Klaus Peter Berger, *The Creeping Codification of the Lex Mercatoria* (The Hague, London and Boston, 1999).

[23] For a discussion, see Klaus Peter Berger, 'Die UNIDROIT-Prinzipien für Internationale Handelsverträge', (1995) 94 *ZVglRWiss* 217 ff. and the contributions by Michael Joachim Bonell, Alejandro M. Garro, Hernany Veytia, Luiz Olavo Baptista and Franco Ferrari in (1995) 69 *Tulane LR* 1121 ff.; Michael Joachim Bonell, *An International Restatement of Contract Law*, 2nd edn (Irvington-on-Hudson, 1997); Michael Joachim Bonell, 'The Unidroit Principles – A Modern Approach to Contract Law', in Hans-Leo Weyers (ed.), *Europäisches Vertragsrecht* (Baden-Baden, 1997), pp. 9 ff.; Arthur Hartkamp, 'Principles of Contract Law', in Hartkamp et al. (eds.), *Towards a European Civil Code*, pp. 105 ff.

[24] Ole Lando and Hugh Beale (eds.), *Principles of European Contract Law* (The Hague, London and Boston, 2000). For a discussion of the first part, published in 1995, see Reinhard Zimmermann, 'Konturen eines europäischen Vertragsrechts', (1995) *JZ* 477 ff.; Reinhard Zimmermann, 'Die "Principles of European Contract Law", Teil I' (1995) 3 *ZEUP* 731 ff.; Hugh Beale, 'The Principles of European Contract Law and Harmonization of the Law of Contract', in *Festskrift til Ole Lando*, pp. 21 ff.; Ralf Michaels, 'Privatautonomie und Privatkodifikation', (1998) 62 *RabelsZ* 580 ff. Generally cf. also the contributions to Weyers (ed.), *Europäisches Vertragsrecht*. A German translation of the Principles of European Contract Law appeared in (2000) 8 *ZEUP* 675 ff. For an evaluation of both the Principles of International Commercial Contracts and the Principles of European Contract Law, from the point of view of German law, see Berger, *Creeping Codification*, pp. 117 ff. and the contributions to Jürgen Basedow (ed.), *Europäische*

Civil law and the civilian tradition

The meaning of civil law

Civil law, the other key term in the title of this chapter, is somewhat ambiguous. *The Oxford Companion to Law*, for instance, lists ten different
meanings.[25] It may refer to the law applied to Roman citizens (as opposed
to the *ius gentium*) or to the traditional core of Roman law, based on the
Twelve Tables and on subsequent legislative enactments (as opposed to the
ius honorarium, i.e. the body of law developed by the praetors). Sometimes
it means Roman law at large, but it is also used as a synonym for private law.
Civil law (as the entire body of state law) can be opposed to canon law, but
it can also (as a common denominator of the Continental European legal
systems) be contrasted to the English (or Anglo-American)[26] common law.
These are probably the most important variations of the term in legal history, comparative law and modern jurisprudence. In the context of modern
comparative jurisprudence we should probably use the last meaning as a
point of departure. Civil law and common law are usually taken today to
designate the two major legal traditions of the western world.[27] In the civil
law, so it is said,[28] large areas of private law are codified. It has already
been pointed out that this was not always the case. Codification is merely
a specific condition in which the civil law currently presents itself. But
there is a second distinctive feature. The civilian legal tradition originated
in medieval Bologna with the rediscovery and intellectual penetration of
the most important body of Roman legal sources, Justinian's Digest. The
English common law, on the other hand, developed more independently
from Roman law (though in neither complete nor noble isolation).[29] Here

---

Vertragsrechtsvereinheitlichung und deutsches Recht (Tübingen, 2000); cf. also the contributions
by Michael Joachim Bonell and Ole Lando to *Making Commercial Law: Essays in Honour of Roy
Goode* (Oxford, 1997), pp. 91 ff., 103 ff.; Roy Goode, 'International Restatements and National
Law', in *The Search for Principle: Essays in Honour of Lord Goff of Chieveley* (New York, 1999),
pp. 45 ff.

[25] David M. Walker, *The Oxford Companion to Law* (Oxford, 1980), p. 222.

[26] On this notion see, critically, Reinhard Zimmermann, '"Common Law" und "Civil Law",
Amerika und Europa', in Zimmermann (ed.), *Amerikanische Rechtskultur*, pp. 1 ff.

[27] Cf., e.g., James Gordley, 'Common Law and Civil Law: eine überholte Unterscheidung', (1993)
1 *ZEUP* 498 ff.

[28] Arthur Taylor von Mehren and James Russell Gordley, *The Civil Law System*, 2nd edn (Boston
and Toronto, 1977), p. 3.

[29] For details, see Peter Stein, *The Character and Influence of the Roman Civil Law* (London,
1988), pp. 151 ff.; R. H. Helmholz, 'Continental Law and Common Law: Historical Strangers

we have the historical connection between civil law as Roman law and civil law as Continental European private law. This connection is based, historically, on a process usually referred to as 'reception': it was the reception of Roman law that constituted European civil law.[30]

Characteristic features of the civil law

European civil law, in the sense of Continental European private law at large, exhibits a number of attributes distinguishing it from the laws of other cultures.[31] It is, in many complex ways, related to moral norms, religious beliefs and political evaluations. At the same time, however, it is quite distinct from morality, religion and politics. It is administered by a body of professional experts who have received a specialised training that qualifies them for their task. The central institution providing such training is typically a university. As a university subject, law is submitted to methodical reflection and analysis: it is the object of a legal science. European legal science, in turn, attempts to demonstrate how individual rules and the decisions of individual cases can be derived from general propositions, and how they can thus be understood and related to each other. A determined effort is made to rationalise the application of the law. Moreover, European law possesses an inherently dynamic character. It is always developing. But it is developing within an established framework of sources and methods, of concepts, rules and arguments. It constitutes a tradition that is constantly evolving. And in spite of many differences in detail, that tradition is characterised by a fundamental unity. It is based on the same sources, has been moving with the same cultural tides, reflects a common set of values and uses common techniques.[32]

or Companions?', 1990 *Duke LJ* 1207 ff.; Reinhard Zimmermann, 'Der europäische Charakter des englischen Rechts', (1993) 1 *ZEUP* 4 ff.; Reinhard Zimmermann, *Roman Law, Contemporary Law, European Law: The Civilian Tradition Today*, Clarendon Lectures, Lecture 3 (Oxford, 2000).

[30] The authoritative analysis is still the one provided by Franz Wieacker: see Wieacker, *A History of Private Law*, pp. 71 ff. He emphasises the intellectualisation and rationalisation of law and public affairs in general, and the creation of a European *ius commune*, as the core features of the impact of Roman law on European legal thinking.

[31] For a succinct summary, see Harold J. Berman, *Law and Revolution: The Formation of the Western Legal Mind* (Cambridge, Mass., 1983), pp. 7 ff.; Franz Wieacker, 'Foundations of European Legal Culture', (1990) 38 *AJCL* 1 ff.; Peter Häberle, 'Europäische Rechtskultur', in Peter Häberle, *Europäische Rechtskultur* (Baden-Baden, 1994), pp. 9 ff. The following paragraphs are based on my foreword to Wieacker, *History of Private Law*, pp. v ff.

[32] See Reinhard Zimmermann, 'Civil Code and Civil Law', (1994/5) 1 *CJEL* 82 ff.

Civil law and civil code

It is important to realise that codification has not brought about an entirely new era within the history of the European civil law. Of course, there have been certain fundamental changes, but they relate to attitude and ideology rather than to substance. The German Civil Code, as has been emphasised already, was drafted in the wake of German national unification and it was taken, at least by some, to be a characteristic expression of the German national spirit. Also, and more importantly, it marked the point where discussion of Roman private law and modern doctrinal scholarship parted company.[33] The codification was attributed sole, supreme and unquestioned authority, and all the energies of those legal academics interested in the application and development of private law were channelled into the task of expounding the code and of discussing the court decisions based on its provisions. As a result, legal scholarship has undergone a process of nationalistic particularisation (which has been denounced, emphatically, as 'undignified' and 'humiliating').[34]

On the other hand, the codification movement was itself a European phenomenon affecting the private law in Germany or Austria as profoundly, and in essentially a similar manner, as in France or Italy. The Prussian Code apart,[35] all European codifications are characterised by a considerable built-in flexibility which has, by and large, made them stand the test of time.[36] Their draftsmen took to heart Portalis' famous observation[37] that the task of legislation is to determine, 'par de grandes vues', the general maxims of law. It has to establish principles rich in implications rather than descend into the details of every question which might possibly arise. The application

[33] This is elaborated in Zimmermann, *Roman Law, Contemporary Law, European Law* (Clarendon Lectures, Lecture One).

[34] For examples of this kind of 'national legal science', see Zimmermann, 'Civil Code and Civil Law', 63 ff. (with reference to the sharp criticism of this state of affairs by Rudolf von Jhering).

[35] See Jan Schröder, 'Das Verhältnis von Rechtsdogmatik und Gesetzgebung in der neuzeitlichen Privatrechtsgeschichte (am Beispiel des Privatrechts)', in Okko Behrends and Wolfram Henkel (eds.), *Gesetzgebung und Dogmatik, Abhandlungen der Akademie der Wissenschaften in Göttingen, Philologisch-historische Klasse, Dritte Folge* (Göttingen, 1989), pp. 43 ff.

[36] This point is further elaborated, as far as the German Civil Code is concerned, in Zimmermann, 'Civil Code and Civil Law', 89 ff.; cf. also Reinhard Zimmermann, 'An Introduction to German Legal Culture', in Werner F. Ebke and Matthew W. Finkin (eds.), *Introduction to German Law* (The Hague, London and Boston, 1996), pp. 8 ff.

[37] As cited in Konrad Zweigert and Hein Kötz, *An Introduction to Comparative Law*, trans. Tony Weir, 3rd edn (Oxford, 1998), p. 90. Cf. also the comments by Herman, 'Schicksal und Zukunft der Kodifikationsidee in Amerika', p. 52 ff.

of the law belongs to the magistrate and lawyer, 'pénétré de l'esprit général des lois'.

Thus, the scene was set for an alliance, not for confrontation, between legislation and legal science;[38] and, as a result, it appears to be generally recognised today that a code has to be brought to life, and has to be kept in tune with the changing demands of time, by active and imaginative judicial interpretation and doctrinal elaboration.[39] In spite of the code, the civilian tradition is still evolving. And it is indeed, fundamentally, still the civilian tradition that is evolving. For while judicial interpretation and doctrinal elaboration have certainly produced some odd quirks of national jurisprudence, they have proceeded from the provisions of the various codes they were supposed to apply. These codes, however, have grown on the same legal soil. Thus, it is well known that those who drafted the German Civil Code did not, by and large, intend their code to constitute a fresh start, a break with the past. On the contrary: they generally aimed at consolidating the contemporary version of the Roman common law: pandectist legal doctrine. Not inappropriately, therefore, the BGB has been referred to as the 'statute book of the historical school of jurisprudence'.[40]

But even the French code civil, carried by the élan of a revolutionary movement, subscribed to traditional conceptions of private law that were,

---

[38] Cf. Okko Behrends, 'Das Bündnis zwischen Gesetz und Dogmatik und die Frage der dogmatischen Rangstufen', in Behrends and Henkel (eds.), *Gesetzgebung und Dogmatik*, pp. 9 ff.

[39] This point is also emphasised by Karsten Schmidt, *Die Zukunft der Kodifikationsidee: Rechtsprechung, Wissenschaft und Gesetzgebung vor den Gesetzeswerken des geltenden Rechts* (Heidelberg, 1985), pp. 67 ff. For further elaboration see, as far as German law is concerned, Zimmermann, 'An Introduction to German Legal Culture', pp. 16 ff. As far as the French and Austrian Codes are concerned, see the famous clauses in art. 4 code civil and § 7 ABGB. For details concerning the relationship between the Code and judicial development of the law in France and Austria, see Heinz Hübner, *Kodifikation und Entscheidungsfreiheit des Richters in der Geschichte des Privatrechts* (Königstein, 1980), pp. 33 ff.; Zweigert and Kötz, *Introduction to Comparative Law*, pp. 89 ff., 160 ff. The Swiss Code has, from the beginning, been renowned for its 'deliberate reliance . . . on judicial amplification' (Zweigert and Kötz, *Introduction to Comparative Law*, p. 175). Its draftsmen have made extensive use of 'general clauses'; cf., e.g., Gmür, *Das Schweizerische Zivilgesetzbuch*, pp. 50 ff. Significantly, the new Dutch Civil Code relies more widely on general provisions than the old one; cf. A. S. Hartkamp, 'Diskussionsbeitrag', in Bydlinski et al. (eds.) *Renaissance der Idee der Kodifikation*, p. 63. Concerning good faith, see M. W. Hesselink, *De Redelijkheid en billijkheid in het Europese Privaatrecht* (Deventer, 1999); Reinhard Zimmermann and Simon Whittaker (eds.), *Good Faith in European Contract Law* (Cambridge, 2000) (with full references).

[40] Paul Koschaker, *Europa und das römische Recht*, 4th edn (Munich, 1966), p. 291. On the reaction of the German courts see the contributions to Ulrich Falk and Heinz Mohnhaupt (eds.), *Das Bürgerliche Gesetzbuch und seine Richter* (Frankfurt am Main, 2000).

as James Gordley[41] puts it very pointedly, almost old-fashioned when the code was enacted. The draftsmen found them in the seventeenth- and eighteenth-century treatise writers, such as Domat and Pothier. The same is true, *mutatis mutandis*, of the other two great 'natural law codes'.[42] For the impact of natural law on the actual content of private law was rather limited.[43] It could be used to make a choice between two or more conflicting solutions, to streamline traditional doctrines or to generalise and round off trends of legal development that had been going on for centuries. But the *ratio naturalis* of natural law did not normally oust the *ratio scripta* of Roman law.[44] Nor, of course, did a code like the Austrian General Civil Code attempt to incorporate the local and regional laws prevailing in the various parts of the monarchy; after all, it was intended to constitute a code that was universally applicable.[45] Predominantly, at least, it is an emanation neither of local custom nor of abstract, universal thought patterns, but of traditional civil law doctrine. The same has remained true of more recent codifications, including the new Dutch Civil Code.[46] They all carry an unmistakably civilian imprint, and the common tradition thus provides the background for an evaluation of their differences and similarities. They all, in a way, used the same legal grammar and, as a result, it is not difficult for those who have learnt that grammar to understand their content. 'Civil law in European codes': this topic, therefore, in essence concerns the fundamental

---

[41] 'Myths of the French Civil Code', (1994) 42 *AJCL* 459 ff.; cf. also Reiner Schulze, 'Französisches Recht und europäische Rechtsgeschichte im 19. Jahrhundert', in Reiner Schulze (ed.), *Französisches Zivilrecht in Europa während des 19. Jahrhunderts* (Berlin, 1994), pp. 12 ff.

[42] Schwennicke, *Entstehung*, has emphasised the extent to which the draftsmen of the Prussian Code followed (and merely rationalised) traditional patterns of the *ius commune*. As far as the Austrian Code is concerned, see the evaluation by Werner Ogris, 'Zur Geschichte und Bedeutung des österreichischen Allgemeinen bürgerlichen Gesetzbuchs (ABGB)', in *Liber Memorialis François Laurent* (Brussels, 1989), pp. 381 ff.

[43] This has been emphasised, in particular, by Klaus Luig, 'Der Einfluß des Naturrechts auf das positive Privatrecht im 18. Jahrhundert', (1979) 96 *ZSS* (Germanistische Abteilung) 38 ff.

[44] Ibid., p. 54.

[45] Wilhelm Brauneder, 'Vernünftiges Recht als überregionales Recht: Die Rechtsvereinheitlichung der österreichischen Zivilrechtskodifikationen 1786–1797–1811', in Schulze (ed.), *Europäische Rechts- und Verfassungsgeschichte*, pp. 121 ff. The same is true, of course, of the French code civil; cf. Schulze, 'Französisches Recht', pp. 23 ff.

[46] This even contains a whole variety of instances where its draftsmen, consciously or unconsciously, have reverted to principles of Roman law even though the old Code had departed from them: cf. Hans Ankum, 'Römisches Recht im neuen niederländischen Bürgerlichen Gesetzbuch', in Reinhard Zimmermann, Rolf Knütel and Jens Peter Meincke (eds.), *Rechtsgeschichte und Privatrechtsdogmatik* (Heidelberg, 2000), pp. 101 ff.

intellectual unity within a diversity of modern legal systems. We will confine our attention to the law of obligations, the most characteristically 'European' of the core areas of private law,[47] although an investigation into property law and testate succession would probably yield similar results. (Family law and intestate succession may not share as much common ground.) And we will take Roman law as our central point of reference. For if it was the 'reception' of Roman law that constituted European civil law, it must also have played a pivotal role in rendering the European civil codes civilian.

Roman roots I: common origins

It is not easy to think of a legal rule expressed in exactly the same way in all European codes. One possible candidate, one would have thought, is the rule that legally or morally offensive contracts must be void. And indeed, the codes invariably tackle this problem by way of general provisions, which (also invariably) use the key concepts of illegality and immorality.[48] All these rules are based on Roman law: the lex Non dubium of Emperor Theodosius,[49] which elevated all statutory prohibitions to the status of a lex perfecta, and the suppression of transactions 'contra bones mores' by the Roman jurists and emperors.[50] But if one looks more closely at the various codes one finds subtle variations. Article 20 I of the Swiss Obligationenrecht (OR) refers to 'contracts with an illegal content', § 134 BGB to 'legal acts violating a statutory prohibition'. The French and Italian codes relate the invalidity of illegal and immoral contracts to their famous doctrines of 'cause' or 'causa'[51] (which in turn derive from medieval jurisprudence but can be traced back ultimately to two fragments in the Digest[52]). The German, Swiss and Austrian Codes contain specific provisions dealing with 'usurious' transactions;[53] the Austrian Code also still retains the institution

---

[47] For an explanation see Reinhard Zimmermann, 'The Law of Obligations: Character and Influence of the Civilian Tradition', (1992) 3 *Stellenbosch LR* 5 ff.

[48] For a comparative overview, see Zweigert and Kötz, *Introduction to Comparative Law*, pp. 407 ff. and Hein Kötz, *European Contract Law*, vol. I, trans. Tony Weir (Oxford, 1997), pp. 154 ff.

[49] Nov. Theod. 9.

[50] For all details, see Reinhard Zimmermann, *The Law of Obligations: Roman Foundations of the Civilian Tradition* (paperback edn; Oxford, 1996), pp. 697 ff., 706 ff.

[51] Cf. art. 1133 code civil; art. 1343 codice civile.

[52] Zimmermann, *Law of Obligations*, pp. 549 ff.

[53] § 138 II BGB (on its historical background, see Zimmermann, *Law of Obligations*, pp. 175 ff., 268 ff.); art. 21 OR; § 879 II n. 4 ABGB.

of *laesio enormis*⁵⁴ (derived from C. 4, 44, 2).⁵⁵ French law does not deal with 'usury' but has a rather different version of *laesio enormis*.⁵⁶ Article 1133 code civil does not refer only to transactions prohibited by law and contrary to the *boni mores* but also mentions those against public policy. The Dutch Civil Code contains a similar provision.⁵⁷ As far as legal consequences are concerned, most codes simply declare the contract to be void. German law, however, displays a somewhat greater degree of flexibility concerning illegal contracts. The transaction is void, unless a contrary intention appears from the statute.⁵⁸ A similar, though not identical, rule was introduced by the Dutch legislature.⁵⁹ This flexible approach, incidentally, is quite in tune with that adopted in classical Roman law before Theodosius enacted the lex Non dubium.⁶⁰

Roman roots II: two sets of rules

Duties and liability of a seller

Not infrequently the Roman sources contain two different sets of rules dealing with the same problem. Both may have found their way into our modern codifications. Under a contract of sale, for instance, the vendor was under no obligation to transfer ownership of the object sold. He merely had to grant the purchaser undisturbed possession and was thus responsible for 'vacuam possessionem tradere' and for sustaining the continued enjoyment of the *res*. Thus, there was an implied warranty of peaceable possession ('habere licere'), for as soon as the true owner, by asserting his title, evicted the purchaser, the latter could hold the vendor responsible.⁶¹ This liability for eviction, as we find it in the law of Justinian, became part and parcel of the *ius commune* and it was also adopted by the code civil.⁶² The situation was different as far as *certam rem dare* obligations (for instance, the promise

---

⁵⁴ § 934 ABGB.   ⁵⁵ See Zimmermann, *Law of Obligations*, pp. 259 ff.
⁵⁶ Art. 1674 code civil.   ⁵⁷ Art. 3:40 I BW.
⁵⁸ § 134 BGB (on which see the discussion by Hans Hermann Seiler, 'Über verbotswidrige Rechtsgeschäfte (§ 134 BGB)', in *Gedächtnisschrift für Wolfgang Martens* (Berlin and New York, 1987), pp. 719 ff.
⁵⁹ Art. 3:40 II BW.   ⁶⁰ Zimmermann, *Law of Obligations*, pp. 697 ff.
⁶¹ For the details, see ibid., pp. 293 ff. and, more recently, Wolfgang Ernst, *Rechtsmängelhaftung* (Tübingen, 1995), pp. 7 ff.
⁶² Artt. 1626 ff. code civil. Cf. also the comparative remarks by Andreas Wacke, 'Die verschuldete Eviktion', in *Festschrift für Hubert Niederländer* (Heidelberg, 1991), pp. 141 ff.

to deliver a certain slave) were concerned. Here the promisor had to transfer ownership and was liable as soon as he was unable to do so.[63] This is the regime that obtains today in modern German law (§§ 433 ff., 440 BGB). It is as 'civilian' as, but nevertheless quite different from, the liability for eviction, no matter that the draftsmen of the German Code had not in fact taken their inspiration from the *obligationes dandi*, but thought (wrongly) that the new regime had organically evolved from the liability for eviction.[64] This explains why, though requiring the vendor to transfer ownership, they still made his liability to pay damages dependent upon eviction.[65]

Breach of contract

Breach of contract presents another example of a significant discrepancy between French and German law. The BGB distinguishes between different types of breach of contract. Of central significance is a highly artificial concept of (supervening) impossibility devised by Friedrich Mommsen, and inspired largely by the Roman regime applicable to *certam rem dare obligationes*.[66] Although, by the time of Justinian, this concept had lost its function, it still featured in the *Corpus Juris Civilis* and has puzzled subsequent generations of lawyers.[67] On the one hand, Mommsen wanted to be faithful to the sources; on the other hand, he attempted on that basis to devise a neat and logically consistent scheme of liability for breach of contract. It is hardly surprising that under these circumstances 'impossibility' became a very broad conceptual abstraction and, as such, a common systematic denominator for a whole range of situations. What Mommsen could not (given the framework of authoritative sources within which he operated) take into consideration was the fact that the modern general law

---

[63] For details, see Ernst, *Rechtsmängelhaftung*, pp. 91 ff.
[64] See ibid., pp. 123 ff.   [65] § 440 II BGB.
[66] Friedrich Mommsen, *Die Unmöglichkeit der Leistung in ihrem Einfluß auf obligatorische Verhältnisse* (Brunswick, 1853). For a discussion, see Christian Wollschläger, *Die Entstehung der Unmöglichkeitslehre: Zur Dogmengeschichte des Rechts der Leistungsstörungen* (Cologne and Vienna, 1970), pp. 123 ff.; Susanne Würthwein, *Zur Schadensersatzpflicht wegen Vertragsverletzungen im Gemeinen Recht des 19. Jahrhunderts: Grundsätze des Leistungsstörungsrechts im Gemeinen Recht in ihrer Bedeutung für das BGB* (Berlin, 1990); Zimmermann, *Law of Obligations*, pp. 783 ff., 809 ff. For a meticulous re-evaluation see now Ulrich Huber, *Leistungsstörungen*, vol. I (Tübingen, 1999), pp. 1 ff.
[67] For a modern example of the confusion obtaining in a legal system based directly on the Roman sources, see W. A. Ramsden, *Supervening Impossibility of Performance in the South African Law of Contract* (Cape Town, 1985), pp. 55 ff.

of contract derives from the consensual contracts of Roman law, not from the law of stipulations entailing 'certam rem dare'.[68] With regard to the former, liability had to be assessed according to the standard of good faith ('ex fide bona'), and there was thus no need for a strict categorisation of specific types of breach of contract.[69] More particularly, supervening impossibility did not have to be dealt with separately. Of central importance was the question whether, and under which circumstances, the failure to perform, or to perform properly, was attributable to the debtor, before he could be made liable for *id quod* interest; and this question was indeed the very question that preoccupied the authors of the older *ius commune*. Following this pattern of the *ius commune* is the French code civil.[70] Its art. 1147 refers to 'inexécution', a broad concept which covers all forms of breach of contract (that is, those cases where one of the parties 'ne satisfera point à son engagement'). The debtor is liable wherever such non-performance is not due to *vis maior* or *casus fortuitus*.[71]

Initial impossibility of performance

As far as initial impossibility of performance is concerned, most modern codes appear to be squarely based on the famous principle that has come down to us under the name of Iuventius Celsus: 'Impossibilium nulla obligatio est'.[72] Thus, for instance, § 306 BGB provides that a contract, the performance of which is impossible, is void. Similar provisions can be found in Swiss[73] and Italian law,[74] and, confined to the law of sale, also in the

---

[68] Cf. Klaus-Peter Nanz, *Die Entstehung des allgemeinen Vertragsbegriffes im 16. Jahrhundert* (Munich, 1985); John Barton (ed.), *Towards a General Law of Contract* (Berlin, 1990); Zimmermann, *Law of Obligations*, pp. 537 ff.; Reinhard Zimmermann, 'Roman-Dutch Jurisprudence and its Contribution to European Private Law', (1992) 66 *Tulane LR* 1689 ff.; Robert Feenstra, 'Die Klagbarkeit der pacta nuda', in Robert Feenstra and Reinhard Zimmermann (eds.), *Das römisch-holländische Recht: Fortschritte des Zivilrechts im 17. und 18. Jahrhundert* (Berlin, 1992), pp. 123 ff.

[69] Zimmermann, *Law of Obligations*, pp. 788 ff., 807 ff.

[70] Cf., e.g., Zweigert and Kötz, *Introduction to Comparative Law*, pp. 496 ff.

[71] A similarly streamlined set of rules, centred around a uniform concept of breach of contract, has been developed in English law. The Vienna Convention on the International Sale of Goods, the German Commission charged with the reform of the law of obligations, the Unidroit Principles of International Commercial Contracts and the Principles of European Contract Law drafted by the Commission on European Contract Law all follow the same approach. Cf. Zimmermann, 'Konturen', pp. 480 ff.

[72] D. 50, 17, 185.   [73] Art. 20 OR.   [74] Artt. 1346, 1418 II codice civile.

code civil.[75] We appear to be dealing here with a rule, not only of venerable antiquity, but also of obvious and even axiomatic validity. However,
'impossibilium nulla obligatio est' merely encapsulates the obvious idea
that nobody can be obliged to perform what he cannot perform. This is
not identical with the assertion that a contract, the performance of which is
impossible, is void; and in the eyes of the Roman lawyers the one did indeed
not necessarily follow from the other.[76] Thus, as far as the contract of sale is
concerned, we find some fragments in the Corpus Juris where a contractual
action for what we would call the positive interest is granted, and where the
contract, to that extent, appears to have been regarded as valid. Stipulations
concerning an impossible performance, however, were invariably held to be
void by the Roman lawyers. This was probably based neither on logic nor
on policy; it simply followed from the way in which the applicable formula
was phrased: for condemnation presupposed the existence of an object, the
value of which could sensibly be estimated.[77]

   Thus, the modern codes perpetuate a rule solely applicable to a type of
contract which has not been adopted by any of them. The responsibility
for this odd anachronism rests in the first place on the natural lawyers.[78]
Discarding the 'subtleties' of Roman law, they found an altogether new
starting point for determining the effect of initial impossibility on contractual obligations in the idea that their content may be attributed to the
promisor only if it is based on the exercise of his free will. The promisor
must have chosen to be bound, and as a rational being he can choose only
what he is able to carry out. A person can will only what lies within the
reach of his volition. The law of contract is based on freedom of will. Ergo: a
contract directed at something impossible must be invalid. This reasoning
could not fail to commend itself to the Pandectists, and thus we find the
(partial) concurrence of views, mentioned above, between the draftsmen
of codifications from both the 'Germanic' and 'Romanistic' legal families.
More recently, however, the rule embodied in § 306 BGB has been regarded
as unsound and unfortunate.[79] Textbooks and commentaries are therefore

---

[75] Art. 1601 code civil.
[76] For details, see Zimmermann, Law of Obligations, pp. 686 ff.; cf. also pp. 241 ff.
[77] See the references in ibid., pp. 689 ff.
[78] For details, see Christian Wollschläger, 'Die willenstheoretische Unmöglichkeitslehre im
    aristotelisch-thomistischen Naturrecht', in Sympotica Franz Wieacker (Göttingen, 1970),
    pp. 154 ff.; Zimmermann, Law of Obligations, pp. 692 ff.
[79] Cf., e.g., Ernst Rabel, Unmöglichkeit der Leistung (1907) and Über Unmöglichkeit der
    Leistung und heutige Praxis (1911), both today in Ernst Rabel, Gesammelte Aufsätze, vol. I

full of exhortations to apply it restrictively and to try wherever possible to avoid the harshness inherent in the unequivocal verdict of invalidity. Quite in line with these developments, the new Dutch Civil Code has completely abandoned the rule.[80] One can hardly refuse the label 'civilian' to this solution. For we are dealing here with the return towards a more flexible regime espoused, already, by the Roman lawyers.[81]

Roman roots III: interpreting the sources

In other cases, considerable variations in the solutions presented by the modern codes are based on the fact that the relevant Roman sources, which have for centuries informed our discussion, are unclear, or even contradictory. This is not at all a rare phenomenon, since the Digest is not a systematically structured piece of legislation but a compilation of fragments from classical Roman legal writings, put together under Justinian in the sixth century AD. It constitutes a gigantic torso of Roman law, which contains case decisions, legal opinions and rules, commentary, disputes, and excerpts from textbooks and monographs. Its overall character is casuistic. Much of it reflects the contemporary position at the various stages of Roman legal history, while other parts were altered to suit the requirements of the sixth century. In addition, we have to take account of the imperial legislation contained in the *Codex Iustiniani* and of the rules contained in an elementary textbook invested with statutory force: Justinian's Institutes.

Vicarious liability

Digesta 19, 2, 25, 7[82] is one of those ambiguous fragments which have been used as the textual foundation for two contradictory solutions. A contractor has undertaken the transport of a column. He uses some servants to carry

---

(Tübingen, 1965), pp. 1 ff., 56 ff.; Zweigert and Kötz, *Introduction to Comparative Law*, pp. 488 ff.; Ulrich Huber, 'Leistungsstörungen', in Bundesminister der Justiz (ed.), *Gutachten und Vorschläge zur Überarbeitung des Schuldrechts*, vol. I (Cologne, 1981), pp. 813 ff.

[80] Cf. A. S. Hartkamp, *Mr. C. Asser's Handleiding tot de Beoefening van het Nederlands Burgerlijk Recht, Verbintenissenrecht*, Part 1, 11th edn (Deventer, 2000), n. 25.

[81] Cf. also § 878, 1 ABGB ('What is *downright* impossible, cannot be the object of a valid contract') and the interpretation placed on this rule by Ernst Rabel, 'Zur Lehre von der Unmöglichkeit der Leistung nach Österreichischem Recht' (1911), in *Gesammelte Aufsätze*, vol. I, pp. 79 ff.

[82] 'Qui columnam transportandam conduxit, si ea, dum tollitur aut portatur aut reponitur, fracta sit, ita id periculum praestat, si qua ipsius eorumque, quorum opera uteretur, culpa acciderit.'

out that obligation. They drop the column and break it. Is the contractor liable not only for his own fault but also for theirs? Or is his liability dependent upon whether he himself was at fault (for instance, in selecting and supervising his servants)? This depends on the interpretation of the clause 'si qua ipsius eorumque, quorum opera uteretur, culpa occiderit'; or, more precisely, on whether the particle 'que' in 'eorumque' has to be understood conjunctively ('and') or disjunctively ('or'). According to the latter interpretation, we would be dealing with an instance of vicarious liability *stricto sensu*, i.e. liability based (merely) on the fault of others. This is indeed how modern Romanists would tend to read the text, for only this interpretation would seem to fit in with the conductor's *custodia* liability.[83] It is this solution that we find, within a delictual context, in art. 1384 code civil: one is responsible, not only for the injury one causes by one's own action, but also for that which is caused 'par le fait des personnes dont on doit répondre'.[84]

Digesta 19, 2, 25, 7 (the 'que' interpreted conjunctively), on the other hand, was one of the key sources upon which nineteenth-century German legal writers relied in order to reject the notion that one person could be held strictly responsible for the acts of others.[85] 'No liability without fault' was one of the great axioms of pandectist doctrine,[86] and the Roman texts tended to be read in such a way as to conform thereto. By the time the BGB was drafted the idea of vicarious liability had gained ground,[87] but ultimately it managed to establish itself only in the contractual context.[88] But when it came to the law of delict, the forces of tradition – a tradition only supposedly going back to the Roman sources! – largely had their way, strongly supported by lobbyists representing the interests of trade, industry and agriculture. The principle laid down in art. 1384 code civil was curtly

---

[83] Rolf Knütel, 'Die Haftung für Hilfspersonen im römischen Recht', (1983) 100 ZSS (Romanistische Abteilung) 419 ff.; Zimmermann, *Law of Obligations*, pp. 397 ff. Contra: Geoffrey MacCormack, 'Culpa in eligendo', (1971) 18 *RIDA* 541 ff.

[84] On the origin of this provision (Domat and Pothier) cf. Alan Watson, *Failures of the Legal Imagination* (Philadelphia, 1988), pp. 6 ff., 15 ff.; on its application, see Zweigert and Kötz, *Introduction to Comparative Law*, pp. 635 ff.

[85] Cf., for example, Bernhard Windscheid and Theodor Kipp, *Lehrbuch des Pandektenrechts*, 9th edn (Frankfurt am Main, 1906), § 401, n. 5.

[86] Cf., e.g., the analysis by Hans-Peter Benöhr, 'Die Entscheidung des BGB für das Verschuldensprinzip', (1978) 46 *TR* 1 ff.

[87] For details of the development, see Hans Hermann Seiler, 'Die deliktische Gehilfenhaftung in historischer Sicht', (1967) *JZ* 525 ff.

[88] § 278 BGB.

rejected by the second commission drafting the BGB as being entirely alien to traditional 'German' notions of justice and fairness.[89] According to § 831 BGB, therefore, liability for the unlawful acts of employees hinges on *culpa in eligendo vel custodiendo vel inspiciendo*.[90] This rule has turned out to be a major source of embarrassment, and has largely been responsible for the extravagant encroachment of contractual remedies on the law of delict, which is such a characteristic feature of the modern German law of obligations.[91]

We are obviously dealing here with an important difference between French and German law. Yet both solutions will have to be labelled 'civilian', for both of them derive from the same intellectual tradition. That tradition has shaped the parameters within which the legal discourse has taken place: the distinction between contractual and delictual liability; the relevance, in principle, of fault as the basis for liability; the possibility of acting through others and the problem, under these circumstances, of how to attribute fault; and the definition of the range of such other persons for whose fault one may be held responsible. Texts such as D. 19, 2, 25, 7 and others deriving from the same intellectual tradition[92] did not, of course, 'determine' whether a legal system opted for vicarious liability or for a strict implementation of the fault principle, but they provided the framework of concepts and arguments for rationalising that decision.

Transfer of ownership and payment of purchase price

For another example we may turn to Justinian's Institutes. They contain an enigmatic rule relating to the transfer of ownership resulting from a contract of sale.[93] Ownership, according to the first sentence of Inst. II, 1, 41, will pass only once the purchase price has been paid (or security given).

---

[89] 'Protokolle', in Benno Mugdan, *Die gesammten Materialien zum Bürgerlichen Gesetzbuch für das Deutsche Reich*, vol. III (Berlin, 1899), p. 1094.

[90] There is, however, as far as this fault requirement is concerned, a reversal of the onus of proof.

[91] Zweigert and Kötz, *Introduction to Comparative Law*, pp. 630 ff.; B. S. Markesinis, *The German Law of Torts: A Comparative Introduction*, 3rd edn (Oxford, 1994), pp. 676 ff.; Reinhard Zimmermann and Dirk A. Verse, 'Die Reaktion des Reichsgerichts auf die Kodifikation des deutschen Deliktsrechts (1900–1914)', in Falk and Mohnhaupt (eds.), *Das Bürgerliche Gesetzbuch*, pp. 335 ff.

[92] For example, Robert-Joseph Pothier, *Traité des obligations*, nn. 121, 456.

[93] Inst. II, 1, 41: 'Sed si quidem ex causa donationis aut dotis aut qualibet alia ex causa tradantur, sine dubio transferuntur: venditae vero et traditae non aliter emptori adquiruntur, quam si is venditori pretium solverit vel alio modo ei satisfecerit, veluti expromissore aut pignore dato. quod cavetur quidem etiam lege duodecim tabularum: tamen recte dicitur et iure gentium, id

In the very next sentence, however, the rule appears to be rendered more or less nugatory: for here it is said to be sufficient that the vendor 'puts his trust in the purchaser'. It is likely that we are dealing with an attempt to reconcile generally accepted notions and practices of Justinian's time with the principles of classical Roman law. Painstaking modern research has revealed the significance and development of both the rule and its fatal qualification within the history of Roman law.[94] The lawyers of the *ius commune*, on the other hand, had to accept the text as they found it. Yet they could never be quite sure how to understand its content.[95] Considerable uncertainty persisted, as is reflected in the fact that all three natural law codes contain a different version of the rule.[96] The draftsmen of the BGB, who at first intended to abandon Inst. II, 1, 41, finally opted for yet another solution (the justification for which is, however, regarded as questionable).[97]

Roman roots IV: different layers of tradition

If Inst. II, 1, 41 provides an example of a notoriously unclear rule, we have only to look at the question of transfer of ownership in general to find two entirely different regimes, both of which can be traced back to – and have in fact been derived from – a contradictory set of sources from Roman law.

The abstract and the causal system

In classical Roman law, transfer of ownership[98] was effected by *mancipatio* for *res mancipi*, by *traditio* for *res nec mancipi*, alternatively by *in iure cessio*

---

est iure naturali, id effici. sed si is qui vendidit fidem emptoris secutus fuerit, dicendum est statium rem emptoris fieri'.

[94] Cf. Zimmermann, *Law of Obligations*, pp. 272 ff.

[95] For all details, see Robert Feenstra, *Reclame en Revendicatie* (Haarlem, 1949), pp. 98 ff., 255 ff.; Coing, *Europäisches Privatrecht*, pp. 307 ff.; Klaus Luig, 'Übergabe und Übereignung der verkauften Sache nach römischem und gemeinem Recht', in *Satura Robert Feenstra oblata* (Fribourg, 1985), pp. 445 ff.; Robert Feenstra, 'Eigendomsovergang bij koop en terugvorderingsrecht van de onbetalde verkoper: Romeins recht en Middeleeuws handelsrecht', (1987) 50 *THRHR* 134 ff.

[96] §§ 224 ff. I 11 PrALR; art. 1582 ff. code civil; § 1063 ABGB.

[97] § 454 BGB. For all details, see the historical discussion by Klaus Luig, 'Das Verhältnis von Kaufpreiszahlung und Eigentumsübergang nach deutschem Recht', in Letizia Vacca (ed.), *Vendita e trasferimento della proprietà nella prospettiva storico-comparatistica*, vol. I (Milan, 1991), pp. 225 ff.

[98] For a general overview of the historical development, see J. H. Dondorp and E. J. H. Schrage, *Levering krachtens geldige titel* (Amsterdam, 1991) (on which, see (1994) 11 *ZSS* (Romanistische Abteilung) 703 ff.).

for both categories of things. *Mancipatio* and *in iure cessio* were 'abstract', i.e. their validity did not depend on whether they were based on a legal ground motivating and justifying such transfer. *Traditio*, on the other hand, was (probably) causal in that it did require a *iusta causa traditionis* (such as a valid contract of sale).[99] Justinian retained only *traditio*.[100] But he incorporated into the *Corpus Juris Civilis* a text by Julian (D. 41, 1, 36), who appears to have dispensed with this requirement; and in a key text of the Institutes (II, 1, 40) he merely stressed the intention to transfer.

For a long time, the *ius commune* was dominated by the causal system: transfer of ownership was seen to depend on what the jurists of the German *usus modernus* referred to as *titulus* (= *iusta causa traditionis*) and *modus* (= the different forms of *traditio*).[101] This regime was incorporated into the Austrian Civil Code.[102] It was not difficult to trace it back to Roman law. Friedrich Carl von Savigny, on the other hand, took his cue from texts such as Iul. D. 41, 1, 36 and Inst. II, 1, 40, and managed, on the basis of a reinterpretation of the Roman sources, to establish his doctrine of the abstract dispositive legal act:[103] transfer of ownership was based on an agreement between the owner and the acquirer that ownership be transferred. This agreement constituted a legal transaction that was completely separate from, and independent of, the underlying obligatory act, and it replaced the *titulus* of the older doctrine. Eventually, this proposition found its way into the BGB,[104] where it contributes to the famous (or infamous) 'abstract' character of the German Civil Code.[105] The differences between

---

[99] Max Kaser, *Das Römische Privatrecht*, vol. I, 2nd edn (Munich, 1971), pp. 412 ff.

[100] Max Kaser, *Das Römische Privatrecht*, vol. II, 2nd edn (Munich, 1975), pp. 282 ff.

[101] For all details, see Coing, *Europäisches Privatrecht*, vol. I, pp. 302 ff.; Italo Birocchi, 'Vendita e trasferimento della proprietà nel diritto comune', in Vacca (ed.), *Vendita*, pp. 139 ff.; Dondorp and Schrage, *Levering*, pp. 31 ff.

[102] § 380 ABGB; on which see Theo Mayer-Maly, 'Kauf und Eigentumsübergang im österreichischen Recht', in Vacca (ed.), *Vendita*, pp. 275 ff.

[103] For details, see Wilhelm Felgentraeger, *Friedrich Carl von Savignys Einfluß auf die Übereignungslehre* (Leipzig, 1927); Filippo Ranieri, 'Die Lehre von der abstrakten Übereignung in der deutschen Zivilrechtswissenschaft des 19. Jahrhunderts', in Helmut Coing and Walter Wilhelm (eds.), *Wissenschaft und Kodifikation des Privatrechts im 19. Jahrhundert*, vol. II (Frankfurt am Main, 1977), pp. 90 ff.; Coing, *Europäisches Privatrecht*, vol. II, pp. 393 ff.; Götz Landwehr, 'Abstrakte Rechtsgeschäfte in Wissenschaft und Gesetzgebung des 19. Jahrhunderts', in Karsten Schmidt (ed.), *Rechtsdogmatik und Rechtspolitik* (Berlin, 1990), pp. 173 ff.

[104] Cf. the discussion by Rolf Knütel, 'Vendita e trasferimento della proprietà nel diritto tedesco', in Vacca (ed.), *Vendita*, pp. 287 ff.

[105] Folke Schmidt, 'The German Approach to Law', (1965) 9 *SSL* 133 ff.; Konrad Zweigert and Hartmut Dietrich, 'System and Language of the German Civil Code 1900', in S. J. Stoljar (ed.), *Problems of Codification* (Canberra, 1977), pp. 34 ff.; Zweigert and Kötz, *Introduction to Comparative Law*, pp. 144 ff.

the abstract and the causal systems of transfer of ownership are not inconsiderable; thus, for instance, the *condictio indebiti* acquires much greater practical significance within a system which allows the transferor to lose his title and requires him to argue that this change of title may have been unjustified. Yet, at the same time, both systems are undoubtedly civilian.

The consensual system

The same is true even of a third system that we find in modern Continental codes. It does not require a separate act of conveyance at all, but allows ownership to pass upon conclusion of a sale.[106] The French code civil provides a fine example. Its art. 1583 reads: 'Elle [sc.: the contract of sale] est parfaite entre les parties, et la propriété est acquise de droit à l'acheteur à l'égard du vendeur, dès qu'on est convenu de la chose et du prix, quoique la chose n'ait pas encore été livrée, ni le prix payé.' This doctrine was propagated most forcefully by Hugo Grotius[107] and other natural lawyers of the seventeenth and eighteenth centuries.[108] But it can already be found in Leonardus Lessius,[109] and even at the time of the Commentators it had been foreshadowed by the introduction of a routine clause into notarial sales instruments which stipulated that the vendor would henceforth possess on behalf of the purchaser.[110] This was interpreted as *traditio per constitutum possessorium*. Similar constructions paved the way to the consensual principle in French law.[111] Thus, the new approach was partly the product of notarial practice and possibly also of the French *droit coutumier*. It was also based on biblical authority: because thought is to be equated to deed, a

---

[106] For comparative evaluations of the different regimes regulating the transfer of property in Europe (abstract, causal and consensual; on the latter cf. the next paragraph in the text), see Franco Ferrari, 'Vom Abstraktionsprinzip und Konsensualprinzip zum Traditionsprinzip', (1993) 1 *ZEUP* 52 ff.; Andreas Roth, 'Abstraktions- und Konsensprinzip und ihre Auswirkungen auf die Rechtsstellung der Kaufvertragsparteien', (1993) 92 *ZVglRWiss* 371 ff.; Ulrich Drobnig, 'Transfer of Property', in Hartkamp et al. (eds.), *Towards a European Civil Code*, pp. 495 ff.; L. P. W. van Vliet, *Transfer of Movables in German, French, English and Dutch Law* (Nijmegen, 2000); Andreas Wacke, 'Eigentumserwerb des Käufers durch schlichten Konsens oder erst mit Übergabe?', (2000) 8 *ZEUP* 254 ff. Neither the abstract nor the consensual system is carried through in practice without exception. Thus there seems to be a trend among the modern legal systems towards a convergence (once again) on the basis of the causal system.

[107] *De jure belli ac pacis*, lib. II, cap. VI, 1.

[108] Cf., e.g., Samuel Pufendorf, *De jure naturae et gentium*, lib. IV, cap. IX.

[109] William M. Gordon, *Studies in the Transfer of Property by Traditio* (Aberdeen, 1970), pp. 172 ff.

[110] Dondorp and Schrage, *Levering*, pp. 49 ff.   [111] Ibid., pp. 83 ff.

promise to transfer ownership must have the same effect as the alienation of property itself.[112] Significantly, however, the consensual theory was couched in terms of traditional civilian learning and thus woven into the fabric of the learned law. Grotius even drew on Roman law in order to provide doctrinal support – both on its *usus modernus* and on the classical law as restored by contemporary legal humanism.[113]

Roman roots V: more ambiguity

Mora creditoris

There are many more examples of this phenomenon: two distinctly different regimes prevailing in the European codes and both of them tracing their pedigree back to Roman law. *Mora creditoris*, for instance, is unknown in some modern legal systems as a specific legal institution. The creditor is liable, in the same way as the debtor, for breach of contract.[114] This was, *mutatis mutandis*, also the view taken by the authors of the *ius commune*: they saw *mora creditoris* as a counterpart, or twin image, of *mora debitoris*.[115] Both were based on fault, and both required the breach of a duty (to deliver in the one case, to receive performance in the other). The concept of *mora creditoris* underlying the provisions of the BGB is quite a different one.[116] For fault as a requirement for *mora creditoris* had lost its basis when it came to be recognised in the second half of the nineteenth century that the creditor is not obliged to receive performance, but only entitled to do so. The institution of *mora creditoris* is merely designed to relieve in certain respects the position of a debtor who has done whatever he could reasonably be expected to do. This doctrine goes back to Friedrich Mommsen;[117] it was emphatically reasserted by Josef Kohler[118] and it impressed the fathers of the BGB.[119] Of course, both Mommsen and the earlier authors of the *ius*

---

[112] Ibid., pp. 70 ff.   [113] Gordon, *Studies in the Transfer of Property*, pp. 173 ff.

[114] Cf., as far as French law is concerned, the discussion by Uwe Hüffer, *Leistungsstörungen durch Gläubigerhandeln* (Berlin, 1976), pp. 61 ff., 87 ff.

[115] Cf., e.g., Christian Friedrich Glück, *Ausführliche Erläuterung der Pandekten*, vol. IV (Erlangen, 1796), pp. 401 ff.; Carl Otto von Madai, *Die Lehre von der Mora, Dargestellt nach Grundsätzen des Römischen Rechts* (Halle, 1837), pp. 227 ff.

[116] §§ 293 ff. BGB.

[117] *Die Lehre von der Mora nebst Beiträgen zur Lehre von der culpa* (Brunswick, 1855), pp. 133 ff.

[118] 'Annahme und Annahmeverzug', (1879) 17 *JhJb* 261 ff.

[119] 'Motive', in Mugdan, *Die gesammten Materialien*, vol. II, pp. 37 ff.; cf. also Hüffer, *Leistungsstörungen*, pp. 14 ff.

commune claimed that their views were derived from, or at least reconcilable with, the sources of Roman law. Contemporary Romanist doctrine tends to side with Mommsen and to attribute the modern, objective construction of *mora creditoris* to the Roman lawyers.[120] Again, however, not all our sources conform to such a general pattern.[121]

Set-off

Or one may look at set-off as a convenient way of satisfying mutual debts. The *magna quaestio* has always been how set-off becomes effective. Modern legal systems deriving from Roman law generally fall into two groups in this regard; § 388 BGB represents a good example of the one, when it states that 'the set-off is made by declaration to the other party'. This rule is based on a tradition dating back to the Glossator Azo.[122] Both French[123] and Austrian[124] law, on the other hand, do not require any such declaration. As soon (and as far) as two debts capable of being set off confront each other, both of them are extinguished *ipso iure*; no account is taken of the will of the two parties concerned. Again, this conception of a set-off can be traced back to the Glossators.[125] How did this dichotomy arise? Because it was not entirely clear how Justinian's compensation worked. 'Ut actiones ipso iure minuant', say the Institutes,[126] and in the *Codex*, too, it is emphasised that 'compensationes ex omnibus actionibus ipso iure fieri'.[127] That is, however, in strange contrast to the language used in other places ('compensationis obici', 'opponi compensationem')[128] and also to the fact that the *ipso iure* effect of *compensatio* is not stressed more strongly in the Digest. And what

---

[120] Cf. Kaser, *Römische Privatrecht*, vol. I, pp. 517 ff.; Wolfgang Kunkel and Heinrich Honsell, *Römisches Recht*, 4th edn (Berlin, Heidelberg and New York, 1987), pp. 247 ff.

[121] For a discussion see Zimmermann, *Law of Obligations*, pp. 819 ff.

[122] For details, see Heinrich Dernburg, *Geschichte und Theorie der Kompensation*, 2nd edn (Heidelberg, 1868), pp. 284 ff. On the notion of retroactivity traditionally attributed to the declaration of set-off cf. now the historical analysis by Pascal Pichonnaz, 'The Retroactive Effect of Set-Off', (2000) 48 *TR* 541 ff.

[123] Art. 1290 code civil.

[124] § 1438 ABGB. For a modern comparative discussion see Reinhard Zimmermann, 'Die Aufrechnung: Eine rechtsvergleichende Skizze zum Europäischen Vertragsrecht', in *Festschrift für Dieter Medicus* (Cologne, 1999), pp. 721 ff.

[125] Dernburg, *Geschichte und Theorie*, pp. 283 ff.   [126] Inst. IV, 6, 30.

[127] C. 4, 31, 14 (Iust.); cf. also C. 4, 31, 4 (Alex.); Paul. D. 16, 2, 4; Paul. D. 16, 2, 21 (all interpolated).

[128] C. 4, 31, 14, 1. Cf. further Siro Solazzi, *La compensazione nel diritto romano*, 2nd edn (Naples, 1950), pp. 166 ff.

is the reason for this ambiguity in our sources? It lies in the distinctly procedural flavour that was one of the most characteristic features of set-off in classical Roman law. Whether, and if so, in which manner and under which circumstances a set-off could be effected, depended entirely on the nature of the formula applicable in a given situation.[129] Thus, the Roman lawyers never developed a uniform and systematic approach to the problem of set-off, and Justinian was faced with a formidable task when he recognised the need to devise a generalised doctrine, that was no longer dictated by procedural niceties. After all, the formulary procedure had been abandoned. In spite of all his efforts, however, he did not manage to eradicate all traces of the older legal layers.

The process of generalisation

Generalisation of rules and institutions, concepts and criteria of Roman law is a characteristic feature of the civilian tradition.[130] Often, that process had already been started by the classical Roman lawyers, who built on the foundations of the ancient *ius civile*; it was carried on by Justinian; and it was further advanced by the jurists of the *ius commune*. Sometimes a reaction occurred against these too far-flung generalities. The codifications, of course, reflect the results of these developments. Set-off provides a rather inconspicuous example. The evolution of the law of delict is much more spectacular.

The evolution of the law of delict

The point of departure was a quaintly worded enactment from the third century BC. Even in Roman law this statute had been extended, adapted and modernised in so many ways that a jurist from the time of its enactment would hardly have recognised the late classical (or Justinianic) delict of *damnum culpa datum* as specifically Aquilian; and any legal advice based

---

[129] For details, see Zimmermann, *Law of Obligations*, pp. 761 ff.
[130] The point is also emphasised by Hartmut Wicke, 'Haftung für Verrichtungsgehilfen in der Europäischen Rechtsgeschichte-Kontinuität durch Generalisierung', in Andreas Thier, Guido Pfeifer and Philipp Grzimek (eds.), *Kontinuitäten und Zäsuren in der Europäischen Rechtsgeschichte* (Frankfurt am Main and Berlin, 1999), pp. 165 ff.; Hartmut Wicke, *Respondeat Superior-Haftung für Verrichtungsgehilfen im römischen, römisch-holländischen, englischen und südafrikanischen Recht* (Berlin, 2000).

merely on the wording of the *lex* would have been hopelessly inadequate. 'Urere frangere rumpere' had been superseded by the all-embracing term 'corrumpere';[131] remedies were granted in cases of indirect causation[132] and even in situations where the substance of the object concerned was not at all affected;[133] fault in the broadest sense of the word became a sufficient basis for liability;[134] the injured party could recover his full 'quod interest';[135] the role of plaintiff was no longer confined to the owner of the object killed or damaged;[136] and the ambit of Aquilian protection had even been extended to damage to freemen.[137]

This process of extension, adaptation and modernisation was carried on by courts and writers of the *ius commune*: almost imperceptibly at first, with small and hesitating steps, but leading, eventually, to the far-ranging, popular and comprehensive remedy described by writers like Samuel Stryk.[138] The famous Enlightenment lawyer Christian Thomasius even set out to pull down 'the Aquilian mask' from the contemporary *actio de damno dato*, which, he said, differed from the Aquilian action as much as a bird from a quadruped.[139] At the same time, however, it was still distinctively civilian. So was the famous general provision of the French[140] and Austrian Codes[141] in which the development culminated. It constituted the statutory version of the 'natural' law of delict as propounded most prominently by Hugo Grotius.[142] 'Ex . . . culpa obligatio naturaliter oritur, si damnum datum est,

---

131 Zimmermann, *Law of Obligations*, pp. 984 ff. For what follows, cf. now also the monographs by Bénédict Winiger, *La responsabilité aquilienne romaine: Damnum iniuria datum* (Basel and Frankfurt am Main, 1997) and Wolfgang Freiherr Raitz von Frentz, *Lex Aquilia und Negligence* (Baden-Baden, 2000), pp. 44 ff.

132 Zimmermann, *Law of Obligations*, pp. 978 ff.   133 Ibid., pp. 986 ff.

134 Ibid., pp. 1005 ff.   135 Ibid., pp. 969 ff., 973 ff.

136 Ibid., pp. 994 ff.   137 Ibid., n. 50, pp. 1014 ff.

138 'Tituli praesentis usus amplissimus est, cum omnium damnorum reparatio ex hoc petatur, si modo ulla alterius culpa doceri possit': *Usus modernus pandectarum*, lib. IX, tit. II, § 1. For details of the development, see Horst Kaufmann, *Rezeption und usus modernus der actio legis Aquiliae* (Cologne and Graz, 1958); Coing, *Europäisches Privatrecht*, vol. I, pp. 509 ff.; Zimmermann, *Law of Obligations*, pp. 1017 ff.; Jan Schröder, 'Die zivilrechtliche Haftung für schuldhafte Schadenszufügungen im deutschen usus modernus', in *La responsabilità civile da atto illecito nella prospettiva storico-comparatistica* (Torino, 1995), pp. 142 ff.; Freiherr Raitz von Frentz, *Lex Aquilia und Negligence*, pp. 71 ff.

139 *Larva legis Aquiliae detracta actioni de damno dato*, 1703, § 1. For a modern edition, with translation and commentary, of that text see Margaret Hewett and Reinhard Zimmermann, *Larva Legis Aquiliae* (Oxford and Portland, Oreg., 2000).

140 Art. 1382 code civil.   141 § 1295 ABGB.

142 On the development from Grotius to the code civil, see Robert Feenstra, *Vergelding en vergoeding*, 2nd edn (Deventer, 1993), pp. 15 ff.; Zimmermann, *Law of Obligations*, pp. 1036, n. 248.

nempe ut id resarciatur', he had postulated,[143] using terms and concepts that were thoroughly familiar to anybody even vaguely acquainted with the tradition of Aquilian liability.

One of the core features of natural law theories concerning delictual liability was, of course, their readiness to provide compensation for purely patrimonial loss. Both § 1295 ABGB and art. 1382 code civil reflect this way of thinking. Even this, however, was not a revolutionary novelty. For a somewhat equivocal phrase in Inst. IV, 3, 16 i.f.[144] could, if taken out of context, be read to imply that according to Roman law any *damnum* was recoverable, irrespective of whether it had flowed from damage to the plaintiff's property or person. This wide interpretation had gained ground in the Middle Ages, and, as a result, Aquilian protection had become available in cases of purely patrimonial loss long before the natural lawyers.[145] The Pandectists of the nineteenth century, on the other hand, predominantly advocated a return to the more limited scope of Aquilian liability in Roman law,[146] and it was this view which found expression in § 823 I BGB: a certain number of specific rights and interests are listed,[147] and it is only by violating one of them that a person may become liable in delict. Neither the German nor the French Codes have conclusively settled the

---

On the history of the relevant provision in the Italian codice civile (art. 2043) see Guido Alpa, 'Unjust Damage and the Role of Negligence: Historical Profile', (1994) 9 *Tulane European and Civil Law Forum* 147 ff.

[143] *De jure belli ac pacis*, lib. II, cap. XVII, 1. On Grotius' general provision of delictual liability, see Robert Feenstra, 'Das Deliktsrecht bei Grotius, insbesondere der Schadensersatz bei Tötung und Körperverletzung', in Feenstra and Zimmermann (eds.), *Das römisch-holländische Recht*, pp. 429 ff.

[144] 'Sed si non corpore damnum fuerit datum neque corpus laesum fuerit, sed alio modo damnum alicui contigit . . . placuit eum qui obnoxius fuerit in factum actione teneri.'

[145] See Kaufmann, *Rezeption*, pp. 46 ff., 62 ff.; Zimmermann, *Law of Obligations*, pp. 1023 sq.; Schröder, 'Zivilrechtliche Haftung', pp. 147 ff. Cf. also, for instance, Thomas Kiefer, *Die Aquilische Haftung im 'Allgemeinen Landrecht für die Preußischen Staaten' von 1794* (Pfaffenweiler, 1989), who draws attention to the continuity between the doctrines of the *usus modernus* and the generalised form of delictual liability in the Prussian Code.

[146] Cf., for example, Johann Christian Hasse, *Die Culpa des Römischen Rechts*, 2nd edn (Bonn, 1838), pp. 26 ff.; Windscheid and Kipp, *Lehrbuch*, §§ 451, 455; RGZ 9, 158 (163 ff.); Hans Hermann Seiler, 'Römisches deliktisches Schadensersatzrecht in der obergerichtlichen Rechtsprechung des 19. Jahrhunderts', in *Festschrift für Hermann Lange* (Stuttgart, Berlin and Cologne, 1992), pp. 256 ff.; Ruth Bilstein, *Das deliktische Schadensersatzrecht der Lex Aquilia in der Rechtsprechung des Reichsgerichts* (Münster and Hamburg, 1994), pp. 19 ff., 28 ff.

[147] For details, see Hans-Peter Benöhr, 'Die Redaktion der Paragraphen 823 und 826 BGB', in Zimmermann et al. (eds.), *Rechtsgeschichte und Privatrechtsdogmatik*, pp. 499 ff.; Zimmermann and Verse, 'Die Reaktion', pp. 320 ff. The list contained in § 823 I BGB can, incidentally, also be traced back to Grotius: cf. Feenstra, *Vergelding*, p. 17.

thorny issue of liability for pure economic loss. Courts and legal writers in the one country have had to restrict the range of application of an all too liberal provision,[148] while in the other country they are devising strategies of extending the scope of an all too narrowly conceived liability regime.[149] While starting from two opposing principles, the systems in actual practice therefore tend to converge.[150]

The evolution of the law of contract

Since Gaius, contract has been perceived as the other main branch of the law of obligations. Here we find a similar development from unimposing origins towards the modern general law of contract, which constitutes a central feature of all civilian jurisdictions.[151] In this case, not even the Pandectists attempted to reverse the position. The Roman rule was 'nuda pactio obligationem non parit'.[152] But by the time of Justinian, a whole variety of agreements had in one way or another become legally recognised. First, there were the four famous consensual contracts, already well established in classical Roman law. Then there were the contracts *innominati* ('*innominati*' even though some of them had actually acquired individual names). Furthermore, consensual agreements were enforceable, if they had been attached to one of the recognised contracts and had been concluded at the same time as the main contract (*pacta in continenti adiecta*). Then, again, there were two groups of agreements, which were not classified as contracts, but which were nevertheless enforceable: the so-called *pacta praetoria* and *pacta legitima*. Other informal arrangements, which did not fall into these categories, could be raised by way of defence; apart from that they could at least be regarded as *obligationes naturales*.

The *Corpus Juris* thus presented a somewhat patchy picture; it was marked by haphazard distinctions and internal inconsistencies. These

---

[148] Cf., e.g., *Canadian National Railway Co. v. Norsk Pacific Steamship Co. Ltd.* (1992) 91 DLR (4th) 289 (320 ff.) and Peter Gotthardt, 'Landesbericht Frankreich', in Christian von Bar (ed.), *Deliktsrecht in Europa* (Cologne and Munich, 1993), p. 16.
[149] Cf., most recently, Karl Larenz and Claus-Wilhelm Canaris, *Lehrbuch des Schuldrechts*, vol. II/2, 13th edn (Munich, 1994), § 75 I 3, 4.
[150] For a similar conclusion, see Helmut Koziol, 'Generalnorm und Einzeltatbestände als Systeme der Verschuldenshaftung: Unterschiede und Angleichungsmöglichkeiten', (1995) 3 *ZEUP* 359 ff.; and see now the comprehensive study by Christian von Bar, *Gemeineuropäisches Deliktsrecht*, vol. II (Munich, 1999), nn. 23 ff.
[151] For details of what follows, see the literature quoted above, n. 68.   [152] Ulp. D. 2, 14, 7, 4.

inconsistencies, of course, presented an intellectual challenge to Glossators, Commentators and the later generations of learned lawyers and triggered off their efforts to establish a more rational scheme. Canon law, the law merchant, supposedly 'Germanic' notions of good faith, Spanish scholasticism inspiring sixteenth-century courts and treatise writers in the southern Netherlands, natural law theories: many factors contributed to the ultimate recognition of the principle 'ex nudo pacto oritur actio' (or: 'pacta (nuda) sunt servanda'). In a way, one can say that it was a triumph of Roman law in spite of Roman law. That contracts based on nothing more than formless consent are, as a rule, actionable is recognised (though no longer always specifically spelt out[153]) in all modern Continental codes.

The evolution of the law of unjustified enrichment

The move towards a general law of contract was bound to have consequences for the law of unjustified enrichment. The Roman system of *condictiones* tied in with and supplemented the contractual system.[154] Particularly important was the *condictio indebiti*, for it covered the paradigmatic situation of 'indebitum solutum'.[155] Recognition of 'ex nudo pacto oritur actio' was bound to extend its range of application even further. The main function of the *condictio indebiti* is still to supplement the law of contract. It has to be available whenever a transfer fails to achieve what it is supposed to achieve: the discharge of an obligation that the transferor had incurred towards the transferee. Not surprisingly, therefore, in all Continental legal systems we find general rules dealing with the restitution of benefits conferred by transfer.[156] The significance of these rules within a given legal system may vary. But whether they subscribe to a consensual, a causal or

---

[153] It is usually taken to be implicit in § 305 BGB. But see, as far as France is concerned, art. 1134 code civil.

[154] For details, see Berthold Kupisch, *Ungerechtfertigte Bereicherung: geschichtliche Entwicklungen* (Heidelberg, 1987), pp. 4 ff.; Zimmermann, *Law of Obligations*, pp. 841 ff.; and see the contributions to Eltjo Schrage (ed.), *Unjust Enrichment: The Comparative Legal History of the Law of Restitution*, 2nd edn (Berlin, 1999).

[155] For details, see Zimmermann, *Law of Obligations*, pp. 834 ff., 848 ff. In both Gaius' and Justinian's Institutes 'indebitum solutum' is the only form of enrichment liability dealt with: Gai. III, 91 (and see Gai. D. 44, 7, 5, 3 read in conjunction with Gai. D. 44, 7, 1 pr.); Inst. III, 27, 6.

[156] For all details, see Reinhard Zimmermann, 'Unjustified Enrichment: The Modern Civilian Approach', (1995) 15 *OJLS* 403 ff.

an abstract system of transfer of ownership, all legal systems provide enrichment remedies, and they all specifically emphasise, and single out, the claim of enrichment by transfer.

Historically, this uniformity of approach is based on the common Roman heritage, for we are dealing here with the modern, extended version of the *condictio indebiti*. Even the new Dutch Civil Code devotes nine sections to 'onverschuldigde betaling', before it deals with other cases of unjustified enrichment.[157] Characteristically, the modern version of the *condictio indebiti* has abandoned, step by step, certain idiosyncrasies of its Roman ancestor; characteristically, too, this gradual development is still reflected in the different codes.[158]

Apart from that, however, there have been, over the last 300 years, repeated attempts to formulate a general enrichment action – a magic formula comprising all instances of unjustified retention even apart from *indebitum solutum*. In France and Germany the decisive advances were launched from two completely different points of departure. The French courts[159] recognised a general enrichment action on the basis of the *actio de in rem verso utilis*, a claim based historically on a single passage in Justinian's *Code*,[160] accepted by the code civil – at best – in a vestigial form, and generalised by a German professor writing a textbook on French private law.[161] Friedrich Carl von Savigny, on the other hand, chose the *condictio sine causa* (*generalis*) as the most suitable means to overcome the Roman fragmentation.[162] But even before the Court de Cassation and Savigny, Hugo Grotius had drawn

---

[157] Artt. 203:6 ff. BW. For an analysis of the historical development see Eltjo J. H. Schrage, 'The Law of Restitution: The History of Dutch Legislation', in Schrage *Unjust Enrichment*, pp. 323 ff.

[158] See the discussion in Zimmermann, 'Unjustified Enrichment', 408 ff.; as far as the law of unjustified enrichment under the *usus modernus pandectarum* is concerned, see Berthold Kupisch, 'Ungerechtfertigte Bereicherung', in Schrage (ed.), *Unjust Enrichment*, pp. 237 ff.

[159] Arrêt Boudier, 15.6.1892, Recueil Dalloz 1892 (première partie), p. 596.

[160] C. 4, 26, 7, 3 (Diocl. et Max.).

[161] See Karl Salomo Zachariä von Lingenthal, *Handbuch des Französischen Civilrechts*, vol. II (Heidelberg, 1808), §§ 399 ff. The astonishing career of the *actio de in rem verso* has been described by Berthold Kupisch, *Die Versionsklage* (Heidelberg, 1965). See further John P. Dawson, *Unjust Enrichment* (Boston, 1951), pp. 85 ff.; Robert Feenstra, 'Die ungerechtfertigte Bereicherung in dogmengeschichtlicher Sicht', (1972) 29 *Ankara Üniversitesi Hukuk Fakültesi Dergisi* 298 ff.; Coing, *Europäisches Privatrecht*, vol. I, pp. 498 ff.; Zimmermann, *Law of Obligations*, pp. 878 ff.

[162] *System des heutigen römischen Rechts*, vol. V (Berlin, 1841), pp. 503 ff. For an analysis, see Horst Hammen, *Die Bedeutung Friedrich Carl v. Savignys für die allgemeinen dogmatischen Grundlagen des Deutschen Bürgerlichen Gesetzbuches* (Berlin, 1983), pp. 187 ff.

together the different threads spun by his predecessors from the material available within the *Corpus Juris*, and had woven them into a single, crisp and comprehensive formula.[163] Even for this formula the Digest, of course, provided a convenient model; it was the general equitable principle enunciated by Pomponius: '... hoc natura aequum est neminem cum alterius detrimento fieri locupletiorem'.[164]

The ambivalence of generalisation

The modern general concept of contract is, ultimately, derived from the consensual contracts of Roman law. On the other hand, one could also describe the modern regime of 'ex nudo pacto oritur actio' as a reversal of the Roman rule of 'nuda pactio obligationem non parit'. This kind of ambivalence is typical of the civilian tradition. One can think of a variety of examples where the second aspect (the gradual erosion of a central principle of Roman contract law by means of Roman learning and, usually, even on the basis of a handful of sources from the *Corpus Juris*) comes out even more strongly.

Specific performance

'Omnis condemnatio pecuniaria' was one such principle. It had been of fundamental importance in classical Roman law.[165] Closely connected with

---

[163] *De jure belli ac pacis*, lib. II, cap. X, 2. For details, see Robert Feenstra, 'De betekenis van De Groot and Huber voor de ontwikkeling van een algemene actie uit ongerechtvaardigde verrijking', in *Uit het recht, Rechtsgeleerde opstellen aangeboden aan mr. P. J. Verdam* (Deventer, 1971), pp. 137 ff.; Robert Feenstra, 'L'influence de la scolastique espagnole sur Grotius en droit privé: quelques expériences dans des questions de fond et de forme, concernant notamment les doctrines de l'erreur et de l'enrichissement sans cause', in Robert Feenstra, *Fata Iuris Romani* (Leiden, 1974), pp. 338 ff.; Zimmermann, *Law of Obligations*, pp. 885 ff.; Daniel Visser, 'Das Recht der ungerechtfertigten Bereicherung', in Feenstra and Zimmermann (eds.), *Das römisch-holländische Recht*, pp. 370 ff.; Robert Feenstra, 'Grotius' Doctrine of Unjust Enrichment as a Source of Obligation: Its Origin and its Influence in Roman-Dutch Law', in Schrage (ed.), *Unjust Enrichment*, pp. 197 ff.

[164] Pomp. D. 12, 6, 14; cf. also Pomp. D. 50, 17, 206. On the origin and background of this principle and its reception into the legal system, see Christian Wollschläger, 'Das stoische Bereicherungsverbot in der römischen Rechtswissenschaft', in *Römisches Recht in der europäischen Tradition, Symposion für Franz Wieacker* (Ebelsbach, 1985), pp. 41 ff.

[165] For what follows, see Coing, *Europäisches Privatrecht*, vol. I, pp. 432 ff.; Zimmermann, *Law of Obligations*, pp. 770 ff.; Karin Nehlsen-von Stryk, 'Grenzen des Rechtzwangs: Zur Geschichte der Naturalvollstreckung', (1993) 193 *AcP* 529 ff.; Wilhelm Rütten, 'Zur Entstehung des

the formulary procedure, it was largely discarded during the ascendancy of the post-classical *cognitio* procedure, but not completely abandoned by Justinian. The *Corpus Juris*, therefore, leaves considerable doubt as to how much ground the principle of specific performance had actually gained in practice. Glossators and Commentators introduced subtle and elaborate distinctions in order to provide some sort of systematic framework for the confusing casuistry of the sources, and even until the days of the *usus modernus* the question continued to be embroiled in disputes. 'Nemo potest praecise cogi ad factum' remained the general maxim applicable for *facere* obligations. Via Pothier[166] it even found its way into the French code civil.[167] In Germany, the last vestiges of *omnis condemnatio pecuniaria* were ultimately overcome in the course of the nineteenth century, and parties to a contract are entitled, as a matter or course, to demand performance of their respective obligations *in specie*. This is implicit in § 241 BGB. By and large, the position in German law is representative of the contemporary civilian approach, for even in France art. 1142 code civil has, for all practical purposes, been rendered nugatory.[168]

Contracts in favour of third parties

'Alteri stipulari nemo potest' is another principle of Roman law that took a long time and much intellectual effort to overcome.[169] It was taken to prevent the recognition of a contract in favour of third parties. Justinian's compilers, however, not only retained – and even emphasised – this principle, but also took over, extended or introduced a number of situations in which it did not apply.[170] Thus they provided convenient levers, which sufficiently imaginative lawyers could use to unhinge the principle altogether.

Erfüllungszwangs im Schuldverhältnis', in *Festschrift für Joachim Gernhuber* (Tübingen, 1993), pp. 939 ff.; Tilman Repgen, *Vertragstreue und Erfüllungszwang in der mittelalterlichen Rechtswissenschaft* (Paderborn, Munich, Vienna and Zurich, 1994).

[166] *Traité des obligations*, n. 160.   [167] Art. 1142 code civil.

[168] For a comparative discussion, see Zweigert and Kötz, *Introduction to Comparative Law*, pp. 475 ff.

[169] For all details of the development, see Zimmermann, *Law of Obligations*, pp. 34 ff.; and see also Hein Kötz, 'Rights of Third Parties: Third Party Beneficiaries and Assignment', in *International Encyclopedia of Comparative Law*, vol. VII (Tübingen, 1992), ch. 13, nn. 4 ff.; Kötz, *European Contract Law*, pp. 245 ff.

[170] Cf., for example, C. 8, 54, 3 (Diocl. et Max.); Ulp. D. 13, 7, 13 pr.; C. 3, 42, 8 (Diocl. et Max.). The latter texts are probably interpolated.

In the course of the seventeenth century, and under the combined auspices of *usus modernus* and natural law, the contract in favour of third parties came to be very widely accepted, albeit on the basis that the third party was required to accept the right which was to be conferred on him. This was a consequence of the emphasis that natural lawyers, and most notably Hugo Grotius,[171] placed on will and consensus as the essential elements of contract law. Even before Grotius, incidentally, Antonius Perezius and Covarruvias had drawn attention to the fact that recognition of contracts affecting third parties followed from the endorsement of 'ex nudo pacto oritur actio'.[172]

It was in the garb of this consensual construction that the contract in favour of a third party made its way into the Prussian, Bavarian and Saxonian codifications. The Austrian Code was more conservative in this respect and retained the 'alteri stipulari nemo potest' principle.[173] So did, under the influence of Robert-Joseph Pothier,[174] the French code civil.[175] It made provision for only two narrowly defined exceptions in art. 1121: a 'stipulation au profit d'un tiers' is valid, 'losque telle est la condition d'une stipulation que l'on fait pour soi-même ou d'une donation que l'on fait a un autre'. It is not difficult to discover the sources from the *Corpus Juris* on which these exceptions were based. French courts have managed to prize open this back door and to introduce into French law – *contra legem*, as it were – the modern contract in favour of third parties.[176] According to the 'théorie de la création directe de l'action' the third party acquires the right directly at the time when promisor and promisee conclude their contract; his own declaration does not have a constitutive effect. This has brought French law into line with modern German law; the 'mature'[177] solutions found in §§ 328 ff. are due to the conceptual clarity achieved by the Pandectists.[178] The Austrian Code, as a result of a revision in 1916, follows a very similar pattern.

---

[171] *De jure belli ac pacis*, lib. II, cap. XI, 18.

[172] See Coing, *Europäisches Privatrecht*, vol. I, p. 425; and see Antonius Perezius, *Praelectiones in duodecim libros codicis*, lib. VIII, tit. LV, n. 9.

[173] § 881 ABGB.   [174] *Traité des obligations*, nn. 57 ff.   [175] Art. 1165 code civil.

[176] Cf. Zweigert and Kötz, *Introduction to Comparative Law*, pp. 462 ff.; Kötz, *European Contract Law*, pp. 249 ff.

[177] Zweigert and Kötz, *Introduction to Comparative Law*, p. 468.

[178] Cf. esp. Windscheid and Kipp, *Lehrbuch*, § 316.

Intellectual unity beyond codification

Roman law, natural law and pandectist legal science

The historical development of the contract in favour of third parties gives rise to two further observations. Firstly, contrary to what is often alleged, the BGB is not necessarily more 'Roman' in its content than the so-called natural law codes. The main thrust of natural law was not directed against the rules and institutions of Roman law as such, but rather against the complexity of sources, the lack of system and transparency, and the great number of intractable doctrinal disputes that had for centuries enveloped its application and bedevilled its comprehensibility. The nineteenth-century Pandectists,[179] on the other hand, who prepared the ground for the BGB were often quite happy to endorse, perpetuate and further refine a development that was clearly moving away from the ancient Roman sources. In essence, they advocated organic development rather than sterile historicism; and while it is easy, today, to criticise their methodology one must not, at the same time, forget that they created a legal framework not only of unequalled sophistication but also suited to the requirements of the first one hundred years of the 'Modern'.[180]

For another illustration of this point we may turn to the problem of the determination of price. Article 1108 code civil requires every contract to have 'un objet certain'. 'Objet' in terms of this rule is also, for instance, the counterperformance to be given for the performance of services, the transfer of an object, etc. As far as a contract of sale is concerned, art. 1591 code civil specifically determines that the price has to be 'déterminé et désigné par les parties'. These rules are based, unmistakably, on Roman law. Article 1591 is the codified version of the 'certum pretium' requirement for the Roman contract of sale.[181] The more general rule of art. 1108, on the other hand, appears to represent an intermediate stage within the

---

[179] For an overview in English, see Mathias Reimann, 'Nineteenth Century German Legal Science', (1990) 13 *Boston College LR* 837 ff.; Wieacker, *History of Private Law*, pp. 279 ff.; Reinhard Zimmermann, 'Heutiges Recht, Römisches Recht und heutiges Römisches Recht', in Zimmermann et al. (eds.), *Rechtsgeschichte und Privatrechtsdogmatik*, pp. 9 ff. For a vindication of their leading representative, Bernhard Windscheid, see Ulrich Falk, *Ein Gelehrter wie Windscheid* (Frankfurt am Main, 1989).

[180] Cf. Paul Johnson, *The Birth of the Modern-World Society 1815–1830* (New York, 1991).

[181] It is discussed in a number of interesting fragments; see my Zimmermann, *Law of Obligations*, pp. 253 ff.

grand development from the fragmented Roman law of contracts (which focused on individual types of contract, the constituent elements of which, as a matter of course, had to be the object of the agreement of the parties) towards the modern, general concept of contract, which emphasises the freedom of the parties to design their own contract.[182] Thus, according to the modern point of view, it only has to be ascertained whether the parties had intended to be bound.[183] This is, indeed, the approach adopted by the BGB.[184] Thus, in particular, determination of the price may be left to one of the contracting parties, whether he has to decide 'in an equitable manner' or even in his free discretion.[185] This obviously represents a deviation from Roman law. It is based on pandectist doctrine[186] which had managed to venture, in Jhering's famous words, beyond Roman law by means of Roman law. In sharp contradistinction to the strict requirements of artt. 1129, 1591 code civil which have given rise to a complex casuistry,[187] §§ 315 ff. BGB appear to have stood the test of time. It is therefore hardly surprising that these more liberal principles are also gaining ground internationally.[188]

Factors counterbalancing nationalistic isolation

The second point relates to the intellectual unity of the civilian tradition. We have emphasised that it existed until the end of the eighteenth century;

---

[182] Cf. Barry Nicholas, *The French Law of Contract*, 2nd edn (Oxford, 1992), pp. 115 ff.

[183] Cf. Wolfgang Witz, *Der unbestimmte Kaufpreis* (Neuwied and Frankfurt am Main, 1989), pp. 89 ff., 155 ff. and the comparative discussion by Barry Nicholas, 'Certainty of Price', in *Comparative and Private International Law: Essays in Honour of J. H. Merryman* (Berlin, 1990), pp. 247 ff.; A. T. van Mehren, 'The Formation of Contracts', in *International Encyclopedia of Comparative Law*, vol. VII ch. 9, nn. 50 ff.

[184] §§ 315 ff. BGB.   [185] § 315 I BGB.

[186] For details, see Hans-Joachim Winter, 'Die Bestimmung der Leistung durch den Vertragspartner oder Dritte (§§ 315 bis 319 BGB) unter besonderer Berücksichtigung der Rechtsprechung und Lehre des 19. Jahrhunderts' (Dr. iur. thesis, Frankfurt, 1979).

[187] See Witz, *Unbestimmte Kaufpreis*, pp. 21 ff.; Christian Larroumet, *Droit civil*, vol. III, 2nd edn (Paris, 1990), nn. 386 ff.

[188] Cf. Artt. 6:104 ff. of the Principles of European Contract Law (for comment see Zimmermann, 'Konturen', 488 sq.); cf. also art. 5.7 of the Principles of International Commercial Contracts (Unidroit). In the meantime, even the Assemblée plénaire of the Court de Cassation has adopted a much more liberal approach to long-term supply agreements and has reversed its previous interpretation of artt. 1129 c.c.: Dalloz 1996, 13; and see the analysis by Claude Witz and Gerhard Wolter, 'Das Ende der Problematik des unbestimmten Preises in Frankreich', (1996) 4 *ZEUP* 648 ff.

and that it has greatly been threatened by the nationalisation of law and legal scholarship resulting from the introduction of codifications within the confines of the modern nation-states. But there have been factors counterbalancing this nationalistic isolation. The most important of them, of course, provides the basis for the present chapter: all these codifications are, and have remained, emanations of one tradition. Characteristically, therefore, neither the French code civil nor the Austrian codifications were intended to be codes of national, specifically French or Austrian, law. They were universalistic in spirit, approach and outlook.[189] The same is true of the German BGB, even if it was caught up in a surge of nationalistic sentiment. For it was only in exceptional instances that this nationalistic attitude, reinforced by a specifically anti-French bias, left its mark on the content of the Code.[190]

The common tradition underlying the modern codifications also contributed to the continued existence of a network of intellectual contacts between them. The code civil, in particular, was able to maintain its dominant position in large parts of Europe even after Napoleon had been defeated.[191] Down to the end of the nineteenth century, for instance, it remained in force in the Prussian Rhine Province and in other German areas on the left bank of the Rhine. The Grand Duchy of Baden adopted the Badisches Landrecht, which was based on a translation of the code civil.[192] One entire division of the Imperial Supreme Court, the second 'senate', dealt with the appeals involving French law. Of course, one did not refer to French but to Rhenish law,[193] and the third senate was therefore dubbed the 'Rhenish' one. Pandectist legal learning, on the other hand, was influential all over

---

[189] Cf. n. 45 above. Interestingly, Hendrik Kooiker even draws attention to a 'third renaissance' of Roman law (after the introduction of the French and Dutch codifications!): *Lex scripta abrogata* (Nijmegen, 1996); cf. also Zimmermann, 'Heutiges Recht', pp. 2 ff.

[190] Cf. the examples provided in Zimmermann, 'Civil Code and Civil Law', pp. 87 ff.

[191] Cf. Elmar Wadle, 'Französisches Recht und deutsche Gesetzgebung im 19. Jahrhundert', in Schulze (ed.), *Europäische Rechts- und Verfassungsgeschichte*, pp. 201 ff.; Schulze, 'Französisches Recht', pp. 23 ff.; and the other contributions in the same volume.

[192] According to Helmut Coing, 'Einleitung', in Staudinger, *Kommentar zum Bürgerlichen Gesetzbuch*, vol. I, 12th edn (Berlin, 1980), n. 24, 16.6 per cent of the population of the German Reich (i.e. more than 8 million persons) in 1890 lived according to French law. Cf. also Diethelm Klippel (ed.), *Deutsche Rechts- und Gerichtskarte* (Goldbach, 1996).

[193] Cf. Hans-Jürgen Becker, 'Das Rheinische Recht und seine Bedeutung für die Rechtsentwicklung in Deutschland im 19. Jahrhundert', (1985) *JuS* 338 ff.; Antonio Grilli, 'Das linksrheinische Partikularrecht und das römische Recht in der Rechtsprechung der Cour d'Appel/Cour Impérial de Trèves nach 1804', in Schulze (ed.), *Französisches Recht*, pp. 67 ff.

Europe: from Sweden[194] to the Netherlands[195] and Italy,[196] and not least of all in France.[197] This reception was not confined to methodology and system; we also find impulses penetrating to the level of private law doctrine. Rudolf von Jhering's famous *culpa-in-contrahendo* doctrine, based on the rather shaky foundations of a handful of Roman sources concerning the sale of *res publicae, res divini iuris* and *liberi homines*,[198] provides just one example.[199]

In view of the similarity of language, German influence on Austrian legal science and on Austrian law was, of course, particularly strong.[200] Thus, for instance, the general provision of delictual liability in § 1295 BGB was reduced, by way of interpretation, into a kind of condensed version of §§ 823 I, 823 II BGB. In 1916 the legislature even added, totally unnecessarily one would have thought, a second subsection to § 1295 ABGB which corresponds to § 826 BGB.[201]

---

[194] Jan-Olof Sundell, 'German Influence on Swedish Private Law Doctrine 1870–1914', (1991) *SSL* 237 ff.

[195] Cf. J. H. A. Lokin, 'Het NBW en de pandektistiek', in *Historisch vooruitzicht, Opstellen over rechtsgeschiedenis in burgerlijk recht, BW-krant jaarboek 1994*, pp. 125 ff.

[196] Cf. e.g. Reiner Schulze (ed.), *Deutsche Rechtwissenschaft und Staatslehre im Spiegel der italienischen Rechtskultur während der zweiten Hälfte des 19. Jahrhunderts* (Berlin, 1990).

[197] See the comprehensive study by Alfons Bürge, *Das französische Privatrecht im 19. Jahrhundert: Zwischen Tradition und Pandektenwissenschaft, Liberalismus und Etatismus* (Frankfurt am Main, 1991), pp. 150 ff.; cf. also Alfons Bürge, 'Der Einfluß der Pandektenwissenschaft auf das französische Privatrecht im 19. Jahrhundert: Vom Vermögen zum patrimoine', in Schulze (ed.), *Französisches Zivilrecht*, pp. 221 ff.; Alfons Bürge, 'Ausstrahlungen der historischen Rechtsschule in Frankreich', (1997) 5 *ZEUP* 643 ff.

[198] Cf. Zimmermann, *Law of Obligations*, pp. 241 ff.; Erich Schanze, 'Culpa in contrahendo bei Jhering', (1978) 7 *Ius Commune* 326 ff.; Dieter Medicus, 'Zur Entdeckungsgeschichte der culpa in contrahendo', in *Iuris Professio, Festgabe für Max Kaser* (Vienna, 1986), pp. 169 ff.; Tomasz Giaro, 'Culpa in Contrahendo: eine Geschichte der Wiederentdeckungen', in Falk and Mohnhaupt (eds.), *Bürgerliche Gesetzbuch*, pp. 113 ff.

[199] Stephan Lorenz, 'Die culpa in contrahendo im französischen Recht', (1994) 2 *ZEUP* 218 ff.; Christian von Bar, *Gemeineuropäisches Deliktsrecht*, vol. I (Munich, 1996), nn. 472 ff.

[200] Cf., e.g., Werner Ogris, *Der Entwicklungsgang der österreichischen Privatrechtswissenschaft im 19. Jahrhundert* (Berlin, 1968); Werner Ogris, 'Die Wissenschaft des gemeinen römischen Rechts und das österreichische Allgemeine bürgerliche Gesetzbuch', in Helmut Coing and Walter Wilhelm (eds.), *Wissenschaft und Kodifikation des Privatrechts im 19. Jahrhundert*, vol. I (Frankfurt am Main, 1974), pp. 153 ff.; Wilhelm Brauneder, 'Privatrechtsfortbildung durch Juristenrecht in Exegetik und Pandektistik in Österreich', (1983) 5 *ZNR* 22 ff.

[201] For a critical evaluation of the assimilation between the German and Austrian laws of delict, see Rudolf Reischauer, in Peter Rummel (ed.), *Kommentar zum ABGB*, vol. II (Vienna, 1984), § 1294, n. 16; for a different view, see Friedrich Harrer, in Michael Schwimann (ed.), *Praxiskommentar zum ABGB*, vol. V (Vienna, 1987), § 1295, nn. 1 ff. Very much the same development, interestingly, appears to have occurred in Swiss law (with regard to the general provision of

Similarly important was the rise of comparative law as a new and independent branch of legal scholarship in the course of the nineteenth century.[202] Comparative research provided a rich source of inspiration for draftsmen of nineteenth- and twentieth-century legislation.[203]

New legal rules

We have been referring to instances where the general current of civilian opinion was drifting away from a principle of Roman law. In other cases new legal doctrines were developed and grafted onto the traditional law of obligations. But although they were new, these doctrines were often crafted of Roman substance. Thus, for example, the medieval lawyers could avail themselves of some building blocks hewn from the Digest[204] in order to establish the notion that only those agreements that rest upon a lawful *causa* are actionable. This was a crucial step facilitating the transition from 'nuda pactio obligationem non parit' to the counter-rule 'ex nudo pacto oritur actio'.[205]

'Fidem frangenti fides frangitur' was a principle of medieval canon law[206] which was transformed by virtue of a suspensive condition read into the contract: 'subintelligitur conditio "si fides servetur"'.[207] People usually promise a performance in order to obtain a counterperformance. If the other party fails to perform, they do not, presumably, want to be

art. 41 I OR); cf. Peter Gauch, 'Deliktshaftung für reinen Vermögensschaden', in *Festschrift für Max Keller* (Zurich, 1989), p. 136.

202 Cf. Zweigert and Kötz, *Introduction to Comparative Law*, pp. 51 ff.; Max Rheinstein, *Einführung in die Rechtsvergleichung*, 2nd edn (Munich, 1987), pp. 37 ff.

203 Cf., in particular, Helmut Coing, 'Rechtsvergleichung als Grundlage von Gesetzgebung im 19. Jahrhundert', (1978) 7 *Ius Commune* 168 ff. Cf. also, for instance, the preparatory drafts for the various parts of the BGB: Werner Schubert (ed.), *Die Vorlagen der Redaktoren für die erste Kommission zur Ausarbeitung des Entwurfs eines Bürgerlichen Gesetzbuches* (Berlin and New York, 1980 ff.).

204 In particular Aristo/Ulp. D. 2, 14, 7, 2; Ulp. D. 2, 17, 7, 4; Ulp. D. 44, 4, 2, 3; further details in Zimmermann, *Law of Obligations*, pp. 549 ff.

205 Cf. n. 68 above. And see the contributions to Letizia Vacca (ed.), *Causa e contratto nella prospettiva storio-comparatistica* (Torino, 1997).

206 Georges Boyer, *Recherches historiques sur la résolution des contrats* (Paris, 1924), pp. 220 ff.; J. A. Ankum, *De voorouders van een boze fee* (Zwolle, 1964), pp. 10 ff.; Friedrich Merzbacher, 'Die Regel "Fidem frangenti fides frangitur" und ihre Anwendung', (1982) 99 *ZSS* (Kanonistische Abteilung) 339 ff.

207 Cf., e.g., Decretales Gregorii IX, lib. II, tit. XXIV, cap. XXV and Boyer, *Recherches historiques*, pp. 220 ff., 240 ff.

bound either. A general right of rescission in case of breach of contract was never recognised in Roman law.[208] Suspensive conditions and the skilful use of legal fictions, however, were.[209] The natural lawyers took up this line of development,[210] which eventually led to the incorporation of a rule into the code civil according to which 'la condition résolutoire est toujours sousentendue dans les contrats synallagmatiques, pour le cas où l'une des deux parties ne satisfera point à son engagement'.[211] The draftsmen of the BGB availed themselves of a tacit *lex commissoria* when they granted the creditor a unilateral right of rescission in cases of impossibility of performance and *mora debitoris*.[212]

The device of an implied condition also stood at the cradle of the *clausula rebus sic stantibus*, a proviso according to which a contract is binding only as long and as far as matters remain the same as they were at the time of conclusion of the contract.[213] It became part of the *usus modernus* as well as of the systematic endeavours of the natural lawyers, and it attained great prominence in the field of private law and far beyond. And if, technically, the *clausula* took the form of a *conditio tacita*, even its substance was inspired by the Roman sources, though in this case not the legal ones. Moral philosophers like Seneca[214] and Cicero[215] had been the first to draw attention to the change of circumstances and thus to sow the seed for a legal principle of great importance.

---

[208] Fritz Schulz very pointedly refers to an 'iron rule of Roman law which the classical lawyers unflinchingly observed'. But see Zimmermann, *Law of Obligations*, p. 578.

[209] Cf. generally Reinhard Zimmermann, '"Heard Melodies are Sweet, but Those Unheard are Sweeter ...". Condicio tacita, Implied Conditions und die Fortbildung des europäischen Vertragsrechts', (1993) 193 *AcP* 121 ff.

[210] For details, see Karl Otto Scherner, *Rüchtrittsrecht wegen Nichterfüllung* (Wiesbaden, 1965), pp. 92 ff.; Coing, *Europäisches Privatrecht*, vol. I, p. 444.

[211] Art. 1184 code civil. On this rule, and its history, see Boyer, *Recherches historiques*, pp. 381 ff., 11 ff.; Hans-Georg Landfermann, *Die Auflösung des Vertrages nach richterlichem Ermessen als Rechtsfolge der Nichterfüllung im französischen Recht* (Frankfurt am Main and Berlin, 1968); Scherner, *Rüchtrittsrecht*, pp. 135 ff.

[212] For details, see Hans G. Leser, *Der Rücktritt vom Vertrag* (Tübingen, 1975), pp. 16 ff.

[213] For details, see Zimmermann, *Law of Obligations*, pp. 579 ff. and, since then, Ralf Köbler, *Die 'clausula rebus sic stantibus' als allgemeiner Rechtsgrundsatz* (Tübingen, 1991); Michael Rummel, *Die 'clausula rebus sic stantibus'* (Baden-Baden, 1991); Zimmermann, '"Heard melodies"', 134 ff.; Klaus Luig, 'Dogmengeschichte des Privatrechts als rechtswissenschaftliche Grundlagenforschung', (1993) 20 *Ius Commune* 193 ff.; Klaus Luig, 'Die Kontinuität allgemeiner Rechtsgrundsätze: Das Beispiel der clausula rebus sic stantibus', in Zimmermann et al. (eds.), *Rechtsgeschichte und Privatrechtsdogmatik*, pp. 171 ff.

[214] *De beneficiis*, lib. IV, XXXV, 3.   [215] *De officiis*, 3, XXV-95.

Main features of a European law of obligations

The main theme of what has been said, so far, is that of considerable diversity within a fundamental intellectual unity — a unity created largely by a common tradition. If we finally try to assess the main features of a common European law of obligations, as derived from Roman law and embodied in the modern codes, we may include the following points.[216] The law of obligations constitutes a body of law that is distinct from property law. The one deals with *iura in personam*, the other with *iura in rem*. Within the law of obligations there is a fundamental distinction between contract and delict. This distinction does not, however, represent an exhaustive basis for the systematic analysis of the law of obligations. In particular, unjustified enrichment and *negotiorum gestio* are recognised as independent sources of obligations. Delictual liability, as a rule, is based on fault. There are, however, also cases of purely risk-based liability. We have a general remedy for the restitution of benefits conferred without obligations, the core features of which are the notions of 'transfer' and 'without legal

---

[216] There is not, to my knowledge, any comprehensive comparative investigation of this nature. As far as German law is concerned, cf., however, Max Kaser, 'Der römische Anteil am deutschen bürgerlichen Recht', (1967) *JuS* 337 ff.; Eduard Picker, 'Zum Gegenwartswert des Römischen Rechts', in Hans Bungert (ed.), *Das antike Rom in Europa* (Regensburg, 1985), pp. 289 ff.; Rolf Knütel, 'Römisches Recht und deutsches Bürgerliches Recht', in Walter Ludwig (ed.), *Die Antike in der europäischen Gegenwart* (Göttingen, 1993), pp. 43 ff.; for Dutch law, see Robert Feenstra, *Romeinsregtelike grondslagen van het Nederlands privaatreg*, 5th edn (Leiden, 1990); Ankum, 'Römisches Recht', pp. 101 ff. Cf. also, under more general aspects, Heinz Hübner, 'Sinn und Möglichkeiten retrospektiver Rechtsvergleichung', in *Festschrift für Gerhard Kegel* (Stuttgart, Berlin, Cologne and Mainz, 1987), pp. 235 ff.; Heinrich Honsell, 'Das rechtshistorische Argument in der modernen Zivilrechtsdogmatik', in Dieter Simon (ed.), *Akten des 26. Deutschen Rechtshistorikertages* (Frankfurt am Main, 1987), pp. 305 ff.; and, under the auspices of European legal unity, Reiner Schulze, 'Allgemeine Rechtsgrundsätze und europäisches Privatrecht', (1993) 1 *ZEUP* 442 ff.; Zimmermann, 'Roman Law and European Legal Unity', pp. 21 ff.; Reinhard Zimmermann, 'Savigny's Legacy: Legal History, Comparative Law, and the Emergence of a European Legal Science', (1996) 112 *LQR* 576 ff.; Rolf Knütel, 'Rechtseinheit in Europa und römisches Recht', (1994) 2 *ZEUP* 244 ff.; Klaus Luig, 'The History of Roman Private Law and the Unification of European Law' (1997) 5 *ZEUP* 405 ff.; Eugen Bucher, 'Gedanken aus Anlaß des Erscheinens zweier Monumentalwerke zum Römischen Recht', (1997) *Aktuelle Juristische Praxis* 923 ff.; Filippo Ranieri, *Europäisches Obligationenrecht* (Vienna and New York, 1999). More specifically on the question of a common system of European law, see Bruno Schmidlin, 'Gibt es ein gemeineuropäisches System des Privatrechts?', in Bruno Schmidlin, *Vers un droit privé européen commun? Skizzen zum gemeineuropäischen Privatrecht* (Basel and Frankfurt am Main, 1994), pp. 33 ff.; Berthold Kupisch, 'Institutionensystem und Pandektensystem: Zur Geschichte des res-Begriffes', (1990–2) 25–7 *The Irish Jurist* 293 ff. (published in 1994); Eltjo Schrage, 'Das System des neuen niederländischen Zivilgesetzbuches', (1994) *JBl* 501 ff.

ground'. Unjustified enrichment also has to be skimmed off, if it has come about in other ways. Taking care of someone else's affairs may lead to a claim for compensation.

There is a general law of contract, and contracts are based, as a rule, on the informal consent of the parties (established by means of offer and acceptance). Only in exceptional situations, and for specific policy reasons, does the law require the observation of certain formalities. The parties are free to decide whether they want to enter into a contract or not, and it is up to them to determine the content of their transaction. Such content may not, however, be illegal or immoral. Equality in the values exchanged is largely immaterial. A party is not bound by his agreement, if he has given it while labouring under a defect of the will (based on or induced by error, *metus* or *dolus*). The parties to a contract are entitled to demand performance of their respective obligations *in specie*. Apart from that, the general law of contract contains rules concerning legal capacity, the interpretation of contracts, the requirements for breach of contract and the remedies available (damages, the right to withhold performance and termination), agency, contracts in favour of third parties and cession, penalty clauses, time, place and other modalities of performance, termination of contractual obligations by means other than *solutio propria* (most notably set-off), extinctive prescription, plurality of debtors and creditors. Most of these rules constitute 'ius dispositivum', i.e. they are not mandatory.

The legal system also makes available to the parties specific contractual paradigms. They range from sale, exchange, donation, *locatio conductio rei*, operis and *operarum*, to suretyship, mandate, deposit and two different types of loan (for use and for consumption). Again, most of the statutory rules concerning these contract types (like the aedilitian remedies in sale) are not mandatory. Also, the parties are free to conclude atypical (or, in traditional civilian terminology, 'innominate') contracts.

Even apart from the structural foundations and the main rules and institutions of the law of obligations, most of the key concepts we use in order to express ourselves are Roman in origin and belong to the common civilian heritage: obligation, contract and delict, debtor and creditor, *dolus, culpa* and *diligentia quam in suis*, risk and *vis maior*, gratuitous and onerous, bilateral and unilaterally binding transactions. The civilian tradition has also seeped into the interstices of the codes: where they do not deal with a matter at all, where they contain a blanket provision or where the solution to a specific problem has expressly been left to legal scholarship.[217] 'Casum sentit dominus', 'interpretatio contra eum qui clarius loqui debuisset', 'venire contra factum proprium', 'dolo agit qui petit quod statim redditurus est', 'nemo auditur propriam turpitudinem allegans': these phrases still belong to the standard repertory of modern private lawyers all over Europe.

And, finally, it has to be remembered that no codification is perfect. Thus, there are bound to be drafting mistakes. In other cases a specific view, espoused by eighteenth- or nineteenth-century legal science, turns out to be, in retrospect, one-sided and unbalanced, somewhat idiosyncratic or too firmly rooted in outdated ideological or doctrinal premises. In many of these cases, courts and legal writers have been able to redress the situation; they have found ways and means to assert more modern views, even in the face of the code. Oddly enough, however, the doctrines thus developed have precursors in the older *ius commune*. Yet this experience is odd only for those who are caught up in the simplistic illusion that a codification can be entirely cut off from the continuity of historical development. For even in a codified legal system the reappearance of ideas is by no means a rare – although it is usually an unacknowledged – phenomenon.[218] In the process, many of the jagged edges and time-bound eccentricities of the codes are worn away. In Germany, for instance,[219] the courts have been prepared to award financial compensation for non-pecuniary harm in all cases where a person's 'general personality right' has been seriously infringed. This is clearly *contra legem*, for the BGB not only does not recognise a 'general personality right', it also explicitly confines the aggrieved plaintiff to a claim for the pecuniary loss that he has suffered. It is, however, in conformity with the civilian tradition as established, in this case, on the basis of the Roman *actio iniuriarum*.[220]

Given some insight into historical background and comparative context, it is not at all difficult for a modern private lawyer from one jurisdiction to

---

[217] For details and examples, see Zimmermann, 'Civil Code and Civil Law', 89 ff., 94 ff.

[218] Theo Mayer-Maly, 'Die Wiederkehr von Rechtsfiguren', (1971) *JZ* 1 ff.; cf. also Peter Stein, 'Judge and Jurist in the Civil Law: A Historical Interpretation', in Peter Stein, *The Character and Influence of the Roman Civil Law* (London and Ronceverte, 1988), pp. 142 ff.; David Johnston, 'The Renewal of the Old', (1997) 56 *CLJ* 80 ff.; Zimmermann, *Roman Law, Contemporary Law, European Law* (Clarendon Lectures, Lecture Two).

[219] For more examples concerning German law, see Zimmermann, 'Civil Code and Civil Law', pp. 101 ff.

[220] For all details, see Zimmermann, *Law of Obligations*, pp. 1050 ff., 1090 ff.; Helge Walter, *Actio iniuriarum: Der Schutz der Persönlichkeit im südafrikanischen Privatrecht* (Berlin, 1996).

understand the rules contained in other civil codes, to recognise similarities and to evaluate differences, and to identify the common foundations underlying all of them. It should not, in principle, be more difficult to devise a European codification today than it was to draft the French or German Codes – not, at any rate, if one confines one's attention, as was the brief of this chapter, to the European continent. What one may well question, however, is the vocation of our time for this ambitious kind of legislation.[221] The code civil would have been unimaginable without the treatises of Domat and Pothier, the BGB equally inconceivable without the work of Savigny and Windscheid. The lesson is obvious. Once again, the essential prerequisite for a truly European private law would appear to be the emergence of an 'organically progressive' legal science,[222] which would have to transcend the national boundaries and revitalise a common tradition.[223]

---

[221] For a discussion see, e.g., Ole Lando, 'The Principles of European Contract Law after Year 2000', in Franz Werro (ed.), *New Perspectives on European Private Law* (Fribourg, 1998), pp. 59 ff. He refers to the modern 'Thibauts' and 'Savigniys'.

[222] Friedrich Carl von Savigny, *Vom Beruf unserer Zeit für Gesetzgebung und Rechtswissenschaft* (1814), in Hans Hattenhauer (ed.), *Thibaut und Savigny: Ihre programmatische Schriften* (Munich, 1973).

[223] For a programmatic statement, see Zimmermann, 'Savigny's Legacy', 576 ff.; for examples of how such a programme may be implemented, see Zimmermann, *Roman Law, Contemporary Law, European Law* (Clarendon Lectures, Lecture Three).

2

'A token of independence': debates on the history and development of Scots law

NIALL R. WHITTY

Introduction

This chapter briefly explores current debates on five aspects of Scots law, namely:

(a) the revision of the 'legal nationalist' history of Scottish private law;
(b) the devolution of legislative power over Scots law to a Scottish Parliament;
(c) the Scottish approach towards ideas of European integration or harmonisation;
(d) the place of Scots law within the Civilian–Common Law dichotomy; and
(e) the future direction of development of Scots law.

A sixth debate, on 'what should be the main vehicle of reform – judicial development, statutory reform or codification?',[1] is excluded since it is considered by Professor Clive's chapter. Criminal law and public law are also excluded.[2]

The United Kingdom: 'parts' and regions

The United Kingdom is divided into three 'parts' each with its own independent system of law and structure of courts, namely (1) England and

---

[1] For the different views in this debate see H. L. MacQueen, 'Judicial Reform of Private Law', (1998) 3 *SLPQ* 134.

[2] Scottish criminal law is uncodified and distinctive. There is no appeal to the House of Lords. For interesting recent surveys, see C. H. W. Gane, 'Criminal Law Reform in Scotland', (1998) 3 *SLPQ* 101; L. Farmer, 'Debatable Land: An Essay on the Relationship between English and Scottish Criminal Law', (1999) 3 *ELR* 32.

Wales, which form one part; (2) Scotland; and (3) Northern Ireland. It is English law that applies within England and Wales: nobody ever talks of Anglo-Welsh law. In the United Kingdom English law is in theory equal in status to Scots law,[3] but in the British colonies it was always English law that was introduced, which thereby became the imperial law.[4]

The debate about revision of the 'legal nationalist' history of Scots law

The debate about the true nature of Scots law and its relationship with the English common law and Continental civilian traditions is bound up with the writing of Scottish legal history, to the dismay of those academically correct historians who would like to keep legal history as a safe (and perhaps even rather dull) discipline immune from modern ideological concerns. The debate is not just a storm in an academic teacup, because legal history can affect the development of the law.

How did Scots law become a 'mixed' system?

English and Continental law, both of which had once been Germanic and feudal, began to diverge in the late twelfth and early thirteenth centuries when Roman law and Romano-canonical procedure started to transform Continental law while at the same time in England, under the Plantagenet kings, a strong but insular common law developed.[5] Scotland became a feudal kingdom on the European pattern in the twelfth century and tended at first to follow a simplified version of the English common law[6] though of course its Church courts applied the general canon law of western Christendom. English attempts to assume sovereignty led to the Wars of Independence in which the Scottish victory at Bannockburn in 1314 was decisive.

---

[3] See *The Laws of Scotland: Stair Memorial Encyclopaedia*, vol. V (Edinburgh, 1987), paras. 711–19, 'Pretensions of English Law as "Imperial Law"' (Sir Thomas Smith).

[4] Ibid., para. 713; Mr Justice J. B. H. McPherson, 'Scots Law in the Colonies', (1995) *Jur. Rev.* 208.

[5] R. C. van Caenegem, *Judges, Legislators and Professors: Chapters in European Legal History* (Cambridge, 1993), p. 114.

[6] The controlling study is H. L. MacQueen, *Common Law and Feudal Society in Medieval Scotland* (Edinburgh, 1993). The diverse origins of Scots law are illustrated by *Regiam majestatem*, a commentary on legal process dating probably from the early fourteenth century. About two-thirds of its contents derive from *Glanville*, some rules from Celtic law and the remainder from the European *ius commune*.

Some time thereafter, the Scottish practice of borrowing from English law greatly diminished or virtually ceased.[7] English law in the late Middle Ages became (in van Caenegem's words) 'an island in the Romanist sea...an anomaly, a freak in the history of western civilisation'.[8] As the *ius commune* moved towards a system organised under headings of substantive law, the English were creating an arcane, complex and idiosyncratic system of substantive law based on the procedural forms of action which subsisted until the nineteenth century.[9] Scotland followed the *ius commune* and Scots lawyers were mainly trained at Continental universities.[10] Our supreme civil court, the Court of Session, was established in 1532 as a college of justice on a Continental model. The earliest unofficial reports of its decisions dating from the 1540s (not yet published) show it (in the words of Professor Dolazalek) acting 'as a fully-fledged Ius-Commune-Court. Texts from *Corpus Iuris Canonici* and *Corpus Iuris Civilis* were applied as if they had been legislated for Scotland, and the respective medieval standard commentaries were read along with them.'[11] Scottish private law attained a fairly high degree of maturity in successive Institutional writings between the first

---

[7] A debate is brewing as to whether borrowing virtually ceased or continued at a significant level.

[8] R. C. van Caenegem, *The Birth of the English Common Law*, 2nd edn (Cambridge, 1988), p. 105.

[9] It seems that the English register of writs grew from about 36 in *Glanville* to about 2,500 in a register of 1531: O. F. Robinson, T. D. Fergus and W. M. Gordon, *European Legal History*, 2nd edn (London, 1994), para. 8.6.10. On the curious characteristics of English 'actional packages' see P. B. H. Birks, 'More Logic and Less Experience: The Difference between Scots Law and English Law', in D. L. Carey Miller and R. Zimmermann (eds.), *The Civilian Tradition and Scots Law, Aberdeen Quincentenary Essays* (Berlin, 1998), p. 167.

[10] In France, Cologne or Leuven and later in the Netherlands, especially Leyden or Utrecht and to some extent Franeker and Groningen: see R. Feenstra, 'Scottish–Dutch Legal Relations in the Seventeenth and Eighteenth Centuries', in T. C. Smout (ed.), *Scotland and Europe 1200–1850* (Edinburgh, 1986), p. 128. P. Nève, 'Disputations of Scots Students Attending Universities in the Northern Netherlands', in W. M. Gordon and T. D. Fergus (eds.), *Legal History in the Making* (London and Rio Grande, 1991), p. 99 states that as far as can be verified from the matriculation lists, about 750 Scots students studied law at Dutch universities. The peak was in the period 1676–1725. The development of legal education in Scotland has been well described in a very fine series of scholarly articles by Dr John W. Cairns. These are too numerous to cite but see, e.g., 'Rhetoric, Language and Roman Law: Legal Education and Improvement in Eighteenth Century Scotland', (1991) *LHR* 31.

[11] Professor Gero Dolazalek, Note dated Spring 1996 introducing unpublished provisional text of *Sinclair's Practicks* based on transcription by Dr Athol L. Murray from the manuscript in Edinburgh University Library (http://www.uni-leipzig.de/jurarom/scotland/dat/inclair.htm). See also A. L. Murray, 'Sinclair's Practicks', in A. Harding (ed.), *Lawmaking and Lawmakers in British History* (London, 1980), p. 90; and G. Dolazalek, 'The Court of Session as a Ius Commune Court – Witnessed by "Sinclair's Practicks", 1540–1549' in H. L. MacQueen (ed.), *Miscellany IV*, Stair Society vol. 49 (Edinburgh, 2002), p. 51.

edition of Stair's *Institutions* in 1681 (a work in the tradition of the northern natural law school)[12] and the fourth and last personal edition of Bell's *Principles* in 1839.[13]

The legal-nationalist view of Scottish legal history and its revision

In the 1950s the dominant view of Scottish legal history was largely the work of Lord Cooper, Lord President of the Court of Session,[14] whose thesis was adopted by among others his disciple Professor Sir Thomas Smith. They were both legal nationalists who passionately believed that one of the ways in which Scots law could be saved from undesirable anglicisation was by returning to its historical roots. In Lord Cooper's view Scots law experienced two great changes of direction (the first at least being a 'false start' and 'rejected experiment'), one in the late Middle Ages away from English law as an external source towards the *ius commune*, the second beginning in the early nineteenth century away from the *ius commune* back towards English law. Cooper and Smith idealised the period of the Institutional writers from 1681 till about 1800 as a golden age. In the view of Cooper, Smith and others,[15] the period after 1800 was one of progressive and to some extent regrettable anglicisation when, in Smith's colourful if somewhat strident language, many civilian principles were ousted by the 'Common Law Cuckoo'[16] and Scots law went 'awhoring after false Gods'.[17]

---

[12] Stair's main sources were Scottish court decisions and custom but he also cites Roman-Dutch and other *ius commune* sources including (Inst. I, 4, 12; I, 10, 5) incidentally Covarruvias and Molina, representatives of the renowned school of late Spanish scholastics who greatly influenced European legal history: J. Gordley, *The Philosophical Origins of Modern Contract Doctrine* (Oxford, 1991).

[13] The main Institutional writings relating to civil (i.e. non-criminal) law are James Dalrymple, Viscount Stair, *Institutions of the Law of Scotland* ([1681], 2nd and last personal edn, 1693); Andrew McDouall, Lord Bankton, *Institute of the Laws of Scotland* (only personal edn, 1751–3); John Erskine, *Institute of the Law of Scotland* (1 and posthumous edn, 1773); Henry Home, Lord Kames, *Principles of Equity* ([1760], 4th and last personal edn, 1800); George Joseph Bell, *Principles of the Law of Scotland* ([1829], 4th and last personal edn, 1839); George Joseph Bell, *Commentaries on the Laws of Scotland* ([1800–4], 5th and last personal edn, 1826). In addition, *Baron Hume's Lectures*, ed. G. Campbell H. Paton (see n. 112 below) have in practice achieved institutional status though this has not yet been formally recognised.

[14] Collated in Lord Cooper of Culross, *Selected Papers 1922–1954* (Edinburgh, 1957).

[15] E.g. A. D. Gibb, *Law from over the Border* (Edinburgh, 1950).

[16] T. B. Smith, 'The Common Law Cuckoo: Problems of "Mixed" Legal Systems with Special Reference to Restrictive Interpretations in the Scots Law of Obligations' (1956) *SALR* 147; T. B. Smith, *Studies Critical and Comparative* (Edinburgh, 1962), p. 89.

[17] T. B. Smith, 'Strange Gods: The Crisis of Scots Law as a Civilian System', (1959) *Jur. Rev.* 119; Smith, *Studies Critical and Comparative*, p. 72. See H. L. MacQueen, '*Regiam Majestatem*, Scots

Cooper's theory of false starts has been attacked by revisionist legal historians[18] who have recently emphasised instead the continuity of historical development[19] but it has also been defended as essentially correct in important respects.[20] Lord Rodger, Lord President of the Court of Session 1996–2001, a powerful critic of his predecessor Lord Cooper and scourge of Scottish (as distinct from British or English) legal nationalism, has attacked the Cooper–Smith idealisation of the Institutional writers in the eighteenth century and instead put forward the late nineteenth century, when the Court of Session opened the door (or floodgates) to English case law, as a period to be admired.[21] This topic overlaps with Professor Clive's chapter because the legal-nationalist view is that the Institutional writings are in substance codifications of Scots law, that Scottish legal thought is based on deduction from principle and that codification 'is the natural product of the civilian method of thought, which always aims at reason methodised and presented systematically and at the application of rationalistic science to law'.[22] By contrast Lord Rodger denies that in Scotland decisions are founded on principle rather than precedent;[23] and argues that 'in truth Scots law has long been built by the working-out of doctrine in our case-law and that this is what gives strength to any statements of principle which

Law, and National Identity', (1995) *Scottish HR* 1 at 25: 'In the twentieth century, this stress on the Civilian tradition became not just a question of history, but more a programme for the renaissance of a Scots law otherwise doomed to irretrievable Anglicisation.'

[18] See, e.g., H. McKechnie, *Judicial Process upon Brieves, 1219–1532*, 23rd David Murray Lecture, Glasgow University Publications (Glasgow, 1956); W. D. H. Sellar, 'The Common Law of Scotland and the Common Law of England', in R. R. Davies (ed.), *The British Isles 1100–1500* (Edinburgh, 1988), p. 82; W. D. H. Sellar, 'A Historical Perspective', in M. C. Meston, W. D. H. Sellar and T. M. Cooper, *The Scottish Legal Tradition, New Enlarged Edition* (Edinburgh, 1991), p. 29; MacQueen, *Common Law and Feudal Society*, pp. 2, 3. MacQueen, '*Regiam Majestatem*', p. 25 describes the view that Scottish legal history began anew on a civilian basis with Stair 'as the modern myth of Scottish legal history', which contains 'much that is true' but 'not the whole truth'. Note, however, that Cooper did not argue that the Middle Ages had contributed almost nothing to the distinctive character of Scots law.

[19] H. L. MacQueen, 'Mixture or Muddle? Teaching and Research in Scottish Legal History', (1997) *ZEUP* 269; W. D. H. Sellar, 'Scots Law: Mixed from the Very Beginning? A Tale of Two Receptions', (2000) 4 *ELR* 3.

[20] N. R. Whitty, 'The Civilian Tradition and Debates on Scots Law', (1996) *TSAR* 227 at 232: 'The evidence still points to the facts that there were indeed two distinct receptions from the English system – one mediaeval and the other modern – and that a colossal divergence between the two systems occurred in the intervening period.'

[21] A. Rodger, 'Thinking about Scots Law', (1996) 1 *ELR* 3 at 16 ff.; A. Rodger, 'The Bell of Law Reform', (1993) *SLT* (News) 339 at 344.

[22] Cooper, *Selected Papers 1922–1954*, p 205.   [23] Rodger, 'Thinking about Scots Law', p. 10.

may from time to time emerge'.[24] So there are two ideals which are difficult to reconcile.

Lord Rodger affirms that the Institutional writers 'could not possibly solve the problems which face a Scots lawyer today'.[25] That must be right. There are however many areas in which the Scottish courts can develop our law along the lines laid down in the Institutional period without resorting to English law as a substitute for analysis.

Historical revisionism has not yet challenged two important historic differences between Scots and English law emphasised by Cooper,[26] namely the unitary character of Scots law as contrasted with the Common Law–equity dualism and its tendency to subordinate the remedy to the right[27] stemming from the fact that it escaped the forms of action.

The devolution of legislative power to Scotland

The Union of the Parliaments (1707)

Though James VI of Scotland succeeded as James I to the throne of England and Wales in 1603, the two Parliaments and the two kingdoms remained separate till the Union of 1707. Traditionally English historians tended to regard the Union of 1707 as if it were little more than the admission to the English Parliament of a relatively small number of Scottish members. By contrast, 'in the Scottish mind, emphasis is placed on the origin of the United Kingdom Parliament in a freely negotiated Union between two equals, the sovereign legislatures of Scotland and England'.[28] To safeguard the minority legal system from assimilation by the majority system, the Treaty of Union provided for the preservation of Scottish private law and the Scottish system of courts though the provisions lacked enforcement machinery.[29]

---

[24] Ibid.

[25] Ibid., pp. 9–10, rejecting the views of Lord Macmillan, 'Two ways of thinking' (Rede Lecture, 1934), in Lord Macmillan, *Law and Other Things* (Cambridge, 1937), 76 ff.

[26] 'The Scottish Legal Tradition', in *Selected Papers 1922–1954*, p. 183. [27] Ibid., pp. 44, 183.

[28] *Written Evidence to the Royal Commission on the Constitution (1969–1973), vol. 5, Memorandum by the Faculty of Advocates*, p. 6, HMSO (London).

[29] Under art. XIX the two highest courts — the Court of Session in civil matters and the High Court of Justiciary in criminal proceedings — were to continue and not to be subject to the jurisdiction of the English courts sitting in Westminster Hall. In fact the House of Lords (which did not sit in Westminster Hall) assumed jurisdiction in civil matters but there is still no appeal to the House of Lords in Scottish criminal proceedings. Under art. XVIII no alteration is to 'be

Devolution to a Scottish Parliament (1998)

Pressure for a 'devolved' legislature in Scotland has come in waves since the late nineteenth century. The last wave began with the rise of Scottish nationalism in the late 1960s and 1970s,[30] was blocked during the Conservative government's rule from 1979 to 1997 and (following the election of Mr Blair's Labour government in 1997) culminated in the Scotland Act 1998 which has re-established a Scottish Parliament for the first time for almost 300 years.[31]

Its very wide sphere of legislative competence includes all matters not expressly reserved to the United Kingdom Parliament.[32] The reserved categories[33] include the constitution and the public service since they concern the integrity of the United Kingdom as a whole. Also reserved are services deemed to be best provided at a United Kingdom level;[34] or which concern maintenance of certain standards throughout the United Kingdom;[35] or which relate to international policy and security;[36] or which

---

made in the laws which concern private right except for the evident utilty of the subjects within Scotland'. While there is a reluctance in Scotland to accept that safeguards in a constitutional document establishing a new state intended to protect important national institutions can simply be amended or swept away as if they were ordinary provisions of an ordinary Act, there is in fact no special constitutional machinery for enforcing these provisions.

[30] Beginning with the Hamilton by-election in 1968 won by the Scottish National Party. The Scotland Act 1978 was passed to establish a Scottish legislature but it failed to get the necessary 40 per cent of votes in a Scottish referendum. See J. G. Kellas, *The Scottish Political System*, 3rd edn (Cambridge, 1989), pp. 144–62. However, over 50 per cent of votes cast supported devolution.

[31] Like the Parliament of an Autonomous Community under the Spanish constitution, the Scottish Parliament has a single chamber. It is elected by proportional representation combining constituency members with additional seats allocated on a regional basis. The result is likely often to be government by coalition.

[32] The reserved matters are based mainly on those functions that are the responsibility of the United Kingdom departments stationed in London as distinct from the Scottish Office stationed in Edinburgh. So they are defined by reference to governmental, administrative or contextual categories rather than the categories of private law.

[33] Set out in detail in the Scotland Act 1998, Sch. 5. For helpful commentary on the Act see, e.g., A. Page, C. Reid and A. Ross, *A Guide to the Scotland Act 1998* (Edinburgh, 1999); B. Hadfield, 'The Nature of Devolution in Scotland and Northern Ireland', (1999) 3 *ELR* 3.

[34] E.g. energy; transport; social security and child support; pensions; the post; broadcasting. Also reserved are a few miscellaneous home affairs topics (e.g. misuse of drugs; data protection; UK and European elections).

[35] E.g. consumer protection; product standard, safety and liability.

[36] E.g. defence, national security, interception of communications, official secrets and foreign affairs.

are required for the integrity of the larger United Kingdom economic unit as a whole.[37]

The devolved matters cover everything which is not reserved including very wide areas of Scottish private law (sufficient to allow a civil code to be enacted) and criminal law and many areas of public law.[38] Scottish private law is defined for some purposes on the same lines as the familiar classification of Justinian's Institutes.[39] The Scottish Parliament is subordinate to the United Kingdom Parliament which in theory could abolish it or legislate within the devolved sphere.[40] In practice the exercise of such powers seems unlikely.

As the Spanish experience might suggest, asymmetrical devolution creates its own momentum.[41] So there is some pressure for devolution to the English regions,[42] but it is presumably unlikely to cover English private law.

The reasons for legislative devolution

I do not pretend to understand the reasons for this momentous change. One plausible and authoritative explanation was given by the late Lord Kilbrandon, one of the main architects of the policy of devolution.[43] He

---

[37] E.g. financial and economic matters; central government taxation; the central bank, currency and banking system; trade and industry including business associations; insolvency and statutory preferences (but not personal bankruptcy and real rights in security); competition; intellectual property; import and export control.

[38] Including home affairs; local government; social work; housing; education; health; agriculture; forestry; fishing; food standards; economic development; town and country planning; environment; natural and built heritage; sports and the arts; and the voluntary sector.

[39] Scotland Act 1998, s 126(4).

[40] The Scotland Act 1998, s 28(7) provides that the Act does not affect the power of the Parliament of the United Kingdom to make laws for Scotland.

[41] Devolution was initially planned only for Catalonia, the Basque country and Galicia but was extended under pressure from other regions.

[42] See, e.g., the Fabian Society's report on *The English Question* (London, April 2000): 'Once a government in Westminster is dependent on Scottish votes to secure English measures, such matters will cease to be merely anomalies and will become the stuff of constitutional crisis.' Hadfield, 'The Nature of Devolution', p. 6, submits that 'it is misleading to regard devolution solely, or even mainly, as a matter for the devolved region/nation', that it was realised in Spain that 'home rule' for the Catalans demanded radical reform and democratisation for the centre; but that lesson had not been learned in the United Kingdom when devolution was introduced.

[43] Lord Kilbrandon, a Scottish judge and chairman of the Scottish Law Commission, was chairman of the Royal Commission of 1969–73 whose *Report on the Constitution* (1973) (Cmnd 5460) led ultimately to devolution.

begins by pointing out that the neglect of Scottish legislative needs could be tolerated in the eighteenth century,

> when the scope of the legislative process was not such as to affect the ordinary citizen, or even the business man, seriously in his private or trading activities. But when the zeal of the 19th century law reformers began to demand modernisation of ancient legal principles, the distinctive character of our law became immediately threatened . . . And as the 20th century rolled on and local administration came under government regulation, standardisation and control through Acts of the Westminster Parliament, it began to appear that by the abandonment of her legislature Scotland had made a sacrifice which she could ill afford, and that the retention of her laws, upon which she had proudly insisted as a condition of union, had become in some sense an illusion.[44]

The establishment in 1885 of the office of Secretary of State for Scotland with wide administrative functions for purely Scottish affairs ultimately increased the anomaly since it was accountable to an absentee parliament in London. As Lord Kilbrandon observed, it would be hard 'to find a parallel for a country which had its own judicature and legal system, its own executive and administration, but no legislature, its laws being made within another and technically foreign jurisdiction, by an assembly in which it had only a small minority of members, but to which its executive was democratically responsible'.[45]

There are, however, deeper forces at work having little to do directly with the machinery of legislation and private law. 'Britain', it has been said, 'is an invented nation, not so much older than the United States'.[46] The factors that moulded Britain as a nation – the perceived need to protect the Protestant succession to the throne; the wars against major European powers; the maintenance of a worldwide empire and commercial supremacy – have largely vanished.[47] New factors have emerged, such as entry into the European Union and the exploitation of North Sea oil. It is perhaps unsurprising that, in adjusting to this new situation, some Scottish

---

[44] Lord Kilbrandon, *A Background to Constitutional Reform*, The Holdsworth Club of the University of Birmingham (Birmingham, 1975), pp. 18–19.

[45] Ibid., p. 10.

[46] Peter Scott, *Knowledge and Nation* (Edinburgh, 1990), p. 168.

[47] L. Colley, *Britons: Forging the Nation 1707–1837* (New Haven and London, 1992), p. 374.

people have reverted to a sense of national identity which is centuries older than Britishness and yet is in some ways more modern.

Whereas language has been a strong element in for example Catalan, Quebecois and Welsh nationalism, it appears a minor element in Scottish nationalism. Gaelic ceased to be the language of the royal court in the eleventh century and has been on the retreat ever since, though it is recognised for naturalisation purposes.[48] In a recent debate in the Scottish Parliament only 2 out of 129 MSPs spoke in Gaelic.[49] Lowland Scots – the language of Robert Burns and of the Acts of the Scottish Parliament before 1707– is a dialect of English but is now ebbing away. From the eighteenth century the Scottish legal profession, in common with much of Scottish 'polite society', suffered from a cultural inferiority complex and self-consciously anglicised its language.[50] Old Scots terms still persist in Scots law as technical legal terms of art[51] but even they are (or were) tending to disappear.[52]

Since some other major European states including Spain are under pressure from a resurgence of relatively small nationalities which once acquiesced in their constitutional position, it may be that the Scottish experience of pressure for devolution should not be attributed exclusively to Britain's own peculiar development.[53]

Legal nationalism distinguished from political nationalism

In Scotland, legal nationalism is not the same thing as political nationalism. It springs from adherence to an intellectual tradition which is independent of political allegiances and ideology. It follows that the creation of a Scottish Parliament could even endanger traditional Scots legal doctrines:

---

[48] Under the British Nationality Act 1981, Sch. 1, para. 1, the Scottish Gaelic language is an alternative to English or Welsh as a prerequisite to naturalisation as a citizen of the United Kingdom.

[49] The signs in the Scottish Parliament premises are in both English and Gaelic.

[50] Cf. D. Daiches, *The Paradox of Scottish Culture: The Eighteenth Century Experience* (London, 1964).

[51] E.g. 'assoilzie' meaning 'to absolve'; the 'ish' (end) of a lease; and 'poinding' (i.e. 'impounding', German *Pfändung*) which now has reference to the attachment by a creditor of his debtor's moveable goods.

[52] E.g. the Bankruptcy (Scotland) Act 1985, s 7 replaced the strong and distinctive old Scots expression 'notour bankruptcy' with the insipid and ambiguous 'apparent insolvency'.

[53] Colley, *Britons*, p. 374.

> If the Scots identity is manifested in outward and visible form only in banknotes, tartans, legal doctrines and forms of religious observance, to these Scots must cleave or lose all sense of identity. If legislative and political power returns to Edinburgh, it can cheerfully be used in pursuit of quite new goals, and with a traditional eclecticism of borrowing, since it will be the Scots' own choice, not something foisted on Scotland from without.[54]

Legislative policy on devolved parts of Scottish private law however will be formulated in a Scottish rather than a British context and therefore is more likely to take proper account of distinctive features of Scots law.

The debate on European legal harmonisation and 'the new *ius commune*'

Within the European Union, there has been a debate as to whether a European code of private law is (1) constitutional in terms of the Treaties of Rome and Maastricht; (2) worthwhile; and (3) feasible.[55]

The European Parliament has twice passed a resolution favouring a common European Code of Private Law[56] and its supporters claim that such a code is essential to the smooth operation of the single market.

In Britain generally, and Scotland in particular, this latter argument tends to lack credibility. The Treaty of Union of 1707 (like the US constitution) established a single economy but no common system of private law.[57] So we find in 1993 Lord Rodger arguing that the Anglo-Scottish experience since 1707 shows that even a close political union does not demand a single system of private law: 'If we in Britain have managed quite happily with two distinct systems for almost three hundred years, it is hard to see why even the most rabid proponent of European union should feel that devising a single system of private law is an urgent priority.'[58]

---

[54] D. N. MacCormick, book review, (1976) *SLT* (News) 303 at 303.
[55] E. Hondius, 'Towards a European Civil Code', in A. Hartkamp et al. (eds.), *Towards a European Civil Code*, 2nd edn (Nijmegen, 1998), p. 8.
[56] *Official Journal of the European Communities* 1989, No. C 158/400, 1; ibid., 1994, No. C 205/518.
[57] T. Weir, 'Divergent Legal Systems in a Single Member State', (1998) *ZEUP* 564 at 565: 'It may be useful to consider how very different, after nearly three hundred years of political unification in an unquestionably single market, the laws of Scotland and England continue to be.'
[58] A. Rodger, 'Roman Law in Practice in Britain', (1993) 12 *Rechtshistorisches Journal* 261 at 262.

The difficulties confronting European integration are graphically illustrated by recent attempts to transpose genetically incompatible English concepts of property law[59] including rights in security[60] into Scots law. These attempts have raised immense difficulties because of profound differences in legal culture and philosophical approach[61] to many fundamental matters.[62] So a unified system of private law will probably be unattainable in Europe in the foreseeable future. Some piecemeal, bureaucratic integration by legislation under European Union directives has occurred even in the heartlands of delict and contract,[63] but this method of integration is now seen to have serious disadvantages.[64]

The rise of a movement to create a new *ius commune* by more organic means seems to have more prospects of success.[65] The immediate aim is not legislative unification but rather, by means of the functional methods of modern comparative law, 'to lay the basis for a free and unrestricted flow of ideas among European lawyers that is perhaps more central to the idea of a common law than that of identity on points of substance'.[66]

In England ideas of European integration are understandably seen by some as threatening English private law. In his recent inaugural lecture in

---

[59] E.g. 'beneficial interest'; 'constructive trust': see G. L. Gretton, 'Constructive Trusts', (1997) 1 *ELR* 281, 408.

[60] Cf. G. L. Gretton 'The Concept of Security', in D. J. Cusine (ed.), *A Scots Conveyancing Miscellany* (Edinburgh, 1987), p. 126.

[61] Cf. R. Goode, 'Commercial Law and the Scottish Parliament', (1999) 4 *SLPQ* 81 at 91.

[62] Such as future security; constitution of real rights; judicial powers to create property rights; the borderline between real rights and obligations, tracing, theories of registration of real rights; and *paritas creditorum*.

[63] E.g. products liability and unfair contract terms.

[64] See H. Kötz, 'A Common Private Law for Europe: Perspectives for the Reform of European Legal Education', in B. de Witte and C. Forder (eds.), *The Common Law of Europe and the Future of Legal Education/Le Droit commun de L'Europe at l'avenir de l'enseignement juridique* (Deventer, 1992), pp. 31–4. The unified rules, for example, often clash with non-unified rules, use common words which actually mean different things in different systems, and, since they are so difficult to amend, tend to become isolated fossils stuck inorganically within the laws of individual states. However, since European instruments have to accommodate both the common law and the civilian approach, they should fit Scots law as a mixed system better than do some English statutes into which segments of Scots law have sometimes been spatchcocked.

[65] See previous note. See also R. Zimmermann, 'Roman Law and European Legal Unity', in Hartkamp et al. (eds.), *Towards a European Civil Code*, p. 21; R. Zimmermann, 'Roman and Comparative Law: The European Perspective (some remarks apropos a recent controversy)', 1995 *JLH* 21; R. Zimmermann, 'Civil Code and Civil Law – the "Europeanisation" of Private Law within the European Community and the Re-emergence of a European Legal Science', (1994–5) *CJEL* 63.

[66] Kötz, 'A Common Private Law for Europe', p. 42.

Cambridge, Professor Jack Beatson confessed that one of his nightmares is that the English 'position as a common law system on the fringe of a civil law continent and our response to international developments will mean that we will only have a marginal influence and will in effect become the Louisiana or, given our relationship with the European Union, the Quebec of Europe'.[67]

In Scotland there are at least two schools of thought. One holds that Scots law has much to gain from the new *ius commune*. 'Its intrinsic intellectual worth is such that it is essential for Scots law to engage with it.'[68] It helps us to understand our own law. While the idea of a European legal science may seem to conflict with the preservation of Scots law as a distinct system, in fact the movement's organic, comparatist approach is already benefiting greatly the literature of Scottish private law.[69]

In Scotland, the opposition to unification of private law within Europe and against the *ius commune* movement is spearheaded by Lord Rodger.[70] The argument that 'as Europe moves towards "an ever closer union", so all our systems of private law should draw closer together' does not attract him.[71] Moreover in his view 'the idea of trying to draw up some legislative code on topics such as family or property law which would apply in all the

---

[67] J. Beatson, 'Has the Common Law a Future?', (1997) 56 *CLJ* 291 at 295. Lord Goff of Chieveley, 'The Future of the Common Law', (1997) 46 *ICLQ* 745 is more optimistic.

[68] E.g. J. Blackie and N. Whitty, 'Scots Law and the New *Ius Commune*', in H. L. MacQueen (ed.), *Scots Law into the Twenty-First Century: Essays in Memory of W. A. Wilson* (Edinburgh, 1996), p. 78.

[69] For examples of what Zimmermann calls 'the living *ius commune*', reference need only be made to the recent contributions on Scots law by him, Professor Evans-Jones and their students in the 1990s. See, e.g., J. E. du Plessis and H. Wicke, '*Woolwich Equitable* v. *IRC* and the Condictio Indebiti in Scots Law', (1993) *SLT* (News) 303; J. Faber, 'Rückforderung wegen Zwecknerfehlung – Irrungen und Wirrungen bei der Anwendung Römischen Rechts in Schottland', (1993) *ZEUP* 279; J. Dieckmann and R. Evans-Jones, 'The Dark Side of *Connelly* v. *Simpson*', (1995) *Jur. Rev.* 90; R. Zimmermann, 'Unjustified Enrichment: The Modern Civilian Approach', (1995) *OJLS* 403; R. Evans-Jones and P. Hellwege, 'Swaps, Error of Law and Unjustified Enrichment', (1995) 1 *SLPQ* 1; R. Evans-Jones and P. Hellwege, 'Some Observations on the Taxonomy of Unjustified Enrichment in Scots Law', (1998) 2 *ELR* 180; J. E. du Plessis, 'Compulsion and Restitution' (Ph.D. thesis, University of Aberdeen, 1997); D. L. Carey Miller and R. Zimmermann (eds.), *The Civilian Tradition and Scots Law: Aberdeen Quincentenary Essays* (Berlin, 1998), p. 167. A doctrinal history of the Scottish law of property and obligations written by twenty-eight lawyers (twenty Scots, six South African and two German) is K. Reid and R. Zimmermann (eds.), *A History of Private Law in Scotland*, 2 vols. (Oxford, 2000).

[70] Rodger, 'The Bell of Law Reform', pp. 342, 343; Rodger, 'Roman Law in Practice in Britain', p. 261; Rodger, 'Thinking about Scots Law', p. 23.

[71] Rodger, 'The Bell of Law Reform', p. 343.

countries of Europe seems wildly impractical. The intellectual effort could be better spent on other projects.'[72] Then again, the modified aim of moving towards a *ius commune* also seems impractical to him since he finds it hard to see states like Germany or France readily casting aside national codes in order to make way for a new *ius commune*.[73]

Lord Rodger points to the unfamiliarity of Scots judges and practitioners with Roman law, comparative law and legal history and to the linguistic difficulties.[74] He argues that while British judges (Scots and English) apply European Union law diligently, they do not make, and should not see it as their duty to make, Scots or English law more 'European' because that 'would be to adopt a particular political view and would fall outside their non-political rôle of safeguarding rights and enforcing obligations by the maintenance and development of English or Scottish law'.[75] Undoubtedly in Scotland there are very great practical difficulties (of language, accessibility and understanding) in borrowing from Roman law and its European descendants. But in Scotland it is difficult to see why borrowing from Europe should be regarded as any more 'political' than borrowing from Commonwealth or indeed from English sources. Time will tell whether Lord Rodger's view is a stable solution suited to the times given the strength of our ties with Europe.

The counter-pull of the Commonwealth

Scots law survived into the eighteenth century as a part of the European *ius commune* from which English law had always stood apart in splendid isolation. But English and British colonial expansion created a new and rival *ius commune* of common law systems now covering one-third of the world's population. So Scots law ceased to belong to a European majority of civilian systems and became one of a minority of mixed legal systems in the English-speaking world. The British empire was then transformed

---

[72] Ibid.   [73] Ibid.

[74] The difficulty of using Roman law or *ius commune* sources to develop modern Scots law is a constant theme of Lord Rodger's writings: see, e.g., 'Molina, Stair and the *Jus Quaesitum Tertio*', (1969) *Jur. Rev.*, 34, 128; 'Roman Law in Practice in Britain', p. 261; 'Roman Law Comes to Partick', in R. Evans-Jones (ed.), *The Civil Law Tradition in Scotland* (Edinburgh, 1995), p. 198; 'Thinking about Scots Law', p. 3; 'The Use of the Civil Law in Scottish Courts', in Carey Miller and Zimmermann (eds.), *The Civilian Tradition and Scots Law*, p. 225.

[75] Rodger, 'Roman Law in Practice in Britain', p. 263.

into a Commonwealth of fifty-three independent states and the common law is perhaps the most enduring link between them.[76] Then by another twist of fate, when the United Kingdom entered the European Economic Community in 1973, it was English law that became a minority and Scots law a minority within a minority, but having an affinity with both the minority and majority.

The Commonwealth exerts a strong gravitational pull against the full participation of the English common law in European legal integration. As Lord Rodger remarks:

> Today practitioners from Manchester in England can and do converse in a common legal language with those from Brisbane in Australia or Bombay in India. They have no difficulty in speaking to American lawyers either. It would be idle to pretend that the Common Law would readily yield up these immense advantages in order to be absorbed into some all-embracing European system, supposing that such a thing could emerge or be devised.[77]

The interests of the English common law in this matter are not the same as the real interests of Scots law.

Bridging the gap between the Civil and Common Law families

'One of the most intractable problems of European legal integration is the reconciliation of the civil law and the common law families.'[78] The Commission on European Contract Law aims 'to provide a bridge between the civil law and the common law by providing rules designed to reconcile their differing legal philosophies'.[79] Some Scots lawyers doubt whether a bridge is wanted.[80] 'A bridge is only worth building, of course, if sufficient people wish to cross from one side to the other at that particular point. So far at least, it is not obvious that many practising lawyers actually wish to cross the chasm which separates the systems.'[81]

---

[76] Lord Goff of Chieveley, 'The Future of the Common Law', p. 746.
[77] Rodger, 'Roman Law in Practice in Britain', p. 262.
[78] O. Lando and H. Beale (eds.), *The Principles of European Contract Law, Part I: Performance, Non-Performance and Remedies Prepared by the Commission on European Contract Law* (Dordrecht, 1995), p. xvi.
[79] Ibid., p. xvii.   [80] Rodger, 'Roman Law in Practice in Britain', p. 261.   [81] Ibid.

In 1925 a French comparative lawyer said that Scots law, as the only mixed system in Europe, could be such a bridge, or 'a picture of what will be, some day (perhaps at the end of this century) the law of the civilised nations, namely, a combination between the Anglo-Saxon system and the continental system'.[82] For long this aim seemed so unrealistic as to be embarrassing.[83] There is a gloomy argument that the factors underlying the creation of the modern Scottish mixed legal system are more indicative of a cultural weakness than strength.[84] There is some truth in that but not enough to make us succumb to defeatism. The fact that, however it happened, Scots law is a mixed system could by scholarly research and analysis become a source of strength in the Europe of today.

Take for example the work on Scottish trust law of Professors Kenneth Reid and George Gretton[85] of Edinburgh University. In the recent book from Nijmegen University entitled *Principles of European Trust Law* which compares the trust laws of nine European countries, the editors (an English and two Dutch lawyers) observe that Scots law 'may prove to be of particular interest to civilians considering the implementation of the trust in their domestic law'.[86] The reason is that Scots law accommodates the trust within a civilian system of property law which observes a strict distinction between real and personal rights, recognises that the real right of ownership is indivisible and rejects the English distinction between legal ownership and equitable ownership. As Professor Kenneth Reid observes:

---

[82] H. Lévy-Ullmann, 'The Law of Scotland', trans. F. P. Walton, (1925) *Jur. Rev.* 370 at 390; see also T. B. Smith, *British Justice: The Scottish Contribution* (London, 1961), p. 228; H. Lévy-Ullmann, 'Le Droit écossais', *Bulletin de la Société de Législation comparée* (1924), as quoted with approval in Cooper, *Selected Papers 1922–1954*, pp. 145, 198.

[83] See, e.g., F. M. B. Reynolds, 'Drawing the Strings Together', in P. B. H. Birks (ed.), *The Frontiers of Liability*, vol. II (Oxford, 1994), p. 160: 'The impression one has as an outsider is that Scots law is a vehicle which could carry developments of great international interest but that, unlike the laws of Australia and New Zealand, perhaps it has not yet started to do so. The most interesting law reform seems usually to be accomplished in small jurisdictions.'

[84] See also R. Evans-Jones, 'Receptions of Law, Mixed Legal Systems and the Myth of the Genius of Scots Private Law', (1998) 114 *LQR* 228.

[85] G. L. Gretton, 'Trust and Patrimony', in MacQueen (ed.), *Scots Law into the Twenty-First Century*, p. 182; G. L. Gretton, 'The Evolution of the Trust in a Semi-Civilian System', in R. Helmholz and R. Zimmermann (eds.), *Itinera Fiduciae: Trust and Treuhand in Historical Perspective* (Berlin, 1999); K. G. C. Reid, next note; K. G. C. Reid, 'Patrimony Not Equity: The Trust in Scotland', (2000) 8 *ERPL* 427.

[86] D. J. Hayton, S. C. J. J. Kortmann and H. L. E. Verhagen (eds.), *Principles of European Trust Law* (Nijmegen, 1999), pp. 3, 4. The 'National Report for Scotland' (ibid., pp. 67–84) was written by Professor K. G. C. Reid.

It is possible to have the trust and yet still remain virtuous. To adopt the
trust is not, or not necessarily, to sink into the arms of equity. A civilian
system cannot readily have the *English* trust, it is true. Probably it would
be ill advised to make the attempt. But there are other models on offer.[87]

There is in particular the Scottish trust in which there is separation of
patrimony without separation of personality. The real right of ownership
is vested in the trustee who has two 'patrimonies' or 'estates', one held
in a personal capacity and the other in a fiduciary capacity: a creditor of
one patrimony has no claim against the other patrimony. So here at least
Scotland might make a substantial contribution to bridge building.

The place of Scots law in the Civilian–Common Law dichotomy

The fourth debate concerns the question of what place Scots law occupies
within the comparative taxonomy of legal systems, and in particular the
civilian–Common Law dichotomy. In the 1950s Cooper and Smith thought
of Scots law as a mixed system in crisis.[88] More recently the question has been
raised whether Scots law is still a mixed system or has become a Common
Law system. Judge Edward of the European Court, for example, has stated
'that, for most practical purposes, the Scottish legal system belongs firmly
within the common-law family, and its most notable peculiarities are home-
grown rather than European'.[89] Others however are equally firm (and much
more correct) in saying that Scots law is – still – a mixed system,[90] albeit
'a mixture in which the ingredients are unevenly distributed'.[91]

If one applies the four relevant criteria of 'style' identified by Zweigert
and Kötz (history; tendency towards abstract or concrete thinking;

---

[87] Reid, 'National Report', p. 67.

[88] E.g. Lord Cooper, 'The Scottish Legal Tradition', in Cooper, *Selected Papers 1922–1954*, esp.
pp. 198, 199; Smith, 'Strange Gods', p. 119; Smith, *Studies Critical and Comparative*, p. 72.

[89] D. Edward, 'The Scottish Reactions – an Epilogue', in B. S. Markesinis (ed.), *The Gradual
Convergence* (Oxford, 1994), p. 264. Cf. R. McCall Smith, 'Scots Law in Comparative Context',
in J. P. Grant (ed.), *Independence and Devolution: The Legal Implications for Scotland* (Edinburgh,
1976), p. 157: 'Scots law is very much more of a common law system than it is a civilian'; S. H.
Amin, 'Scottish Legal System Revisited', (1982) *SLT* (News) 137 argues that the only important
respect in which Scots law is still a mixed system lies in the absence of the distinction between
law and equity.

[90] E.g. R. Evans-Jones, 'Some Reflections on the Condictio Indebiti in a Mixed Legal System',
(1994) *SALJ* 759.

[91] K. G. C. Reid, '*Sharp v. Thomson*: A Civilian Perspective', (1995) *SLT* (News) 75.

distinctive legal institutions; and sources of law)[92] to which Markesinis adds 'judicial style',[93] Scots law is still a mixed system by virtue of its separate history, to some extent the mode of thinking (though that is problematic) and especially its institutions. With only very slight exaggeration, the law of property has been described as 'entirely civilian in character. There is a *numerus clausus* of real rights. The real right of ownership is indivisible. And there is no place for the distinction between legal ownership and equitable ownership.'[94] But a maverick decision of the House of Lords[95] is causing problems. The law of obligations is a mixture of English, civilian and indigenous elements.[96] The future course of the law on obligations redressing unjustified enrichment is uncertain.[97] So the battle for the civilian soul of Scots law continues.

The direction of the future development of Scots law

The fifth debate concerns the ideology that should govern the future direction of the development of Scots law. In any mixed system, there will be conflicting pressures. The most significant example of conflict is perhaps the South African Purist-Pollutionist-Pragmatist *bellum juridicum* of the 1950s to 1980s. In Scotland, on the eve of devolution, there were many views spread across a wide spectrum as to the best path of development including (a) legal unionism in the form of the anglicisation of Scots law; (b) cross-border assimilation taking the best of each system; (c) pragmatism which can take the form of (i) pragmatic drift; or (ii) 'forward-looking development within a regional and international context'; (d) neo-civilian

---

[92] K. Zweigert and H. Kötz, *An Introduction to Comparative Law*, trans. T. Weir, 3rd edn (Oxford, 1998), esp. ch. 5 (pp. 63–73) on 'The Style of Legal Families'. Another mark of style – ideology – has reference to political or economic doctrine or religious belief and is irrelevant here.

[93] B. S. Markesinis, 'A Matter of Style', (1994) *LQR* 607. See also S. Levitsky, 'The Europeanisation of the British Legal Style', (1994) 42 *AJCL* 347.

[94] Reid, 'National Report', p. 67; for a full survey see K. G. C. Reid, *The Law of Property in Scotland* (Edinburgh, 1996); *The Laws of Scotland: Stair Memorial Encyclopaedia*, vol. XVIII (Edinburgh, 1993), s.v. 'Property'.

[95] *Sharp* v. *Thomson* 1997 SC (HL) 66 deciding that for some purposes 'ownership' of immoveable property passes to a transferee on delivery of the disposition instead of its registration in the land registers (which alone creates a real right in the disponee).

[96] For a recent survey, see *The Laws of Scotland: Stair Memorial Encyclopaedia*, vol. XV (Edinburgh, 1996), s.v. 'Obligations'.

[97] Evans-Jones and Hellwege, 'Some Observations on the Taxonomy', p. 180; cf. *Shilliday* v. *Smith* 1998 SC 725 at 727.

irredentism (i.e. reinstating civilian rules in anglicised areas of law) or resistance to anglicisation; (e) non-ideological adherence to civilian doctrine;
(f) non-civilian resistance to anglicisation; and (g) patriotic conservation-
ism. The following quotations illustrate the spread of views that existed on
the eve of devolution.[98]

Anglicisation and cross-border assimilation

In a debate on the paucity of Scottish legal literature in 1960, one soli-
citor wrote: 'It is manifestly absurd that two peoples, speaking the same
language, living as neighbours under the same constitution, having almost
complete community of interest in industry, finance and social welfare and
a dozen other fields, should have two systems of law – and what is equally
important – separate systems of legal administration.'[99]

Pragmatic drift

Lord Rodger does 'not foresee the Scottish courts positively embracing the
Civil Law, as the South African courts did, particularly during the *bellum
juridicum* of the 1950s and 1960s'.[100] Instead, they are likely to continue
with their century-old practice of displaying their independence 'by a certain eclecticism in adopting English doctrines rather than by any positive
hostility to English law or any positive rush to embrace Roman law...
even if this does indeed mean that Scots law is left without any very certain guiding principles'.[101] Professor Joe Thomson remarked that 'modern Scots law cannot be systematically expounded as a set of interlocking,
internally consistent principles.'[102] ... 'The study of the Civilian tradition

---

[98] For a fuller survey, see Whitty, 'The Civilian Tradition and Debates', pp. 442–8.

[99] Letter by Mr S. Scott Robinson, (1960) *SLT* (News) 35; see also letter by H. R. Aylmer, (1960)
      SLT (News) 28: 'This small country cannot afford in the middle of the twentieth century to have
      its own legal system.' For the anti-assimilationist reaction, see letters by Mr. R King Murray,
      (1960) *SLT* (News) 40 and Professor A. Dewar Gibb, (1960) *SLT* (News) 47.

[100] Rodger, 'Roman Law in Practice in Britain', p. 271.

[101] Ibid. Rodger, 'Thinking about Scots Law', p. 24: 'Our predecessors do not appear to have worried
      too much about which element of the Scottish mixture they called into service at any particular
      moment, but rather let the law develop as seemed best-suited to the demands and fashions of
      the times. We could do worse than follow their rather pragmatic example.'

[102] J. Thomson, 'When Homer Nodded?', in MacQueen (ed.), *Scots Law into the Twenty-First
      Century*, p. 26.

[cannot] still provide the rational foundations of contemporary Scots law.'[103]

Against these propositions contrast the warning of the late Professor W. A. Wilson: 'A legal system which has no doctrinal foundation must drift. It may be under the delusion that it is proceeding in the light of pure reason.'[104]

Forward-looking development within a regional and international context

Professor Clive favours forward-looking development within a regional and international context and 'rational, principled and socially responsive development'. In an antidote to legal nationalism, he remarks: 'A distinctive legal system is about as desirable as a distinctive system of weights and measures.'[105]

Neo-civilian irredentism or resistance to anglicisation

Lord Normand (Lord President of the Court of Session 1935–47) stated: 'Unless our law continues to grow in accordance with [the Roman] tradition it will run a grave risk of becoming a debased imitation of the Law of England, stumbling and halting before every problem where we have no English precedent to guide us.'[106]

Responding to Professor Clive's rejection of distinctiveness, Professor Robert Black emphasised 'the role of the institutional and civilian components in our legal heritage as furnishing the bedrock of rationality and principle which gives to Scottish private law the coherence which entitles it to be described as a system'.[107] 'If what makes a legal system distinctive is also what gives it coherence, then . . . distinctiveness is worth tolerating.'[108]

---

[103] Ibid.

[104] W. A. Wilson, 'The Importance of Analysis', in D. L. Carey Miller and D. W. Meyers (eds.), *Comparative and Historical Essays in Scots Law* (Edinburgh, 1992), p. 171.

[105] E. M. Clive, 'Scottish Family Law', in Grant (ed.), *Independence and Devolution*, p. 173.

[106] Lord Normand's foreword to J. S. Muirhead, *An Outline of Roman Law* (Edinburgh, 1937). He continued: 'From that fate our law students and future practitioners can save us by a right appreciation of the Roman tradition in the Law of Scotland and by accepting it as an active principle of natural growth and development.'

[107] R. Black, 'Practice and Precept in Scots Law', (1982) *Jur. Rev.* 31 at 45.   [108] Ibid., p. 46.

Non-ideological adherence to civilian doctrine

In particular areas of Scots law, the resurgence of the civilian tradition may not be inspired by a perceived need to resist uncritical anglicisation. The Scots law of property for example was not, or not yet, seriously threatened with anglicisation: it was simply in a muddle and the best way of sorting out the muddle was, and is, by way of developing the civilian tradition.[109]

Non-civilian resistance to anglicisation

An eminent English jurist conjectures: 'Perhaps the future for Scottish private law is to free itself from any connection with English law and develop freely in accordance with its own genius. That is what Commonwealth countries have done, and are doing.'[110]

The late W. A. Wilson remarked:

> Can there be a profitable analysis of the circumstances surrounding, and justification for, such rhetoric as 'It is ridiculous that the law on X should be different on each side of the border'? Are the rules which prevail in England suitable for a country with a somewhat different economic and social structure? Professor Willock asserts that employment and social security – both UK based – are the central areas of the system now. Are rules which change with each government law of the same order as principles which have stood for a thousand years?[111]

Patriotic conservationism: Hume's castle

The great novelist Sir Walter Scott was an advocate and later a sheriff (local judge). He was taught Scots law by Professor (later Baron) David Hume of Edinburgh University, the nephew of another David Hume, the celebrated philosopher of the Scottish Enlightenment. Scott copied the whole of Hume's law lectures[112] twice in his own hand, a gargantuan task, and in a famous passage Scott described them in glowing terms:

---

[109] See the comments on 'neo-civilianism' by K. G. C. Reid, 'Sharp v. Thomson: Property Law Preserved', (1995) SLPQ 53 at 56.

[110] Reynolds, 'Drawing the Strings Together', p. 160.

[111] W. A. Wilson, 'Knowing the Law and Other Things', (1982) Jur. Rev. 257 at 271.

[112] These were published posthumously by the Stair Society: Baron Hume's Lectures 1786–1822, 6 vols. (Edinburgh, 1939–58). Hume had forbidden publication.

I can never sufficiently admire the penetration and clearness of conception which were necessary to the arrangement of the fabric of law, formed originally under the strictest influence of feudal principles, and innovated, altered, and broken in upon by the change of times, of habits and of manners, until it resembles some ancient castle, partly entire, partly ruinous, partly dilapidated, patched and altered during the succession of ages by a thousand attritions and combinations, yet still exhibiting, with the marks of its antiquity, symptoms of the skill and wisdom of its founders, and capable of being analysed and made the subject of a methodical plan by an architect who can understand the various styles of the different ages in which it was subjected to alteration. Such an architect has Mr Hume been to the law of Scotland.'[113]

Both Hume and Scott were legal patriotic conservatives and their viewpoint is still strong in the Scottish legal profession. It was articulated by the Scottish Law Commission in the debate on devolution:

At the outset, however, the Commission wish to emphasise the importance which Scots lawyers, in common with other informed persons, attach to their own legal system and the maintenance of its integrity. This is not solely, or even mainly, because the Scottish legal system, as a language might be, is an important focus of national identity for Scotsmen in general. It is because Scots lawyers, who in their daily practice come into frequent contact with English law and legal institutions, are convinced that their own system is better adapted to Scottish needs and in certain respects, arguably, to those of the United Kingdom as a whole.[114]

Conclusion

In conclusion, I would make two points. First, I respectfully agree with Professor Jacques du Plessis of Stellenbosch who contends that in developing mixed systems, we should as far as possible take into account the character and historical foundations of the specific area of law which is to be developed and then build on these foundations to maintain the integrity

---

[113] Walter Scott, 'Autobiographical Fragment', in J. G. Lockhart, *The Life of Sir Walter Scott*, vol. I, 2nd edn (Edinburgh, 1839), pp. 81, 82.

[114] Scottish Law Commission Memorandum No. 32, *Comments on White Paper 'Our Changing Democracy: Devolution to Scotland and Wales'* (1975), pp. 54, 55.

of the structure.[115] In that way a mixed system achieves equipoise (harmony in balance) between its constituent elements.

Finally, if it be asked why small nations like Catalonia and Scotland should have their own legal systems in a complex world in which globalisation and the economies of scale matter so much, I would answer that a legal system can be a legitimate object of national pride which can add a priceless dimension to national life. Moreover, from the wider perspective of legal science and generally the good of mankind, I would invoke the views of Professor John Blackie of Strathclyde University, who

> considers it desirable to keep a large degree of variety and independence among legal systems, since they are like the constituents of the gene pool in the natural world. One certainly would not seek to cover the widest possible geographical area with one set of rules. Variety promotes elaboration and evolution. Furthermore the conservationist requires convincing that we should seek uniformity. To use another simile the historic building is worth renovating because of its independent value. One puts into it lifts and heating systems and so on. But it may in fact be also that one puts up with certain ongoing disadvantages if they are minor and justified by the whole.[116]

In his view and mine, the advantages of continuing to use and develop Hume's castle within the international context provided by the new European *ius commune* greatly outweigh the disadvantages.

---

[115] J. du Plessis, 'The Promises and Pitfalls of Mixed Legal Systems: The South African and Scottish Experiences', (1998) *Stellenbosch LR* 338 at 344.

[116] Professor Blackie's views were first stated in Whitty, 'The Civilian Tradition and Debates', p. 442.

3

The Scottish civil code project

ERIC CLIVE

The nature of the project

The Scottish civil code project is at present an unofficial project, based in the University of Edinburgh. The Scottish Minister for Justice and his officials know of the project but they have neither fully endorsed it nor rejected it. The present position is that the Minister has asked me to prepare a further paper explaining the scope of the project and an illustrative draft of a family law code. I have already submitted an illustrative draft of a general part. So links to the government remain open and work can proceed, even if on a slightly speculative basis for the time being.

The Scottish Law Commission, the statutory body charged with making law reform recommendations in Scotland, also knows of the project and expresses support for it in its latest programme of law reform. It presumably suits the Commission to have this long-term work undertaken outside the Commission because its resources are fully committed to more urgent projects, particularly in the field of property law.

I should emphasise that the aim of the project is a legislated code – enacted by the Scottish Parliament – and not simply a model code or unofficial restatement. It is therefore essential that the government is involved and interested.

Background

Attitudes of the legal community

Support from the legal community for the idea of codification cannot be taken for granted in Scotland. Indeed until a few years ago there was very little support for the idea and much opposition to it. It seems clear that the opposition is not to statutory reorganisation of the law as such. I have never heard anyone object to consolidating and reorganising those branches of the law that are already statutory. The opposition to codification appears to be an attachment to the case-law method in those areas where it survives. This attachment is perhaps understandable. There is an intellectual pleasure in working from an existing body of case law to solutions to new problems. There is also a flexibility in the method. The inconsistency and incoherence of case law can be used by skilled lawyers to reach just results in particular cases and to effect changes, sometimes quite dramatic changes, in the law. However, pleasure and flexibility are dearly bought – at the expense of the citizens who have to pay for an inefficient and unsatisfactory process. There is also a fundamental constitutional question whether it is right that important questions of social policy – such as whether certain classes of people should be prevented from claiming damages for losses caused to them by the carelessness of others – should be determined by unelected judges, often more or less overtly on policy grounds, or by the country's elected legislature.

I think, however, that attitudes are changing. One reason is the existence of the new Scottish Parliament with very wide legislative powers. It seems appropriate that Scotland's own legislature should be seen as the source of the basic rules of Scottish law. Also, the legislative process is much more local and accessible. Another possible reason may be the changed nature of legal practice in Scotland. Many lawyers already work in areas dominated by statute law. This is true of tax lawyers, planning lawyers, property lawyers, employment lawyers, agricultural lawyers, family lawyers, social welfare lawyers and others. All Scottish lawyers are now perfectly familiar with the idea of a body of law based on statute but supplemented by cases and commentary. Another reason, I suspect, is the more open approach now adopted in preparing legislation. There is a great deal of consultation. Lawyers can have an input. Indeed, the legal community as a whole, through its representative bodies, can have more influence on legislation than on case law. The Law Society of Scotland is recognised as one of the most effective lobbying organisations in the country. A fourth reason for a change in attitudes towards codification is the explosion of information retrieval technology. There is so much information – so many undigested cases available at the click of a mouse – that the demand now is for this mass of raw information to be organised. The best way of organising the law is to have a code.

Opinion among legal academics appears to be mixed. Some are enthusiastic about the idea of codification. Others are doubtful about the need or even opposed to the idea. However, there have been some significant recent converts to the idea and I do detect an interest and enthusiasm which were not there a few years ago. Law students I have spoken to about the project appear to be enthusiastic.

I do not want to give the wrong impression. Some judges, including Lord Rodger of Earlsferry, are strongly opposed to codification. Attitudes within the wider legal community are mixed. However, I do believe that attitudes have changed recently and are changing and that there is a tide flowing in favour of codification. I also believe strongly that people should have the opportunity of seeing what a draft code would look like before they express a definitive view. Many people might quite sensibly adopt the position 'Well, I would be in favour of a code if it was well done but I would be against one which was badly done.'

Attitudes of the wider community

So far as I know, no public opinion survey has been done on public attitudes to codification in Scotland. I suspect that there would be widespread indifference but, in so far as there was a view, support for the idea of making the law of Scotland more accessible and more understandable. Some people might say that lawyers have a certain interest in preserving the delights and mysteries of the common law, although I do not personally believe that that is the case. No one would say that the general public has any such interest.

It was clear to me during my time at the Scottish Law Commission that those non-legal professional people who have to work with the law – such as social workers, company directors and financial advisers – prefer statute law to case law. Case law to them is alien, mysterious and dangerous. They do not know what is there. They need the opinion of a lawyer, but even then they are not safe because lawyers can have different opinions.

The same may well turn out to be true for Members of the Scottish Parliament. Already, in debates on important Bills, they have been presented with conflicting legal opinions on basic questions of common law. A debate can be influenced, or at least temporarily confused, by a legal opinion from an advocate presented by a pressure group which has paid for that opinion. It is my guess that members of the Parliament would feel much more in control of their own legislative process if they had a text which all could read.

In short, I believe, although I cannot prove, that the wider community of public and politicians in Scotland would be in favour of codification. I hope I am right because ultimately power rests with the wider community of citizens and politicians and not with the unelected senior judges who appear to be the main opponents of the idea.

The scope of the project

The meaning of 'codification' in the present context

By codification I mean a more or less comprehensive, organised, statutory statement of the law on a subject, whatever the existing nature of that law and whether or not it is changed. A civil code would therefore be a more or less comprehensive, statutory reorganisation and restatement of the civil law. The words 'more or less' comprehensive are important. It is neither sensible nor practicable nowadays to aim for a completely comprehensive statute.

Structure and contents in general

There is much to be said, on grounds of familiarity and accessibility, for adopting a fairly traditional approach to the structure and contents of a civil code. However, if the Scottish civil code is to be enacted as an Act of the Scottish Parliament it will have to be divided into parts and sections, rather than books, titles and articles. That is not important but it will have some effect on the structure. I envisage provisionally that the code might contain a general part, followed by a group of parts on persons, a group of parts on rights and obligations, a group of parts on property, trusts and succession, and a group of parts on private international law. A very provisional layout (with some parts in need of expansion) might be:

Part 1 – General

Part 2 – Natural persons
Part 3 – Juridical persons
Part 4 – Unincorporated associations
Part 5 – Family law

Part 6 – Rights and obligations in general
Part 7 – Contracts
Part 8 – Unjustified enrichment
Part 9 – Delicts
Part 10 – Other obligations

Part 11 – Property
Part 12 – Succession
Part 13 – Trusts

Part 14 – Private international law[1]

Existing comprehensive statutes: incorporate or make reference?

One difficulty so far as contents are concerned is knowing what to do about existing comprehensive statutes dealing with important areas of private law – existing mini-codes, in effect.

What, for example, should be done about the extensive legislation on companies, partnerships, sale of goods, bills of exchange or bankruptcy? So far as Scotland is concerned it seems clear that most of these existing statutory codes should be left out of a new civil code. In some cases[2] the subject matter is beyond the competence of the Scottish Parliament. In other cases it would be inefficient to re-enact legislation recently passed after much deliberation and, sometimes, much difficulty.

The position is more difficult in relation to family law. Here too there is a lot of modern legislation but it is fragmented and there is a strong argument for including it in the code in a new coherent form. What about the law

---

[1] This list covers most substantive law topics contained in the definition of Scottish private law in s 126(4) of the Scotland Act 1998 which set up the Scottish Parliament and determined its competence. The definition is

   (a) the general principles of private law (including private international law),
   (b) the law of persons (including natural persons, legal persons and unincorporated bodies),
   (c) the law of obligations (including obligations arising from contract, unilateral promise, delict, unjustified enrichment and negotiorum gestio),
   (d) the law of property (including heritable and moveable property, trusts and succession), and
   (e) the law of actions (including jurisdiction, remedies, evidence, procedure, diligence, recognition and enforcement of court orders, limitation of actions and arbitration).

[2] Such as companies and partnerships.

on the registers of civil status? There is much on that in the French Civil
Code. We have comprehensive statutes in Scotland on the registration of
births, marriages and deaths but the subject matter seems to me to be more
administrative than substantive and my provisional view would be to omit
this material.

We have in Scotland a new comprehensive statute on adults with
incapacity,[3] which takes into account the recent Council of Europe Recommendation on this subject[4] and the recent Hague Convention on the
International Protection of Adults. Some parts of that Act were quite difficult and controversial. Some parts of it deal with procedures and remedies,
and public law controls, rather than substantive private law. It forms a coherent whole. It would not be sensible to re-enact it in a new code or to split
it up into parts, even although some sections would belong very naturally
in a section on incapacity in the law of persons. So again my inclination
would be to leave it out.

Of course, each decision to omit something diminishes the compre-
hensiveness of the code but that is perhaps not such a serious objection
nowadays. There can be a reference in the code to the other statutes, as is
sometimes done in the Spanish Civil Code, and for those using the text in
electronic form there can be hyperlinks to the other statutes which would
enable immediate access to be obtained to them.

Difficulties and opportunities in producing a new civil code at this time

More and different law

One of the difficulties in trying to produce a new civil code at the beginning
of the twenty-first century is that there is much more law to take into
account. It would have been easier to codify Scottish private law in 1800
than in 2000. However, that is not a serious problem and can even be seen
as an advantage. There has been more time for problem areas to emerge and
for solutions to be found.[5] There has been more time for archaic sections
of the law to be cleared away entirely. For example, a new Scottish civil code

---

[3] The Adults with Incapacity (Scotland) Act 2000.
[4] *Principles Concerning the Legal Protection of Incapable Adults*, Recommendation No. R (99) 4 and
explanatory memorandum.
[5] This is particularly apparent in the law of delict.

will not have to contain a voluminous and archaic part on the feudal system of land tenure. This has, fortunately, been swept away by the Abolition of Feudal Tenure Etc. (Scotland) Act 2000. Most of Scottish private law is reasonably up to date. The Scottish Law Commission has, after all, had it under review since 1965 and most of its recommendations for reform have been enacted. We are not in the position that the Dutch codifiers were in at an early stage of their project. We would not have to submit fifty questions to Parliament, some of them on quite fundamental questions of social policy, before beginning work.[6] We can concentrate on the form rather than the substance of the law with, however, some ironing out of inconsistencies and anomalies.

A more serious problem is that there is now much more public law and that many areas of the law which might traditionally have featured in a civil code are now a mixture of public and private law. I have already mentioned one example – the law on adults with incapacity. There are others – such as the law on the protection of children; the law on adoption; employment law; the law on unfair trade practices; the law on leases, whether agricultural or urban; the law on banking and financial advice, the law on the registration of titles to land. It is now realised and widely accepted that the best solution to a problem may not be to set out private law rights and obligations and let people litigate when problems arise. The best solution may be to prevent problems arising by some public law regulation and to provide some effective public law remedies or alternative methods of dispute resolution for cases of difficulty. Again it seems to me that a good deal of judicious omission and use of cross-references is called for.

A similar problem is presented by the growing volume of supra-national law, from the European Union in particular but also in the human rights field. This, of course, is not just a problem for a new civil code. It is a problem for existing laws and existing codes as well. Much supra-national law will, I believe, have to remain outside the code. Some of it will no doubt influence the content of the rules in the code.

What all this comes to is that when we say that a code is a more or less comprehensive statement of the law we now have to accept that it will inevitably be less comprehensive than it might once have been and that a great deal of the law regulating people's lives in important ways will lie

---

[6] See J. Dainow, 'Civil Code Revision in the Netherlands: The Fifty Questions', (1956) 5 *AJCL* 595–610.

outside the code. That does not mean that a civil code is not worth having. It means that a civil code has to be seen as just one part of the system of rules and that its relationship to other parts has to be carefully considered.

More pressure groups

The legislative process is much more open and democratic than it was 200 or even 100 years ago. It is to be expected that pressure groups and special-interest groups of various kinds will follow closely any proposed legislation which might affect their interests or special concerns and will attempt to influence the outcome. On the one hand, that makes the whole process of enacting a code much more difficult and stressful. On the other hand, the input of pressure groups and special-interest groups must surely be welcomed. A code is not enacted for, or at least not only for, professors or judges or lawyers. It is enacted for the people affected by it and it is, in my view, an entirely good thing that those people should have every reasonable opportunity to influence its contents. Indeed, an advantage of codifying now is that rules of law which have lain buried and unnoticed for a long time will be exposed to informed scrutiny and, perhaps, challenged from a functional and practical point of view. Lawyers may, for example, take some of the traditional rules on joint and several liability for granted. Those affected by them may say, 'Wait a minute! That rule operates unfairly in the situations in which we commonly find ourselves. We think it should be changed.' Special interests have to be weighed against opposing special interests and public interests but it must be better that they should be taken into account than that they should be unheard.

International and comparative models

One very definite advantage of codifying at the present time is that there are excellent international and comparative models on which to draw. Not only are there the older codes, still of immense interest and value, but there are also new and newly revised codes which respond quite consciously to the needs and values of the present time. I might mention the new Dutch Civil Code and the new Quebec Civil Code as examples – both highly impressive but rather different in style and approach. I have also been very interested in, and impressed by, the Catalonian Family Code of 1998. Having spent some years at the Scottish Law Commission working on the modernisation of Scottish family law, I recognise the problems and appreciate the way in which the solutions adopted respect the principle of equality between the spouses and the rights of the child.

In the area of contract law we are particularly fortunate in having three marvellous international instruments on which to draw – the United Nations Convention on Contracts for the International Sale of Goods, the Principles of European Contract Law produced by the Lando Commission and the Principles of International Commercial Contracts produced by Unidroit.

The pace of change

The pace of legal change is now much greater than it was 100 or even 50 years ago. Where our predecessors may have considered with some justification that they were legislating for centuries we must be modestly aware that we are legislating for decades. A clear recognition of this fact is an advantage because it helps to avoid false expectations of permanence and because it helps to counter the argument that a civil code would somehow petrify the law and prevent future development. It seems clear to me that a civil code would no sooner be enacted than a continuing process of review would have to be initiated. That is no different in substance from the present position, where the law is constantly under review. The difference in technique would be that the law to be reviewed would often be more apparent. The challenges for anyone devising a new draft code for this time of rapid change are to try to build in flexibility and to ensure that there is a strong logical structure capable of absorbing frequent changes of content.

Easier communications and information retrieval

Electronic access to local, comparative and international materials is improving all the time. This is an undoubted advantage of codifying now. The actual process of codification ought also to be greatly eased by electronic methods of communication. Once drafts have reached a certain stage they can be published on the Web and opened for comment by interested parties. It ought to be possible to have fewer physical meetings and organisational structures and thereby to cut down delay and expense.

Once the code is in place, electronic links to other relevant statutes, cases and commentary could easily be provided and constantly updated. There is an advantage in making a fresh start at a time when all related cases and commentary on the code, for example, and all new legislation having a bearing on it, can be made available in electronic form.

What might a new Scottish civil code be like?

It is probably rash to venture any opinion on what a Scottish civil code might look like. It is certain that any initial draft would undergo many changes as a result of further consideration, consultation and compromise.

It seems likely, however, that the code would be quite recognisable as a European type of civil code. The layout, as mentioned, would be in parts and sections but would otherwise be fairly typical. The style would, so far as possible, be general and conceptual. The subject matter would be recognisably the normal core areas of civil law in a modern European country. However, because the code would be making a fresh start, because there is no one model which political or historical considerations would indicate for adoption, and because the code would have to grow out of and reflect the existing law, it is likely that the result would be novel in some respects.

The code would be enacted primarily for functional rather than cultural purposes. Government ministers and Members of the Scottish Parliament are unlikely, for example, to have much interest in making Scottish law more civilian or jurisprudential in character. They would have an interest in setting out existing laws, reformed and modernised where necessary, in a clear and understandable way for the benefit of the citizens. There should of course be a clear conceptual and intellectual basis but I doubt whether the code should appear on its face to be a 'learned code' aimed at professors and the most senior judges. Ideally it should have a lot of hidden learning in it but should be presented in a popular way. The two aims of conceptual clarity and clear presentation are not, in my view, incompatible. Clear and logical underlying principles lead to an easier and more readable presentation.

Some questions

Should there be a general part?

My own view is that there should certainly be a general part. Indeed, there already is a tentative draft of such a part. It contains rules on the interpretation of the code; on its relationship to other enactments; on its relationship to common law rules; and on a judicial power to create exceptions to rules where justice so requires. It also contains definitions of some essential concepts – such as persons; juridical acts; juridical relationships; rights; obligations; remedies; property; abuse of rights and waiver of rights. And it contains some general rules that apply to all juridical acts – including rules on interpretation and rules on requirements of writing. Currently it also contains rules on prescription and limitation but I now think these rules should probably go in a later part on rights and obligations generally.

Good faith

There is some reason to suppose that the introduction of a general concept of good faith, either in the general part or in the part dealing with rights and obligations in general or in the part on contracts, would meet with opposition in Scotland. People would argue that too much uncertainty would be introduced and that litigants and judges would simply be invited to spend a lot of money and a lot of time on clarifying the role of the new provision in many different contexts. It will be absolutely necessary to have some flexibility in the code but I suspect that a way of providing it other than a general concept of good faith will have to be found. I have already mentioned that the general part will, at least provisionally, have a provision enabling the court to recognise exceptions to rules where this is manifestly required in the interests of justice. It will also have rules on 'personal bar', a potentially wide doctrine[7] already well recognised in the law of Scotland whereby a person who has a right or remedy may be prevented from exercising it if, for example, that person has represented to the other party that the right or remedy would not be exercised and the other party has acted on that representation to his or her prejudice. And the draft code will have rules on abuse of rights. Particular rules will also refer, where appropriate, to what is fair and reasonable. Good faith will be there but probably not as a general provision capable of directly supplementing, limiting or interpreting other provisions or rights and obligations.

---

[7] Akin to some forms of estoppel in English law.

How much should be said about juridical persons?

It seems clear that the part on juridical persons would have to be very brief and general and that, partly because of limitations on the competence of the Scottish Parliament but partly also for reasons of space and efficiency, the detailed rules on companies and partnerships should be left to United Kingdom statutes. The part on juridical persons might therefore be confined to some basic rules on how personality is acquired, name, domicile, habitual residence, capacity, representation and how personality is lost.

Unincorporated associations

It would, however, be useful to have in the code a section on unincorporated associations. This branch of the law turns largely on case law and a few rules of procedure. It is badly understood and yet is important in practice. There is a lot of underlying difficulty in the law on the liability of ordinary members of the association, on the ownership of property held as association property and on bringing or defending actions on behalf of the association. Codification could here be very useful. The area is currently untouched by statute law.

Family law

Scottish family law has been thoroughly modernised in recent years and is now very largely in modern statutes which just need to be brought together. There are still some outstanding recommendations from the Scottish Law Commission for reform,[8] and some other areas where reform might be considered, but the Scottish Ministers have the whole area under review[9] and there seems a reasonable prospect of further reforming legislation in the not-too-distant future. Once that is done, codification would be a question of reorganising the existing statute law into a coherent whole rather than

---

[8] See the Scottish Law Commission Report on Family Law (Scot. Law Com. No. 135, 1992).
[9] A consultation paper on *Improving Scottish Family Law* was issued in March 1999 and a further paper, taking account of the responses to the consultation, *Parents and Children: The Scottish Executive's Proposals for Improving Scottish Family Law*, appeared in September 2000. See also *Parents and Children: Responses to the Scottish Executive's Proposals for Improving Scottish Family Law* (September 2001) and the website http://www.scotland.gov.uk/justice/family law.

changing the content – still a difficult task but by no means an impossible one.

What about private international law?

It would, in my view, be highly desirable to include a part on private international law. This is an important branch of the law but it is not compulsory for students and many practitioners have had no comprehensive instruction in it. It still depends largely on case law,[10] and Scottish writers and judges place great reliance on English cases in this field. The problem is that if it is not included as a separate part then there will be pressure to include particular rules throughout the code in relation to particular topics so as to make it clear when the Scottish rule applies. That would be an undesirable way of proceeding because it would provide only half the answers. It would not say when one of two potentially applicable non-Scottish rules should apply.

What about contract?

Contract would have been potentially one of the most difficult areas of the code. Fortunately a lot of work has been done by others already. The English and Scottish Law Commissions worked on a British Contract Code in the late 1960s and 1970s. They abandoned the project at a late stage but much of their work remains valuable and available.[11] More importantly, there are the international instruments I have mentioned already. The Principles of European Contract Law produced by the Lando Commission are the most relevant for Scottish purposes because they apply to all contracts, not just to sales and not just to international commercial contracts. My hope is that these principles could be very heavily relied on, and indeed to a large extent simply adopted, in the new Scottish civil code. In fact, that would not be too difficult or too revolutionary because the Scottish law on contract is already remarkably similar to that in all these international instruments.

---

[10] There are now, however, statutory provisions on several matters, including choice of law in delict and the recognition of foreign divorces and nullity decrees.

[11] Harvey McGregor, who acted as a consultant to the English Law Commission on the project, has published the draft which he produced for the English Law Commission. See H. McGregor, *Contract Code: Drawn up on Behalf of the English Law Commission* (Milan, 1993).

This is perhaps because it has already for a long time had to accommodate civil law and English common law ideas.

What about delict?

Codifying the law of delict could be difficult. It is a highly developed branch of the law, of daily application and importance, and yet its foundations seem to be unstable. It is not even clear in Scotland whether we have a law resting on any general principle or a law of specific delicts liable to be affected by every pronouncement of senior English judges. It is also an area of the law in which there are powerful interest groups, including trade unions, insurance companies, the construction industry, the oil industry, tobacco companies and the press, to name but a few.

Any hope of a brief, elegant law must probably be abandoned. It will probably be necessary to try to reproduce the existing law, preferably in a reasonably principled and understandable way while trying to avoid purely temporary developments or swings of the pendulum – no easy task.

What I would provisionally envisage would be a general rule for delicts based on fault saying something like

> A person who, intentionally or by negligence, and without lawful justification, causes harm to another person by infringing a legally recognised right or interest of that person commits a delict.

This could then be supplemented by provisions explaining negligence, lawful justification, harm, and legally recognised rights or interests. These provisions would have to be framed in such a way as to leave some room for development of the law.

Then I would envisage provisions on the extent of liability for intentional delicts and on the extent of liability for negligent delicts.

There would then have to be provisions on delicts not based on fault, including sections on liability for animals, liability for dangerous things and situations, product liability and defamation. And there would have to be rules on vicarious liability for employees, on who could recover what for the death of a relative, and on the transmissibility of certain types of claim. Various restrictive rules of the present law would also have to be incorporated. Fortunately some of these matters, including liability for animals and damages for death, are already regulated by statute.

The result would be a much longer set of provisions than those found in most European codes but I do not think that anything shorter or more general would be acceptable to the politicians or the interest groups. Even something on these lines would be a considerable improvement on the present law because there would be a framework of principle and Scottish law would no longer be entirely at the mercy of sudden shifts in English judicial opinion.

One of the many points on which I am still uncertain is whether we would need to have a provision on reckless delicts. It is rather unfashionable at present in the United Kingdom even to mention recklessness or gross negligence in this context but it does seem to me that if you have special rules for intentional delicts then the same rules ought to apply at least sometimes to reckless delicts. The policy reasons that justify some restrictions on liability for negligence, simply to keep liability for careless conduct within acceptable bounds and to prevent useful activities from being confined by a legal straitjacket, do not always apply to intentional or reckless delicts. In the criminal law, recklessness is often equiparated to intentional wrongdoing and it is difficult to see why the same should not sometimes apply also in the civil law on delict. This is something on which I would like to consult at an early date.

Unjustified enrichment

This area has been well worked over in recent years by my colleague Niall Whitty and others. The Scottish courts have now recognised that the law is based on the underlying principle that a person who is, without legal justification, enriched at the expense of another is, in general, bound to redress the enrichment.[12] This recognition of a single underlying principle giving rise to an obligation of redress[13] puts the law in a fine state for codification. Model provisions based on this principle already exist.[14] So it

---

[12] See *Dollar Land (Cumbernauld) Ltd* v. *CIN Properties Ltd* 1996 SC 331 at 348–9; *Shilliday* v. *Smith* 1998 SC 725 at 727: 'a person may be said to be unjustly enriched at another's expense when he has obtained a benefit from the other's actings or expenditure, without there being a legal ground which would justify him in retaining that benefit'.

[13] See *Shilliday* v. *Smith* 1998 SC 725 at 727 where the Lord President said that where there was unjustified enrichment the significance was that it triggered, in general, a right to have the enrichment reversed.

[14] See, e.g., the draft provisions in A. S. Hartkamp et al. (eds.), *Towards a European Civil Code*, 2nd rev. and exp. edn (Nijmegen, 1998), ch. 25, pp. 393–4; or the more elaborate *Draft Rules on*

would not be hard now to include a fully developed section on unjustified enrichment in the draft code. Of course, there would then be argument about it but this will be true of any interesting part of the draft.

What about property?

I must confess that I have given very little consideration to the parts on property. I am hoping that my colleague Professor Reid might be tempted to do something in this area when he has time! I would hope that, with the abolition of the feudal system of land tenure, we could in Scotland begin with the assumption that the core rules of property law are the same for moveable and immoveable property. Again, as I have mentioned, it would probably be wise to leave many of the modern administrative, social and regulatory rules to their own special statutes. It seems likely that the Scottish Parliament will soon consider important Bills on the law on the relations between the owners of different flats in a building[15] and on title conditions which run with the land. These matters could usefully be included in the code along with provisions on joint and common property, servitudes, rights of way and other matters.

Trusts

Scotland has a law on trusts even although it does not have, and never has had, separate systems of law and equity, as in English law. The essence of the Scottish law on trusts is that the trustee owns the trust property as a sort of separate patrimony, not liable for the trustee's own debts as an individual, but owes fiduciary duties to the beneficiary, including an obligation to account to the beneficiary. Trusts are very important in practice in Scotland and there is a great need to have the law clarified and clearly set out in statute. Without that there is a danger that some of the wilder and more unacceptable English developments in the area of constructive trusts will creep into Scottish law without enough consideration being given to

---

Unjustified Enrichment and Commentary prepared by the author and appended to the Scottish Law Commission's Discussion Paper No. 99 on Judicial Abolition of the Error of Law rule and its Aftermath (1996).

[15] Buildings divided into different flats are called tenements in Scotland and the relevant branch of the law is called 'the law of the tenement'. See the Scottish Law Commission Report on the Law of the Tenement (Scot. Law Com. No. 162, 1998).

their effects in practice. The difficulty at present is that some English judges have shown a tendency to invent a constructive trust to remedy any kind of apparent injustice presented to them. The problem is that remedying an apparent injustice in one case by inventing a new type of trust of general application may not only create injustices in other cases, not presented to or considered by the court, but may also create uncertainty in commercial relations and undermine other areas of the law carefully developed to balance different interests in a reasonably fair and certain way.

Succession

The Scottish Law Commission produced a major report on the law of succession in 1990. This covered intestate succession and what we call legal rights – that is, the forced share of the widow or widower and descendants. The main thrust of the Commission's recommendations was an improvement in the legal position of the surviving spouse. In many estates of ordinary size the surviving spouse would take everything on intestacy. This corresponds to what testators do and to what, according to public opinion surveys, people think is appropriate. Once the policy is decided by the government it should not be too hard to codify the law on intestate succession and legal rights. Much of the work has already been done – and, indeed, the law on intestate succession is already statutory. Testate succession would be slightly more difficult and would take a bit of work.

Tactics

I have been talking so far in terms of a complete civil code. That is the ultimate dream, the grand design. It is useful to have in mind what a complete code would look like. However, as a matter of tactics it may well prove to be more practicable to codify in stages, as is being done in Catalonia. The reasons are fairly clear. To enact a whole civil code in one Act, in one Parliamentary session, would be too demanding a task. It would impose intolerable pressures on the civil servants, on the parliamentarians[16] and on the bodies and people, such as the Law Society of Scotland, the Faculty of Advocates, the judges and various pressure groups and special-interest groups who would wish to submit comments and influence the outcome. A

---

[16] Particularly the members of the already hard-pressed Justice Committees.

much more realistic prospect would be to enact self-contained codes – e.g. first family law; then succession law; then contracts; then unjustified enrichment; then delict; then property; then trusts; then private international law; and so on. Over time, techniques and smooth working practices could be established and, if a momentum could be built up and sustained, the result would still be a massive reorganisation and modernisation of Scottish civil law. I would be most interested to learn more of the experience of codification in Catalonia, particularly from the point of view of the civil servants and Members of Parliament who have to handle the work. I am sure there are valuable lessons that Scotland could learn.

Where does the criminal law fit in?

There is also in Scotland a criminal law codification project. Again this is an unofficial project being undertaken by a small group of professors from the universities of Edinburgh, Aberdeen and Dundee.[17] It is more advanced than the civil law project because work has already been proceeding for a number of years. A draft text and commentary were published in 2000. One advantage of the tactic of codification in parts, on the lines I have just mentioned, is that it would enable a criminal law code to be fitted into a rolling codification programme at some convenient point. From some points of view, including human rights, the enactment of a criminal code in Scotland is probably more urgent than the enactment of a civil code.

Assessment of prospects

The situation in Scotland is significantly different from that in the other countries and territorial units represented in this volume. The question for us is not 'How can we modernise our code?' but 'Should we attempt to introduce a code?' However, the fundamental benefits, both functional and cultural, of having an organised and up-to-date set of laws enacted by our own Parliament are the same in Scotland as in the other countries and territorial units represented here and my own assessment is that, once a draft is available for scrutiny, those benefits will become increasingly apparent.

---

[17] Professor Gane, Aberdeen; Professor Ferguson, Dundee; Professor McCall Smith, Edinburgh; Sir Gerald Gordon QC and the author of this chapter.

The first task is to produce a draft. Fortunately, I am in a position to devote virtually my whole time to this project and I am confident that, with the support of enthusiastic colleagues, a complete tentative draft can be produced within a few years. Individual parts, such as a part on family law, could be produced much more quickly, in months rather than years. I do not for one minute imagine that a first draft would be anything more than the beginning of a long and difficult process but the important thing is to get started and produce something for people to discuss and improve.

As for the ultimate prospects of enactment, I think it is too early to say. A lot will depend on political and parliamentary considerations in a few years. I am absolutely convinced that the enactment of a Scottish civil code, or even of substantial parts of it, would be a magnificent and worthwhile achievement for the new Scottish Parliament, precisely the sort of thing which it could do well and which could never have been done by the London Parliament. However, more pragmatic considerations are also likely to be important and the support of bodies such as the Law Society of Scotland will be vital. What is clear is that unless a draft exists it will not be possible to seize any opportunity which might be presented by a favourable combination of circumstances.

4

Scots law in Europe: the case of contract

HECTOR L. MacQUEEN

Introduction

It is a crucial aspect of the history of Scots private law that in its history in-fluences from the common law of England have been unavoidable from the beginning and waxed particularly strong after the Union of the Parliaments of the two kingdoms, with a common legislature, final court of appeal (the House of Lords) and the familiarity that comes from proximity, accessibility and a common language. But unlike English law, Scots law was also open from the very beginning to what was to become the Continental European *ius commune* (common law). The substance of the law was much affected by the universal law of the church (the canon law) and the Roman or Civil law taught in the Continental universities at which until the eighteenth cen-tury many Scots lawyers underwent their initial legal education. A further effect was that when Scots lawyers wrote treatises on their law, they used the systematics and concepts of the learned laws of Europe, further reinforcing its *ius commune* characteristics. If this Civilian dimension weakened after the 1707 Union, and in particular from the Victorian era on, Scots private law nonetheless remains significantly distinct from that of England, and in comparative law terms it is correctly classified as a 'mixed' system.[1]

In 1924 the distinguished French comparatist Professor Lévy-Ullmann observed that 'Scots law gives us a picture of what will be some day the law

---

An earlier version of this chapter appeared as *Scots Law and the Road to the New Ius Commune*, Ius Commune Lectures in European Private Law, ed. M. Hesselink et al., No. 1, Universities of Maastricht, Utrecht, Leuven and Amsterdam (Amsterdam, 2000).

[1] For a more detailed survey with literature references see H. L. MacQueen, 'Mixture or Muddle? Teaching and Research in Scottish Legal History', (1997) 5 *ZEUP* 369, responding to N. R. Whitty, 'The Civilian Tradition and Debates on Scots Law', (1996) *TSAR* 227 and 442; see further W. D. H. Sellar, 'Scots Law: Mixed from the Very Beginning? A Tale of Two Receptions', (2000) 4 *ELR* 3.

of the civilised nations, namely a combination between the Anglo-Saxon and the Continental system'.[2] Fifty years later two equally distinguished German comparatists, Professors Zweigert and Kötz, wrote: 'It is clear that Scots law deserves particular attention from comparative lawyers as a special instance of the symbiosis of the English and Continental legal traditions; this may be of some assistance to those who embark on the great project of the future, namely to procure a gradual approximation of Civil Law and Common Law.'[3]

However, it is, I think, fair to say that despite these very flattering remarks Scots law has not in fact received much attention from comparative lawyers outside Scotland itself.[4] Thus it is not altogether surprising to find that, in the recent renaissance of interest in the idea of harmonising and unifying the private law of Europe, perhaps even in the form of a European civil code, relatively little attention has been given to Scots law as a potential model for (in the words of Zweigert and Kötz) 'a gradual approximation of the Civil Law and Common Law'. Indeed, Scots lawyers themselves seem at times to lack faith in the merits of being a mixed system and to see only a future of gradual assimilation within the Common Law.[5]

The first argument which I want to offer here, therefore, is that more heed should be given to the words of Lévy-Ullmann, Zweigert and Kötz by those following the road to what is sometimes described as the new *ius commune* of Europe. Indeed, I would go further and suggest that it is not only Scots law, but also the world's other mixed legal systems, that should receive attention in this regard.[6] The argument is based upon an analysis

---

[2] H. Lévy-Ullmann, 'The Law of Scotland', trans F. P. Walton, (1925) *Jur. Rev.* 370 at 390.

[3] K. Zweigert and H. Kötz, *Introduction to Comparative Law*, trans T. Weir, 3rd edn (Oxford, 1998), p. 204. The statement also appeared in the first and second editions.

[4] But see H. David, *Introduction à l'étude du droit écossais* (Paris, 1972) and H. Weber, *Einführung in das schottische Recht* (Darmstadt, 1978). Other non-Scots to write extensively about Scots law include Klaus Luig (Cologne) and Peter Birks (Oxford). Recently Reinhard Zimmermann (Regensburg) and a number of South African scholars have begun to take a comparative interest in Scots law: see K. G. C. Reid and R. Zimmermann (eds.), *History of Private Law in Scotland*, 2 vols. (Oxford, 2000).

[5] See most recently R. Evans-Jones, 'Receptions of Law, Mixed Legal Systems and the Myth of the Genius of Scots Private Law', (1998) 114 *LQR* 228–49. Cf., however, T. Weir, 'Divergent Legal Systems in a Single Member State', (1998) 6 *ZEUP* 564, emphasising 'how very different, after nearly three centuries of political unification in an unquestionably single market, the laws of Scotland and England continue to be' (at p. 565).

[6] For a recent collection on mixed legal systems see E. Örücü, E. Attwooll and S. Coyle (eds.), *Studies in Legal Systems: Mixed and Mixing* (The Hague and London, 1996). Note Örücü's comments at pp. 350–1: 'Mixed systems can be regarded as points of reconciliation and as models of the

of the outcome so far of the new *ius commune* project in which I have
been involved myself, namely the Commission on European Contract Law
chaired by Professor Ole Lando. The Commission is a private initiative, with
a membership drawn from all the legal systems in the European Union.
I have been the Scottish representative since 1995, when I succeeded the
late Professor W. A. Wilson. The aim of the Commission is the production
of a set of rules — the Principles of European Contract Law — which will
represent an ideal system of contract law.[7]

The intellectual origin of the Principles lies in the successful conclusion in
1980 of the Vienna Convention on the International Sale of Goods (CISG),
which includes a number of rules on general contract law reconciling the
conflicting traditions of the Common and the Civil Law.[8] But CISG applies
only to sale contracts, and one aim of the Lando Commission is to create
a system for all contracts in the context of the European Union. A similar objective with regard to the global market-place has been successfully
pursued by Unidroit, the International Institute for the Unification of
Private Law, which published its Principles of International Commercial
Contracts in 1994.[9]

Although the very similar Unidroit and Lando Principles may one day
be the basis for the contract law of a unified Europe, that is not their immediate goal. They are also designed to be capable of adoption by contracting
parties engaging in cross-border transactions but anxious not to tie them
to particular systems for purposes of either the applicable law or dispute
settlement. The Principles may thus take effect in international commercial

---

symbiosis of legal systems. They may even be depicted as the "ideal systems" of the future ...
They have not yet become the ideal systems of the future as was hoped, however.' See also
J. du Plessis, 'The Promises and Pitfalls of Mixed Legal Systems: The South African and Scottish
Experiences', (1998) 3 *Stellenbosch LR* 338.

[7] The Principles (henceforth PECL) are only partly published. Part I (Performance, Non-
performance and Remedies) appeared in 1995 (O. Lando and H. Beale (eds.), *Principles of
European Contract Law* (Dordrecht, 1995)). This part was revised and another part, dealing
with formation, agency, validity, interpretation, contents and effects, added (O. Lando and
H. Beale (eds.), *Principles of European Contract Law Parts I and II* (Dordrecht, 1999)). A final
part was published in 2003 (O. Lando, E. Clive, A. Prum and R. Zimmermann (eds.), *Principles
of European Contract Law Part III* (Dordrecht, 2003)).

[8] For the text of CISG see F. D. Rose (ed.), *Blackstone's Statutes on Commercial and Consumer Law
1997–8* (London, 1997), pp. 468–85.

[9] Unidroit, *Principles of International Commercial Contracts* (Rome, 1994). See M. J. Bonell, *An
International Restatement of Contract Law: The Unidroit Principles of International Commercial
Contracts*, 2nd rev. edn (Irvington, N.Y., 1997).

arbitrations. They are also expected to influence law reform in the member states and by the European Community itself, and to be a basis for teaching in the law schools.[10]

The work of the Lando Commission is now drawing to a conclusion, with the publication of parts I and II of the Principles at the end of 1999, and of part III early in 2003. The time is therefore ripe to examine its results and to consider how far they reflect the position in the Scots law of contract. My approach will be to draw attention to some major rules in the Principles which can be said to approximate to those of the modern Scots law of contract but on which there are significant divisions between the approaches of the Civil Law and the Common Law. I will divide the discussion according to whether the rules are of Civilian or Common Law origin.

Rules of Civilian origin

No consideration: the unilateral promise

The Principles state that a contract is concluded if (a) the parties intend to be legally bound and (b) they reach a sufficient agreement. There is no further requirement (art. 2:101). Thus the English requirement of consideration (to say nothing of the French *cause*) plays no part in the Principles, any more than it does in Scots or German law.[11] One consequence in Scots law is the enforceability of the unilateral or gratuitous promise;[12] and likewise the Principles hold that 'a promise which is intended to be legally binding without acceptance is binding' (art. 2:107).

Irrevocable offers and postal acceptances

The Principles, while stating a general proposition that offers are revocable, allow them to be made irrevocable by an indication to that effect (art. 2:202). The Scots law concept of promise allows a party to make offers irrevocable

---

[10] See H. Beale, 'Towards a Law of Contract for Europe: The Work of the Commission on European Contract Law', in G. Weick (ed.), *National and European Law on the Threshold to the Single Market* (Frankfurt am Main, 1993); H. Beale, 'The "Europeanisation" of Contract Law', in R. Halson (ed.), *Exploring the Boundaries of Contract* (Aldershot, 1996).

[11] For the comparative position see Zweigert and Kötz, *Introduction to Comparative Law*, pp. 389–99.

[12] See most recently W. W. McBryde, 'Promises in Scots Law', (1993) 42 *ICLQ* 48.

or 'firm' by an appropriate statement in the offer.[13] In French law offers are revocable but nonetheless an offeree may have a claim in damages if the offeror abuses his right, while in Germany offers are irrevocable unless otherwise stated. Offers are always revocable in English law, however, unless the offeree provides consideration. The problems this limitation creates are overcome to some extent by the distinctive rule of English law, under which a postal acceptance concludes a contract at the time and place of posting rather than when and where it is communicated to the offeror.[14] This rule has also been received into Scots law, although the Scottish Law Commission has recommended its abolition in a report published in 1993.[15] Given that the Principles start on the basis that offers are revocable, it has to do something to protect offerees where the parties are not dealing face to face; the solution is to provide that offers can no longer be revoked once the offeree has dispatched an acceptance (art. 2:202(1)), but the contract is not concluded until the acceptance reaches the offeror (art. 2:205(1)).

Contracts for the benefit of third parties

The Principles follow the Continental and Scots legal systems in recognising that contracting parties may create enforceable rights for third parties by appropriate terms in their contract (art. 6:110).[16] English law by contrast has traditionally started from the doctrine of privity, under which only the contracting parties can acquire rights under a contract, even if they intend to confer a benefit upon a third party. The Law Commission of England and Wales produced a report on this subject in 1996, recommending the abandonment of privity and the introduction of a system of third-party rights.[17] Significantly, one of the reasons for this change given by the Commission was the need for English law to be brought into harmony with the approach elsewhere in Europe. Even more significantly, on the highly symbolic date

---

[13] W. W. McBryde, *The Law of Contract in Scotland* (Edinburgh, 1987), pp. 65, 68–70; *The Laws of Scotland: Stair Memorial Encyclopaedia* (Edinburgh, 1987–1996, henceforth *SME*), vol. XV, para. 617.

[14] For all the foregoing see Zweigert and Kötz, *Introduction to Comparative Law*, pp. 356–64.

[15] Report on Formation of Contract: Scottish Law and the United Nations Convention on Contracts for the International Sale of Goods (Scot. Law Com. No. 144, 1993).

[16] For third-party rights in Scotland see *SME*, vol XV, paras. 824–52; for the Continent Zweigert and Kötz, *Introduction to Comparative Law*, pp. 456–69.

[17] Report on Privity of Contract: Contracts for the Benefit of Third Parties (Law Com. No. 242, 1996).

of 11 November 1999 (the anniversary of Armistice Day) the report was given effect as law when the Contracts (Rights of Third Parties) Act received Royal Assent.

Performance as the primary right of a creditor

The Principles provide a range of remedies for breach of contract, or non-performance, as the Lando Commission has preferred to term the matter. First among them is the aggrieved party's entitlement, or right, to specific performance of the other party's obligation (art. 9:102(1)). Here again the model being followed is that of the Continental systems,[18] and under Scots law too the creditor's primary remedy is an order for specific implement.[19] In English law, by contrast, the aggrieved party is not entitled to specific performance, which is an equitable remedy subject to the discretion of the court and which will not be granted in a number of circumstances. Scots law has been influenced by English law in this area, to the extent that the courts exercise an equitable control over the grant of the remedy and have borrowed many of the rules that limit specific performance in England. Moreover, in practice on the Continent specific performance is granted only relatively rarely. This means that the outcome in particular cases is often much the same in England, Scotland and on the Continent. The Principles reflect this, and indeed the development of Scots law, when they qualify the right to specific enforcement with a number of exceptions mainly drawn from the English rules on the subject (art. 9.102(2)). Nevertheless that a difference exists between a system where specific performance is a right and one where it is a remedy within the discretion of the court is suggested by the contrasting outcomes of recent cases in Scotland and England on so-called 'keep open' clauses in commercial leases. In both countries commercial leases are typically of several years' duration. In the cases, changing commercial circumstances led the tenants to withdraw prematurely from the leases. In England the House of Lords refused to grant specific performance to the landlords, on the grounds that the order could not be used to compel

---

[18] Zweigert and Kötz, *Introduction to Comparative Law*, pp. 472–9; G. H. Treitel, *Remedies for Breach of Contract: A Comparative Account* (Oxford, 1988), pp. 43–63 (note also pp. 71–4 on mixed systems).

[19] McBryde, *Law of Contract*, pp. 509–14. See also A. D. Smith, 'Some Comparative Aspects of Specific Implement in Scots Law' (Ph.D. thesis, Edinburgh University, 1989).

someone to trade at a loss,[20] whereas the Scottish courts upheld the landlords' claim and ordered the tenants to continue to implement the contract.[21] While there may seem to be economic inefficiency in compelling a party to trade at a loss and against its will, the Scottish approach seems preferable to me in upholding the sanctity of contract and the overall risk allocation in long-term bargains; it also means that the onus of finding a new tenant falls on the existing tenant rather than the landlord – that is to say, the contract-breaker pays the costs of breach up front, rather than later in a claim for damages.

The exceptio non adimpleti contractus: *retention*

Another remedy in the Principles (art. 9:201) which is found in Scots and Continental contract laws is the right to withhold performance until the other party performs — the *exceptio non adimpleti contractus* (defence of the unperformed contract).[22] The remedy is in the nature of a suspension of performance, and there is no precise equivalent in the English law of remedies,[23] which emphasises termination and damages, although its rules on conditions precedent and subsequent and on order of performance provide some analogues.[24]

Rules of Common Law origin

Unified concept of breach

In general the Principles and Scots law adopt a unified approach to breach or non-performance of contract; that is to say, the remedies apply to any failure to perform in accordance with the contract, whether by total or partial non-performance, delayed or late performance, or defective performance

---

[20] *Cooperative Insurance Society Ltd* v. *Argyll Stores (Holdings) Ltd* [1998] AC 1.

[21] *Retail Parks Investments Ltd* v. *The Royal Bank of Scotland Ltd (No. 2)* 1996 SC 227; *Highland Universal Properties Ltd* v. *Safeway Properties plc* 2000 SC 297. See further H. L. MacQueen and L. J. Macgregor, 'Specific Implement, Interdict and Contractual Performance', (1999) 3 *ELR* 239, and A. D. Smith, 'Keep on Keeping Open', (2000) 4 *ELR* 336.

[22] The comparative position receives detailed treatment in Treitel, *Remedies*, pp. 245–317. For the Scots law of retention and mutuality see McBryde, *Law of Contract*, pp. 303–9, and for comment on the latest cases (*Bank of East Asia* v. *Scottish Enterprise* 1997 SLT 1213 and *Macari* v. *Celtic Football Club* 1999 SC 658), see W. W. McBryde, 'Mutuality Retained', (1996) 1 *ELR* 135–9 and J. M. Thomson, 'An Unsuitable Case for Suspension', (1999) 3 *ELR* 394.

[23] Treitel, *Remedies*, pp. 299–317.   [24] Ibid., pp. 255–99.

(see generally Principles, chs. 8 and 9). This is essentially the approach of English law and indeed of modern French and Dutch law; however, it contrasts with German law, where remedies for non-performance depend upon whether it results from delay or impossibility. This limitation has given rise to great difficulties in Germany, only partially alleviated by the development in the courts of the further idea of 'positive breach of contract'.[25] Before the nineteenth century Scots law showed some signs of developing a similar idea of non-performance as either delay or impossibility, but this was given up largely under English influence.[26] Impossibility came to be treated quite separately from breach, under the heading of frustration (another concept borrowed from English law). The Principles do not go quite this far: a concept of non-performance excused by an impediment beyond a party's control is deployed instead (art. 8:108), and under this head, the remedies of specific performance and damages are precluded but those of withholding performance and termination (see below) are allowed. Apart from this, however, the Principles do not impose any requirement of fault before remedies for non-performance become available, and again this is akin to the position in Scots and English law. A final point under this heading is that the Principles follow Scots and English law in allowing the cumulation of remedies so long as they are not incompatible with each other (art. 8:102). Again there is a contrast with the German position under which, for example, an aggrieved party must choose between termination and restitution, on the one hand, and damages protecting its expectation or performance interest, on the other.[27]

Repudiation as breach

Breach of contract by repudiation – that is, refusal to perform including anticipatory refusal before performance has fallen due – is an invention of English law which is not exactly paralleled in the Continental systems.[28] A party may consequently be released from its contract by the refusal without having to wait to see whether or not it is fulfilled when performance is due. It is a doctrine of immense value in commercial situations which Scots

---

[25] For all the foregoing see Zweigert and Kötz, *Introduction to Comparative Law*, pp. 487–515.
[26] See H. L. MacQueen, 'Remedies for Breach of Contract: The Future Development of Scots Law in its European and International Context', (1997) 1 *ELR* 200–24, at 203.
[27] §§ 325, 326 BGB.   [28] Treitel, *Remedies*, pp. 379–81.

law received in the later nineteenth century, and it is recognised in several articles of the Principles (e.g. arts. 8:105, 9:101(2), 9:201(2), 9:304).

'Self-help' remedies for non-performance

Another distinctive characteristic of the English law of remedies for breach which has only limited parallels on the Continent is the informal and 'self-help' nature of some, such as termination, meaning that it is not necessary in law to go to court or to give the other party special notice to invoke them.[29] This means that the remedies can be exercised speedily and without immediate cost, again features attractive to commerce. Once more Scots law borrowed the English approach here in the nineteenth century, and the Principles follow suit with regard to their remedies of withholding performance and termination of the contract (see Principles, ch. 9, ss 2 and 3).

Undisclosed principal in agency/representation

Moving away from remedies, a final example of an English doctrine based upon commercial utility rather than strict conceptual purity which has found its way into Scots law and the Principles, but not into Continental systems, is that of the undisclosed principal in cases of agency.[30] The gist of this doctrine is that an agent who has not revealed to his co-contractant that he is an agent may nonetheless bind together in a contract his principal and the other party (Principles, ch. 3 s 3).

Scots law and European law

These examples suffice to make my basic point, which is the simple one that in a number of important respects the mixed Scots law of contract has anticipated the position arrived at by the Lando Commission in considering what is the best rule of contract law to deal with particular situations. The same might be said of other mixed systems, such as that of South Africa, which likewise rejects consideration, gives immediate effect within limits to postal acceptances, allows third-party rights, favours specific performance,

---

[29] Ibid., pp. 323–40.
[30] Zweigert and Kötz, *Introduction to Comparative Law*, pp. 433–44, 436–41. For Scots law see *SME*, vol. I, paras. 616–23, 625–7, 637, 657.

adheres broadly to a unified concept of breach, and has adopted the doctrines of repudiation, self-help remedies and the undisclosed principal.[31] Of course it is not suggested that all the Lando Commission had to do was codify the Scots law of contract – in fact, its deficiencies and gaps are highlighted by much of the Commission's work – but it might have provided a useful point of departure, perhaps alongside some of the other mixed systems.

Another interesting dimension is that Scots law reached its position largely through the decisions of the courts, i.e. it reflected problems that actually arose in practice. There was no worthwhile systematisation of contract law by a text writer until 1914,[32] by which time many of the modern features had been laid down by the judges. Some of the nineteenth-century developments show the flexibility of approach that may not be possible with a code. The law of breach provides a particularly good example: the move to adopt some major characteristics of the English system took place quite suddenly in the middle of the century, and provides a striking contrast to the difficulties of German law, hampered by its ossification in the concepts of the BGB of 1900. There are other examples in areas of contract law which I have not so far mentioned. For instance, it was judicially noted in 1868 that Scots law knew only five grounds for the reduction of a contract – incapacity; force and fear; facility and circumvention; fraud; and error.[33] Eleven years later, the same judge presided in the court that borrowed a sixth ground from English law, namely undue influence.[34] Similarly, challenges to contracts based on the originally English doctrine of misrepresentation gained ground in Scotland in the latter part of the nineteenth century, overlapping confusingly with the established rules of error,[35] while fraud was significantly narrowed down by acceptance of the English doctrine laid down by the House of Lords in 1889 in *Derry v. Peek*.[36]

---

[31] For discussion of these points see R. Zimmermann and D. Visser (eds.), *Southern Cross: Civil Law and Common Law in South Africa* (Oxford, 1996), pp. 165–80, 303–34, 342–4. Note that offers are generally revocable in South Africa.

[32] W. M. Gloag, *The Law of Contract: A Treatise on the Principles of Contract in the Law of Scotland* (Edinburgh, 1914). The second edition of 1929 remained the only book-length treatment of the subject until the late 1970s. Before 1914 there were only treatments within more general works on private law.

[33] *Tennent v. Tennent's Trs* (1868) 6 M 840 at 876 per Lord President Inglis. Facility and circumvention is really a sub-category of fraud. Compare with the Inglis list the classical Civilian grounds of invalidity: incapacity, violence, fraud and error. Note also PECL, artt. 4.103–4.108.

[34] *Gray v. Binny* (1879) 7 R 332.   [35] McBryde, *Law of Contract*, pp. 187–203.

[36] (1889) 14 App Cas 337; McBryde, *Law of Contract*, pp. 207–9.

The factors underlying this reception of English law in the nineteenth century, which can be paralleled in areas of the law other than contract, have often been discussed, and were most likely multiple: as already mentioned, they probably included a common language, ready access to sources and texts of English law contrasting with a relative paucity of indigenous material, and the existence of a common appeal court in the House of Lords. In addition, there may well have been a judicial perception that the unified commerce and increasingly unified culture of a great imperial nation required at the least a harmonised or common approach to legal issues.[37] A further possibility which has not yet received the attention it probably deserves is the influence, or even reception, of Civilian concepts and thinking in nineteenth-century English law,[38] which may have made it seem more intelligible to lawyers brought up in another tradition altogether.

Legislation, from Westminster since the 1707 Union and from Brussels since 1973, has also been a factor in the convergence of Scots and English contract laws, although mainly at the level of particular contracts such as sale of goods. In many areas of legislation, in particular those associated with commerce, employment, welfare and taxation, it is increasingly difficult to see any specifically Scottish dimension, and it is possible to talk properly of United Kingdom law, or indeed European Community law. But in the traditional areas of private law, legislation has in recent times often contributed to the continuation of a distinct Scottish dimension. This can be attributed largely to the existence since 1965 of the Scottish Law Commission, which has greatly improved Scottish legislation in private law. The Commission works by detailed research on Scots law and the comparative position, wide consultation and the presentation of generally well-argued reports and draft Bills. In contract law, the Commission has been responsible for the modernisation of the rules on requirements of writing;[39] the undoing of the parole evidence rule, another piece of nineteenth-century borrowing from England;[40] and the de-anglicisation of the sale of goods legislation to some extent by the removal of ambiguous references to the condition/warranty

---

[37] A recent discussion is A. F. Rodger, 'Thinking about Scots Law', (1996) 1 *ELR* 1.

[38] See, e.g., A. W. B. Simpson, 'Innovation in Nineteenth-Century Contract Law', (1975) 91 *LQR* 247–78.

[39] Requirements of Writing (Scotland) Act 1995. For the background see Report on Requirements of Writing (Scot. Law Com. No. 112, 1988).

[40] Contract (Scotland) Act 1997, s 1. For the background see Report on Three Bad Rules in Contract Law (Scot. Law Com. No. 152, 1996).

dichotomy in the rules on implied terms and buyer's remedies.[41] In addition the Commission has proposed adoption of a number of the general contract formation rules in the Vienna Convention,[42] and has been examining the rules on the interpretation of contracts, penalty clauses and breach of contract with the Unidroit and Lando Principles very much in mind.[43]

At least in the domain of contract law, therefore, it is already possible to query the pessimism of Zweigert and Kötz when they write:[44]

> It is an open question whether Scots law will be able in the long run to resist the influence of Common Law and whether in the future the area within which it can develop its own solutions may not become more and more restricted. One must realise that Scots law is not reinforced by codification, as the law of Louisiana is, nor by using a separate language, like the law of Quebec; nor is Scotland in the position of South Africa of being its own legislator, for Scotland must often trim its legal sails to the winds blowing from Westminster.

Moreover, there is a further new factor in the Scottish legal scene to qualify the last observation in this quotation – the devolved Parliament which from July 1999 has sat in Edinburgh with power to legislate in the field of Scots private law. Pleasingly, this is defined in terms reflecting the traditional divisions of the law into persons, things and actions, as

> the following areas of the civil law of Scotland –
> (a) the general principles of private law (including private international law),
> (b) the law of persons (including natural persons, legal persons and unincorporated bodies),
> (c) the law of obligations (including obligations arising from contract, unilateral promise, delict, unjustified enrichment and negotiorum gestio),

---

[41] Sale and Supply of Goods Act 1994. For the background see Report on Sale and Supply of Goods (Scot. Law Com. No. 104, 1987).

[42] Report on Formation of Contract: Scottish Law and the United Nations Convention on Contracts for the International Sale of Goods (Scot. Law Com. No. 144, 1993).

[43] Report on Interpretation in Private Law (Scot. Law Com. No. 160, 1997); Report on Penalty Clauses (Scot. Law Com. No. 171, 1999); Report on Remedies for Breach of Contract (Scot. Law Com. No. 174, 1999).

[44] Zweigert and Kötz, *Introduction to Comparative Law*, p. 204. The same statement appears in the first and second editions.

(d) the law of property (including heritable and moveable property, trusts and succession), and

(e) the law of actions (including jurisdiction, remedies, evidence, procedure, diligence, recognition and enforcement of court orders, limitation of actions and arbitration).[45]

What can the Parliament do with this power? The attentive reader will have noted the time-lag which often exists between the making of Scottish Law Commission reform proposals and implementing legislation, and that some reports remain unenacted years after their publication. Moreover, scrutiny at Westminster has often been cursory in the extreme. Scottish law reform should therefore be quicker, yet more thoroughly examined, in an Edinburgh Parliament. Some limitations on the available possibilities will have to be recognised, at least for the time being: schedule 5 of the Scotland Act 1998 excludes from the competence of the Parliament some important areas affecting private law, such as the law of business associations, their insolvency, competition, intellectual property and consumer protection.

The possibility of going further than reform and codifying the law was specifically recognised in a provision of the original Scotland Bill which has not survived in the final Act.[46] Nevertheless, there is certainly interest in this, albeit far from universal, in Scotland,[47] and schedule 4 paragraph 7 of the Scotland Act allows for the possibility of an Act of the Scottish Parliament to 'restate' the law. The Scottish Law Commission already has a statutory duty to consider the codification of the law.[48] Much of its work has tended in this direction, although it is clear that a civil code, or codification of particular parts of the law, is not at present a priority.[49] Nevertheless, the work of the Commission, the completion of the twenty-six-volume *Laws of Scotland: Stair Memorial Encyclopaedia*, and a massive growth in research and writing on Scots law mean that much of the basic research on the current position of the law has been done.

---

[45] Scotland Act 1998, s 126(4); see further ss 28–30.   [46] Scotland Bill, clause 28(9).

[47] See in particular E. M. Clive, 'A Scottish Civil Code', in H. L. MacQueen (ed.), *Scots Law into the Twenty-First Century* (Edinburgh, 1996). Contrast, however, in the same volume A. D. M. Forte, 'If it Ain't Broke, Don't Fix it: On Not Codifying Commercial Law'.

[48] Law Commissions Act 1965, s 3(1).

[49] W. W. McBryde, 'Law Reform: The Scottish Experience', (1998) 3 *SLPQ* 86, at 90–3. But see the Scottish Law Commission's Sixth Programme of Law Reform (Scot. Law Com. No. 176, 2000), paras. 1.30–1.33, in which the Commission states that it is 'taking a close interest' in the Clive codification projects referred to below, text accompanying n. 50.

However, the Members of the Scottish Parliament will be pursuing political agenda rather than those of reformers of private law as such, and a codification project may lack the voter appeal to commend it as a legislative priority. An alternative possibility is a private initiative along the lines of the Lando Commission, producing what would be in effect a 'restatement' of Scots private law which would test the feasibility of a code, offer a model up for substantive criticism and development, and, in whole or in part, provide material which, if found acceptable, could in due course be enacted by the Scottish Parliament. Such an initiative is already under way at the Edinburgh Law School, under the leadership of Professor Eric Clive.[50] It might even be best left outside positive law, as a restatement would be more capable of adjustment over time and would avoid the rigidity and inflexibility associated with formal codes.

Another benefit that such a restatement could bring, enacted or not, is to make Scots law more accessible to comparative study. As a system based on a jumble of statute and judicial decision, and in which textbook writing has focused principally on a domestic audience, Scots law has not lent itself to study by outsiders, nor has it been easy for insiders to broadcast its merits beyond the jurisdiction. That a code can change this picture is well demonstrated by the European attention attracted to a draft codification of the Scots law of unjustified enrichment compiled by Eric Clive in a private capacity when a Scottish Law Commissioner and published by the Commission in 1996.[51] Presenting other areas of Scottish private law in codal form might well prove similarly attractive for comparative study. An example that comes to mind is the law of trusts, which has developed in Scotland despite the absence of the divide between law and equity which is supposed to be the lifeblood of the institution in the system of its origin, England.[52] In the recently produced *Principles of European*

---

[50] See his contribution to the present volume, and note also the Scottish criminal code project, in which Professor Clive, along with others, is involved.

[51] The draft code appears as an appendix to Scottish Law Commission Discussion Paper No. 99, Judicial Abolition of the Error of Law Rule and its Aftermath (February 1996). Other versions of the text may also be consulted in F. D. Rose (ed.), *Blackstone's Statutes on Contract, Tort and Restitution 1997–8* (London, 1997), pp. 444–51, or in E. M. Clive, 'Restitution and Unjustified Enrichment', in A. S. Hartkamp et al. (eds.), *Towards a European Civil Code*, 2nd edn (Nijmegen, 1998), pp. 383–96.

[52] The Scots law of trusts gives ownership to the trustee and confers a personal right upon the beneficiary with certain privileges. The concept goes back to the early modern period, and English influence has affected its development less than might be expected. These points are

Trust Law, the introduction, written by one English and two Dutch lawyers, states:

> The experience of two legal systems is especially interesting. Scots law and Roman-Dutch law in South Africa both provide examples of civilian systems which have been exposed to heavy English influence. Neither knew the institutional separation of law and equity. Both have a law of property based on Roman concepts. Both Scots law and South African law have today a vigorous law of trusts, recognizable as such and named as such despite being in some important respects different in detail from the English law. However, though on each case the influence of English case law is undeniable, both Scots law and Roman-Dutch law see their law of trusts not as an artificial implant from an alien system, but as part of a civil law inheritance. In large measure we are witnessing the revivification of the familiar Roman institutions of *fiducia* and *fideicommissum*. In the present volume, the Scottish National Report may prove to be of particular interest to civilians considering the implementation of the trust in their domestic law.[53]

The Lando Commission has completed its work on contract; but what we have discovered, as we work on such matters as assignation, prescription, plurality of debtors and creditors, and illegality, is that increasingly we are straying beyond the boundaries of contract into property, delict and un-justified enrichment. From within the group has therefore come a move to work towards a European civil code, which has now commenced as a project at Osnabruck in Germany and at Utrecht, Tilburg and Amsterdam in the Netherlands. Funding has come from the German and Dutch equivalents of the British research councils; these and other British funding bodies have so far shown no willingness to join in, unfortunately. I find myself on the project's Coordinating Committee; so far as I know, the only other Scots lawyers involved are John Blackie of Strathclyde, in the Delict group and Eric Clive in the Enrichment one. Its first full meeting was at Utrecht in December 1999, with a second in Rome in June 2000, a third in Salzburg in December 2000, a fourth in Stockholm in June 2001, a fifth in Oxford in

---

expounded in depth by my colleague, G. L. Gretton, 'Scotland: The Evolution of the Trust in a Semi-Civilian System', in R. H. Helmholz and R. Zimmermann (eds.), *Itinera Fiduciae: Trust and Treuhand in Historical Perspective* (Berlin, 1998).

[53]   D. J. Hayton, S. C. J. J. Kortmann and H. L. E. Verhagen (eds.), *Principles of European Trust Law* (The Hague, 1999), pp. 3–4. The 'National Report for Scotland' is by K. G. C. Reid and is at pp. 67–84.

December 2001, a sixth in Valencia in June 2002 and a seventh in Oporto in December 2002. The project is exciting and hugely ambitious; perhaps overambitious. Grand projects for European unity or harmonisation are not getting, nor perhaps always deserving, a good press at the moment. Yet the beauty of this being an academic project, rather than for real, like monetary union, may be that a model will be created which can be tested and criticised, and then put into use should the time ever seem ripe to do so.

What can Scots law contribute? If there is ever to be a European civil code, whether as positive law or in 'restatement' form, it will have to be equally accessible to the Common and the Civil Law traditions; in other words, it will have to be 'mixed'. The possibility that a more acceptable model could be provided by the only existing 'mixed' system in Europe is surely one that deserves to be put to the test. But we Scots must put our house in order, in terms both of making our law accessible to those who would examine it from the outside, and of reforming it to the standards that are now being set by deliberations in Europe and around the world. It is a challenge to which our judges, legislators, law commissions and, perhaps above all, our academics must rise as Scots law prepares to enter the twenty-first century. If we do, then perhaps we will at last be able to say, with Lévy-Ullmann, that Scots law does indeed give us a picture of the law of the civilised nations.

5

Scottish property: a system of Civilian principle. But could it be codified?

DAVID L. CAREY MILLER

Introduction

This chapter is restricted to the principles of derivative acquisition applying to the voluntary transfer of corporeal property, the most important part of any system of property law. The regulation of the passing of property will be considered on the basis of the prerequisites of derivative acquisition and by reference to the exceptions to these requirements. Given the objective of a conclusion as to the feasibility of code provisions applying to the transfer of ownership only matters of property law as such will be considered. Issues of the law of obligations, or of other areas of law, will not be dealt with.

The chapter will proceed on the premise – having outlined its basis – that in Scots common law the essential principles of derivative acquisition apply to the voluntary transfer of both moveable and immoveable (Scot. 'heritable') subjects. In seeking to demonstrate that the common principles concerned are essentially civilian the categories of moveable and immoveable property will be dealt with together with relevant differences noted as necessary.

In respect of both categories the applicable principles of the common law (of Scotland) will be considered under the following headings: the requirement that the parties are in a position to pass and acquire ownership (entitlement); the requirement that the parties intend the passing of ownership and the basis on which this requirement operates (intention aspect); the requirement of delivery (delivery); the circumstances in which ownership passes regardless of the prescribed requirements not being met (positive exceptions); the circumstances in which ownership does not pass in a final sense regardless of the prescribed requirements being met (negative exception).

In relation to moveables the chapter will consider the Sale of Goods Act of 1893 (now 1979) from the perspectives of two separate and mutually inconsistent issues: (a) the extent to which the legislation amounted to a departure from the principles of Scots law, and (b) to what extent the Act represents a codification of the basics of Scottish derivative acquisition. In relation to immoveable property particular consideration will be given to the 1990s decisions in *Sharp* v. *Thomson*.

The chapter will conclude by posing the question as to whether a general codification of the principles of derivative acquisition could be put in place without the removal of the Sale of Goods Act and, if so, whether this would be desirable.

Common Civilian factor

Scots property law reflects, to a significant extent, the influence of both Civilian and feudal law. This factor caused the perpetuation of an attitude for a long period in the history of the system which sought to identify the law relating to moveable property as Civilian but that applying to heritable subjects as feudal.[1] The extent to which this thinking became entrenched in Scottish legal education has been demonstrated by Professor Kenneth G. C. Reid, principal author of the property volume of *The Laws of Scotland: Stair Memorial Encyclopaedia*: 'There is no modern work giving a systematic and unitary exposition of the law of property, and in its absence the general principles of the subject have tended to be lost sight of, where they have not been disregarded altogether.'[2]

Arguably, at any rate in the context of derivative acquisition, it is inaccurate to perceive of moveable property as civilian based while matters of

---

[1] The significance of the feudal factor in the land law of Scotland is acknowledged by jurists, but modern scholars tend to give emphasis to its decline. In 1961 Professor Sir Thomas Smith QC in his Hamlyn Lectures, *British Justice: The Scottish Contribution* (London, 1961), p. 182, commented: 'In short the land law of Scotland remains perhaps the most feudal in the world.' Some thirty years later in *The Laws of Scotland: Stair Memorial Encyclopaedia*, vol. XVIII (Edinburgh, 1993), para. 45, Professor George L. Gretton wrote: 'Only in one country in the world does feudalism survive in any real sense, albeit attenuated to an extreme degree. That country is Scotland.'

[2] *Stair Memorial Encyclopaedia*, vol. XVIII, para. 1.

heritable property are assumed to be founded upon feudal principles. In this regard it should be noted that the defining features of feudal law – long of declining significance in Scotland[3] and, at the time of writing, about to be finally removed[4] – are primarily concerned with the basis under which property is held rather than with the means by which it is acquired. In a focus suggested by co-editor Professor Reid, my chapter in the *History of Private Law in Scotland*[5] sets out to identify the basis of the derivative acquisition of rights in land. The conclusion of this study is that the process – commonly known as 'conveyancing' – is essentially civilian.[6]

A wider consideration concerns the use of the label 'civilian'. In the context concerned this should include an acknowledgement that the system of transferring property evolved in the long history of the development of the civil law in fact represents the natural and rational method of doing so. This is acknowledged by Scottish writer David Hume who occupied the Chair of Scots Law at Edinburgh from 1786 to 1822:[7] 'The natural way of transferring property, whether moveable or immoveable, is by an agreement to convey as in property, followed by delivery, real or symbolical,

---

[3] George L. Gretton, ibid., para. 45: 'The decline of feudalism was already in progress in the fourteenth century, but the progress was slow.'

[4] At time of writing see Scottish Law Commission, Report on Abolition of the Feudal System (Scot. Law Com. No. 168) February 1999 and the Abolition of Feudal Tenure (Scotland) Bill, 2000; developments on the basis of a manifesto commitment which became a political priority of the context of Scottish devolution and which have since been enacted.

[5] 'Transfer of ownership', in K. G. C. Reid and R. Zimmermann (eds.), *History of Private Law in Scotland* (Oxford, 2000).

[6] In this regard it is significant that Scotland's seventeenth-century institutional writer on feudal law Thomas Craig rejected the notion of usufruct to identify the nature of the right acquired through feudal title, preferring the simple idea of the division of the right of ownership in terms of *dominium directum/dominium utile*. See Sir Thomas Craig of Riccarton, *Jus Feudale*, 3rd edn by J. Baillie trans. Lord Clyde ([1732] Edinburgh, 1934), 1.9.11. As a distinguished modern commentator has noted, the most compelling reason for Craig's conclusion 'is that the notion of a vassals's right, transmissible to his heirs, being a mere usufruct was unacceptable to Scottish landowners who regarded themselves as proprietors of their estates'. See J. M. Halliday, 'Feudal Law as a Source', in D. M. Walker (ed.), *Stair Tercentenary Studies*, Stair Society Publications (Edinburgh, 1981), pp. 136–7; see also Professor W. M. Gordon's treatment of feudal law in *Studies in the Transfer of Property by Traditio* (Aberdeen, 1970), pp. 190–209 and Professor George L. Gretton's treatment of the matter in the *Stair Memorial Encyclopaedia*, vol. XVIII, paras. 47–52.

[7] On Hume's contribution to thinking on Scottish property law see the comments of Professor Kenneth Reid, above, n. 2.

of the thing. These two circumstances (I have said) must concur in any case towards transference of the real right.'[8]

The Court of Session in the case of *Sharp* v. *Thomson*[9] sought to clarify the basis under which property passes in the context of the sale of heritable property – i.e. a 'conveyancing' transaction involving the sale of land. Although the House of Lords reversed the decision of the Court of Session it is significant for present purposes that it sought to do so without challenge to the fundamental conclusions concerning principles of property law arrived at by the court *a quo*. Lord Clyde articulated this point in a dictum consistent with the narrow and technical basis under which the Lords decided the case.

> As the argument before this House developed it became clear that no challenge was being made of the careful analysis made by the judges of the First Division of the basic concepts of Scottish law which apply in the area of heritable property. A basic distinction between real rights and personal rights was not questioned. It was not suggested that there is any kind of hybrid right somewhere between a real right and a personal right. It was accepted that Scottish law holds a unitary theory of ownership by which only one real right of ownership can exist in respect of any one thing at any one time.[10]

The opinion of Lord President Hope, as he then was, in the First Division of the Court of Session is particularly instructive as to the fundamentals of Scots property law. The learned Lord President, referring to Professor Kenneth Reid's *Stair Memorial Encyclopaedia* text,[11] emphasised the strength of the civilian factor giving a clear and well-understood distinction between real and personal rights. On the basis of the system enunciated by the Institutional writers of Scotland,[12] 'it is not until the transaction is completed by delivery that the real right is transferred', and pending this event there is no support for the existence of 'an intermediate, or incomplete, right which

---

[8] G. C. H. Paton (ed.), *Baron David Hume's Lectures 1786–1822*, Stair Society Publications, vol. III (Edinburgh, 1952), p. 245.

[9] 1995 SLT 837.   [10] 1997 SLT 645.

[11] *Stair Memorial Encyclopaedia*, vol. XVIII, paras. 1–3.

[12] The Lord President refers to Stair, *Institutions of the Law of Scotland*, 6th edn, ed. D. M. Walker ([1681] Edinburgh, 1981) and J. Erskine, *An Institute of the Law of Scotland*, 8th edn, ed. J. B. Nicholson ([1773], 1871, repr. Edinburgh, 1989).

lies between the personal right on the one hand and the real right on the other'.[13]

The starting point, in modern Scots doctrinal writing, of an articulated recognition of the civilian credentials of Scots common law as to the passing of title to property is Professor W. M. Gordon's seminal *Studies in the Transfer of Property by Traditio*.[14] As indicated, the *Stair Memorial Encyclopaedia* volume, under the principal authorship of Professor Kenneth G. C. Reid,[15] has established, to convincing effect, the complete picture of civilian influence in Scots property.[16]

On the basis of the material referred to this chapter will proceed on the premise that the civilian factor is, indeed, a source of influence in relation to the derivative acquisition of both moveable and immoveable property in Scots law.

Relevant principles

In this core part of the chapter the relevant controlling principles of the law of property will be identified. The passing of property on a voluntary basis[17] involves an interplay between obligations and property with other areas of law having possible implications. The label 'contract and conveyance',[18] applied to identify the critical area of derivative acquisition, is relevant in terms both of the distinction between the separate aspects of contract and conveyance and of their interplay. The aim of this chapter is to identify and consider the relevant active aspects of the law of property without dealing with other areas of law.

---

[13] 1995 SLT 844.

[14] *Stair Memorial Encyclopaedia*, vol. XVIII, esp. paras. 210–35.   [15] Above, n. 1.

[16] See also D. L. Carey Miller, *Corporeal Moveables in Scots Law* (Edinburgh, 1991); D. L. Carey Miller, 'Systems of Property: Grotius and Stair', in D. L. Carey Miller and D. W. Meyers (eds.), *Comparative and Historical Essays in Scots Law* (Edinburgh, 1992), p. 13; D. L. Carey Miller, 'Derivative Acquisition of Moveables', in R. Evans-Jones (ed.), *The Civil Law Tradition in Scotland* (Edinburgh, 1995), p. 128; 'Stair's Property: A Romanist System', (1995) 107 *Jur. Rev.* 70.

[17] A basis involving the consent of the transferor; this being distinct from involuntary derivative acquisition in which the law confers the title formerly held by one party upon another party, as in the case of succession; see *Stair Memorial Encyclopaedia*, vol. XVIII, paras. 597, 663.

[18] Ibid., para. 606. The word '*causa*' in the context of a *causa* preceding a conveyance has a wider meaning than 'contract' in the contract/conveyance dichotomy; see, e.g., W. W. Buckland and A. D. McNair, *Roman Law and Common Law*, 2nd edn, ed. F. H. Lawson ([1936], Oxford, 1974), pp. 111–12.

Entitlement

Voluntary derivative acquisition must be possible in the sense that the transferor is entitled to pass property to the transferee; in Hume's compellingly simple negative formulation: 'No one can convey a better or more ample right to another, than he has in his own person.'[19] The fundamental dogmatic imperative in this regard is reflected in the brocard 'nemo plus iuris ad alium transferre potest quam ipse habet, frequently represented in modern law in its truncated version 'nemo dat quod non habet'.[20] A rational amplification of this principle is that entitlement to transfer is a matter of the prevailing position at the relevant point in time; hence, it is of no moment that the transferor's position is open to challenge provided a state of entitlement to transfer subsists at the time of the act of transfer. As Professor Reid has noted: 'It makes no difference for this purpose whether the title of the transferor is subsistent and absolutely good or subsistent but voidable, for a voidable title subsists until it is reduced.'[21] Although fundamental and normally prevailing the entitlement prerequisite is subject to exceptions in which ownership passes even though the transferor lacks entitlement – referred to below under 'positive exceptions'.

The voluntary disposal of property by one in principle entitled to do so necessarily involves the issue of capacity[22] but because this is not a property issue as such it is enough to note its role in the present context.

The position of the transferee with regard to entitlement is subject to a particular property law consideration noted below under 'negative exception'.

Intention aspect

Because the act of transfer involves the motivation of two parties its constitution, as a single identifiable legal act, must necessarily be founded upon a concurrence between transferor and transferee. Well-established doctrine recognises that this essential identification of the parties' agreement that property shall pass can be on either a 'causal' or an 'abstract' basis.[23] In

---

[19] Paton (ed.), *David Hume's Lectures*, vol. III, p. 232.
[20] *Stair Memorial Encyclopaedia*, vol. XVIII, para. 669.   [21] Ibid.   [22] Ibid., para. 599.
[23] In respect of Scots law see ibid., paras. 608–11, and Carey Miller, *Corporeal Moveables in Scots Law*, paras. 8.06–8.10; see also generally Reinhard Zimmermann, 'The Civil Law in European Codes', in D. L. Carey Miller and R. Zimmermann (eds.), *The Civilian Tradition and Scots Law:*

the former the necessary consensual basis is found in the parties' underlying agreement which gives rise to their intention to transfer the property concerned; in the latter the underlying contract is ignored and the analysis requires a separate self-contained agreement specifically to transfer ownership. The better view is that in Scots law derivative acquisition operates on the basis of the abstract form, in relation both to heritable[24] and to moveable property.[25] Arguably, this is the only rational conclusion in respect of a system which, in principle, requires a separate legal act of delivery (*traditio*) to effect the passage of property;[26] this is because the criterion of a 'separate' legal act is one motivated by acts of will of the parties specifically associated with the act.[27]

Delivery

It is trite that the common law of Scotland requires a separate identifiable legal act of conveyance or delivery to effect the passing of a proprietary right in relation to both heritable and moveable subjects. As indicated the identification of the system of transfer as 'abstract' is a necessary conclusion drawn from the long-standing certainty of the delivery requirement. But while it is apparent that the associated intention aspect is fundamental, what is in fact required in terms of the physical act of delivery? It would appear that this must be something sufficient to justify the conclusion that a change of possession has occurred. Thus Stair equates 'tradition' with 'the delivery of...possession'[28] and in his next section goes on to note that possession being 'the accomplishment of the disposition of real rights' it is 'not the first disposition, but the first possession' that counts.[29] The opinion of a five-judge bench in a nineteenth-century case identified the prerequisite of a change of possession – while at the same time suggesting that considerable latitude exists – in its denial of the occurrence of delivery in the circumstances: 'There was not only no ordinary delivery from hand to hand, but there was no delivery of any kind, no change of possession, or power over the subject held by the seller, into

Aberdeen Quincentenary Essays (Berlin, 1997), pp. 274–5; L. P. W. van Vliet, *Transfer of Movables in German, French, English and Dutch Law* (Nijmegen, 2000), pp. 24–5.

[24] *Stair Memorial Encyclopaedia*, vol. XVIII, para. 611.

[25] Ibid., para. 609.   [26] See Gordon, *Studies*, pp. 210–36.

[27] Carey Miller, *Corporeal Moveables in Scots Law*, para. 8.06.

[28] Stair, *Institutions*, 3.2.5.   [29] Ibid., 3.2.6.

possession or power over the subject held by the buyer, in any mode or form whatever.'[30]

The distinction between personal and real rights as a matter of distinct and fundamental difference in kind[31] necessarily calls for identification as either one or the other with no possibility of a partial or provisional make-up. The dogma of a requirement of tradition subscribed to by Scots law is only consistent with the real (or proprietary) right coming into being at a particular and identifiable point in time. Whether this is achieved by actual delivery, by some form of constructive delivery or by a prescribed formal act of registration,[32] the process is always one of specific actuation of the transmission of title from transferee to transferor. This feature has caused Professor Kenneth Reid to observe, under the heading of 'instantaneous effect of transfer', that 'Scots law, following Roman law, is "unititular"'.[33] The learned writer goes on to explain the consequences of this.

> So if property is being transferred from A to B, there can never be a stage where ownership is partly with A and partly with B; and since ownership is a real right, ownership cannot be with B in a question between transferor and transferee but with A in a question with third parties. Either A is the owner, or B is; and the rule is that A remains owner until the final act of transfer has been performed when ownership passes at once to B. Up until the moment of transfer, A remains full owner with power to burden the property or to transfer it to someone else, although to do either is usually to break his contract with B; and the property also remains vulnerable to A's creditors. But once the moment of transfer arrives B becomes owner in turn and A's rights in the property are extinguished immediately and absolutely.[34]

---

[30] *Gibson* v. *Forbes* (1833) 11 S. 916, 925.

[31] Stair, *Institutions*, 2.1.pr.: 'For as obligation is a right personal, as being a power of extracting from persons that which is due; so a real right is a power of disposal of things in their substance, fruits or use.' See also 2.1.27, distinguishing possession, on the basis of some lesser right, and title: 'Possession, as distinct from right, is ascribable only to that title by which it did begin.' Reference should also be made to Erskine, *Institute*, 3.1.2, distinguishing a *jus in re* and a *jus ad rem*; this classic passage is quoted by Lord President Hope in *Sharp* v. *Thomson* 1995 SLT 837, 843.

[32] See Stair, *Institutions*, 3.2.6: 'This possession is not alike in all cases, for in some real, in others symbolical, possession is requisite, which cannot be supplied by real possession itself, as in property of lands or annual rents by infeftment, wherein the disposition and natural possession makes no real right without seasin.'

[33] *Stair Memorial Encyclopaedia*, vol. XVIII, para. 603.   [34] Ibid.

In this regard one should also note the conclusion of Lord President Hope following an exhaustive review of the relevant authority on this issue in the context of the transfer of title to land.

> In my opinion it is plain . . . that Scots law does not recognise a right which lies between the personal right on the one hand and the real right on the other. A personal right, once created, is of course a species of incorporeal property, which can be transmitted from one person to another by assignation. But it remains at all times a right based solely on the law of obligations, until it is replaced by a real right which alone invests the grantee with a right of property in the thing which is the subject of the transaction. Various steps are necessary to complete the transaction from start to finish, and each step is different. But there is no such thing as a real right which is imperfect or incomplete. Until the real right is transferred the matter rests entirely upon personal obligation.[35]

In the context of a system which functions on the basis of a controlling distinction between personal and real rights, essentially without room for slippage or blurring, it must necessarily be that a means exists to identify the particular point in time, in any given transaction, at which the personal right becomes a real right. The requirement of delivery serves this purpose and, arguably, this is its primary function if not its *raison d'être*. Accepting that the necessary determination of the point in time at which the critical change occurs is the essential rationale of delivery explains the scope for a wide range of forms. Even the so-called *constitutum possessorium*[36] – envisaging the passing of property in a thing remaining in the natural possession of a transferor, but one holding, as from an identifiable point in time, on a basis other than that of owner – is acceptable in terms of this rationale.

Positive exceptions

Any defining statement of the fundamental prerequisite of derivative acquisition as the right to pass property – commented above under 'entitlement' – must be qualified to the extent of noting the existence of an established limited category of exceptions applicable in particular circumstances. The diverse nature of the exceptions defies their specific identification in direct

---

[35] *Sharp v. Thomson* 1995 SLT 837, 847.
[36] *Stair Memorial Encyclopaedia*, vol. XVIII, para. 623; see also Carey Miller, *Corporeal Moveables in Scots Law*, paras. 8.23–25.

qualification of a statement of the 'nemo dat quod non habet' principle, but any attempt to formulate the basics of derivative acquisition must include a global reference to the existence of the exceptions which, of course, have to be identified to give a complete picture of the operation of derivative acquisition.[37]

Negative exception

The position of the transferee is subject to particular property law consid-erations. While it would not be accurate to speak of a requirement of the transferee being 'entitled' to receive in the same sense as the transferor must be entitled to pass transfer, the position of the transferee, in this regard, is not simply a matter of the presence of the necessary capacity to receive. In certain circumstances of the transferee's particular knowledge he or she is disabled from entitlement to receive in a final sense. In particular, knowl-edge by the transferee of an existing obligation binding the transferor to transfer the subject concerned to another party[38] or knowledge of a defect in the transferor's subsisting title makes the title passed vulnerable to ter-mination (Scot. 'reduction') or limitation at the instance of, or in favour of, a third party.[39]

Sale of Goods Act

Traditional thinking is to the effect that the Sale of Goods Act 1893 (now 1979) represents a major inroad into the principles of Scots property law

---

[37] What is included by way of exception depends, of course, upon the particular scope and focus of the *nemo dat* concept; in the present context of its application to voluntary derivative acquisition deriving from a subsistent title the category of exceptions is a prescribed one limited to the notion of personal bar (see Carey Miller, *Corporeal Moveables in Scots Law*, para. 10.19) on the basis of a potential transferor allowing circumstances to prevail which justify preclusion of the right to deny the occurrence of derivative acquisition. Regarding the *nemo dat* rule, its scope and exceptions from a wide perspective: see Reid, in *Stair Memorial Encyclopaedia*, vol. XVIII, paras. 669–83.

[38] See *Stair Memorial Encyclopaedia*, vol. XVIII, paras. 690, 695–700 concerned with the rule against 'offside goals'; in *Rodger (Builders) Ltd* v. *Fawdry* 1950 SC 483, 501, Lord Justice-Clerk Thomson applied this footballing metaphor to the circumstances of a transferee disabled from acquisition on the basis of knowledge of another's prior right to acquire.

[39] See *Stair Memorial Encyclopaedia*, vol. XVIII, para. 601. Regarding this and the previous ('offside goal') situation in which a transferee is subject to a requirement of being in good faith see D. L. Carey Miller, 'Good Faith in Scots Property Law', in Angelo D. M. Forte (ed.), *Good Faith in Contract and Property Law* (Oxford, 1999), pp. 104–10.

which could be identified in terms of the imposition of English law upon Scotland in a United Kingdom context. The late Professor Sir Thomas Smith, probably the major figure in the twentieth-century revival of the identity of Scots law, observed that the legislation introduced 'the doctrine that real rights may be transferred by agreement' – a doctrine revolutionary to Scots law – 'which had long been accepted in English law'.[40] Professor J. J. Gow referred to the 'avowed purpose' of draftsman Sir Mackenzie Chalmers 'to reproduce as accurately as possible the existing English law'.[41] More recently, scholars have drawn attention to the non-partisan interest of the late nineteenth-century Scottish commercial community – a very significant part of the wider Victorian commercial empire – in a uniform body of United Kingdom commercial law.[42]

But is the system of the transfer of property introduced by the Sale of Goods Act 1893 fundamentally different from the common law of Scotland? The system under the Act, as one would expect, accords with the common law in respect of the basic requirements that the parties are in a position to pass and acquire ownership and that they both intend that it should pass. Derivative acquisition necessarily involves these essentials. But the Act departs from the common law in not requiring a separate act of delivery as such. What are the implications of this in terms of any rational system of transfer? As a legal act giving effect to the transmission of property, delivery is clearly an optional requirement – rather than a fundamental prerequisite in the manner of the requirements of entitlement and intention. The passing of property is provided for as follows in the Act:

(1) Where there is a contract for the sale of specific or ascertained goods the property in them is transferred to the buyer at such time as the parties to the contract intend it to be transferred.

(2) For the purpose of ascertaining the intention of the parties regard shall be had to the terms of the contract, the conduct of the parties and the circumstances of the case.[43]

---

[40] *Property Problems in Sale* (London, 1978), p. 39. Professor J. M. Halliday, *Conveyancing Law and Practice in Scotland*, vol. I (Edinburgh, 1985), p. 251 noted that the legislation 'altered the Scottish common law and substituted the English rules whereby the property in specific or ascertained goods passes when the parties to the contract of sale intend it to pass'.

[41] *The Mercantile and Industrial Law of Scotland* (Edinburgh, 1964), p. 75.

[42] See esp. A. F. Rodger, 'The Codification of Commercial Law in Victorian Britain', (1992) 108 *LQR* 570.

[43] Section 17 of the Sale of Goods Act 1979.

With regard to the essential aspects of the actual transfer of ownership s 17(1) envisages a separately identifiable legal act supported by the specific mutual intention that property should pass. A legal act on the basis of which the party entitled to property against the seller acquires a proprietary right is what appears to be provided for. The system of the Act recognises and functions in terms of the distinction between real and personal rights with property passing to the buyer at a particular identifiable point in time.[44] The relevant provisions are directed towards this in a set of rules which aim to bring a measure of uniformity, at least in the more common commercial contexts, in ascertaining the intention of the parties as to when property in the goods sold should pass from seller to buyer.[45]

That the legislation requires the identification of a particular point in time at which the buyer's right changes from a personal one to a real one is of greater significance than the fact that the relevant time is established by reference to the parties' intention rather than on the basis of an act of delivery. Arguably, in fact, the respective delivery and intention bases are interchangeable as criteria in the critical matter of determining the time of transmission – and simultaneous acquisition – of a proprietary right from an existing contractual form. This, of course, does not gainsay the obvious truth that intention must always be present as the factor ultimately controlling transmission, as, indeed, it is in systems which require delivery.

It is submitted that it is of no significance that in a particular case under the Act property may pass on the basis of the agreement of sale, as provided for in rule 1 under s 17. With the proprietary intention factor – rather than a delivery requirement – controlling, the elapse of a period of time between the conclusion of the underlying contract and the acquisition of the subject sold by the buyer can be avoided.[46] When this occurs the legal analysis perspective of the coincidence of contract and conveyance must be the simultaneous occurrence of two separate acts rather than the notion of a unitary transaction. Given the premise of the need to identify

---

[44] A leading modern textbook, P. S. Atiyah, *The Sale of Goods*, 9th edn, ed. J. N. Adams (London, 1995), p. 271 is entirely clear on this: 'The *exact moment* [my emphasis] at which the property passes depends upon whether the goods are specific or unascertained.'

[45] Section 18 of the Sale of Goods Act 1979 (rules 1–5).

[46] Arguably, in the everyday situation of the simple purchase of consumer goods the coincidence of contractual and proprietary intentions provides a more workable analysis than that of delivery.

a specific point in time at which a pre-existing contractual right becomes
a proprietary right the analysis must necessarily involve the two separate
events of conclusion of contract and passing of property even if, in a particular case, the two events are compacted together in a unitary factual
situation.[47]

The Sale of Goods Act maintains a clear distinction between contract and property in that from the position of a personal right a proprietary right comes into immediate being in a legal act occurring at
a particular point in time; to this important extent, the Act is in conformity with Scots common law.[48] The better view is that this conformity
is more important than the departure from a delivery requirement and
the adoption of the parties' coincident intent as the identifying factor of
conveyance.

On one view the Sale of Goods Act in fact represents a shift from the
English common law position to the Scottish one. This would appear to be
true in so far as the Act leaves behind the distinction between equity and
common law which, in the present context, produced a qualification of the
notion of the unitary passing of property as described above. Prior to the
passing of the Sale of Goods Act there was support in English law for equity
having a role in relation to unascertained goods through the transfer of an
equitable interest in future property in circumstances in which the common
law, insisting upon identification, denied the passing of property.[49] The issue
of the possible role of equity in the Sale of Goods Act was authoritatively
pronounced upon by Atkin LJ in 1927 in denying any role in relation to

---

[47] Professor Kenneth Reid, writing in the *Stair Memorial Encyclopaedia*, vol. XVIII, para. 606,
notes that the intention provided for in s 17(1) 'is separate from the intention required for the
conclusion of the contract' but that 'in practice the distinction is blurred by s 18 and in particular
by rule 1 of that section which provides that in certain circumstances ownership passes when
the contract is made'. The critical point for present purposes is that there must, in principle, be
two separate intention factors.

[48] See Professor Reid's statement, ibid.: 'In common with other Civilian systems, Scots law makes
a clear distinction in the transfer of ownership between, on the one hand, the conveyance and,
on the other hand, the contract which in many cases precedes the conveyance. Only in the
sale of goods, where the law has been anglicised by statute, is the distinction not fully observed,
although even here transfer of ownership requires an act of intention which, at least in principle,
is separate from the contract of sale.' For present purposes the learned writer's final qualifying
statement is significant.

[49] Atiyah, *The Sale of Goods*, p. 298 refers to a *dictum* of Lord Watson in *Tailby* v. *Official Receiver*
(1888) 13 App Cas 523, 533 and comments that 'it seems to have been thought that physical
identification or ascertainment might not be required in equity so long as the thing sold belonged
to an identified bulk or whole'.

the transfer of unascertained goods under the Act even if such a role had existed prior to the legislation.

> It would have been futile in a Code intended for commercial men to have created an elaborate structure of rules dealing with rights at law, if at the same time it was intended to leave, subsisting with the legal rights, equitable rights inconsistent with, more extensive, and coming into existence earlier than the rights so carefully set out in the various sections of the Code.
>
> The rules for the transfer of property as between seller and buyer, performance of the contract, rights of the unpaid seller against the goods, unpaid seller's lien, remedies of the seller, remedies of the buyer, appear to be complete and exclusive statements of the legal relations both in law and equity.[50]

It would accordingly appear that while the Sale of Goods Act may represent a codification of the late nineteenth-century English commercial law, in the area of property it happens not to reflect an aspect that would have been wholly incompatible with Scots law. At the same time, the better view would appear to be that the much-criticised abandonment of a delivery requirement is an inroad into Scottish legal principles only in a relatively minor degree because it represents a change which is more apparent than real.

Sharp v. *Thomson*

Detriment which the much-maligned Sale of Goods Act did not cause for Scots law may, unfortunately, have been done by the House of Lords decision in *Sharp* v. *Thomson*.[51] As indicated in the previous section the sale code avoids any role for the English law dichotomy of equitable ownership and ownership proper; indeed, the legislation maintains a clear distinction between contract and property in a system in which, on a correct analysis, property is acquired on the basis of a separate unitary act. In this respect the legislation is compatible with Scots law.

---

[50] *Re Wait* [1927] 1 Ch 606, 635–6. It may be noted that Atiyah, *The Sale of Goods*, p. 299, n. 154 comments that in view of subsequent authority 'this point would appear to be settled beyond doubt'. The learned writer cites the following: *London Wine Co (Shippers) Ltd* (1986) PCC 121; *Leigh & Sullivan Ltd* v. *Aliakmon Shipping Corp Ltd* (*The Aliakmon*) [1986] AC 785; *Re Goldthorp Exchange Ltd* [1994] 2 All ER 806; *Re Stapylton Fletcher* [1994] 1 WLR 1181.

[51] 1997 SLT 636.

In the House of Lords decision in *Sharp*, early in Lord Jauncey's opinion, the concept of 'beneficial interest' is brought into the reckoning in an interpretation of authority leading to the conclusion that, in the circumstances, such an interest had passed from the sellers in advance of the legal act of conveyance.[52] There has been much learned comment on this decision[53] but, for present purposes, two associated observations would appear to be especially relevant.

In the first place, while the decision of the First Division of the Court of Session, the highest court in Scotland in the context concerned, was at pains to emphasise that fundamental considerations leave no room for a blurring of contractual and proprietary rights in Scots law,[54] the decision of the House of Lords allowed this to happen, albeit on a basis which the court sought to ring-fence in terms of the factor of a floating charge under the Companies Act of 1986 which was seen to be the cause of the difficulty.

My second observation arises from this apparent aim of the House of Lords to limit the scope of the decision as a precedent. Arguably, in this regard, the decision of the case necessarily required a legal finding concerning the issue of the passing of property in circumstances entirely analogous to the familiar situation of a dispute between an insolvent transferor's creditors and a transferee as to whether or not property has passed from the insolvent estate. In this regard it is significant that the role of a case as precedent is determined by what the court has to decide – judicial observations unnecessary for the purposes of the decision are *obiter dicta*. The courts of England and Scotland have not accorded themselves with the capacity to prescribe the scope of a precedent in terms of how the *ratio* of the decision will impact on subsequent matters – in the manner of the American device of 'prospective overruling'[55] – and, indeed, it may well be that any attempt to claim such a power would be in breach of the principle of separation

---

[52] See at 639 B-C and 643 K-L.

[53] See esp. the following: K. G. C. Reid, 'Jam Today: Sharp in the House of Lords', 1997 *SLT* (News) 79; K. G. C. Reid, 'Equity Triumphant: *Sharp* v. *Thomson*', (1997) 1 *ELR* 464; and K. G. C. Reid, 'Obligations and Property: Explaining the Border', (1997) *Acta Juridica* 225. See also R. Evans-Jones, 'Receptions of Law', (1997) 114 *LQR* 228.

[54] 1995 SLT 837. On this decision see K. G. C. Reid, '*Sharp* v. *Thomson*: Property Law Preserved', (1995) 1 *SLPQ* 53.

[55] See Andrew G. L. Nicol, 'Prospective Overruling: A New Device for the English Courts', (1976) 39 *Modern LR* 542.

of powers.[56] It would accordingly appear that the decision does have major implications for Scots property law; in the present writer's view, as already indicated, with greater potential detriment than the abandonment of delivery by the Sale of Goods Act.

Feasibility of codification

Professor Sir Thomas Smith QC[57] perceived of the contribution of Stair in terms of rational systematisation under the influence of the civil law.[58] While, in principle, all systems are open to codification, Scots law had a definite contemporary affinity with the European development[59] which led to codification.[60] Stair's remarkable text, in its lucidity and structure, is the basis of any claim that eighteenth-century Scots law could be placed somewhere on the road to codification. Stair's stated position is consistent with the principal justification for codification as a jettisoning of unnecessary historical baggage: 'There is little to be found among the commentaries and treatises upon the civil law, arguing from any known principles of right; but all their debate is a congestion of the contexts of the law.'[61]

Moving from the general to the particular, it is arguably the case that Stair's treatment of the principles of voluntary derivative acquisition reflects strengths of rationality and structural integrity which might be seen as the

---

[56] This, of course, is not to deny the latitude open to a court in giving effect to a binding precedent; a matter which differs between English and Scots law: see Smith, *British Justice*, pp. 84–5; Rupert Cross, *Precedent in English Law* (Oxford, 1968), p. 16.

[57] See Smith, *British Justice*, p. 12–13.

[58] The issue of the extent of the civil law influence in the development of Scots law has become increasingly controversial. See R. Evans-Jones, 'Civil Law in the Scottish Legal Tradition', in Evans-Jones (ed.), *The Civil Law Tradition in Scotland*, pp. 3–12; N. R. Whitty, 'The Civilian Tradition and Debates on Scots Law', (1996) *TSAR* 227–39 and 442–57; Hector L. MacQueen, 'Mixture or Muddle? – Teaching and Research in Scottish Legal History', (1997) 5 *ZEUP* 369–84; R. Evans-Jones, 'Receptions of Law, Mixed Legal Systems and the Genius of Scots Private Law', (1998) 114 *LQR* 228–49; and now W. D. H. Sellar, 'Scots Law – Mixed from the Very Beginning? A Tale of Two Receptions', (2000) 4 *ELR* 3.

[59] Identified by Zimmermann, 'The Civil Law in European Codes', p. 258, as a 'specific historical phenomenon that originated in late 17th and 18th century legal science'.

[60] Even if the system seems unlikely to have any role as a bridge between the civil and common law systems of Europe in any European civil code project: see Hector L. MacQueen, *Scots Law and the Road to the New Ius Commune*, Ius Commune Lectures on European Private Law, ed. M. Hesselink et al. (Amsterdam, 2000) p. 1.

[61] Stair, *Institutions*, 1.1.17.

necessary foundation for codification.[62] An example is Stair's rejection, as a matter of principle, of the Justinianic rule which, in the case of sale, made the passing of property subject to payment or a credit or security arrangement: 'Sale being perfected, and the thing delivered, the property thereof becomes the buyer's, if it was the seller's, and there is no dependence of it, till the price be paid or secured, as was in the civil law, neither hypothecation of it for the price.'[63]

The foundation provided by Stair may be a suitable one, but is there scope for codification of the principles that regulate the voluntary derivative acquisition of corporeal property in modern Scots law? If there is, would it serve any useful purpose?

It would appear that there is scope for codification in the form of a statement of the core and essential principles applicable to the process of the derivative acquisition of corporeal property. To be complete such a statement would need to include a restatement of the positive and negative exceptions – as referred to above – found in diverse aspects of common law and legislation.

A code statement would, arguably, have beneficial effect in two respects. First it would lay to rest, on a definitive basis, the precedent of a non-unitary concept of ownership *ex facie* applicable from the House of Lords decision in *Sharp* v. *Thomson*. While it may well be that a subsequent court would find a means of reverting to the position of the Court of Session, it is impossible to know how long a period of uncertainty would prevail. On one view, even without formal correction, the criticism of the eventual outcome in *Sharp* v. *Thomson* has been such that the decision could well 'wither on the vine', but this also is a scenario which involves uncertainty. A second positive consequence of the contemplated form of code would be clarification regarding compatibility with the property principles of the Sale of Goods Act 1979.

Draft

Foundation provisions controlling system of voluntary derivative transfer of ownership in corporeal property (part I)

---

[62] See Carey Miller, 'Systems of Property: Grotius and Stair', p. 15.
[63] Stair, *Institutions*, 1.14.2.

I (1) The real right of ownership in corporeal property, including a share in corporeal property, passes from a party in a position to dispone to one in a position to acquire on the basis of a legal act of transfer.

(2) The passing of ownership from disponer to disponee, as provided for in (1), takes place in full in a process not open to incomplete or partial acquisition on a limited or provisional basis.

(3) The legal act of transfer must be in a form prescribed by law which reflects the disponing party's intention to dispone and the receiving party's intention to acquire; the act must be identifiable by date and time which will constitute the date and time of transfer.

(4) Subject to certain exceptions, as provided for in II,[64] only the owner or a party legally entitled to act on behalf of the owner has the right to dispone corporeal property by act of transfer.

(5) Knowledge of another party's existing better right to acquire makes acquisition by act of transfer open to reduction at the instance of the other party pending effective disposal.

---

[64] Not dealt with in this chapter.

6

'...Quae ad ius Cathalanicum pertinet': the civil law of Catalonia, *ius commune* and the legal tradition

FERRAN BADOSA COLL

The following chapter offers a synthesis of the long-standing relationship between the two fundamental components of current Catalan law. On the one hand, we have Catalan law as it has been developed by Catalan institutions; and on the other, the European *ius commune*, canon and Roman law, as adopted and incorporated into Catalan law by Catalonia's institutions.

The introduction refers to the period just before the initial reception of Roman law, and is followed by four further sections, which focus on the period after the reception process began. The first of these four sections refers to the *ius commune* as current law in Catalonia; the second to the situation of Roman law with regard to the *Decreto de Nueva Planta* (1716); the third to the Spanish Civil Code of 1889; and the fourth refers to the legislative systems in Spain's autonomous regions (1932, 1978).

'Gothicæ leges fuerunt prima Cathalanorum iura'[1]

The Liber Iudiciorum

The Latin terms *Liber Iudiciorum* (book of trials) and *Liber Iudicum* (book of judges) were used without distinction to refer to the written law applied in Catalonia before and after it was invaded by the Moors, between 715 and 720, following the key Battle of Guadelete in 711. In Spanish it was known as *Fuero Juzgo*. It had been laid down (*c*.654) by the Visigoth king Rescesvint (649–72), to provide a single law for the Visigoth and Roman populations of the Iberian peninsula.[2] It was very widely disseminated

---

[1] Antonius Olibanus (1534–1601), *Commentarii de actionibus in duas summas partes ... pars prima* (Barcelona, 1606), lib. III, cap. I, no. 1.
[2] Karl Zeumer, *Historia de la Legislación Visigoda* (Barcelona, 1944), pp. 82 ff.

within Catalonia, a fact to which the fifty or so extant copies give ample testimony.[3]

Trial and inheritance records of the time bear witness to its application. There are two trials that can be cited.[4] One of these was presided over by Salomon, Count of Urgell-Cerdanya-Conflent, at the town of All (Cerdanya, 26 August 862) 'in mallo publico, una cum iudices suos', on the question of the thirty-year prescription (which would later incorporate the *usatge* 'Omnes causae'). A second trial (at some time between 1040 and 1060) was presided over by two people of the same name, 'Isarnus', one a judge, the other the Lord of Caboet, at the church of Coll de Nargó, for an attack on a woman.[5]

As for hereditary law, one need only look through the numerous wills lacking an heir, in which the testator orally expresses his desire that his estate be distributed among the executors (*elemosinarii*), which was then carried out by judicial order in an 'ad hoc' procedure: the so-called *causa elemosinaria*.[6]

The Usatges de Barcelona

It is from this period under Gothic law that the *Usatges de Barcelona* came to take effect. I will not enter into the debate about their exact dates. The

---

[3] On the diffusion of the *Liber Iudicum* in Catalonia, see Anscari Mundó, 'Fragment del *Llibre Jutge*, versió catalana antiga del *Liber Iudiciorum*', in *Miscel·lània Aramon i Serra*, vol. IV (Barcelona, 1984), p. 160. Diffusion also included translation in Catalan. Mundó, 'Fragment del *Llibre Jutge*', pp. 155 ff., contains a one-page parchment transcription (MS 1109 in the Library of Montserrat), corresponding to a copy dating from between 1180 and 1190. Even older is the text described by Cebrià Baraut and Josep Moran, 'Fragment d'una altra versió catalana antiga del "Liber Iudiciorum" visigòtic. I. Edició, contingut i datació. II. Estudi lingüístic', (1996–7) 13 *Urgellia* 7. This is a fragment (MS 187.1 from Capitular Archive of the Cathedral of la Seu d'Urgell) which Baraut dates to the year 1150. Forthcoming within the collection *Textos jurídics catalans* is the publication of the codex of the Barcelona judge Homobonus ('Liber iudicis popularis', from around 1010), active between 987 and 1024.

[4] See Joan Bastardas, 'Dos judicis antics (s.IX i X)', in *Documents jurídics de la història de Catalunya* (Barcelona, 1991), pp. 24 ff.

[5] More textual quotations from the *Liber* in documents edited by Petrus de Marca, *Marca Hispanica sive Limes Hispanicus* (Paris, 1688; repr. Barcelona, 1972), pp. 760 ff., concerning legal proceedings, litigations ('perquisivimus in lege Gothorum', docs. 34, 143, 151, 181, 204 and 240) and in reconstructions of lost texts (docs. 39, 40 fin., 41, 133, this on the occasion of the destruction of Barcelona by al-Mansur, in 985).

[6] Antoni Udina, *La successió testada a la Catalunya Altomedieval* (Barcelona, 1984), collected or transcribed 137 of them between 840 and 1025. For a study of Catalan wills of the period cf. Jean Bastier, 'Le testament du IXe au XIIe siècle: une survivance visigothique', (1973) *Revue historique du droit français et étranger* 373.

traditional thesis attributes them to Ramon Berenguer I and his wife Almodis, around 1068, while the more recent one argues for their instigation under Ramon Berenguer IV, around 1170, though they were based on an older model.[7]

The references to the *Liber* are to be found in the *Usatges* 1 ('Antequam Usatici') and 3 ('Cum dominus Raymundus'), which considered it insufficiently clear. *Usatge* 3 refers to the 'potestas regia' (see *Fuero Juzgo* 2-I-1) of the Count of Barcelona as the basis of the *Usatges*.

At the same time, the *Usatges* contain references to Roman law. For example, *Usatge* 69 ('Item statuerunt') includes the principle 'Quod Principi placuit, legem habet vigorem' (D. 1, 4, 1 pr.). The 'Principat' of the Count of Barcelona is firmly established in *Usatges* 43 ('Si quis in curia'), 60 ('Omnes quippe naves' which speaks of 'Principis Barchinonae'), 61 ('Item statuerunt' primer), 63 ('Constituerunt etiam'), 64 ('Quoniam per iniquum Principem'), 65 ('Simili modo'), 68 ('Princeps namque'), 69 ('Item statuerunt'), 71 ('Per bonum usaticum'), 75 ('Si quis iudeo'), 76 ('Auctoritate et rogatu' primer), 79 ('Possunt etiam'), 80 ('Iudicium in curia datum'), 81 ('Iudicia curiae'), 84 ('Stabilierunt), 91 ('Auctoritate et rogatu' segon), 96 ('Laudaverunt'), 121 ('Siquis dixerit'), 125 ('Item constituerunt'), 129 ('Statuerunt siquidem'), 130 ('Statuerunt etiam').[8]

Of these, the most interesting is *Usatge* 81 ('Iudicia curiae') in which the sources of law are presented in hierarchical order for the first time in Catalan legal history: 'E per ço las cosas fetas o a fer, constituiren los dits princeps que sien jutjadas segons lo usatge; e aquí hon no bastaran los Usatges torna hom a las Leys gotiques e al arbitre del Princep e a son juy de la Cort.'[9]

---

[7] See the summary by Jesús Fernández Viladrich and Manuel J. Peláez, in the prologue to Fernando Valls Taberner (ed.), *Los Usatges de Barcelona* (Barcelona, 1984). On the period, Pierre Bonnassie, *Catalunya mil anys enrera (segles X–XI)*, vol. I (Barcelona, 1979), vol. II (1981), which deals with the origins of the *Usatges* in the court of Ramon Berenguer I and Almodis in vol. II, pp. 162 ff.

[8] Catalan political doctrine on the Principality of the Count of Barcelona is explained by Olibanus, *De actionibus*, lib. III, cap. II, no. 11 ff. The starting point was that the Count of Barcelona, despite his title, 'tametsi Rex non dicatur' was the 'Princeps Cathaloniae' and had veritably royal powers: 'hic enim Comes Barcinonae dumtaxat regiam potestatem habebat'. Therefore, 'immo est quasi Imperator in sua Provincia' 'ex quibus efficitur Comitem Barcinonae non recognoscere superiorem in sua provincia'. This is repeated in no. 17, 'Quia Comes Barcinonae regiam potestam habens, superiorem non recognoscens'.

[9] Constitutions y Altres Drets de Catalunya (CYADC), I.1.14, *Us*. 2. In *Us*. 81 the 'arbitrium Principis' and the 'eius iudicium atque curiae' were according to Roman laws 'tamquam aequas et iustas' (Olibanus, *De actionibus*, lib. III, cap. II, no. 21). Nevertheless, according to Thomas Mieres (fl. 1400–74), *Apparatus super constitutionibus generalibus Curiarum Generalium Cathaloniae*,

Ius proprium and *ius commune*

The *ius proprium* and *ius commune* duality arises from the First Book of the Institutions of Gaius (I.1, transcribed in D. 1, 1, 9 'Omnes populi'). The text states that all the cities ruled by laws and customs, 'in part' use their 'own' law or 'civil law', and 'in part' the law common to all men.

This duality, which was consolidated during the reception of Roman law, explains the situation of the law in the different European kingdoms up until the time of the codification. During this period, Catalan lawyers came to consider that *ius commune* no longer referred to Gothic law, but exclusively to Roman law.[10]

Reception in Catalonia

The reception period is generally thought to have been during the reign of Alfonso I (1162–96).[11] The first legal testimonies to the fact are from the time of the reign of his son and heir, Peter I (1196–1213). These are found in *Usatge* 143 which applies 'imperial laws' to the question of the neutrality of witnesses and, more importantly, in one of the constitutions enacted at the Parliament of Barcelona of 1210 (CYADC I.4.36.1), which mentions the dual use of the *Usatges de Barcelona e Constitutio*, on the one hand, and '*comú dret*', on the other. What is more, in 1213 (the year in which the king was killed at the Battle of Muret) there is mention of the presence at the University of Bologna of one 'Pontius de Ilerda...sacrarum legum interpres', considered to be its first teacher of Catalan origin.[12]

Catalan local laws recognised the *ius commune* widely as supplementary. In the *Consuetudines Ilerdenses* (compiled in 1228), the chapter 'De legibus romanis' states: '...pluribus utimur, pluribus non, ut in cotidianis tractatibus causarum liquere potest'. The Customs of Perpignan (in the version granted by Jaume II King of Majorca in 1267, whose kingdom also included Rousillon and Sardinia) excluded the *Usatges* and Gothic law and referred

vol. II (Barcelona, 1621), coll. 9, ch. 10, no. 12, recourse to the veritable 'arbitrium boni viri' was necessary when Roman laws were too tough.

[10] Olibanus, *De actionibus*, lib. III, cap. II, no. 21.

[11] The first traces of Roman law in Catalonia are found two centuries before. After studying these, Aquilino Iglesia Ferreirós, in 'La difusión del Derecho común en Cataluña', in Aquilino Iglesia Ferreirós, *El Dret Comú i Catalunya* (Barcelona, 1991), pp. 95 ff, concludes that the date limit must be 1210.

[12] Guido Rossi, *La 'Summa Arboris actionum' di Ponzio da Ilerda* (Milan, 1951).

back to the 'jura'. In the *Consuetudines Dertusae* (compiled in 1272), the 'Costuma' 9.25.19 established the following hierarchy: 'Custumes escrites de Tortosa...Usagies...dret civil e comú'. In *Recognoverunt Proceres* of Barcelona (1283), Roman law is presupposed in chapters 44 and 104. In the Customs of Horta de Sant Joan (1296), chapter 17 established that on the subject 'de maleficiis' judges had to decide 'secundum Usaticos et jus commune'. In the Customs of Miravet (1319), chapter 29 states that where the constitutions and *Usatges de Barcelona* are found lacking 'sie recorregut al dret comú'.[13]

The contrary reactions to Roman and canon law are symbolised in a constitution by James I (*Corts* of Barcelona, 1251, CYADC III.1.8.1; it must be borne in mind that vol. III contains the repealed texts) which attempts to exclude the influence of foreign law in secular courts: 'no sien rebudas, admesas, judicadas ne allegadas...las leys Romanas o Gotigas, drets e decretals'. Catalan law is to be used exclusively: 'mes sien fetas en tota causa [secular allegations] segons los usatges de Catalunya e segons las aprovadas costumas de aquell lloc on la causa sera agitada e, en defalliment de aquells, sie proceit segons seny natural'. Clearly, the 'arbitrium principis' of *Usatge* 81 had disappeared.

The exclusion of Roman law was not successful, however. A *pragmatica* by Peter III (1380, CYADC II.1.10.1) stated that in the city of Tortosa there were doubts 'an Constitutiones Cathaloniae Generales iuri scripto canonico vel civili debeant praeferri vel anteponi', given that both laws 'pro legibus habentur'. The king established that, where customs were lacking, the constitutions of Catalonia came before Roman law. Moreover, it was recalled that Roman laws and constitutions only had to be observed 'if and to the extent we so wish' and that they did not have a greater authority than the 'pacted' constitutions.

The exclusion was successful as regards Gothic law, basically as it had fallen into disuse thanks to Roman law. One example of a conflict between

---

[13] Cf. *Els Costums de Lleida* ([1228], repr. 1997). The Customs of Perpignan are quoted from the transcription of Guillermo M. de Brocà, *Historia del Derecho de Cataluña especialmente del Civil y Exposicion de las instituciones de Derecho civil del mismo territorio en relacion con el Código civil de España y la Jurisprudencia* (Barcelona, 1918; repr. 1985), p. 196. The *Costums de Tortosa* are quoted from the edition by Jesús Massip (Tortosa, 1996). The Recognoverunt Proceres is in CYADC II.1.13. XIII. The *Costums d'Horta* are quoted from the edition by Josep Serrano (Horta de Sant Joan, 1996). The *Costums de Miravet* are from the transcription by Ana Maria Barrero, 'Las Costumbres de Lérida, Horta y Miravet', (1974) *Anuario de Historia del Derecho Español* 519.

the two, where Gothic law predominates for the moment, is found in the *Consuetudines Ilerdenses* (1228), in which the compiler, Guillem Botet, gives preference to the Gothic will, with appointment of executor, over the Roman will with appointment of an heir.[14] The presence of Gothic law in Catalan law was reduced to five instances,[15] of which only the thirty-year prescription has survived.

The ordination of the sources of law

Capítol de Cort 2 of the Parliament of Barcelona of Martí l'Humà (1409) imposed the following order on the different laws applied in Catalonia. Firstly, the general civil law of Catalonia: 'Usatjes de Barcelona e Constitutions e Capitols de Cort de Cathalunya'. Secondly, local law, whether written or not: 'Uses, Customs, Privileges, Immunities and Liberties... of the Universities and their inhabitants'. Lastly, 'Roman law, equity and common sense' (CYADC I.1.38.2).

As to the system of sources of 1409, with reference to general Catalan law, it was not founded upon the Roman concept of royal power ('Quod Principi placuit legis habet vigorem', D. 1, 4, 1, *Us.* 69), so much as the idea of the 'pact'.[16] Legislative power resided with the king but with the

---

[14] The chapter 'De heredibus' explains the conflict and the preference: 'Non instutuuntur heredes nominatim per consuetudinem, sed fiunt manumissores in testamento qui rogantur sic', 'precor ut dividant omnia bona mea sicut inferius apparebit'. However, 'in legitimam observamus legem romanam de triente et semisse'. This is the *novissima* of Justinian (Nov. 18, ch. 1) which assigns a third ('triens') to up to four children and a half ('semis') for four or more children. Catalan law did not finally choose this option (ch. 94 of the Parliament of Montsó 1585, held by Philip I (CYADC I.6.5.2), generalising a privilege granted to Barcelona by Peter III in 1343 (CYADC II.6.3.1) which is the classical Roman portion of a quarter in all cases (Inst. II, 18, 6).

[15] On the five cases of Gothic law, Mieres, *Apparatus*, coll. 5, chs. 7 and 28, no. 8. See also Olibanus, *De actionibus*, lib. III, cap. II, no. 21.

[16] Pacting is the most important characteristic of Catalan political thought (cf. the discussion by Jaume Sobrequés i Callicó and Juan Vallet de Goytisolo in *El pactismo en la Historia de España* (Madrid, 1980), pp. 49 ff. and 75 ff.; and, above all, Victor Ferro, *El Dret Públic Català: Les Institucions a Catalunya fins el Decret de Nova Planta* (Vich, 1987), pp. 272 ff. and 290 ff.).

Pacting can be seen from two perspectives: a political one, and a legal one. In political pacting, its main characteristic is a negation of the legislative power of the King. Cf. Jacobus Cancerius, *Variarum resolutionum iuris caesarei, pontificii et municipalis Principatus Cathaloniae pars tertia* (Lyons, 1670); Olibanus, *De actionibus*, lib. III, cap. II, no. 14; Joannes Petrus Fontanella, *Decisiones Sacri Regii Senatus Cathaloniae*, vol. II (Lyons, 1668), dec. 283, no. 7. It is also visible in submitting royal powers to the laws of the land (Fontanella, *Decisiones*, vol. I, dec. 3, no. 23).

In the legal area, it is clear in the exercise of judicial power. Its basis was *Usatge* 124 'Alium namque', where the 'Principes' imposed on themselves certain obligations, among which 'approval and consent' of the Parliament divided into its three branches – ecclesiastical, military and royal – or those of free cities. The official origin of law by consent is found in the *Corts* of Peter II in Barcelona in 1283.[17] However, Catalan lawyers traced it back to the Assemblies of 1056 in which Ramon Berenguer I and Almodis granted the original *Usatges*.[18]

The application of Roman law within Catalonia also raised the question of the basis of its legitimacy. Once the principle 'rex in regno suo est imperator' was affirmed, Catalan lawyers went on to extract the consequence: '...recurramus ad leges romanas...non tamen legibus romanis subditi sumus, nec illas sequimur ut latas a principe superiore comite Barcinonae, sed ut rationabiles rationes et decisiones continentes' (as stated in the above-mentioned *pragmatica* of Peter III in 1380, CYADC II.1.10.1).[19]

Catalan law also questioned the order of the component parts of the *ius commune*. This included both canon and Roman law, with each compiled in its respective corpus. Nevertheless, canon law took precedence over Roman law.[20]

Finally, Roman law could not ensure a complete system of sources, as it is incomplete in itself. Beyond its sources, one could still recur to the concepts of equity and good sense.

was that 'tenerent iustitiam et iudicarent per directum'. That is to say, 'according to the law'. See Cancerius, *Variarum resolutionum*, cap. 3, no. 44; Gabriel Berart et de Gassol, *Speculum visitationis secularis* (Barcelona, 1627), cap. 12, no. 22; Fontanella, *Decisiones*, vol. II, dec. 530, no. 23; Josephus Ramonius, *Consiliorum una cum Sententiis et Decisionibus Audientiae Regiae Principatus Cathaloniae Primum Volumen* (Barcelona, 1628), cons. 37, no. 273; Joannes Paulus Xammar, *De officio iudicis et advocati Liber Unus* (Barcelona, 1639), Pars 1, qu. 18, no. 19).

[17] This is a general affirmation. See, for all, A. A. Ripoll, *Variae iuris resolutiones* (Lyons, 1630), cap. 4, no. 119; Luys de Valencia, *Ilustración de la Constitución VII, Tít. De la eleccion de los Dotores de la Real Audiencia* (Barcelona, 1674), cap. 3, no. 8.

[18] This origin resides in *Us.* 3 'Cum dominus Raymundus' and specifically in the fact that the Count acts 'laudo et consilio suorum proborum hominum, una cum prudentissima et sapientissima coniuge sua Adalmoda'. Olibanus, *De actionibus*, lib. III, cap. II, no. 13 says later: 'Modus condendi leges, quem Raymundus Comes observavit, hodie...necessarius factus est'. Thus, the seventh feudal obligation, the *consilium* of the lord (Karl Lehmann (ed.), *Consuetudines Feudorum* (repr. Aalen, 1971), 2–6: 'De forma fidelitatis': 'restat ut in sex praedictis, consilium et auxilium domino praestet, si beneficio vult dignus videri et de fidelitate esse salvus'), became the right to participate in the legislative power.

[19] Olibanus, *De actionibus*, Pars 1, lib. III, Ad P. Curare, no. 3.

[20] The supplementary character of canon law in relation to Catalan law is evident from the admission of bad faith in the three-year prescription or in the preference of canon law over Roman law in calculating the degree of relatedness (Fontanella, *Decisiones*, vol. I, decs. 12, no. 2 and 152, no. 1 respectively).

This situation was modified to some extent by chapter 40 of the Parliament of Philip II of Aragon and Catalonia (Philip III of Castile) of 1599 (CYADC I.1.30 – 'Del Dret se a de seguir en declarar les causes' – 1). The constitution substitutes the four-way division of the law for another: general Catalan law, canon law, Roman law and equity, with the total disappearance of local laws. These are ordered as follows: firstly, 'the disposition of the *Usatges*, Constitutions and Chapters of Court of the present Principality together with the Crown possessions of Rousillon and Sardinia'; secondly, 'and in cases where legislation was lacking', the unity of Roman law would break down in favour of 'the disposition of Canon Law' 'and where that is incomplete (reference would be to) Civil law and the legal writings of Doctors of law'. Another innovation is the reduction of 'equity': it is no longer an equity freely arrived at, but rather one 'que sia regulada y conforme a les regles del Dret comú y que aporten los Doctors sobre la materia de equitat'.[21]

However, this restriction on equity did not pass without some argument. In the unsuccessful Parliament of 1632, a representative of military law proposed the total repeal of written law, both Catalan and Roman, and the application of equity alone.[22]

The above-mentioned notion of 'pact' became a fundamental obstacle to the uniformist pretensions of later kings of the house of Austria (which ended with the childless death of Charles II in 1700).[23] Catalonia's rebellion resulted in the recognition of Louis XIII of France as the Count of Barcelona (Treaty of Ceret of 24 September 1640 and the pacts agreed with the three branches of the Parliament on 23 January 1641, with the king accepting and swearing to observe them on 18 September 1641.[24] The War of Separation lasted until 1653 with the surrender of Barcelona to John of Austria, son of Philip IV, who recognised the continuing existence of the Catalan constitutions.

The question of respect for the Catalan constitutions is equally a determining factor in the conflicts between Catalonia and the first king of the house of Bourbon, Philip V, who was crowned in 1701, and the

---

[21] A. Bosch, *Sumari, index o epitome dels admirables y nobilissims titols de honor de Cathalunya, Rossello y Cerdanya* (Perpignan, 1628), lib. 5, cap. 22.

[22] Explained by Xammar, *De officio*, Pars 1, qu. 16, no. 1, 2.

[23] See J. H. Elliott, *La revolta catalana, 1598–1640*, 2nd edn (Barcelona, 1989).

[24] Cf. José Sanabre, *La acción de Francia en Cataluña (1640–1659)* (Barcelona, 1956), with transcriptions of the pacts on pp. 648 ff.

consequent choice of Archduke Charles of Austria during the War of the Spanish Succession in the Pact of Geneva on 20 June 1705 between the Catalan sympathisers and Mitford Crowe, the plenipotentiary of Anne, Queen of England.[25]

'En todo lo demás que no está prevenido en los capítulos precedentes de este Decreto, mando se observen las Constituciones que antes havía en Cataluña; entendiendose que son de nuevo establecidas por este decreto'[26]

This quotation is from chapter 42 of the Royal Decree (16 January 1716) by Philip V on the Establecimiento y Nueva Planta de la Real Audiencia de Cataluña, the new judicial and political body (ch. 37, 'si fuere perteneciente a justicia o gobierno, correrá en adelante a cargo de la Audiencia') which, presided over by a captain general, governed life in Catalonia.[27]

The Decree's importance resides in the change marked in the foundation of its own legitimacy, in that both the old political organisation (the *Generalitat* and the Catalan Parliament – *Corts*) and the administrative one were finally suppressed. The old Audience of Catalonia was also substituted by the *Real Junta Superior de govierno y Justicia del Principado de Cataluña* (15 September 1714).

Civil, mercantile, criminal and procedural law were all maintained. Nevertheless, they were not affirmed through a pact, but rather by the

---

[25] Joaquim Albareda i Salvadó, *Els catalans i Felip V, de la conspiració a la revolta (1700–1705)* (Barcelona, 1993), pp. 59 ff. and 159 ff. respectively. The pact and its preliminary documents are in Josep. M. Torres i Ribé (ed.), *Escrits polítics del segle XVIII*, vol. II (Vich, 1996), pp. 68 ff.

The defection of England was criticised in two works, among others, from the time of the defeat: *The Case of the Catalans Consider'd* (London, 1714) and *The Deplorable History of the Catalans* (London, 1714) (both published and translated by Michael B. Strubell, *Consideració del cas dels catalans* (Barcelona, 1992), pp. 23 ff. and 83 ff. respectively). Later there appeared the anonymous *Record de l'aliança fet al Srm. Jordi August Rei de la Gran Bretanya. . . . amb un carta del Principat de Catalunya i ciutat de Barcelona* (1736, printed according to the printers' inscription in Oxford), pp. 66 ff.

[26] 'Regarding that which is not foreseen in the preceding chapters of this Decree, I command that the former Constitutions of Catalonia be observed; by which it is to be understood that they are established anew by this Decree.'

[27] See Josep M. Gay Escoda, 'La gènesi del Decret de Nova Planta a Catalunya. Edició de la consulta original del "Consejo de Castilla" de 13 de juny de 1715', (1982) *RJC* 8 and 263.

absolute power of the king, being legitimated retroactively (ch. 42, 'entendiendose que son de nuevo establecidas'),[28]

This is a concept of absolute power which, while referring to the past, projects itself much more into the future. The lands that made up the Crown of Aragon were defeated in the War of the Spanish Succession and the 'right of conquest' was applied to them, with the total suppression of their laws, in the cases of Valencia and Aragon (Decree of 29 June 1707), though they were partially re-established by a later decree (3 April 1711), and their maintenance in Majorca (Royal Decree of 28 November 1715).

Supplementary law in Catalonia up to the Napoleonic Wars

The fact that Roman law was supplementary, according to chapter 40 enacted at the Parliament of 1599, created problems in Catalonia. The currency of chapter 40 was reinforced by chapter 42 of the Decree of *Nueva Planta*.[29] At the same time, however, the law of Castile, which described itself as 'Derecho Real' (royal law), also tried to be considered supplementary, and therefore, also as supplementary to Catalan law. Catalan law had described itself as *ius municipale*, but exclusively in relation to Roman law.

Royal Decrees after the Decree of *Nueva Planta* varied between upholding chapter 40 of the enactment of 1599 and applying Castilian law as supplementary (1768, referring to feudal cases, compiled in the *Novísima Recopilación* (1805) 5.9.4: 'gobernandose a falta de leyes municipales no revocadas, por las leyes generales del Reyno'). This Royal Decree was upheld in the *Real Cédula* of 2 October 1785.[30]

---

[28] For the list of decrees immediately following the conquest of Barcelona (11 September 1714), see Josep M. Gay Escoda, *El Corregidor a Catalunya* (Madrid, 1997), pp. 76 ff. Also Santiago Sobrequés (ed.), *L'onze de setembre a Catalunya* (Barcelona, 1976), pp. 87 ff.

[29] See Josep M. Gay Escoda, 'Notas sobre el derecho supletorio en Cataluña desde el decreto de nueva planta (1715) hasta la jurisprudencia del Tribunal Supremo (1845)', (1990) 34/35, 2 *Per la storia del pensiero giuridico moderno* 805 ff.

[30] On the origin of this Decree in relation to the defence of the royal prerogatives concerning the *monitorium* of Pope Clement XIII (30 January 1768) which attempted to affirm the superiority of the papacy over kings, see Gay Escoda, 'Notas sobre el derecho supletorio en Cataluña', p. 815. Against the supplementary application of Castilian law, see José Solsona in the response (24 September 1809) to the *Consulta al País* (see below, pp. 152–4) (transcribed by Miguel Artola, *Los orígenes de la España contemporanea*, vol. II (Madrid, 1976), pp. 571 ff.).

This *Resolución* is significant for the way it compares Catalan law as a 'municipal law' with Castilian law as 'general law of the Kingdom'. This comparison emerges even more clearly in the systematisation of the *Novísima Recopilación* (1805): the only 'laws' considered as such were those of the Kingdom of Castile (book 3, title 2), while non-Castilian laws were limited by their description as 'Fueros Provinciales' (book 3, title 3).

On the other hand, chapter 40 had been upheld in its entirety by Catalan case law, with the supplementary character of both canon and Roman law.[31]

Raising doubts about supplementary laws and their resolution in favour of the law of Castile was the responsibility of the professor of the University of Cervera, Joan Antoni de Mujal. In this, he was opposed by the Chancellor of the same university, Ramon Llàtzer de Dou i de Bassols, who defended the *ius commune* as supplementary law, an opinion which became prevalent.[32]

Catalan law during the Napoleonic Wars (1808–14)

To understand the developments in Catalan law during this period, two historical occurrences must be borne in mind: namely, the occupation of Catalonia by French forces (the occupation of Barcelona, which had begun on 13 February 1808, was made official in the Decree of General Duhesme on 13 September 1808, Girona surrendered in December 1809, and Tarragona was occupied on 28 June1811), followed by the annexation of Catalonia by France (Napoleon's Decree of 26 January 1812, preceded by the Decree of 8 February 1810 which had established a specific form of government).[33]

---

[31] See Santiago Espiau Espiau and Pere del Pozo Carrascosa, *L'activitat judicial de l'Audiència de Catalunya en matèria civil (1716–1834)* (Barcelona, 1996). Testimonies of the belief in the application of Roman law as a supplementary (not in chronological order) are to be found on pp. 32 (1808), 243 (1783), 327 (1810), 476, 477 (1792). There are also those in favour of the law of Castile: pp. 103, 105 (1798, lawyer's demand).

[32] The imputation that Mujal (Joannes Antonius Mujal et de Gibert, *Noviter Digestae Justiniani Institutionum et Patrii Cathalauniae Annotationes* (Cervera, 1781), p. 9) had raised the question was made by P. N. Vives y Cebriá, *Traducción al Castellano de los Usatges* (repr. Barcelona, 1989), vol. I, p. 109. Dou's account is in Ramon Lázaro Dou y de Bassols, *Instituciones del Derecho Público general de España, con noticia del particular de Cataluña y de las principales reglas de gobierno en cualquier estado*, vol. I (Madrid, 1800; repr. 1975), pp. 76 ff.
The *communis opinio* on the question is to be found in Solsona (see n. 30 above).

[33] On this period, from the French point of view see Juan Mercader Riba, *Barcelona durante la ocupación napoleónica (1808 a 1814)* (Madrid, 1949), and Maties Ramisa, *Els catalans i el domini napoleònic* (Barcelona, 1995).

The former system of law was embodied in the continuity of the old Audience of Catalonia which, after its expulsion from Barcelona, established itself in various parts of Catalonia, and in the political and military resistance embodied in the *Junta Superior del Principado de Cataluña*. The Audience of Catalonia was made up of judges who had fled Barcelona, and its headquarters varied as the French occupation progressed, moving from Tarragona (1810) to Vich (1811), and then to Manresa (1812).[34]

The political reaction to the French occupation is also of great importance. The first reaction came to Napoleon's calling for a deputation of 150 people to Bayonne (from May to July 1808) where the first constitution for Spain was set forth (6 July 1808). The city hall of Barcelona gave a memorandum to its representative, José de Vega y de Sentmenat. In one of its sections, it required 'that, in all the provinces which have their own laws, these be upheld religiously by all the Parliament, and that for the laws of Catalonia, as they are mostly written in Catalan, there be made a translation into Spanish, to be printed beside the original, to aid the comprehension of those judges who are unfamiliar with the original language'.[35]

The second reaction came in the form of the *Junta Superior del Principado de Cataluña* (formed in Lleida on 18 June 1808) which took charge of civil and criminal administration, and laid down that the 'leyes, constituciones municipales y fueros de Cataluña' ought to be applied.[36]

The third, and most important, response came in the form of the calling of the Parliament (termed 'extraordinary' by the Decree of 1 January 1810, and begun in Cadiz on 24 September 1810), where the overall situation of Spanish law was under consideration. As regards Catalan law, the most important document was the *Exposición* of the *Junta Superior*

---

[34] Espiau and del Pozo, *L'activitat judicial de l'Audiència de Catalunya*: at Tarragona, p. 330; at Vich, pp. 507, 510; and at Manresa, pp. 229 and 511.

[35] Literal fragments were published (quotes here come from these) by Federico Camp, 'Memoria del Ayuntamiento de Barcelona a las Cortes de Bayona sobre las aspiraciones de Cataluña', (1916) 15 *Estudio* 271. Vega de Sentmenat was professor at the University of Cervera and never got to Bayonne, being detained as he left Barcelona. However, José Garriga, who was pro-French, went of his own accord and requested of the *Junta española* called by Napoleon (session 27 June 1808) that the 'local laws and specific constitution' of Catalonia be upheld. The answer of the *Junta*'s president, Miguel Jose Azanza, was that Catalonia had no official representative and that 'Catalonia has no specific Constitution' for political purposes (Carlos Sanz Cid, *La Constitución de Bayona* (Madrid, 1922), p. 146).

[36] Federico Rahola y Tremols, *Los Diputados por Cataluña en las Cortes de Cadiz* (Barcelona, 1912), p. 11.

del Principat to the Catalan representatives at the *Cortes* of Cadiz
(Tarragona, 13 August 1810). The 'consideration' given is clearly political in its nature:

> While the obvious political advantages accruing from imposing uni-
> formity on the legislation and rights of all the provinces of the monarchy
> must be recognised, in order to avoid the body of law being too heteroge-
> nous in character; with all considered, when the plurality of opinions do
> not coincide on this issue, or when insuperable obstacles are in oppo-
> sition to the realisation of this healthy measure, in such circumstances,
> Catalonia should not only preserve its privileges and current laws, but
> also recuperate those laws which it enjoyed at the time that the Throne of
> Spain was occupied by the august House of Austria.[37]

In other words, Catalonia should recover its public law.

As for the system of law imposed by the French, this was primarily judi-
cial, to be followed later by administrative legislation (the aforementioned
Decree of 26 January 1812 divided Catalonia into four *Départements* – Ter,
Segre, Montserrat and Bouches de l'Ebre – and thirteen *Arrondissements*).[38]
The definitive French judicial organisation (by the Governor of Barcelona,
Maurice Mathieu, 21 October 1810) had magistrates' courts, county courts,
the Court of Appeal, the *Conseil de Requettes* and the *Consejo de Reposición*
who advised the governor. The law they applied was derived from a recognition of chapter 40 of the Parliament of 1599. Thus Catalan law was applied
in preference to Roman law, with the latter acting as supplementary where
necessary, and with the suppression of equity. Canon law was also applied,

---

[37] It is 'la Exposición de las principales ideas que la Junta Superior del Principado de Cataluña
cree conveniente manifestar a los señores Diputados de la Provincia que en representación
de la misma pasan al Congreso de las próximas Cortes' (the exposition of the principal ideas
which the *Junta Superior* of the Principality of Catalonia consider it convenient to present to
the gentlemen representatives of the province, who in representation of the same, will go to the
Congress of the next *Cortes*), published as an appendix by Rahola, *Los Diputados por Cataluña*,
pp. 51 ff.

[38] Federico Camp, 'História jurídica de la Guerra de la Independencia', (1918) *RJC* 353. The
supreme territorial organ was the *Conseil de Requettes* (with Melchor de Guardia, José de Campá
and Andrés López de Frías as its members). The Court of Appeal was presided over by Tomás
de Puig.

On the performance of each of these courts, see Espiau and del Pozo, *L'activitat judicial de
l'Audiència de Catalunya*, pp. 605–43 which transcribes twelve cases (mostly verdicts, the first
in Catalan) of the Court of Appeal, between 1810 and 1813. On the magistrates' courts, pp. 616,
632, 636, 645; on the county court, pp. 88, 599, 612, 615, 623, 625, 628, 637, esp. pp. 632, 633;
on its powers, p. 617; on the *Consejo de Reposición*, p. 626.

except for the case of divorce. The Napoleonic Code as it coincides with Roman law was taken into account, but not in opposition to Catalan law (e.g., the concept of emphytheusis *(emphytéose)* was upheld, where it had been repealed in France by the Decree of 18–29 December 1790).[39]

Supplementary law in Catalonia after the Napoleonic Wars

The question of supplementary law is one that was thrown into sharp relief outside the university, after the armistice between Suchet and Wellington on 19 April 1814, and the departure of Napoleon's forces from Barcelona on 29 April 1814. It is first raised in a *Consulta* to the Audience by Juan Manuel de Moya in the *Alcalde Mayor* (the equivalent of the present-day county court) of Figueres (6 July 1815). De Moya's argument was founded on that of the aforementioned *Resolución* of 1768, the aim of which was to replace Roman law with the law of Castile.[40]

The consultation went as far as the Council of Castile, which, in an *Auto Acordado* (8 February 1816), decided to create an 'instructional proceedings on the origins and history of the custom and practice of the judges of

---

[39] Espiau and del Pozo, *L'activitat judicial de l'Audiència de Catalunya.* As for the applicability of chapter 40 of the Parliament of 1599, p. 631; on the application of Catalan law, pp. 619, 626 and 630; on that of Roman law, pp. 611, 613, 614, 616, 619, 626, 630 and 635; on the abolition of equity, pp. 630 and 631; on the application of canon law, p. 638 and its negation, p. 641; on the application of the Code Napoleon, pp. 614, 616, 635 (for being 'even more indulgent' than Roman law) and 641. On upholding emphytheusis, pp. 613 and 614.

As regards French legislation for Catalonia, the Decree of 26 November 1810 is considered an extract of the *Code de procedure civile* of 29 April 1806. The *hereus de confiança* (confidence heirs) were also repealed (Decree of 11 June 1812). On the attempts to translate the Napoleonic Code into Catalan, see Camp, 'Història jurídica de la Guerra de la Independencia', p. 3; Ramisa, *Els catalans i el domini napoleònic*, p. 258.

[40] Moya complains that 'Desde que en Mayo de este año tomé posesión de la vara de Alcalde Mayor de esta Villa no experimento más que transgresiones a la Real Orden citada y un empeño decidido en alegar y sostener las leyes Romanas con preferencia a las de la Novisima Recopilación, desconocida para alguno de los letrados de este país' (Since taking up the office of the mayor of this City in May of this year, all I have experienced have been transgressions against the cited Royal Order and a decided effort to allege and uphold Roman laws in preference to those of the *Novísima Recopilación*, which are unknown to certain lawyers in this country). The Royal Order he mentions is that of 15 July 1805 acclaiming the *Novísima Recopilación*. Moya bases his argument on a *Resolución* of 1768 (Nov. Rec. 5.9.4), not on chapter 42 of the Decree of *Nueva Planta*, which upholds the continuing existence of chapter 40 of the Parliament of 1599. Thus, he admits that 'se de antelacion a las Leyes Municipales o Constitucionales de Cataluña no derogadas según previene la ley 4, lib. 5, tit.5', (preference is given to the unrepealed municipal or constitutional laws of Catalonia, as foreseen in Ley 4, lib. 5, tit.5) but not to the supplementary law.

Catalonia of citing Roman law in preference to those of the Kingdom [of Spain] and on the usefulness or inconvenience which such a practice and custom occasions'. The most important part of this document was the Report on the Local Legislation of Catalonia (November 1819), which was favourable to upholding the practice in question.[41] The proceedings were interrupted thanks to the three-year constitutional period (which began with the Decree of Fernando VII of 7 March 1820, which restored the constitution of 1812, and ended with Fernando's Decree of 1 October 1823, which re-established the absolute power of the monarchy). However, during the so-called liberal three-year period, it was taken as given that the regional laws of Spain were different from the law of Castile.[42]

During the new period of absolute power (which ended with the death of Fernando VII on 2 September 1833) the question of supplementary law was raised again, this time in relation to the so-called *guerra dels malcontents* (1827), in reference to the ultra-royalist Catalan followers of Fernando VII who considered him to be under the influence of the liberals. One of the causes of the war was judicial malpractice in Catalonia, and this, in turn, was caused by confusion over the sources of law.[43] During his stay in Barcelona in 1827, the king nominated a 'Consultative Board'. One of its members was the almost ninety-year-old Chancellor of the University of Cervera, Ramon Llàtzer de Dou. Dou produced a report in favour of the maintenance of canon and Roman law; however, the proposals by the members of the Board were not unanimous and the question remained unresolved once again.[44]

---

[41] Published in (1881) *Revista de Derecho y del Notariado* 19. The recommendation is that 'it must become an indisputable maxim . . . that the preservation of the uses and customs, of practices and provisions received by a people or province is both necessary and useful . . . from which can be deduced the usefulness of preserving in Catalonia the customs and practices which are firmly founded and consolidated on the common law'.

[42] 'Discurso Preliminar' for the frustrated Civil Code draft (of 14 October 1821): 'Without going far into Spain's past, its different provinces present a very varied picture, amidst the unity of its political principles: Navarre, the provinces of the Basque Country, Aragon, Catalonia, the Balearic Islands are different from the two Castiles in this particular, much more so than in their climate or produce' (see Juan Francisco Lasso Gaite, *Crónica de la Codificación civil española*, vol. IV, part 2 (Madrid, 1970), p. 24).

[43] On the complaints about the administration of justice in Catalonia, see the documents collected together by the Seminario de Historia Moderna in *Los agraviados de Cataluña* (Pamplona, 1972).

[44] On the *Junta*, see Seminario de Historia Moderna, *Los agraviados de Cataluña*, vol. III, pp. 319 and 331. The 'Informe sobre la observancia de las Constituciones Municipales de Cataluña' by Dou was published in the aforementioned *Revista de Derecho y del Notariado* 3, pp. 60 ff. Dou

After the death of Fernando VII, with the arrival of the liberal regime, it was assumed that Roman law was the supplementary law of Catalonia. There is an example of this in the projected Civil Code of 15 September 1836 and in the case law of the Spanish Supreme Court (the first being in the judgment of 21 May 1845).[45]

> 'Las Provincias y territorios en que subsiste derecho foral, lo conservaran por ahora en toda su integridad, sin que sufra alteración su actual regimen jurídico por la publicación del Código que regirá tan solo como supletorio del que lo sea en cada una de aquellos por sus leyes especiales'[46]

The upholding of supplementary laws was one of the most long-awaited victories of the Spanish civil codification process, and the subsistence of non-Castilian laws, despite the Spanish Civil Code, was a key prerequisite.

The movement towards codification

The movement towards codification gathered pace during the period of Napoleon's domination of Spain, with Fernando VII in France after his renunciation of the Spanish Crown (1808–14), and his subsequent replacement by Joseph I, Napoleon's brother. It began at the time of the *Cortes* called on 1 January 1810 by the *Junta Central suprema gubernativa del Reino* (formed on 25 September 1808 by bringing together representatives of the

focuses on the argument of the Castilian judges who come to Catalonia: 'Siendo corto el número de jueces que han de venir de otras provincias respecto de la población de sus súbditos . . . es mas fácil instruirse ellos con los libros que ya se dice haber en el país que no el que novecientas mil almas que habrá en Cataluña deban mudar sus costumbres y práctica' (p. 63) (As the number of judges having to come from other provinces is small in relation to the population of their subjects . . . it is easier to instruct them with the books which there are said to be in the country [(i.e. Catalonia] than to oblige the nine hundred thousand people living in Catalonia to change their customs and practices).

[45] This affirmation is in the preamble of the Civil Code draft of 1836: 'and thus it is that in Catalonia, where by local law or custom Roman law is still followed in various points of the legislation' (Lasso Gaite, *Crónica de la Codificación civil española*, vol. IV, part 2, p. 112). The verdicts of the Spanish Supreme Court are mentioned in Guillermo M. de Brocà y Montagut and Juan Amell y Llopis, *Instituciones del Derecho civil catalan vigente*, vol. I, 2nd edn (Barcelona 1886), p. 106.

[46] Article 5, *Ley de Bases del Código Civil* of 11 May 1888 (In the provinces and territories in which there are still in force regional laws, these will be preserved in their entirety, without the publication of the Code, which only acts as supplementary legislation to those special laws in each of those territories, implying any change to their current legal regime).

various provincial governing bodies as part of the resistance against the French army).

The call to Parliament had been organised by a commission of the *Cortes* known as the *Junta Central* (22 May 1809). A Royal Decree of the same day passed a *Consulta al País* (nationwide consultation) requiring that rulings be produced on how the *Cortes* should be celebrated. The fifth section of the *Consulta* referred to reform of the legal system, which was tantamount to raising the question of a possible unified legal code for the whole of Spain. Thus, for Catalonia, this was not a question of supplementary law, but rather of the continuing existence of Catalan law itself. The answers to the consultation coming from Catalonia ranged from full acceptance of a civil code for the whole of Spain to demands to uphold Catalonia's own laws.[47]

Given that Andalusia was still almost completely under French control, the *Cortes* were held on the island of Leon, off Cadiz, opening on 24 September 1810, and were presided over by Dou y de Bassols. The *Cortes* began by declaring the sessions 'general and extraordinary', and affirmed that 'in them resided the sovereignty of the nation'.

In the session of 9 December 1810, José Espiga y Gadea, representing the *Junta Superior de Cataluña*, requested the formation of five commissions, 'one for the reform of civil legislation, another for criminal legislation, a third for the Treasury system, a fourth for commerce and a fifth for planning education and public instruction'. Thus, there was no mention of codes, and Catalan members of the *Cortes* opposed any regulation on Catalan law.[48]

---

[47] A lengthy extract from the *Consulta*, with extracts also from the answers, is to be found in Artola, *Los orígenes de la España contemporánea*, pp. 125 ff. This transcription is from this source.

  The opinions emanating from Catalonia that were favourable to the single Code are those of the Chapter of the Cathedral of Tortose (p. 274) and of the Marquis of Castellet (p. 445). Those opinions in favour of upholding Catalan law belong to the Chapter of the Cathedral of Tarragona (p. 271), the Chancellor of the University of Cervera, Ramon Lázaro de Dou (p. 420), and Fra José Rius, of Balaguer (p. 432).

  The longest and most important is the opinion already considered above (n. 30) of José Solsona (pp. 571 ff). After describing the differences between Catalan law and Castilian law, he concludes that there needs to be 'a single legal code for all the provinces', adding that this is due to the fact that 'sometimes, the inequality between them is inevitable'. Therefore, he recommends 'passing special statutes for those instances which are peculiar to each province' (p. 585). One similarly eclectic solution is that offered by José Sala (p. 440).

[48] In the session of 5 February 1811, Dou alleges that 'we have our bodies of law neither here, nor in Cadiz'. Felip Aner de Esteve said, with reference to the Civil and Penal Codes: 'I approve of both commissions only if there is an attempt to reform the legislation of Castille; but if it is in order to reform the general legislation of Spain, Your Majesty must nominate a commission for every province, as in each of them the uses are different.' Additionally, the *Exposición* of

The Political Constitution of the Spanish Monarchy (384 articles) was proclaimed on 19 March 1812. In art. 258 the unity of the legal codes was established as a constitutional requisite ('The Civil, Criminal and Commercial codes will be the same throughout the Realm, without prejudicing the distinctions which because of particular circumstances the *Cortes* may draw'). The unity of the legal codes was presented as a requisite based on the principle of equality among the Spanish people (artt. 6–9).[49] It would go on to become a permanent requisite in all the subsequent Spanish constitutions of the nineteenth century: in the constitutions of 1837 (art. 4); of 1845 (art. 4); of 1869 (art. 52); and of 1876 (art. 75); the only exception was the Royal Statute of 1834.

The first three of the five commissions demanded by Espiga were approved in the session of 1 October 1813. On 23 March the designated members included, apart from Espiga, the Catalans, Ramon Utgés, professor at the Universitat de Cervera, and Antonio Tamaro, a lawyer from Barcelona.

Nevertheless, the constitutional demand would have to wait. Fernando VII had recovered the crown from Napoleon on 11 December 1813. In the Decree of 2 February 1814, the *Cortes* demanded that he swear to uphold the constitution (required by art. 173) in return for their recognising him as king. However, Fernando issued a Decree on 4 May 1814 that annulled the constitution and the Decrees of the *Cortes*.

The initiative to codify the law was taken up again during the so-called 'liberal three-year period' (1820–3). In response to the *Pronunciamiento* by Rafael de Riego (1 January 1820), Fernando VII promised to swear to uphold the constitution of 1812 (Decree of 7 March 1820) which he did two days later. On 9 July 1820 the *Cortes* opened, and after a month a commission was nominated to formulate the civil code. This code consisted of a preamble and 476 articles (dated 14 December 1821). Laws other than the law of Castile were downgraded to 'uses and customs' ('there may be some merit in preserving and generalising various uses and customs which are used to

the *Junta* to the *Catalan* representatives who went to the Cortes of Cadiz must not be forgotten (Tarragona, 13 August 1810); see n. 37 above and related text.

[49] Cf. Agustin Argüelles, 'Discurso Preliminar leído en las Cortes al presentar la Comisión de Constitución el proyecto de ella' (in three parts, 17 August 1811, 6 November 1811 and 24 December 1811), in *Colección de Constituciones*, 2nd edn (Madrid, 1836). The 'variations' mentioned in art. 258 do not take into consideration the territory of the peninsula, but are rather 'certain modifications that are of necessity required by the difference of so many climates to be found within the vast bounds of the Spanish Empire and the prodigious variety of its territories and their produce' (p. 163).

govern certain classes of interests in some provinces'). Although the wording of article 258 of the constitution allowed a more flexible interpretation, any territorial variation was rejected, specifically on questions of succession law.[50]

The liberal three-year period, and with it the attempt at producing a civil code, ended with the re-establishment of an absolute regime by the Decree of 1 October 1823 (with French help backed by the Congress of Verona, 10 December 1822).

The decade of absolute monarchy that followed ended with the death of Fernando VII. He was succeeded by his three-year-old daughter, Isabel II, with her mother, Maria Cristina de Bourbon, acting as Regent Queen-Mother.

A newly projected Civil Code was developed by a commission set up by the Minister of 'Grace and Justice'. This commission was not instigated by Parliament but rather by the government. The *Project*, presented on 15 September 1836, had a preamble and 2,458 articles. It was uniformly applicable to all the territories of Spain, whose own laws were degraded to the status of special laws and customs (art. 12: 'Against the laws of this Code cannot be alleged . . . the custom or local law of any region which were observed before the Code's proclamation'; and art. 816 states: 'Any other legal obligations fall before the strength and vigour [of the Code] . . . as may have existed in the divers provinces of Spain as ordinations of their local laws and customs, which are declared valid until the enactment of a Rural Code').[51]

The planned civil code of 5 May 1851

The Decree of 19 August 1843 called for the formation of a 'General Codification Committee', under the auspices of the Ministry of Grace and Justice, to consider purely technical aspects and to coordinate the development of the different bodies of law. It was divided into four sections: for the

---

[50] See Lasso Gaite, *Crónica de la Codificación española*, vol. IV, part 2, pp. 8 ff. The sections in quotation marks are from Argüelles, 'Discurso Preliminar' (pp. 14 and 24). The history of the 1821 draft is in Lasso Gaite, *Crónica de la Codificación españo la*, vol. IV, part 1, pp. 62 ff.

[51] Lasso Gaite, *Crónica de la Codificación española*, vol. IV, part 2, pp. 130 and 198. Shortly before his death, Fernando VII charged Manuel Maria Cambronero with writing a civil code (by Royal Decree of 9 May 1833), which was interrupted by the author's death (cf. ibid., vol. IV, part 1, pp. 98 ff. and 4–2, pp. 73 ff).

civil and criminal codes and the respective judicial procedures. Six 'general bases' were given (20 September 1843). Of these, the one referring to the constitutional demand for a unified civil code is of some interest (base 2: 'the Codes will not recognise any special local law'), as it operated at the expense of laws other than the law of Castile (base 4: 'The Civil Code will embrace those provisions considered convenient so that in being applied in those provinces which have their own special legislation neither are acquired rights harmed, nor even such hopes as have been created by those same legislations').

Fifty-three specific Basic Principles were also established (7 March 1844). Of those, some acted against certain deeply rooted institutions within Catalan law. The most important was the generalisation of the Castilian concept of forced heirship of descendants (base 35) which was extensive (four-fifths of the sum of the *relictum* and *donatum*) and which favoured the uneconomical division of the inheritance between all the children. In contrast, the compulsory share, according to Catalan law, was limited to a quarter of the estate (as in Inst. II, 18, 6), which allowed family farms to remain in the hands of a single heir, thereby maintaining their economic viability. Base 47 suppressed the concept of lesion 'ultradimidium' and base 20 limited parental power 'post mortem' in making the family council compulsory.[52]

The result was a draft (sent to the Minister of Grace and Justice on 5 May 1851) which was unifying, in favour of the law of Castile.[53] It provoked the opposition of Catalan lawyers because of those regulations that they

---

[52] On the creation of the Comisión General de Codificación and the specific bases of the Civil Code, see ibid., vol. IV, part 1, pp. 152 and 157. The general bases are in José Antonio Elías, *Derecho civil general y foral de España*, vol. I (Madrid and Barcelona, 1875), p. xcvi.

Forming part of the Commission was a Catalan lawyer based in Madrid, Domingo Maria Vila, who pointed out to the Commission the dangers of a single code for the 'various important provinces of Spain, which are today prosperous and flourishing in the shadow of their protecting law'. The fragment is in Lasso Gaite, *Crónica de la Codificación española*, vol. IV, part 1, p. 155. Vila's intervention dates from 20 September 1843 and was published in the journal *El Faro Nacional* (Madrid 1852), pp. 401 ff.

[53] The Royal Order of 11 June 1851, sent to the Commission, stated in its second point: 'The existence of local laws and special legislations, uses and varying and complex customs in what are not only certain specific territories of the Crown, but were formerly independent States... considerably increases the difficulties and obstacles in publishing and putting into practice a general Code.' The third point insists on the protection of acquired rights of those people likely to suffer the extinction of their own 'provincial or local legislation'.

On the will to get rid of non-Castilian legal codes, see art. 1237 (the same as art. 1390 of the French Civil Code): 'A husband and wife cannot agree in a general way that their properties

considered uneconomical. Their protests centred on the aforementioned application of the Castilian concept of forced heirship (art. 642) as well as the suppression of emphyteusis (artt. 1547 and 1563 under the influence of the French Civil Code). The latter was unanimously considered the best means of exploiting the land by allowing non-owners access to it, and the reason that a poor country such as Catalonia was much more developed agriculturally than Castile.[54]

This opposition had been foreseen in the Royal Order of 11 June 1851 which announced the so-called 'period of statutes' (point 3: 'without prejudicing the Government's presenting to the *Cortes*, of course, such opportune drafts regarding certain subjects of well-known convenience or regarding such as offer no grave obstacles or difficulties in their general application').

In the first period, the most important of these special statutes were the Ley Hipotecaria (dealing with mortgages and the Land Registry, of 8 February 1861, amended in 1869) and the Notary Act (28 May 1862, which is still in force). The second period began with the so-called 'September Revolution' and the disenthronement of Isabel II (30 September 1868), and was the period in which the Acts of the Civil Register (17 June 1870) and of Civil Marriage (18 June 1870) were passed.

The subsistence 'for the time being' of law other than the law of Castile

This was an idea proposed at the Congress of Lawyers in Madrid (27–31 October 1863). Question one was as follows: 'At what moment in the life of a people should codification take place? What are the presiding principles of a codification process?' Conclusion five stated on the unity of codes: 'This unity must be verified by avoiding the extreme of allowing one legislative code to prevail over all those others which are in force within Spain, and by taking, according to rational criteria, that which is most acceptable from each of those codes.' Conclusion six proposed 'to locate beside the general provisions, other special ones which allow for a freedom to pursue the ancient laws of each province on specific issues'. Possible examples of this

should be governed by local laws or customs which until the present have been in force in different provinces or counties of the Kingdom' (cf. also artt. 1263 and 1264).

[54] The protests of Catalan lawyers are summarised in Ferran Badosa Coll (coord.), *Compendi de Dret Civil català* (Madrid and Barcelona, 1999), p. 36. For much more detail, see Pablo Salvador Coderch, 'El Proyecto de Código Civil de 1851 y el Derecho Civil Catalán', in Pablo Salvador Coderch, *La Compilación y su Historia* (Barcelona, 1986), pp. 10 ff.

variety were, according to conclusion seven: 'the dowry system, the system of property during marriage, and the law of succession'.[55]

It was accepted in the Royal Decree of 2 February 1880. It reduced those laws other than that of Castile to 'principles and institutions of local law' which 'must be included in the General Code as exceptions'. Catalonia, Aragon, Navarre, the provinces of the Basque country, Galicia and the Balearic islands were all officially considered territories with their own civil law. As previously mentioned, Catalonia, Aragon and the Balearic islands had been defeated during the War of the Spanish Succession (1705–14). Nevertheless, Philip V had re-established their legislative systems. Valencia had also been defeated, but did not recover its law by the Decree of 7 September 1707. Navarre and the Basque country upheld their law in the statute of 25 October 1839, as a consequence of the Treaty of Vergara (31 August 1839), which ended the First Carlist War. The law of Galicia was recognised because it was the homeland of the Minister.

The legislative translation of the Royal Decree of 1 February 1880 was the Project for the *Ley de Bases* for the Civil Code, presented on 9 September 1881 by the liberal Minister of Grace and Justice, Manuel Alonso Martinez. It foresaw the inclusion into the Civil Code of those *'foral* institutions' that were susceptible to becoming 'general laws' (base 17). In order for it to be accepted by the Catalan lawyers, emphyteusis was re-established (base 11) and the descendants' compulsory share was reduced (base 12). But, above all, it established that 'in those provinces with their own laws, for the time being and until a special bill is presented, those well-established traditions will be preserved'.[56]

In his draft of the *Ley de Bases*, presented before the members of Congress on 7 January 1885, the conservative Minister of Grace and Justice, Francisco Silvela, planned a civil code which was exclusively based on the law of Castile. The law of Castile was the only law to be codified (bases 1, 9, 11 and 12), and also the only one to be repealed (base 27). The inclusion of institutions belonging to laws other than the Castilian into the Civil Code was limited to servitudes (base 12). In general, however, it established that in 'those provinces and territories where a *foral* law exists', its sources which constitute the current body of law 'will remain active for the time being',

---

[55] There is a summary in 23 *Revista General de Legislación y Jurisprudencia* 273.
[56] The 1881 draft was published in Lasso Gaite, *Crónica de la Codificación española*, vol. IV, part 1, pp. 386 ff.

including the supplementary Roman and canon law. It was foreseen that in the future 'Appendices to the Civil Code' would be drafted, containing those 'local institutions which may be conveniently retained' (art. 6).[57]

Alonso Martínez, after becoming Minister a second time, took on this project in the Act of 11 May 1888 'by which the Government is authorised to publish a Civil Code, according to the conditions and bases' that the Act enshrined. On that basis, the current Spanish Civil Code was published (by Royal Decree of 6 October 1888, later modified by Royal Decree of 24 July 1889). Its fifth base stated that the Preliminary Title of the código civil and the duality – canonical and civil – of forms of marriage were obligatory for the whole of Spain.

Laws other than that of Castille were upheld provisionally, 'for the time being' (art. 6, Ley de Bases of 1888 and art. 12.2, código civil). However, this expression would take almost eighty years to disappear, thanks to the modification to the preliminary title of the código civil (Decree of 31 May 1974) when 'for the time being' was removed from article 13 (which substituted the repealed art. 12).

The government of Catalonia 'will hasten its labours... in order for the Legal Assessment Commission to make available the Projected text so that the Civil Code of Catalonia may be passed by this parliament'[58]

Appending Catalan law to the Civil Code

The appending of Catalan civil law never happened, despite several attempts to do so. The first one was the very important Memorandum on the Institutions of the Civil Law of Catalonia by Manuel Duran y Bas (1882), an attempt to respond to the demands of the Royal Decree of 2 February 1882. Duran's document set forth a fundamental idea for later Catalan legislation: the *juris continuatio*, in other words, the concept that a new law does not repeal the previous law (art. 2 which establishes the subsistence of ch. 40 of the Parliament of 1599).[59]

---

[57] The 1885 draft was published in ibid., vol. IV, part 1, pp. 427 ff.

[58] Joan Lluhí i Vallescà, Prime Minister of the *Generalitat* of Catalonia, speech in the Catalan Parliament, 20 December 1932.

[59] Manuel Duran y Bas, *Memoria acerca de las instituciones del Derecho civil de Cataluña, escrita con arreglo a lo dispuesto en el artículo 1 del Real Decreto de 2 de febrero de 1880* (Barcelona, 1883; repr. 1995). On upholding the supplementary character of the *ius commune* and its consequences for Catalan law, see pp. xxxiv and lxv.

The appendix was not even carried out when Duran y Bas became Minister of Grace and Justice in 1899, even though he set up 'Special commissions for the formation and revision of Projected legislation containing regional institutions' within the 'General Codification Committee' (Royal Decree, 17 May 1899). After the Civil Code there only existed officially a 'Draft for Appending Catalan Law to the Civil Code' (1930, reformed in Madrid in 1931, once the Second Republic was established). Also, four private members' drafts were brought forth (1896, 1902 and 1915).

Nineteenth-century opposition to the codification process had its roots in the ideology of the historical school of law and its rejection of codification. This influence is clear in the setting up in Barcelona of a 'Spanish Committee' linked to the Savigny Foundation of Berlin, under the honorary presidency of Pere Nolasc Vives i Cebrià, although Duran y Bas was effectively its leader. It was this Committee that requested a change in the statutes of the Foundation (12 September 1871) so that studies written in Spanish might be accepted.[60]

In his *Memoria*, Duran brought the ideas of the historical school to the Spanish civil codification, as he considered that Spain had not yet reached the moment for codifying its civil law because, while there was 'political unity', there was no 'social unity'. A second reason for Duran's rejection of the opportunity was that he considered that 'we have no national school of law'.[61]

---

[60] On 'ein Spanisches Savigny-Comite' founded at the College of Lawyers of Barcelona on 11 July 1869, see Karl Georg Bruns, 'Die Savigny Stiftung', (1880) 1 *ZSS* 6 (1) (I am grateful to Prof. Dr José M. Miquel, Professor of Civil Law at the Universidad Autónoma de Madrid, for finding this reference).

In a letter of 12 September 1871, the Barcelona Committee requested the modification of art. 16 of the statutes of the Savigny Foundation, to include Spanish among the '*Kultursprachen*'. In its reply of 29 December 1871, the Foundation set out the difficulties this entailed, as modification of the statutes required the approval of the Science Academies of Berlin, Munich and Vienna as well as the authorisation of the Kaiser. Nevertheless, the *Curatorium* of the Foundation admitted papers and *Konkurrenzschriften* in Spanish, although the latter would have to be accompanied by a translation into one of the official languages which were Latin, German, English, French and Italian.

There was still no answer in 1880. However, a communication from the German Consul in Barcelona, Richard Lindau, on 12 July 1877, stated that the Spanish Committee under the presidency 'des Professors Durand' continued to work without interruption 'in erfreulicher Weise'.

[61] Quoted from Duran, *Memoria*, pp. xxiv and xlv.

An evaluation on the state of the legal sciences in Spain in relation to the 'Tratado elementar del Derecho Civil Romano y Español' by the Catalan Professor Ramon Martí d'Eixalá (Barcelona, 1838) is to be found in the critical study by Gustav Hanel, 'Ueber römisches Civilrecht in Spanien', (1847) 19 *Kritische Zeitschrift für Rechtswissenschaft und Gesetzgebung des Auslandes* 16. After

Apart from the appendix required by the Civil Code (art. 6, *Ley de Bases* of 11 May 1888) the codification of Catalan civil law bore a heavy political burden. Given the lack of Catalan political power, it was thought that legislation on Catalan civil law should not be left in the hands of non-Catalans.[62]

So much is clear from the formation of the *Mancomunitat* of Catalonia by Royal Decree on 18 December 1913. Despite being ostensibly an administrative body, formed by bringing together representatives of the four Catalan provinces, it was required to exercise legislative powers in civil law.[63] The Assembly of 26 May 1918 declared that the new *Codex Iuris Canonici* proclaimed by Benedict XV (27 May 1918) was not to be equated to the *ius commune* in Catalonia.[64] On 28 May 1918, the Assembly charged the Permanent Council with fixing 'those legal provisions which together make up the Catalan body of law, codifying them either in parts by institutions, or in their totality'.[65]

The Statute of Autonomy Bill passed by the Assembly of Catalan City Halls on 26 January 1919 demanded that the civil law fall within the competence of the 'regional power'. An Autonomy Bill developed in Madrid by an 'extraparliamentary commission' (21 January 1919) made mention for the first time of a *Generalitat de Catalunya*, also with competence in civil law.[66]

Political power also included judicial power. The *Tribunal Supremo* was the Supreme Court for the whole of Spain, even when Catalan law was

---

giving a detailed description of the work, the conclusion (p. 41) is that it is a work of purely local interest and of no interest at all in Germany. Hanel accuses Martí of making no use of foreign law or of legal history.

[62] The Royal Decree of 2 February 1880 provoked the celebration of the Primer Congrés Catalanista (9 October–14 November 1880), one of the topics of which was opposition to the single Civil Code. Once the Civil Code was enacted, the Unió Catalanista (founded 15 March 1891) held a congress at Manresa where the 'Bases per a la Constitució regional catalana' (March 1893) were passed. The Seventh Basic Principle gave the Catalan Parliament power over 'civil, criminal, mercantile, administrative and procedural legislation'.

[63] The autonomy movement in Catalonia was encouraged by the fourteen points of American President Woodrow Wilson (8 January 1918), which proclaimed the principle of nationalities.

[64] See this text in (1921) *RJC* 489. There is an extract in Leopold Perels, 'Das rezipierte kanonische Recht und der Codex iuris canonici in Katalonien', (1920) 41 *ZSS (KA)* 291.

[65] Mancomunitat de Catalunya-Oficina d'Estudis Jurídics, *El Dret Català i la Codificació* (Barcelona, 1919), p. 8.

[66] The statute draft, passed 26 January 1919, established a double list for attributing legislative powers to the Spanish state or to Catalan political legislative power. The criterion for this distribution was the duality of functions divided along 'legislative' and 'executive' lines (artt. 6 and 8). It is the same division used in artt. 10 and 11 of the new constitution of Austria (1 September 1920).

applicable. Its decisions were openly centralist in that they favoured the extension of the Civil Code to all those territories of Spain with their own laws, by excluding the supplementary application of the *ius commune* to the benefit of the Civil Code.[67] There was an outburst of protest in Catalonia against three decisions by the Supreme Court, which applied the Civil Code on the question of inheritance when this was already regulated by regional laws. These occurred in December 1918, on the 10th (on behalf of Catalan law) and twice on the 13th (on behalf of the laws of Aragon and of Majorca). In the Catalan case, the Supreme Court was unaware of a regional precept on the special succession of impuberates (CYADC I.6.2.2). This provoked the Academy of Law and Jurisprudence of Barcelona (1920) into asking that 'the territory of Catalonia be removed from the jurisdiction of a court which offers the people of Catalonia neither protection nor guarantees'.[68]

These attempts came to nothing as a result of the dictatorship of General Miguel Primo de Rivera (1923–9). In the last year of the reign of Alfonso XIII the aforementioned plan for appending Catalan law to the Civil Code (1930) was sent to Madrid. In it, the idea of the *iuris continuatio* was affirmed (artt. 3 and 4) which upheld the Chapter of 1599 in order to resolve the contradictions between the appendix and the Civil Code and as criteria for its construction.

The Statutes of Autonomy

The Second Spanish Republic was declared on 14 April 1931. Its constitution (9 December 1931) anticipated the 'autonomy' of those 'regions' that wished to establish themselves as such (art. 8). It recognised their legislative power on questions of civil law, while reserving four areas for the state (art. 15.1, which inspired art. 149.1.8 of the current constitution). With the Decree of 21 April 1931, the provisional Republican government reinstated the

---

[67] On the unifying character of the *Tribunal Supremo* case law, see Guillermo M. de Brocà, *Historia del Derecho de Cataluña especialmente del civil y Exposición de las instituciones del Derecho civil del mismo territorio con el Código Civil de España y la Jurisprudencia* (Barcelona, 1918; repr. 1985), pp. 489–98.

[68] The Academy's protest ((1921) *RJC* 115) was taken to the Spanish Parliament by the representative of the Lliga Regionalista (Regional League) Josep M. Trías de Bes in the form of a proposed Act of 15 April 1920, with the aim that the Spanish government 'adopt urgently and propose as soon as necessary the measures that it considers essential in order to avoid that legal practice diminish or alter the regime of regional laws which may be modified by the legislative power alone, reserved by the constitution for the *Cortes* and the King'.

Generalitat, which had been abolished in the Decree of *Nueva Planta* of 1716. During a ten-day period in June 1931 a commission wrote up the statute (known as the Statute of Núria). On 2 August it was put to the people and it was definitively enacted by the *Generalitat* in the Decree of 11 August 1931. On questions of civil law, art. 11 only reserved 'the legal forms of marriage and the ordination of the Civil Register' to be legislated by the state.

As the statute had anticipated the Republic's own constitution, it was presented before the *Cortes Contituyentes*, on 14 August 1931. The debate on it began on 6 May 1932 and it was passed, in a much more limited form than the original text, on 9 September 1932. With respect to the application of the Spanish Civil Code in Catalonia, the new legislation regained the old concept of 'ownership': Catalan law as the law of Catalonia (artt. 11, 9). The Catalan language was also established explicitly as the language of Catalonia in art. 3, Act of 26 May 1933, Internal Statute of Catalonia.

The *Generalitat* exercised full legislative power over civil law, leaving aside the enactment of an appendix to the Spanish Civil Code. Thus it legislated by means of statutes, such as the Majority and Emancipation Act, the Rent Charges Act or the Intestacy Act.[69]

After the Spanish Civil War (1936–9), the autonomy of Catalonia was abolished by General Franco (Act of 4 April 1938), as was the autonomy of the Basque country, and the legislation of the *Generalitat* was repealed (Act of 8 September 1939).

The idea of the appendices to the Civil Code was brought back, though substituting it for the broader concept of providing compilations of regional laws, as a step towards their 'definitive regulation and ordination' as part of a projected 'General Code of Spain' (Decree of 23 May 1947).

In the preliminary attempts at a Catalan compilation (in 1953, 1955 and 1956) the idea of *juris continuatio* was retained. The Compilation was defined as a mere 'Recasting of the Current Law of Catalonia'. The old sources of law would be used as a means of interpretation and to fill in any legal gap, along the lines of the constitution of 1599. This attempt was frustrated by the General Codification Commission which reduced the transcription of the 1599 constitution to a vague description as 'Catalan legal tradition,

---

[69] The statutes passed by the *Generalitat* during the Republic, as well as the decisions of the Court of Cassation of Catalonia (Act of 10 March 1934), have been published in Maria-Encarna Roca Trias, *El Dret civil Català en la Jurisprudència, Vol. IV. Anys 1934–1937* (Barcelona, 1974).

embodied in its ancient laws, customs and doctrine', to be used only for interpretation purposes, and not to fill in any legal gap (art. 1.2, *Compilation of the Special Civil Law of Catalonia* of 21 July 1960). *Juris continuatio* was reduced to a verbal resource: the Compilation did not repeal but rather was a 'substitute' for the previous law (First Final Provision). Yet, in reality, the *ius commune* was repealed as supplementary law, with its place being taken by the Civil Code (art. 1.1 and First Final Provision CDCC). If anything was to remain of the *ius commune* it would be in the opinions of Catalan scholars who had always based their works on it.

With the reinstatement of the monarchy on the death of General Franco in 1975, the Act of 29 November 1977 repealed the Act of 5 April 1938, and thus re-established the *Generalitat de Catalunya*. The new constitution of 1978 once again gave autonomous status to all those regions that wanted it (art. 137). Nevertheless, art. 149.1.8 only gave competence on private law to those regions where a different civil law was in force. Six areas of the civil law were considered as exclusive competence of the state, along the lines of art. 15 of the Republican constitution.

The new Statute of Autonomy of Catalonia (Act of 18 December 1979) gave legislative power on private law to the *Generalitat* (art. 9.2). The Compilation passed from being state law to Catalan law (Act of 20 March 1984). Catalan law ceased being a collection of isolated institutions to become a true system of law (artt. 1, 2 and Fourth Final Provision CDCC).

In view of the increase in Catalan law through statutes and sectorial codes, such as the Code of Succession (1991) and the Family Code (1998), the question of which is the supplementary law, whether the *ius commune* or the Spanish Civil Code, becomes less vexed. Nevertheless, it is important to draw a distinction between the two laws currently in force in Catalonia. Only Catalan law is Catalonia's *own* law, according to art. 26.2 of the Statute of Autonomy, just as Catalan is Catalonia's *own* language, according to art. 3.1 of the same.

7

The codification of Catalan civil law

NÚRIA DE GISPERT I CATALÀ

Introduction

To examine the present position of civil law in Catalonia, and to compare it with the position of civil law in nations that show similarities with Catalonia, is a task that we consider to be of importance, in so far as an idea that must inspire – effectively inspire – the action of the government of Catalonia is understanding the civil law of Catalonia both as a feature that shapes the Catalan national identity, and also as a tool of social progress.

With respect to civil law as a feature that shapes our national identity, it should be remembered that, as stated by the Commission concerned with the review of the Compilation, at the beginning of the 1980s, 'Civil Law represented, together with the language, one of the most important cultural products of the Catalan people, one of the principal exponents of their identity as a people, and therefore one of the essential reference points in identifying Catalonia as a product of a specific historical process'. We cannot – nor do we – view the cultivation and promotion of Catalonia's own legal system and language as an element of confrontation, but as a factor conducive to personal and collective coexistence and enrichment.

As for civil law considered as a tool of social progress, it should be borne in mind that the legal system, which shapes and indeed consolidates social relations, seeks to put forward peaceful and appropriate solutions to the conflicts that arise in every type of community. In this respect, we must promote – as we are promoting – legislation, in so far as society accepts and demands specific regulations or formulae, and we must be able to offer society technically viable solutions born of calm reflection and analysis, solutions that are at all times open in character and adapted to new times, with new demands and new challenges.

The development of the Catalan civil law

Much has been achieved in the last two decades since the recovery of self-government in Catalonia. And it is worth making brief reference to the Spanish constitution of 1978, which has permitted and promoted a collective course of development in democracy on two fronts: through the effective recognition of fundamental rights and the autonomous state, which represents a project – perhaps incomplete, but heading in the right direction – of decentralisation and recognition of the national plurality of the Spanish state.

As far as the civil law of Catalonia is concerned, to all effects the constitution of 1978 and the Statute of Autonomy of Catalonia of 1979 consecrated a plurilegislative conception of the state and of respect for the rights of those peoples such as the Catalan that had, and have, their own civil laws. Thus the idea of schedules and compilations was abandoned, and, in the case of Catalonia, there was an urgent need to tackle the process of adjustment to the constitutional principles of the Compilation of Catalan Civil Law, passed in 1960 at the height of the Franco era, and with all its conditioning features. This first process, which was completed in 1984, was succeeded by a subsequent phase of updating our legal system, which is where we find ourselves today.

And it must be said that, at all events, the action taken by the Catalan government has reflected an aim of making the Catalan legal system not only an element of national construction, but a system that can harmoniously combine modernity and identity, clearly opting for social progress and the reinforcement of links within our European context.

This justifies the attention devoted in recent years to the development of our civil law, in deployment of the provisions of art. 9.2 of our Statute of Autonomy. The twenty-nine civil laws passed by the Catalan Parliament in the last two decades are powerful evidence of this.

I will highlight three of these, due to their importance from the point of view of the action taken by the government (by dint of their content and their social impact), and in terms of the development of the civil law of Catalonia, in so far as they have notably enriched our collective legal heritage.

Firstly, Act 40/1991 of 30 December concerning the Code of Succession by reason of death in Catalan civil law. It aims 'to show particular respect towards classical principles and recent legal tradition', and therefore preserves the important principles of Roman law, so established in Catalan succession law, such as the need for an heir in succession, the universality of the title of heir, the incompatibility of successory titles, the prevalence of the voluntary title (while respecting, however, the principle of priority of pacted succession over testamentary succession), and the perdurability of the successory title.

Secondly, Act 9/1998 of 15 July concerning the Family Code. Its guiding principles are the protection of the family (considered at all times as the prime social unit and a basic and central institution at the heart of our society), *favor filii* and the autonomy of will in recognition of individual personality and civil liberty, while maintaining respect for local rights, which establish special economic regimes arising out of a matrimonial relationship for some *comarques* (administrative districts) of Catalonia.

And finally, Act 10/98 of 15 July concerning stable relationships between couples, a pioneering law within the cultural context of Latin countries in Europe, which provides a legal response to an emerging social reality: that of both heterosexual and homosexual de facto couples.

Our aim to codify

In the context of the legislative development of Catalan civil law, what is the role played by our aim to codify?

Bearing in mind that codification is the legislative process pursued from the nineteenth century by legal ordination in developed countries that are masters of their own destiny, it must be said that the craft of codification has never lacked antecedents or tradition in Catalonia. And that if the Decree of the New Plan imposed by Philip V, with the abolition of our courts, had not destroyed the material sources of Catalan law in 1716, our legal system would now be completely standardised, and therefore codified.

The International Congress on Comparative Law held in Brussels in 1964 demonstrated a general trend towards codification. And between 1949 and 1985, thirty-seven codes appeared – one code every year. Catalonia would not have been an exception here.

We might recall *els Usatges* (Usages), the first European feudal code, begun in the mid-eleventh century; or the book of the *Costums de Tortosa* (Customs of Tortosa) of 1279, which even by today's standards constitutes a genuine code; or, to provide just one more example, *el Llibre del consolat de mar* from the fourteenth century, a maritime code applied to the entire Mediterranean.

The desire for codification has reappeared and been most evident during the periods when Catalonia has enjoyed a certain degree of freedom.

We are now in a position to overcome this historical servitude and to make up for the time lost in these last three centuries of fossilisation through a codifying project – already begun – which is planned to culminate in the short term in a single civil code of Catalonia, in which the two codes already passed (on succession and on family) and the one that is planned (on patrimonial law) will become fundamental books, bound together by a preliminary title that includes a new regulation of the system of sources of Catalan law and personal law. The First Act of the civil code of Catalonia (Act 29/2002) was enacted on 30 December 2002.

The intention here, as it has been up until now, will be to legislate, in the genuine sense of the verb: that is to say, focus our efforts on the creation of new law and not on the establishment, preservation and mere amendment of pre-existing law.

Codifying policies are often accompanied by an intention to absorb and to standardise, and, in this context, the code appears as an emanation of public power that imposes the future order. An example of this manner of proceeding would be the Napoleonic Code.

In Spain, the codification movement also began with a marked tendency towards standardisation, with the expression 'the same Codes for the entire monarchy', and it ended in the promulgation of a Civil Code that was Napoleonic and centralist in character.

In Catalonia, the legislative style has always been a different one (characteristic of a democratic nation): the law has been understood as the legal expression of the way that the nation goes about its business. In the words of an eminent Catalan jurist: 'Law is not created, it is only discovered.'

The two applicable codes fully correspond to this conception of law, which, despite introducing all those innovative measures demanded by the Catalan society of today, has showed respect towards the classical principles of our law on inheritance and the family.

In producing the civil code of Catalonia, efforts will be made to fully achieve the essence of the craft of codification, which seeks unity (and not uniformity, so alien to our ideological and national focus), completeness and systematisation, in developing in a single code all the regulations of civil law that need to be established and can be established, and which are duly classified and coordinated. Simplification in the application of the law and legal certainty will surely be two prime benefits here.

This point clearly highlights the purpose, the need and the expediency of the codification that we are undertaking, as we move into the new century. It is a codification that we vindicate and consider to be technically viable and desirable.

The effective codification of Catalan civil law must be understood as a symbol, as a milestone and as a tool of progress. Above all, it is a clear indication of legal normality, which Catalonia has claimed and deserved.

Towards a Catalan civil code

In 2000 we commenced the work that needs to be undertaken in order to draw up what we consider to be a priority task: the code of patrimonial law, or to be more exact, the code of property law and contract law, by means of special laws that will update some of the institutions established in the codification, regulate others by connection, and propose the possible regulation of various atypical contracts.

In this respect, two Bills (one on usufruct, use and habitation; the other on periodical pensions) have already been presented to the Parliament of Catalonia.

Furthermore, at the beginning of the 1990s, four Acts concerning property were passed: the Act of Annual Pensions (Act 6/1990); the Act of Negatory Action, Immissions, Servitudes and Neighbourhood Rights (Act 13/1990); the Act of Possessorial Guarantees on Movable Goods (Act 22/1991); and the Act modifying the Codification of Civil Law of Catalonia in respect of sale with a letter of respite (Act 29/1991).

At this point, I would like to emphasise a reflection that I consider to be particularly relevant: at present, we are in a position to make a qualitative leap, which coincides symbolically with the turn of the century. This qualitative leap must permit us to attain a state of legal normality, as a culmination of the process of standardisation of our own legal system. That process has entailed, and continues to entail, overseeing the adaptation of Catalan civil law to constitutional principles, aspiring to make this law complete and seeking to update it.

As the jurist Ramon M. Coll i Rodés foresaw as long ago as 1931, 'with stabilisation immediately defined, the second stage of definitive reconstitution will commence, since legal life in Catalonia would not be fully restored until we have completed the future Civil Code of Catalonia'.

Now that the efforts have been made to do what was necessary and we have attained many important goals, we are in a position to embark on a second stage from a position of strength, in which we may give priority to what is expedient.

I shall now present some lines of action that will surely make a decisive contribution to the legal normality that we seek, and which lies within our reach, if, all together, we are able to combine political will, dedication and sensible decisions.

Firstly, there is the Observatory of Private Law in Catalonia, which we have created to provide advice and a response to the growing complexity of legal relationships governed by private law, monitoring private legal regulation at autonomous, state and European community level. Family law, succession law, property law and civil law of procedure will be considered from Catalonia and with a Catalan focus.

But we have gone one step further. Therefore, secondly, within the Observatory of Private Law, we have created the 'Codifying Commission', which is intended to be permanent, with a dual purpose: to revise legal texts and shape the civil code of Catalonia. Lawyers, who for a long time have been the conscience of Catalan law, will now play a fundamental role in its development. Therefore, we will need a Catalan legal doctrine that is solid, receptive and militant. This will not lead to the relaxation of exigency and rigour, but on the contrary, to the reinforcement of these qualities.

At the beginning of the twenty-first century, I am convinced that the Catalan codification movement must represent an effort to attain normality and to affirm ourselves as a nation, while, of course, maintaining a direct link with modernity.

It should be pointed out that the civil code of Catalonia will not only be a compiled text, but also a fundamental landmark in a highly ambitious project: to ensure that national normality is also brought to the field of private law in Catalonia. And this will take place, in so far as the civil code of Catalonia becomes an exponent of different, European and solid law.

Indeed, we seek a different legal process, because the political circumstances and the state of evolution of Catalan civil law enable us to overcome the obsession with the Spanish Civil Code and its specific legal solutions.

However, our fundamental challenge, which we all have to face with resolve, is to ensure that our legislative authorities meet social demands and expectations.

We also want a European legal system, one that is decidedly outward-looking, without limitations or complexes, and a system that is solid, in so far as it may become a useful tool for social development, offering stability and validity.

Two temptations will, of course, have to be avoided: that of making Catalonia the anthropological reserve of private law, and that of making it the ideal test-tube in the hands of doctrine, in which new and audacious formulae may be tested.

In this respect, it will be advisable to adopt a judicious intermediate position. Without abandoning the construction of a leading society that is linked with modernity and open to innovation, we must be very aware that the legal system is dependent on the society of a particular time, and not the other way round, and that civil law must therefore follow closely behind society, while respecting the classical principles of our legal process.

On the basis of all these considerations, we may conclude that it is necessary to build a legal system that is impregnated with society, of which it must be sufficiently aware. Therefore, it is important that public authorities, doctrine and legal players seek to spread knowledge of our historical legal system, and even more importantly, of the present position of Catalan law.

Thus it is appropriate to stimulate a participatory legal system, one that is rich in participation, in which doctrine will play a fundamental role. This is not only because the abundant debate that will be aroused will provide the political class with tools to develop Catalan law in a calm, solid and uninhibited manner, but also, and essentially, because the involvement of everyone and the achievement of a social consensus are necessary, in order to move forward with our self-government in a field that is a very sensitive one for our community, in so far as it affects our identity as a nation and as a people.

I am convinced that the future civil code of Catalonia, which must represent the civil legal system of all the Catalans, is a legal infrastructure that is necessary for the Catalan society of the twenty-first century, which shows itself to be demanding and in need of what we might describe as a 'modern identity'.

Consequently, the civil code of Catalonia becomes a question of society. In the light of these conditions, the Observatory of Private Law in Catalonia and the Codifying Commission must attain the highest standards, in order to guarantee the correct and lasting development of codification.

In short, the civil code of Catalonia will doubtlessly have a great symbolic value. But our aim is not a *coup de théâtre*, or a gesture void of content. We do believe, however, that this is an emblematic project undertaken by our autonomous government that obliges us to act with special care and resolve, while encouraging participation. In fact, the civil code of Catalonia is not, nor can it be, a party or a government project, but rather society's project. It is no exaggeration to view the civil code of Catalonia as the future pillar of Catalonia – a point from which a return is neither possible nor wished for.

We must debate, reflect and act with a clear perspective of the civil code of Catalonia, on the understanding that we do not see it as the final destination of a collective journey, but as a very important milestone in the history and the life of the Catalan people.

Therefore, we wish to produce a civil code of Catalonia that is at once a code of quality, by dint of its legal craft, a potential point of reference in comparative law, and a code appropriate to the social reality of Catalonia, a code that is attuned to Catalan society in the early twenty-first century and to the men and women who wish to play their part as citizens and develop in human terms within a nation that is facing the challenges of a new century.

I would like to end this chapter by expressing my conviction that this is now a positive and hopeful time in Catalonia, not least with respect to justice and the legal system. The new century is replete with challenges, but also opportunities, which we will be able to fully and effectively explore, in so far as we know where we wish to go and how we are to get there.

An eminent Catalan jurist, Ramon Maria Roca i Sastre, described law as 'the greatest poetry of life'. As in poetry, we must strive to harmoniously combine sensitivity and craft in our task of promoting the modernisation of Catalan civil law.

8

Unification of the European law of obligations and codification of Catalan civil law

Scope and terms of comparison

Scope of comparison: the law of obligations

The topic of the present chapter, 'Unification of the European law of obligations and codification of Catalan civil law', has been chosen for several reasons. Firstly, there is the prospect of a future Catalan patrimonial law code, in relation to which the legislative competence of the Catalan Parliament (*Generalitat de Catalunya*) as regards obligations and contracts will still – presumably – arouse controversy. Secondly, there is the growing importance within Community law of regulations devoted specifically to this matter. And finally, there is the conviction that, in the exercise of its legislative competence, the *Generalitat* must not only adapt to social reality and adjust to the 1978 constitution, but also embrace the principles that underpin a Community legal system which, little by little, is consolidating progressively.

Terms of comparison

The expressions 'European law' and 'Catalan civil law' lend themselves to various interpretations, and the first thing is to clarify, right at the outset, their significance.

The expression 'European law' is confined to Community law created by and at the instance of the bodies and institutions of the European Union. In the first instance, this means Community directives; but reference will also be made to the Principles of European Contract Law (PECL), drawn up by the Lando Commission, under the patronage of the Commission of the

European Community, and endorsed by both resolutions of the European Parliament.[1]

For its part, the expression 'Catalan civil law' is used in the sense attributed to it by Professor Badosa Coll: it is limited to the civil law enacted by the *Generalitat* and exclusively enforced in Catalonia, thus distinguishing it from the civil law applicable to Catalonia, which includes state legislation.[2] That is why reference is made only to compiled law[3] and to the regulations enacted by the *Generalitat de Catalunya* as regards obligations and contracts in exercise of their legislative competence, but not to state legislation existing on such matters, even when it is also in force – but not exclusively – in Catalonia and, at times, is also applicable.

However, it is a matter not just of clarifying the significance of the two legal systems – European law and Catalan civil law – juxtaposed, but also of highlighting the different ways they are manifested in regulations: unification, in the case of European law; and codification, with respect to Catalan law. Although reference is thereby made to processes which pursue the same result – to work out a single regulation for a specific sector of the legal system – the starting point is different, as are the procedures used to try and achieve such a result. Unification presupposes the existence of different laws – those of the member countries of the European Union – and is geared to laying down some basic rules or principles which allow the harmonisation of their respective rules. Codification, on the contrary, starts out from the existence of a single, separate body of law, whatever way it is reported in miscellaneous statutes, and tries to reform and systematically embody it in a unitary legal text.

Also, the significance of the process differs in the two legal systems. While unification of European law is not just a process aiming at its formation,

---

[1] The law made up of agreements or treaties signed by the member states of the European Community is not therefore going to be dealt with, although there are within them such important treaties in contract matters as the Treaty of Rome, of 19 June 1980, on the law applicable to contractual obligations (OJEC L 266/1980, of 9 October). The reason is clear: in the context of the unification of Community law, it is worth waiting, before and above all, for the law derived from the exercise of the actual regulatory powers of the Community institutions.

[2] Cf. Ferran Badosa Coll (ed.), *Compendi de dret civil català* (Madrid and Barcelona, 1999), p. 3.

[3] Originally reported in the Compilation of the Special Civil Law of Catalonia, Act 40/1960, of 21 July; Act 13/1984, of 20 March, on the Compilation of Civil Law of Catalonia. The concern was not only to bring it into line with constitutional principles, but also and in particular to incorporate the 1960 regulatory text into the legal system.

codification of Catalan civil law assumes the consolidation of a lengthy process, the final stage of which starts with the granting by the 1978 constitution of exclusive legislative powers in civil matters to the *Generalitat de Catalunya*. However, the processes are likely to be interrelated: although it is true that the codification of Catalan civil law must not ignore the principles that underpin unification of European law, it is also true that, as a consolidated legal system, Catalan law meets the requirements for partaking in such a process of unification and adding criteria and solutions which contribute to strengthening such.

Unification of the European law of obligations

Community bodies and institutions have responded to the requirement to harmonise European law by way of two different procedures. In the first place and preferably, by means of directives geared to harmonising the different laws of the member states of the Union in specific matters, in particular with reference to the ambit of consumer protection law. But a call has also gone out from the European Parliament to the Commission 'for work to be commenced on the possibility of drawing up a Common European Code of Private Law' (Resolution of 26 May 1989, restated by another of 6 May 1994). The PECL fall within this second process.

Sector-based Community directives   In the unification of European law on obligations and contracts, Community institutions have opted preferably for a sectorial harmonisation of different state laws by way of various directives. As is common knowledge, the directive is only binding on individuals as from its transposition into domestic law by national authorities: it imposes on states the obligation to adopt, within the time-limit set by the directive itself, the measures necessary to achieve the result it pursues, but leaving the freedom to such states of 'choice of the form and means' necessary for the purpose (cf. art. 189.3 EC Treaty).

According to this arrangement, the addressees of the directives are the member states of the European Union. However, this claim does not deny the autonomous communities such status as addressees, particularly if their respective statutes contain any provision relating to the 'enforcement' of international treaties and conventions as happens in art. 27.3 EAC (Statute on the Autonomy of Catalonia), and such treaties and conventions refer to matters over which the autonomous community has jurisdiction.[4]

Within the scope of the law of obligations and contracts, Community directives have been limited to a very specific sector: that of consumer protection. In this context, this includes regulations geared to regulating and harmonising national laws relating to liability for defective products;[5] to contracts negotiated away from business premises;[6] to consumer credit;[7] to package travel, package holidays and package tours;[8] to the control of unfair terms in consumer contracts;[9] to contracts relative to purchase of the right to use immoveable properties on a time-share basis;[10] to consumer protection in matters of contracts negotiated at a distance (distance selling);[11] or to specific aspects of the sale of consumer goods and associated guarantees.[12]

One consequence of all of these directives has been the introduction or consolidation of a whole series of changes in the traditional arrangement of the contract. In effect, the 'consumer contract' does not fit the concept of 'contract' as the supreme manifestation of the principle of free will and which assumes a relationship between equals, freely assumed and concluded by way of respective declarations of intent of offer and acceptance. In the contractual relationship between consumer and trader, the dominant position the latter holds is likely to encourage a situation of abuse of power, in particular when the terms of the contract have been previously framed by the trader and the consumer has no option other than to agree and accept it wholesale or reject it. With this in mind, therefore, Community directives

---

[4] On the matter, Alegría Borràs Rodríguez, arts. 27.3 and 5, in *Comentaris l'Estatut d'Autonomia de Catalunya*, vol. III (Barcelona, 1990), pp. 53 ff.; generally, Araceli Mangas Martín and Diego J. Liñan Nogueras, *Instituciones y derecho de la Unión Europea* (Madrid, 1996), p. 554.

[5] Council Directive 374/1985, of 25 July, OJEC L 210/1985, of 7 August.

[6] Council Directive 577/1985, of 20 December, OJEC L 372/1985, of 31 December.

[7] Council Directive 102/1987, of 22 December 1986, OJEC L 42/1987, of 12 February.

[8] Council Directive 314/1990, of 13 June, OJEC L 158/1990, of 23 June.

[9] Council Directive 93/13/EEC, of 5 April, OJEC L/95/1993, of 21 April.

[10] Directive 94/47/EC of the European Parliament and Council, of 26 October, OJEC L280/1994, of 29 October. The Directive does not deal with the legal nature of such 'right to use'; its object is to approximate the regulations of the member states as regards 'contracts relating, directly or indirectly, to the purchase of the right to use one or more immovable properties on a time-share basis' (cf. art. 1).

[11] Directive 97/7/EC of the European Parliament and Council, of 20 May, OJEC L144/1997, of 4 June.

[12] Directive 99/44/EC of the European Parliament and Council, of 25 May, OJEC L171/1999, of 7 July.

are geared to trying to guarantee and maintain a certain relationship of
equivalence between the rights and obligations vested in the contracting
parties.

The *Principles of European Contract Law*   In 1980, a group of lawyers
from different European countries set up, on the initiative of Professor Ole
Lando, and sponsored by the Commission of the European Community, the
'Commission on European Contract Law'.[13] Its objective was to lay down
and formulate some common principles of contract law to make possible
the legal uniformity required by unification of the European market. As a
result of its work, a first digest of such principles was published with the title
Principles of European Contract Law and, in 1998, a second one, revising
and supplementing the previous one.[14] A third part was published in 2003.

Unlike directives, which fundamentally affect a specific sector of contract
law – that of contracts concluded by consumers – the PECL deal with the
contract in the abstract without, however, any enactment being devoted
to specific contract types nor, either, to 'consumer contracts'.[15] And also,
unlike the directives, which – even after the appropriate transposition –
affect and are binding on individuals and constitute applicable law, the
PECL are only binding on them if they themselves agree to incorporate
them into the contract they enter into or they decide expressly to make
it subject to their regulations: their applicability depends on the intention
of the parties who frame the terms of the contract – as voluntary terms,
thus – with their own provisions.

The PECL seek to achieve different objectives. In the first place, to serve as
a basis for a future common European code of private law. Yet they are also
a way forward as a source for modelling possible Community regulations,
as well as of the laws of the different European countries, in the process
of modernising or regulating their contract law.[16] Certainly, they include
those of eastern and central Europe,[17] which need to bring their legislation
into line with the needs of a market economy; and also those that, like

---

[13] For the origins of such Commission, its composition, tribulations and modus operandi, see
Ole Lando and Hugh Beale (eds.), *The Principles of European Contract Law. Parts I and II* (The
Hague, London and Boston, 2000), pp. ix–xiv.
[14] The second version has 9 chapters and 131 articles.
[15] 'They do not deal with any specific types of contract, nor do they make special provision for
consumer contracts' (Lando and Beale (eds.), *Principles of European Contract Law*, p. xxv).
[16] Cf. ibid., pp. xix–xxiv.   [17] Cf. ibid., pp. xix and xxiv.

Catalonia, are still lacking in a unitary and systematic set of regulations in this respect.

Codification of Catalan civil law

The 1889 Spanish Civil Code recognised the 'co-existence of different civil laws' on Spanish territory and sanctioned – albeit on a restrictive basis and provisionally in nature – their subsistence. One of these 'civil laws' was Catalan civil law which, though considered in 1880 as a set of 'customs and traditions converted into laws' (preamble of the Royal Decree of 2 February 1880), has gone on – in just under one century – to make up 'the legal system of Catalonia' (art. 1 CDCC 1984) as a result of a process of 'preservation, reform and development' of the Catalan civil law (art. 149.1.8 CE) and ending up in the enactment of the Code of Civil Law of Catalonia (as stated in the preamble to Act 9/1998, of 15 July, of the Family Code, I, 9).

The coexistence of different legal systems within a single state territory and the tendency to its affirmation and consolidation by maintaining its autonomy is likely to arouse some perplexity in a European context which – as has just been pointed out in the previous paragraph – tends to legislative unity. However, there is no contradiction in this. Codification of Catalan civil law is coterminous with its very existence and development and, in any event, does not negate fitting it into a wider context, inspired by the idea of European unification. Furthermore, Catalan law claims its part in this process. But it wants to do so from the angle of its own identity and own institutions, contributing its own approaches to European law and taking from the latter such criteria as make harmonisation of distinct national laws possible. Reciprocally, European law, as much as it aims at unity, does not deny diversity either, not just with respect to the different state legal systems, but also with reference to the very existence of regional laws.[18]

Compiled law   The Compilation of the Special Civil Law of Catalonia, cataloguing certain institutions of Catalan law, was enacted in 1960 – by Act 40/1960 of 21 July. Book IV is geared to specifically regulating matters

---

[18] See art. 19 Treaty of Rome of 19 June 1980; although, as has already been pointed out, the treaty does not constitute European Community law in the sense which is given here to this expression. The principle alluded to is illustrative of a specific attitude in this respect.

relating to obligations and contracts, without being concerned to establish either a general theory of obligations or a general theory of contract.[19] It is also true that either would have to differ, to a small extent, from those reflected in Spanish civil law, as the Roman tradition on which it is modelled also constitutes the foundation of Catalan law. However, in any event, the truth is that book IV CDCC constitutes a group of unconnected rules, rather than a set of rules modelled on the systematic criteria that might be expected from a body of law.

From the sparse constituent regulations, two sets of rules deserve to be singled out: those that are devoted to rescission for lesion *ultra dimidium* (artt. 323–5), and those devoted to a gift *inter vivos* (artt. 340 and 341), sanctioning the non-opposability to the donor's creditors of gifts made after their credits arise.

The legislative competence of the *Generalitat de Catalunya* as regards obligations: the 'development' of Catalan civil law and the 'bases of contractual obligations'   Article 149 1.8 CE recognises the competence in civil law both of the state and of the autonomous communities. Rule 8 of the constitutional precept is a good example of how not to draft a statutory provision: it is not only couched in tortuous terms, but also uses expressions whose ambiguity makes their interpretation difficult. Add to that the fact that political criteria have, on many occasions, prevailed over strictly legal criteria in such interpretation, and it must come as no surprise that this precept has turned out to be one of the most controversially worded in the constitution.

Article 149 1.8 CE starts out from a general rule: power in 'matters of civil legislation' is vested in the state exclusively. Immediately afterwards, it imposes an exception to the rule: the autonomous communities in which a civil law is in force have – equally exclusive – competence to legislate on 'preservation, reform and development' of this law. However, the competence of the state is acknowledged 'in any event' – exception to the exception – in relation to the rules relating to the application and effectiveness of legal rules, civil law relations relating to marriage formalities, arrangement of registers and public instruments, bases of contractual obligations, rules for resolving conflicts of law and determination of sources

---

[19] Which has recently been chronicled by Juana Marco Molina, in her study of obligations and contracts in Catalan law, 'Obligacions i contractes', in Badosa Coll (ed.), *Compendi*, p. 125.

of law. And a final saving is still made in relation to this competence: as regards sources of law, its exercise by the state has to respect the rules of regional law.

In the Statutes of Autonomy of the communities with a civil law of their own, the question has been approached with a far simpler test: 'The *Generalitat de Catalunya* – states Art. 92 EAC – has exclusive competence' as regards 'preservation, reform and development of Catalan Civil Law'. This provision is supplemented with the provisions contained in art. 26.3 EAC:

1. As regards the exclusive competence of the *Generalitat*, Catalan Law is the one applicable on the territory in priority over any other one.
2. In default of its own Law, the Law of State will be subsidiarily applicable.
3. In the determination of the sources of Civil Law, the State is to respect the rules of Catalan Civil Law.

The scope and significance of two expressions is discussed, in particular, in the interpretation of the constitutional rules: that of 'development' of regional law, the competence for which is exclusively vested in the autonomous community; and that of 'bases of contractual obligations', in respect of which such competence is negated – even in relation to the development of regional law – as the legislation relating to the same is vested in the state 'in any event'.

'Development' of its own civil law   While the competence of the *Generalitat de Catalunya* with a view to 'preservation' and 'reform' of its own civil law has not aroused excessive controversy, its power to 'develop it' has been a keen subject for debate and referred to in constitutional case law, in particular in Constitutional Court Cases 88/1993 and 156/1993. The approach of the Constitutional Court has been very restrictive, basically because such regional law is unjustifiably identified with the one contained in the Compilation, so that its 'development' is confined to that of previously compiled institutions.[20]

However, art. 149 1.8 CE, in vesting in the communities exclusive legislative competence to 'preserve, reform and develop', refers it to the 'civil law' of Catalonia, but not to its 'compiled law'. And it is patent that such 'civil law' is not mixed up or exhausted in the one reflected – at a very specific time and

---

[20] On the matter, see Ferran Badosa Coll, 'La recent jurisprudència sobre les competències de les CCAA en Dret Civil', (1994) *Iuris* 11 ff., who is followed in the present statement.

historical circumstances – in the respective compilations. Consequently, and with respect to the competence of the *Generalitat de Catalunya* with a view to the 'development' of its own law, such 'development' is predicated on the Catalan legal system in its entirety and not on the compiled law.

The 'bases of contractual obligations'   The legislative competence of the autonomous communities – and, within them, their exercise by the *Generalitat de Catalunya* – for 'preserving, reforming and developing' its own civil law, albeit 'exclusive', is not 'absolute'. In effect, there exist certain matters on which the autonomous community is unable to legislate and in respect of which the state is granted competence 'in any event': including those referring to the 'rules relating to...the bases of contractual obligations' (art. 149 1.8 CE).[21]

The question of what such rules are and, in particular, of to what they refer has been resolved by the Constitutional Court also with enormously restrictive criteria prejudicial to the autonomous communities and this – to my mind – without too much justification. In the main, this is because it has ignored the literal tenor itself of the constitutional precept, which is confined solely and exclusively to the 'bases' of 'contractual obligations'. In spite of this, the Constitutional Court has extended the jurisdictional limit of the autonomous communities in 'matters' of civil legislation to every class of obligations, in particular to those that have their origin in tort. And, on the other hand, waving away with a magic wand the institution referred to – 'obligations' – it has substituted for it one of its possible sources – 'contracts' – also extending to them the competence of the state (Constitutional Court cases of 22 July 1993 and 22 January 1998).

This interpretation is open to criticism and is at odds with the literal tenor itself of art. 149 1.8. The legislative competence of the state refers to 'the rules relating to the bases of contractual obligations', not to the rules relating to the 'bases of the obligations', nor to the rules relating to the 'bases of the contracts'. Therefore, the autonomous communities, in exercise of their competence in 'preserving, reforming and developing' their own civil law, are able to legislate on 'non-contractual obligations' and,

---

[21] Prof. Badosa Coll has dealt on various occasions with the 'bases of contractual obligations'. Cf., in particular, 'La competència de la Generalitat i les bases de les obligacions contractuals', unpublished lecture (1990).

needless to say, on the contract in general and on different types of contract in particular.[22]

The question to be resolved is what, and which ones, are the 'bases of the contractual obligations' in respect of which the state has exclusive competence 'in any event'. The Constitutional Court has believed it has found the 'bases of the contractual obligations' in art. 1091 Sp. CC and defined them in their effectiveness 'with force of law between contracting parties' and in the need for their strict performance, having regard to the tenor of the contract.[23] However, these two propositions are more than 'bases'. They are institutional corollaries of the concept of 'contractual obligation' and, therefore, notions which are inferred from the concept itself and without which the category of the 'contractual obligation' would not exist.[24]

To my mind, the concept of the 'bases of the contractual obligations' could be found in the Act of 11 May 1888 (*Ley de Bases del Código civil*), to which the wording of the Spanish Civil Code had to be adapted. After establishing that 'both the Government and the Commission are to adhere in the drafting of the Civil Code to the following *bases*',[25] it enumerates the questions to which refer the ones relative to the 'obligations': nature, effects, methods of discharge and evidence (bases 19). Certainly, these 'bases' refer to obligations in general and not to 'contractual obligations'. But the same generality with which they are considered makes it possible for them also to be predicated on these: the 'bases of the obligations' are common to every obligation, irrespective of their origin. The 'contractual' nature classifies the 'obligations', not the 'bases'.

It should then be asked what the idea of 'contractuality' adds to the 'bases of the obligations'. Firstly, a reference to its origin: 'contractual obligations' are those that arise from the contracts (art. 1089 CC); to which could be added a second aspect: 'contractual obligations' are those in which not only their creation, but also the structure of its legal system, depend on the intention of the individuals. It is true that the latter can also happen in 'non-contractual obligations', but only in relation to particular aspects

---

[22] On the same lines, ibid., pp. 8 ff.

[23] Cf. Constitutional Court cases 28 July 1981 (see *BOE* 193, 13 August 1981); 26 January and 27 July 1982 (*BOE* 36, 11 February and 197, 18 August 1982); 30 September 1986 (*BOE* 253, 22 October, 1986); and 22 March 1988 (*BOE* 89, 13 April, 1988).

[24] Cf. Badosa Coll, 'La competència', p. 1; he develops his criticism on pp. 11 ff.

[25] In the context of the precept, the expression 'bases' refers not only to the different 'bases' which it enumerates afterwards, but also to the contents of the same, in that they reflect 'basic principles or criteria of the different institutions to which they refer'.

of such scheme. And, in any event, what is needed for this is an express act on those lines; distinct, moreover, from the act or event that causes the creation of the obligation. On the other hand, in 'contractual obligations', the contract is, at the same time, the source of the obligation from which they arise and the rule that imposes and controls its legal scheme.

To these two characteristics has to be added a third one. 'Contractual obligations' are, above all, those of contractual origin and character. This idea refers the category to the obligations arising from synallagmatic contracts. The relationship between these obligations and such consequences as derive therefrom occurs only in 'contractual obligations' looked at that way. On the other hand, it is not fitting in 'non-contractual obligations' and this would justify the specialisation of contractual obligations within the wider category of 'obligations' in general.

However, the conclusion it is important to reach in this section, whatever the interpretation given to the expression 'bases of the contractual obligations', is that the reservation of competence established in the state's favour neither limits on the same nor excludes the possible legislative action of the *Generalitat de Catalunya* as regards contracts (in particular, as regards consumer contracts), nor as regards non-contractual obligations (in particular, as regards obligations arising in tort).

Exercise of the legislative competence of the *Generalitat de Catalunya*
The *Generalitat de Catalunya* has exercised its legislative competence as regards obligations and contracts in two ways: one, geared to 'reforming' the Compilation, adapting it to the 1978 constitution and also bringing it into line with the requirements of social reality; the second, of 'development' of Catalan civil law, by way of statutes, the substance of which refers, whether in whole or in part, to 'civil matters'. The ultimate purpose is to enact, following its appropriate revision, the 'patrimonial code' of Catalonia.

Even so, the *Generalitat*'s legislative activity has shown a preference for the task of 'developing' Catalan law, whether on the basis of institutions referred to directly or indirectly in the Compilation or regulating matters unrecognised by the compiled text. An example of the first would be Act 24/1984, of 28 November, on cattle-raising contracts, and Act 22/1991, of 29 November, on possessory securities over chattels (LGP). With respect to this Act which regulates pledge and retention, the relationship with the Compilation is more obvious in the latter institution than in the first,

in which it is utterly remote.[26] Although this is an Act referring specifically to real rights, the right of retention is a legal guarantee of the credit
granted to someone who has carried on a specific activity over a chattel,
has paid the expenses required for its preservation and management, or has
suffered damage while he held it in his possession (art. 4 LGP). The non-
performance of such obligations authorises sale by notarial public auction
of the property. Moreover, the creditor is entitled to pay off his claim out
of the proceeds obtained, also being able to claim it if it is not disposed of
at any of the three auctions provided by law (art. 6 LGP).

However, it has undoubtedly been within the sphere of 'consumer law'
that the *Generalitat de Catalunya* has engaged in legislative activity which
has had the greatest impact in the contractual sphere. However, the basis
of competence relied on by the *Generalitat* has not been the 'development'
of civil law, but 'the organising of internal trade and the protection of
consumers' to which art. 12.1.5 EAC alludes. The result of this is that,
although the statute vests in the *Generalitat de Catalunya* exclusive competence in such matters, there is – as has been underlined by the Constitutional
Court – a competence shared with the state, whose duty it is to organise and
manage general economic policy (art. 149.1.13 CE). In accordance with this
interpretation, the Catalan legislature's action must, therefore, be limited
to supplementing, specifying and developing state regulations.[27]

Therefore, the effectiveness of this regulation is doubtful. Essentially
programmatic in content, its terms are, at times, nothing but a mirror of
state regulations. It suffers from the competence and – as a consequence
of the same – from the need to bring it into line 'with the bases and the
general economic organisation' that is vested in the state. Moreover, such
competence causes the Catalan regulation to be an administrative regulation and, consequently, to envisage and preferably impose solutions –
sanctions – of this nature, and not civil in nature, in the event of breach
of its terms. It would be different if the Catalan legislature would exercise
its powers with a view to the 'development' of the law. By acting as
it has done, it has limited its own possibilities of action. Nevertheless,
it is highly probable that, were it to exercise them, the Constitutional

---

[26] See Antoni Vaquer Aloy, 'Los conceptos de "conservación", "reforma" y "desarrollo" del art' art.
149 1.8 de la Constitución: – su interpretación por el legislador catalán', (1994) *Derecho Privado
y Constitución* 239, 249.

[27] In this respect see Marco Molina, '*Obligacions i contractes*', p. 143.

Court would affirm the exclusive competence of the state, in reliance on its idiosyncratic interpretation of art.149.1.8 CE.

European law of obligations and Catalan civil law

Community directives and Catalan civil law

Community directives on obligations and contracts have been slanted preferentially to consumer protection. In this area, the regulatory action of European institutions has concentrated on two points: first, on the regulation of liability for damage caused by defective products; second, on the so-called 'consumer contract', looking at the 'consumer contract' in the abstract, but without thereby disregarding the issues that may be raised by certain – the commonest – 'consumer contracts'.

The *Generalitat de Catalunya* has legislative competence in both respects. As has already been noted, the power to 'preserve, reform and develop' Catalan law as regards obligations and contracts has no limit other than that determined by the 'bases of the contractual obligations'. Yet this means that, both with reference to non-contractual obligations – for example, liability for defective products – and with reference to contract in general and contracts in particular, the *Generalitat de Catalunya* does have competence to bring to a head the process of codification it is carrying out.

The principles underpinning Community directives

With respect to liability for defective products, Community law is modelled on the basic principles of strict liability and of extension of such liability to anyone who takes part in the production or the distribution of defective products. The consumer protection system is assured by excluding exemption clauses.[28]

Concerning consumer contracts, Community law sets a whole series of principles which modify the traditional law of contract; thus, for example, the prohibition on misleading information, and the binding force of the same. The information is included within the terms of the offer and forms an integral part of the contract (art. 3 Directive 314/1990 and art. 3.2 Directive 94/47/EC). In relation to this, the right of unilateral withdrawal of the contract for the sole benefit of the consumer is also worthy of note, as a

---

[28] Cf. Directive 374/1995, in particular artt. 3, 4, 5 and 12.

result of failing to supply him with the statutory information or as a result of this being incomplete or inaccurate. It is not a question of breach of contract, but of a breach produced during the process of formation of the contract. This right of withdrawal is therefore pre-contractual in nature (art. 6 Directive 94/7/EC and art. 5 Directive 97/47/EC).

Community directives also give consumers the power to withdraw *ad nutum* from the contract in specific cases, without there having been any breach of contract (artt. 5 and 7 Directive 577/1985, art. 6 Directive 94/7/EC and art. 5 Directive 94/47/EC). The right of unilateral withdrawal of unfixed-term contracts, or contracts with a term of more than one year, is also recognised under certain conditions (art. 5.1 Directive 97/7/EC).

On the other hand, Community regulation takes into account the supervening alteration of circumstances existing at the time of concluding the contract, giving the consumer the right to opt for either 'withdrawing of the contract without penalty' or adapting its terms to the new situation (artt. 4, 5 and 6 Directive 314/1990).

Finally, clauses that unbalance the parties' rights are ineffective.[29] However, the unfairness of the clauses will not refer to the object of the contract, nor the relationship between its market value and the value paid for the same (art. 4.2 Directive 13/1993). The possible unfairness that can arise in such respects is irrelevant. When the alternative is between consumer protection and the requirements of a market economy, the choice to opt for the latter appears plain.

Community directives and Catalan civil law

As has been pointed out, the Catalan legislature has not fully exercised the competence in consumer law. It has not legislated on liability for defective products nor on the 'consumer contract' in the abstract. It has only dealt with regulating some typical contracts contained in Community directives. Thus, contracts concluded away from business premises (Directive 577/1985), package tour contracts (Directive 314/1990) and distance selling (Directive 97/7/EC).

Contracts concluded away from business premises have been the subject of regulation by the Catalan legislature on two occasions: first, in

---

[29] Generally, Directive 93/13/EC; particular statements in art. 6 Directive 577/1985, 53 Directive 314/1990, art. 8 Directive 94/47/EC and art. 12 Directive 97/7/EC.

Act 1/1983, of 18 February, on administrative regulation of certain commercial premises and special selling, and afterwards, in Act 23/1991, of 29 November, on domestic trade. The point of view adopted by the Catalan legislature has been substantially different from that underpinning Community regulations, although both share the common purpose of restoring the necessary balance between the parties when the contract is negotiated away from business premises. While, for Act 1/1983, pre-dating Directive 577/1985, consumer prejudice arises from 'the absence of a basic factor for the *identification* and for the *liability of the trader*, as is a permanent premise' (preamble, para. 5), as far as the Directive is concerned, it is due to the fact that 'as a rule it is the trader who initiates the contract negotiations, for which the consumer is unprepared or which he does not except' (preamble, para. 5).

Consistently with this, the solutions will be equally different. Catalan law establishes an administrative regulation of contracts negotiated away from business premises, which is reflected in a control of the activity of the trader, which is subject to certain requirements and licences. However, breach of the terms of Act 1/1983 amounts to administrative penalties, so that the consumer protection which derives from this regulation is an indirect protection. Conversely, the Directive sets a far more effective means of protection of consumers, since the consumer has a seven-day period to withdraw from the contract.

Instead, Act 23/1991 does incorporate the approach of the Community Directive, enabling the buyer's unilateral withdrawal (art. 11). Nevertheless, it does not abandon the system of administrative protection set up by Act 1/1983. Consequently, it establishes a scheme of administrative penalties (artt. 21–25) concentrated on the trader's activity within which are contemplated, among other types of conduct deserving of sanction, 'the withholding of information from the consumer relating to the cooling-off period' (art. 21.1 f.).

With respect to package-tour contracts, the terms laid down in Decree 168/1994, of 30 May, regulating travel agencies – pre-dating State Act 21/1995, of 6 July, regulating Package Tours, which is therefore non-applicable to Catalonia – are directly modelled on Directive 314/1990. The main principles are that advertising must not contain misleading information (art. 14.1 Decree and art. 3.1 Directive) and the binding force of information supplied for the organiser of the package tour (art. 14.3

Decree and art. 3.2 Directive). The same should be said about the right of withdrawal without penalty if the organiser finds that before departure he is constrained to alter significantly any of the essential terms of the contract (art. 21 Decree and 4.5 and 6 Directive). Conversely, the right of unilateral withdrawal given to the consumer – 'at any time' – by art. 18 Decree was not foreseen by the Directive. It constitutes an innovation in the regulation of a package-tour contract which does not appear as an event of withdrawal *ad nutum* since, if it does not require any supporting reason and gives 'a right to return of the monies [the consumer] has paid', it does not exempt him from the duty to compensate the travel agency.

Finally, as regards distance selling, the regulation in force in Catalonia is to be found in Act 23/1991, previous to Directive 97/7/EC. Nevertheless, both regulations are similar. Thus, art. 12 of the Act and artt. 4 and 5 of the Directive refer to the information the consumer has to be supplied with. Article 12 e of the Act, which alludes to the 'cooling-off period' of no less than seven days 'during which the consumer is able to return the product and recover the amount paid', is reflected in art. 6 Directive, according to which the latter may 'withdraw from the contract without any penalty and without giving any reason'. Article 7 of the Directive, relating to the performance of the contract within a thirty-day period from the day following that on which the consumer forwarded his order to the supplier, is nothing but a concretion of the 'maximum time for delivery or making available to the consumer the product or services which are the object of the transaction, from the time of receiving the order', to which art. 12 d of the Act refers. Finally, the prohibition on unsolicited goods specified in art. 13.2 of the Act can also be found in art. 9 of the Directive.

Worthy of note, therefore, in this connection is a virtually absolute match between the principles of Community law and the principles of Catalan civil law on consumer protection. This is above all because the latter has been directly modelled on the former principles, but also because – albeit to a lesser extent – Community law has at times adopted the same principles that, previously, had likewise underlain the action of the Catalan legislature. The relationship between Community law and Catalan law may provide an important incentive to the development of the latter, in particular if the *Generalitat de Catalunya* fully exercises its competence. At the same time, it has to be an incentive for the Catalan legislature to participate in the process of drafting European law.

Principles of European Contract Law and Catalan civil law

As has already been indicated, the PECL are held out as a basis for a future European contractual code. But, as has also been indicated, the PECL are also a way forward for the legislatures of European countries to regulate or modernise their contract law and do so, also, with unitary criteria. The Catalan legislature may also use them in the exercise of its legislative competence as regards obligations and contracts. Certainly, such competence is not absolute, excluding all possibility of regulating issues which affect the 'bases of the contractual obligations'; but there is nothing to prevent contracts and contractual principles being legislated on. It goes without saying that it is in this area that recourse to the PECL is likely to be useful.

Principles of contract law and bases of contractual obligations

This possibility, and the restrictions with which its legislative competence is hedged, suggest the advisability of trying to distinguish, within the scope of the PECL, between the 'principles or bases of contract' and 'principles or bases of contractual obligations'. Needless to say, the drafters of the PECL did not apply themselves to expressly formulating the distinction; but the same certainly underlies its regulation. Although it is conceivable that the rules that make it up deal only with contractual principles, strictly the PECL regulate not only such principles, but also those of the 'contractual obligations'. Further, perhaps the significance of this expression can be gauged from the precepts devoted to the same.

The PECL refer specifically to the 'contractual obligation' for the first time in art. 6:101, which refers to events which give rise to the creation of a contractual obligation. In this way, the PECL not only state that 'contract' and 'contractual obligation' are distinct concepts, which must not be mixed up, but add a first aspect to the structure of the 'contractual obligation'. Contractual obligations arise from *consensus in idem* or from acts which, due to their special significance, are considered equivalent to an agreement.

The systematic locating of art. 6:101 in chapter 6 PECL, relating to the content and effects of the contract, adds a second aspect. In effect, such location alludes to two possible points of view from which the obligation can be considered in relation to the contract. As content, the obligation lacks autonomy and still forms part of the contract, from which it is not distinguished. As an effect, the obligation separates itself from the contract and acquires a life of its own.[30] Strictly speaking, the 'contractual obligation' exists only as such when it appears as an effect of the contract. Consistently with this point of view, some chapters of the PECL refer to performance (ch. 7) and to non-performance and to remedies for non-performance (chs. 8 and 9). These vicissitudes refer not even to the contract, but to the obligation that arises from such contract.

The provisions relating to the performance and non-performance of the 'contractual obligation' have just profiled the concept of such. The provisions on performance of 'contractual obligations' bring out the relevance and primacy of the parties' intention. Creditor and debtor set the rules concerning performance, and only in default of agreement do the provisions of the PECL apply.[31]

Yet perhaps it is the rules referring to non-performance of 'contractual obligations' that reveal their essential characteristic, as the impact of the parties' intention on the scheme of specific performance may also be brought out in obligations of non-contractual origin. The PECL are fundamentally geared to the protection of the creditor's interest and start out from a very wide concept of non-performance, which includes defective or delayed performance. Moreover, it is not necessary to prove fault in order to prove non-performance (art. 1:301 (4)). The existence of an excuse (art. 8:108 (1)) does not exclude non-performance; what happens is that the means the creditor is able to use for remedying the consequences of such non-performance vary. If non-performance is not excused, the creditor may claim specific performance, withhold its own performance, terminate the contract, reduce its own performance, and claim damages (art. 8:101 (1)). On the other hand, a performance which is excused does not give the creditor the right to claim specific performance or to claim damages; but the other remedies may be available (art. 8:101 (2)). Therefore, if the non-performance is excused, the creditor is able to choose and decide on its own – principle of 'self-help'[32] – the remedy to fit its needs, without having to obtain a court order. Conversely, if the non-performance is not excused,

---

[30] The distinction between the obligation as content and the obligation as an effect of the contract has been explained by Badosa Coll, 'La competència', p. 10.

[31] This happens, e.g., with respect to the place (art. 7:101) and to the time (art. 7:102) of performance, but also in terms of the quality of the performance which has to be tendered by the debtor (art. 6:108).

[32] Cf. Lando and Beale (eds.), *Principles of European Contract Law*, p. xxviii.

judicial intervention is necessary in order to obtain specific performance or to calculate damages.

The consequences that arise from non-performance of the 'contractual obligations' – withholding performance, termination and price reduction – denote a final and definite characteristic of this category of obligations. 'Contractual obligations' are the those that arise from synallagmatic contracts. Although it is not expressly affirmed, the idea is implicit, not only in the provisions that regulate the non-performance of contractual obligations, but throughout the articles of the PECL.

Therefore, the distinction – within the PECL – between the 'bases of the contracts' and 'bases of the contractual obligations' can be established with some sharpness. To the first one belong all matters relating to the contract as an act: that is to say, and basically, the ones that refer to the formation and externalisation of contractual declarations of intention, to their content, validity and interpretation. The second ones deal with the effects of the contract: performance and non-performance of the obligations that arise from it. In broad outline, this distinctive criterion is equally reflected in the systematic arrangement of the PECL: after a chapter 1 containing the 'general provisions' on the matter, the next four reflect the 'bases of the contracts', while the last four are devoted to the 'bases of the contractual obligations'.

Principles of European Contract Law and Catalan civil law

The 'contractual principles' contained in the PECL are likely to serve as a source of inspiration to the Catalan legislature with a view to development of the Catalan law of contracts, enabling it, at the same time, to create a contract law capable of being integrated within the process of European legal unification.

The PECL start out from the idea of a contract based on the principle of freedom of contract, both in its creative function and in its regulatory function (art. 1:102), and guided by the general principle to act in good faith (art. 1:201) and the duty of cooperation between the parties (art. 1:202). According to the general rules, the contract is concluded by the combination of offer (art. 2:201) and acceptance (art. 2:204), being completed when the latter reaches the offer, or if by his fault he has prevented it from reaching him (art. 2:205).

The PECL also deal with preliminary negotiations, excluding any idea of liability when negotiations do not culminate in an agreement (art. 2:301 (1)). However, a party that breaks off the negotiations contrary to good faith – when there is no true intention to conclude the contract – may be held liable to the other party (art. 2:301 (2) and (3)). Breach of a duty of confidentiality in the course of negotiations makes the person committing the breach also liable in damages (art. 2:302).

The validity of the contract depends on the absence of vices of consent: mistake (artt. 4:103 and 4:104), fraud (art. 4:107) and threats (art. 4:108), to which should be added – also as a cause of invalidity – excessive benefit, or unfair or unjust advantage gained by one party (art. 4:109).

Particularly noteworthy in the regulations of the PECL on vices of consent is the treatment of mistake, due to its extent and thoroughness and the restrictive way in which it is interpreted. A legally relevant mistake may be as to facts or law. A party may avoid a contract if (i) the mistake was caused by information supplied by the other party; (ii) the other party knew or ought to have known of the mistake and it was contrary to good faith to leave the mistaken party in error; (iii) the other party made the same mistake. Moreover, its essential nature is equally required: if the contracting party affected by the mistake had not made it, he would not have entered the contract or would have done so only on substantially different terms. But not only that: it is also required that the other party knew or ought to have known of such circumstances. The mistake has to be also inexcusable. Finally, for the contract to be voidable, it is even required that the aggrieved party was under no duty to assume the risk of the mistake.

Also worthy of note, in the regulation of the PECL, is excessive benefit and unfair advantage on one party, as a ground of nullity of the contract. Under art. 4:109, this circumstance arises when one of the parties finds himself in a situation of weakness or inequality in relation to the other and the latter, knowing this or being able to know this, takes advantage thereof unfairly or obtains an excessive benefit. The state of weakness or inequality may be due to different causes: the confidential relationship of one party with the other, urgent needs or economic hardship when contracting, inexperience or lack of bargaining skill. This detail in description of the key causes of the state of inferiority contrasts with the lack of definition of the consequence: being aware of the situation, the other party obtains 'an excessive benefit'. Certainly, in order to determine such, art. 4:109 requires the circumstances and purpose of the contract to be looked at; but this does not clarify the issue too much. What appears to sanction the provision is the need for a balanced relationship between the parties and, in the final instance, breach of the duty of good faith which must underlie the action of the parties (cf. art. 1:201). But it neither excludes nor negates the possible existence of a certain amount of inequality, provided it is not 'excessive', nor the consequence of an unfair act.

Generally, the existence of vices of consent, excessive and unfair benefit on one of the parties allows the aggrieved party to avoid the contract. Avoidance must be by notice to the other party (artt. 4:112 and 4:113 (1)). However, the vice of consent must have been caused, induced or known by the other party. The contract is also voidable when the vice of consent is caused by a third person if the unaffected party knew or ought to have known of the relevant facts (art. 4:111 (2)).

One consequence of nullity of the contract is the mutual restitution of benefits (art. 4:115). The aggrieved party may also recover damages from the other party, as a penalty for having caused the ground for avoidance or for having taken advantage thereof (art. 4:117).

Even so, both in the event of mistake and of excessive benefit, the invalidating lack or defect does not necessarily entail nullity of the contract, but possibility of its subsistence is contemplated, as if the defect had not arisen. The principle of preservation of the contract underlying this approach enables the contract to be considered concluded on the terms and conditions taken into account by the party entitled to avoid the contract in the case of mistake, if the other party indicates its willingness to perform or renders such performance. In the case of excessive benefit, at the instance both of the aggrieved party and of the party receiving notice of avoidance, a court may adapt the contract in order to bring it in accordance with what might had been agreed had the requirements of good faith been followed (art. 4:109 (2) and (3)).

The PECL also deal with unilateral termination of the contract. Contracts for an indeterminate or indefinite period may be ended by either of the contracting parties, without any requirement other than giving notice of reasonable length (art. 6:109). This is a right of termination *ad nutum.* The foundation of the same is to be found in the same unfixed term of the contract and in the need to avoid a situation of the parties being indefinitely or perpetually bound. The requirement of pre-notice is coterminous with the general duty to act in accordance with the requirements of good faith (art. 1:201).

Finally, chapter 5 of the PECL is devoted to interpretation of contracts. The guiding principle is that of primacy of the common intention of the contracting parties, even if it does not appear suitably reflected or differs from the literal meaning of the words (art. 5:101). The means of interpretation the interpreter has to use to enquire into such common intention are diverse: *inter alia*, the parties' preliminary negotiations and conduct, even subsequent to conclusion of the contract (art. 5:102). The rules of interpretation are the traditional ones on the matter: the rule *contra proferentem* (art. 5:103), rule of preference of clauses negotiated over those which have not been (art. 5:104), rule of interpretation of the contract as a whole (art. 5:105), and rule of useful interpretation (art. 5:106). On the other hand, the PECL make reference to a question of particular importance: the divergences between the different linguistic versions of a contract. However, if none of them has been attributed priority, there is a preference for the interpretation according to the version in which the contract was drawn up (art. 5:107).

In broad outline, these would be some of the bases underlying the regulation of the PECL. All of these bases and principles which develop them are capable of adoption by Catalan law and can be reflected and developed, in their turn, by the regional legislature. Thus, the PECL afford the Catalan legislature the possibility of passing an 'Act on Contracts' which serves not only to develop Catalan law, but to do so in accordance with the same principles that underpin the process of European contractual unification.

Principles of the Catalan law of obligations and European contract law

The ups and downs Catalan civil law has gone through and the controversy that surrounds the exercise of the legislative competence of the *Generalitat de Catalunya* as regards obligations and contracts make it difficult to define the 'principles of Catalan law' which underlie it. Moreover, Catalan law is ascribed to the Roman law tradition of *ius commune* and, accordingly, adopts a good part of the principles that underlie Continental European law. On the other hand, the subsidiarity of state legislation and the 1889 Spanish Civil Code also implies that its instructive principles apply as part of a law applicable in Catalonia which is not Catalan law.

The principle of economic equivalence of contractual obligations   The Catalan law of obligations is based on peculiar principles of its own, some already rooted in its legal tradition and others of far more recent formulation.

The first one worthy of note within the first group is that of balancing or economic equivalence of the prestations of the parties, which enables rescission by lesion (*laesio ultra dimidium*), which the CDCC currently regulates in its artt. 321–5.[33]

Lesion is an institution which directly impacts on the 'basis of the contractual obligations'. The characteristic relationship of dependency of this category of obligations also requires a balanced relationship or economic equivalence to exist between the value of the prestations of the parties so that, when this equivalence does not occur or is broken, the prejudiced contracting party may seek rescission of the contract. The effect of rescission is the mutual restitution of benefits.

Lesion does not apply to any onerous contract, nor may it be invoked by any of the parties. Article 321 CDCC confines it to contracts 'related to immoveables', therefore excluding the possibility of its application to such contracts as are made over moveable property; and vests the faculty to rescind in the transferor only.

The circumstance that causes breakdown of the prestations of the parties occurs when the price paid for an immoveable is less than one-half – *laesio ultra dimidium* – of its fair price, such meaning 'the sale value the articles had, at the time of the contract being made, in relation to other articles in circumstances identical or similar to the particular place, although the contract is completed afterwards' (art. 323.2 CDCC).

The transferor may waive the action for rescission (art. 322 CDCC), but only once the contract has been concluded.[34] Therefore, advance renunciation is unacceptable, consistently with the principle – already sanctioned by European legislation – of exclusion of waivers prejudicial to the party who makes them. However, although the transferor is granted the faculty to rescind the contract, upon all the preliminaries and requirements provided by Catalan legislation being met, the decision on the subsistence or otherwise of the same is a matter, ultimately, for the acquirer. Article 324 CDCC, modelled on the principle of preservation of the contract, enables the acquirer to avoid rescission if he offers a pecuniary supplement of the full price, with interest thereon.

---

[33] Cf. Miquel Martin Casals, arts. 321 to 325 CDCC, in Manuel Albaladejo García (ed.), *Comentarios al Código civil y Compilaciones Forales*, vol. XXX (Madrid, 1987), pp. 451 ff.

[34] Exceptionally, the rule is not applicable 'to Tortosa and its former territory, where the waiver may be made in the contract itself' (art. 322 CDCC, final subsection).

The principle of non-opposability of gifts against the donor's creditors
The principle of non-opposability to the creditors of the donor of gifts made by the latter also fits within Catalan legal tradition. This principle, which affords a special level of protection for creditors' benefit, is contained in art. 340.3 CDCC, in sanctioning the 'non-prejudice' of the creditors of the donor as against gratuitous alienations made by the latter.[35] What exactly such 'non-prejudice' consists of has been discussed in legal literature. Majority opinion is inclined to consider that 'non-prejudice' results in the non-opposability of the disposal to the creditors, so that the latter may ignore it and execute the gifted asset as if it were still in the debtor's property. The gift is valid, but becomes ineffective, in whole or in part, in a particular case: when the donor has creditors whose rights pre-date the gift and is without any assets to pay it off. However, once the remedy is satisfied, the balance, if any, still belongs to the transferee.[36]

The principle of non-opposability of the gratuitous alienations is a remedy which fits within the 'bases of the obligations', leaving out the origin and characteristics of the concrete obligation. This is expressly borne out by art. 340 CDCC itself in establishing that the granting of the gift has to post-date the date of the 'event' (non-contractual obligation) or of the 'act' (contractual obligation) from which the creditors' rights arise. Creditors who are not prejudiced by the debtor's gifts are, therefore, creditors both of a 'contractual obligation' and of a 'non-contractual obligation'.

The principle of retention of property in restitutional obligations   The principle of retention of property, unlike the two previous ones, is of recent date. It is gathered from Act 22/1991, of 29 November, of possessory securities over chattels, and may be considered a manifestation of a wider principle: the principle of 'self-help' which enables a creditor who, in his turn, is a debtor of his debtor, to refuse to perform his obligation until such time as the latter fulfils his obligation.

In effect, art. 3 LGP provides that the possessor in good faith of a chattel belonging to the other party may retain it as security for the payment of his

---

[35] On the issue, Antoni Vaquer Aloy, 'Inoponibilidad y acción pauliana (La protección de los acreedores del donante en el art.340.3 de la Compilación del Derecho Civil de Cataluña', (1999) *ADC* 1491.

[36] See ibid., pp. 1510 ff. Juan Egea Fernández, art. 340 CDCC, in Juan Egea Fernández (ed.), *Comentarios al Código civil*, vol. XXX, pp. 821–2.

claims as a result of having incurred expenses necessary in its preservation or management, or as a result of having incurred any damage, or having conducted any activity over it (art. 4.1 a, b and c LGP). The right of retention also extends to the interest arising from any of the previous obligations (art. 4.1, d LGP), as well as to '[any] other debt to which the law expressly grants such security' (art. 4.1 e LGP).

Act 22/1991 constitutes an important landmark in the arrangement of the right of retention. The Catalan legislature has tended to consider the right of retention as a real right (preamble, para. 3, LGP) enforceable *erga omnes* (art. 5 LGP) and capable of performance (art. 6 LGP). Thus, the right of retention has a greater level of effectiveness enabling the creditor, as it does, to abandon the abstentionist or negative position its consideration as a defence forces him to maintain. As a real right, the creditor adopts a positive attitude, making possible the satisfaction of his claim on its own, by way of sale of the object retained in a notarial public auction.

Even so, this is not – at least, for the Catalan legislature – the most important innovation added by Act 22/1991. In its own words 'the most important point lies in the fact that it is the party exercising the right who, unilaterally, decides the value of the claims which cause the right of retention' (preamble, para. 2 LGP). This faculty constitutes a new manifestation of the principle of self-help which underpins the institution, and the only requirement which is imposed for enforcing it is the one to communicate notarially to the debtor or, where appropriate, to the owner of the thing, the decision to retain, the account taken and the resulting proceeds (art. 4.2 LGP). Debtor and owner may go to court to resist the retention and/or determination of the value secured for three months, with effect from notice thereof. If they do not do so, or the court sanctions the claim of the retainer, the latter may – with effect from three months of such notice – auction the property (art. 6.1 LGP).

However, as a prerequisite to notarial specific performance, art. 6.2 LGP requires the valuation of such object by mutual agreement between the retainer and the owner. This requirement, possibly thought up to counterbalance the creditor's excessive influence, cuts down in a notable way the effectiveness of the right of retention,[37] since, if the owner refuses to reach such agreement, the legislature has not provided any procedure substituting

---

[37] As already pointed out by Professor Lluís Puig i Ferriol, *Institucions del Dret civil de Catalunya'*, vol. I, 5th edn (Valencia, 1998), pp. 397–8.

it. Thus, the creditor's security is reduced to mere retention and, where appropriate, to the antichretic effect referred to in art. 2.1, b) LGP.

The right of retention regulated in Act 22/1991 constitutes a means of protection and security of credits which does not impact necessarily, or exclusively, on the 'bases of the contractual obligations'. At times, the obligation whose performance is secured may be a 'contractual obligation'; but will not always be so. In fact, of the obligations described in art. 4 LGP, it is only 'the compensation for the activity carried on by reason of the thing, on instructions of the lawful possessor, provided he has given him an accepted estimate and the activity conducted matches this' (art. 4.1 c LGP). But both the compensation for necessary expenses (art. 4.1 a) and for 'damages caused by reason of the thing to the person bound to delivery' (art. 4.1 b) are obligations of legal origin and therefore belong to the category of non-contractual obligations. Therefore, the principle of retention of property in restitutional obligations protects every creditor, both if his remedy arises from a 'contractual obligation' and if it arises from a 'non-contractual' obligation.

The principles of the Catalan law of obligations and its adaptation to European contract law   The confirmation of the existence of principles of Catalan law of obligations raises the question about its inclusion and impact on a European contract law in the process of formation.

With respect to the principle of the economic equivalence of contractual obligations and *laesio ultra dimidium*, I believe that it will be difficult to fit in within European law, at least taking into account Catalan law currently in force. The CDCC starts out from a purely objective consideration of lesion, based on the idea of a 'fair price' and the need for a correlation between the price agreed and the market price. This idea was already disputed at the end of the eighteenth century, in connection with the codification of French civil law, and at the present time it is wholly and utterly lacking in foundation.

Article 4:110 PECL and art. 4.2 Directive 93/13/EC, on unfair terms in consumer contracts, anticipate a response on these lines. The adequacy of value of one party's obligations compared to the value of the other party's obligations is not an unfair term. Consumer law provides an additional argument for excluding lesion: the contracting party benefiting from the same is the seller or the transferor, not the acquirer, who is the one who occupies the position that corresponds to the consumer.

However, if from an objective point of view lesion does not appear to have too much of a future, something else could happen if it is considered from a subjective perspective, looking at the 'excessive benefit' or at the 'unjust advantage' gained by one party. In such a case, the PECL accept the possibility of avoiding the contract. A rescission for lesion guided by subjective criteria is likely to accommodate itself to this new European law of contract, if a possible reform of Catalan law occurs on such lines.

Turning to the two other aforementioned principles of the Catalan law of obligations, its adaptation to European contract law appears less of a problem. Both the principle of non-opposability to creditors of gifts made by the debtor and that of retention of property are for one purpose – protection of the creditor's interest – which also underpins European law and which is contained in its provisions. With respect to the non-opposability of gifts, this is a mechanism for protection of creditors existing in various European laws.[38] The same does not happen in relation to the right of retention, in respect of which Catalan civil law has assumed an innovative role. But as definition of a wider principle accepted in the PECL – the principle of 'self-help' – it might be taken into consideration by the Lando Commission and be incorporated among the means of protection of creditors.

---

[38] See Antoni Vaquer, 'From revocation to non-opposability: modern developments of the Paulian action', below, pp. 199–220.

9

From revocation to non-opposability: modern developments of the Paulian action

ANTONI VAQUER

Preamble

Any serious attempt to harmonise the various European civil laws needs to take into account the different regional laws, such as those of Scotland or Catalonia. Taking the Paulian action as an example, and adopting a historical and comparative approach, this chapter aims to demonstrate that most modern legal systems tend to coincide in some of the remedies they provide, and also that the regulations found in Catalan regional civil law can act as a model for a future unified regulation of the legal protection of the right of credit.

Roman law: *fraus* and *restitutio*

The origins of the *actio pauliana* – an action that originated in Roman law for the protection of creditors against the diminution of assets brought about by their debtors – is not at all clear. Having said that, lengthy discussions founded on fragmentary and contradictory Roman sources have taken place within classic law about the identity and number of available remedies for the defence of creditors against fraudulent acts by their debtors, and the effects of such remedies. Current opinion seems to suggest that the phrase *actio pauliana* conceals a Justinian fusion of two classic remedies for the protection of creditors: (i) *in integrum restitutio ob fraudem*; and (ii) *interdictum fraudatorium*.[1] Paulian action, forged in Justinian's

---

[1] Theodor Kipp, 'Impugnación de los actos "in fraudem creditorum", en Derecho romano y en el moderno Derecho alemán, con referencia al Derecho español', (1924) *RDP* 1 ff.; Antonio Butera, *De l'azione pauliana o revocatoria* (Turin, 1934), pp. 25–7; Hans Ankum, '"Interdictum fraudatorium" et "restitutio in integrum ob fraudem"', in *Synteleia Vincenzo Arangio-Ruiz*, vol. II

compilation, presupposed two assumptions: (i) *eventus damni* or detriment to the creditor – arising from the debtor's diminution of assets as a result of an act of gratuitous alienation by the debtor; and (ii) *consilium fraudis* or intention by the debtor to defraud the creditor's rights by diminishing the debtor's saleable assets, generally thought to occur in conjunction with the acquirer's knowledge of such intention or *scientia fraudis*.[2]

As for the effects of the remedy, it would seem that the Paulian action involved the reconstruction of the debtor's assets, given that any goods transferred from it had to be restored. The classic remedy had at least an unequivocal restitutory character,[3] which was probably transferred – both in relation to the alienated goods and, to some extent, to their fruits – to the current action as a result of the reforms carried out by Justinian.[4] It should also be noted that this remedy was not only granted to the *curator bonorum*, but also to creditors themselves.[5] The uncertainty that surrounds the nature and function of the Paulian action, and the multiplicity of views defended by authors[6] over the centuries, provide an explanation for some of the discrepancies that exist among modern legal systems that contain some modern version of the *actio pauliana*.

Objectivation of the protection of creditors and *ius commune*

In the medieval *ius commune*, the Paulian action remained the basis for the protection of creditors' interests against gratuitous alienation of assets by their debtors. Authors, from Glossators to Post-commentators, showed no doubt in their appreciation of the revocatory character of the Paulian

(Naples, 1964), pp. 145–6; Biondo Biondi, *Istituzioni di diritto romano* (Milan, 1972); Giovanbattista Impallomeni, 'Azione revocatoria (diritto romano)', *Novissimo Digesto Italiano*, vol. II, pp. 148–9; Max Kaser, *Das römische Privatrecht*, part 2 (Munich, 1975), pp. 94–5; Vincenzo Arangio-Ruiz, *Istituzioni di diritto romano* (Naples, 1976), pp. 145–6; Mario Talamanca, 'Azione revocatoria' (dir. rom.), in *Enciclopedia del diritto*, vol. I, pp. 883 ff.; Antonio Guarino, *Diritto privato romano*, 10th edn (Naples, 1994), pp. 1028–9.
[2] Kipp, 'Impugnación', p. 7; Biondi, *Istituzioni di diritto romano*, p. 354; Impallomeni, 'Azione revocatoria', p. 149; Talamanca, 'Azione revocatoria', p. 886; Xavier d'Ors, *El interdicto fraudatorio en el derecho romano clásico* (Rome, 1974).
[3] Butera, *De l'azione pauliana*, p. 22; Impallomeni, 'Azione revocatoria', p. 148; Talamanca, 'Azione revocatoria', p. 886; Biondi, *Istituzioni di diritto romano*, p. 353; Arangio-Ruiz, *Istituzioni di diritto*, pp. 145–6; D'Ors, *El interdicto fraudatorio*, pp. 189 ff.
[4] Doubtful, Kipp, 'Impugnación', p. 9. On the contrary, Angelo Maierini, *Della revoca degli atti fraudolenti fatti dal debitore in pregiudizio del creditori* (Florence, 1874), pp. 30 ff.
[5] D'Ors, *El interdicto fraudatorio*, p. 25.
[6] A summary of these in Antonio Butera, 'Pauliana (Azione)', in *Digesto Italiano*, vol. XVIII.

action. This is translated into the reconstruction of the debtor's patrimony by the restitution of those goods unduly transferred from his or her estate and held by the acquirer.[7]

However, throughout the Middle Ages, with the development of commercial activities, there was an increasing need to find more flexible and agile methods of protecting creditors' interests than the Paulian action. As mentioned previously, the success of this action required evidence of the debtor's intention to defraud (*animus fraudandi*) and the acquirer's knowledge of the fraud (*scientia fraudis*). Thus, across the whole of Europe, and beginning with local laws, a clear tendency emerged to objectivate the protection of creditors and gradually abandon fraud as a decisive element for the right to protection, and to focus more on the notion of patrimonial detriment arising from acts of alienation carried out by debtors.[8]

The methods employed to strengthen the position of creditors were varied. In Germany, for example, several local laws (Magdeburg, Bamberg, Lübeck) dealing with the disappearance of the debtor declared void any alienation of property to third parties, allowing creditors to pursue the goods being held by those.[9] In Italy, presumptions of fraud proliferated within local statutes in order to facilitate recourse to the Paulian action.[10] In England, despite the fact that the Paulian action was never received, a statute of Edward III (50 Edward III, c. 6 (1376)) imposed a series of provisions aimed at avoiding fraud arising from gifts to friends and family, which eventually only applied to merchants (Law of 13 Elizabeth, c. 7 (1571)) and finally led to the regulation of bankruptcy.[11] Although we will come back to this emerging English law, we must first return our attention to an

---

[7] See the vital study by Vincenzo Piano Mortari, *L'azione revocatoria nella giurisprudenza medievale* (Milan, 1962), *passim*.

[8] See, in general, Kipp, 'Impugnación', pp. 10–11; Federico de Castro, 'La acción pauliana y la responsabilidad patrimonial. Estudio de los arts. 1.911 y 1.111 del Código civil', (1932) *RDP* 203; Salvatore Pugliatti, *La trascrizione*, vol. I (Milan, 1957), pp. 154–7; Biondo Biondi, *Le donazioni* (Turin, 1961), pp. 433–4; Ramon Maria Roca Sastre, 'L'acció pauliana i la Constitució "Per tolre fraus"', (1935) *RJC* 128–30; Ángel Rojo, 'Introducción al sistema de reintegración de la masa de la quiebra', (1979) *RDM* 40–4; Rolf Möhlenbrock, *Die Gläubigeranfechtung im deutschen und spanischen Recht* (Frankfurt, 1996), pp. 18–22.

[9] Alfred Schultze, 'Über Gläubigeranfechtung und Verfügungsbeschränkung des Schuldners nach deutschem Stadtrecht des Mittelalters', (1920) 41 *ZSS (germanistische Abteilung)* 210 ff.; Möhlenbrock, *Die Gläubigeranfechtung*, pp. 32–3.

[10] Piano Mortari, *L'azione revocatoria*, pp. 175–83.

[11] Louis Edward Levinthal, 'The Early History of English Bankruptcy', (1919) 67 *UPLR* 1 ff.; Sir William Holdsworth, *A History of English Law*, vol. IV (repr. London, 1966), pp. 480–1, vol. VIII (repr. 1966), pp. 229 ff.; Ian F. Fletcher, *The Law of Insolvency*, 2nd edn (London, 1996), pp. 6–10.

institution of Roman law which was applied to a new purpose: the insinuation of gifts.

Insinuation of gifts as a means of protection of creditors

In Roman law, insinuation was seen as an instrument for the protection of
donors themselves. Nevertheless, because of the publicity that it gave to the
donation, it could serve other purposes including, although indirectly, the
protection of a third party's interests.[12] On the other hand, in late medieval
and modern European law, the objective is to protect the donor's creditors[13]
by establishing a means of publicising donations made by debtors in order
that potential creditors had the opportunity to be made aware of the real
status of their assets.

In France, in the Dauphiné in particular, Louis XI ordered (1456) that donations be made public in order to prevent fraud, in the presence of 'bailluii
iudiciis aut castellani loci sive parrochie domicillis donatoris'; otherwise,
such donations were 'nullas atque irritas'. Of greater importance, however,

---

[12] In addition to protecting donors themselves by preventing the irreflective character of the
donation, Reinhard Zimmermann, *The Law of Obligations (Roman Foundations of the Civilian
Tradition)* (Oxford, 1996), pp. 492–3 (and p. 495), refers to the ease of obtaining evidence and
the prevention of free disposal of a third party's goods by non-authorised persons, denying
that this has a financial purpose, as maintained by Kaser, *Das römische Privatrecht*, p. 395, and
John P. Dawson, *Gifts and Promises: Continental and American Law Compared* (New Haven
and London, 1980), pp. 23–4 (this author adds as purpose the provision of authenticity to
the donation). It can be noted, for example, that in Roman-Dutch law only (R. G. McKerron,
'Registration of Gifts', (1935) 52 *SALJ* 24 ff.) Joannes Voet, *Commentariorum ad Pandectas
libri quinquaginta* (Venice, 1828), after deciding for the currency of the Roman insinuation,
indicates its function in relation to avoiding creditors' fraud: 'nec quicquam in Hollandia contra
juris civilis dispositionem cautum appareat, nec ratio est, cur apud nos cessaret insinuatio, ubi
tot dolosae in fraudem creditorum alienationes saepe confinguntur, magis iuri civili standum
videtur'. This relates to the same issue in South Africa, where insinuation originating in Roman
law – as has happened in Catalonia (*see* n. 45 below) – has remained current until very recently
(abolished by the General Law Amendment Act 70/1968, according to Zimmermann, *Law of
Obligations*, p. 500, n. 144), jurisprudence having considered that the protection of creditors
was the only reason for maintaining the institution (McKerron, 30 and n. 55, and 17–23 for a
series of judicial decisions).

[13] Catalan authors expressed it thus. For example, Joannes Petrus Fontanella, *Tractatus de pactis
nuptialibus sive capitulis matrimonialibus* (Geneva, 1684), cl. IV, gl. XXIX, n. 12: 'nostra iura
municipalia aliud proculdubio in his insinuationibus respexerunt, quam ius commune: non
enim curant de interesse donantis, ad quod ius commune attendisse visum est, sed imo ad
interesse creditorum eorum, qui donationes fecissent'; Antonius Olibanus, *Commentarii de
actionibus* (Barcelona, 1606), pars 1, lib. 3, ad § rei quaedam action, n. 6, qualified this insinuation
as 'special', because it is introduced 'ad effectum ut creditores donatoris notitiam habere possint
huiusmodi donationum'.

was the subsequent *Ordonnance* of Villers-Cotterets (1539) by Francis I, who in art. 132[14] sanctioned the obligation to insinuate across the country any donation *inter vivos* in order to make them known to creditors.[15] This rule was completed with the Declaration of February 1549 and the *Ordonnance* of Moulins in 1566. With the Edict of Louis XIV in 1703, insinuation[16] became compulsory for any act of transfer of immoveables, onerous or gratuitous, even though this Edict was in place mainly for fiscal purposes.[17]

A similar development occurred in Catalonia. The first step was the *pragmatica* of John I[18] in 1384, which included a presumption of fraud where the donor retained possession of the transferred property.[19] Nonetheless, it is after all a fraud that arises from a presumption of simulation, and its

---

[14] 'Nous voulons que toutes donations qui resont faites cy-après par & entre nos subjets, soient insinuées & enregistrées en nos Cours, & Jurisdictions ordinaires des parties, & de choses données: autrement seront reputées nulles, & ne commençeront à avoir leur effet que du jour de ladite insinuation. Et ce quant aux donations faites en la presence des donataires & par eux acceptées' (as transcribed by Carolus Molinæus, *Commentaires et annotetions sur l'ordonnance du roy François I du mois d'Aoust mil cinq cent trente-neuf, verifiée en Parlement le 6 septembre ensuivant*, in Carolus Molinaeus, *Omnia quæ extant opera*, vol. II (Paris, 1681), p. 787.

[15] Géraud de Maynard, *Notables et singulieres questions du droict escrit, decises ou preiugees par arrests memorables de la Cour Souveraine du Parlament de Tholose par . . .* (Paris, 1604), book 2, ch. 53, n. 2: 'l'insinuation fuit introduite pour obvier au dol fraude, & circomventions clandestines . . . pour n'ignorer la qualité du donateur, avec lequel ils viendroient apres à contracter, & pour y adviser sans danger'. Equally, Olivier Martin, *Histoire de la coutume de la Prévôté et Vicomté de Paris* (Paris, repr. 1972), p. [486], also indicates fiscal purposes and the protection of heirs' interests; Paul Ourliac, J. de Malafosse, *Histoire du droit privé*, vol. III (Paris, 1968), p. 465; Xavier Lagarde, 'Reflexions sur le fondement de l'article 931 du code civil', (1997) *RTDC* 26 and n. 6, quoting J. M. Ricard, *Traité des donations entre vifs et testamentaires*, vol. I (Paris, 1683), n. 1084. Dawson, *Gifts and Promises*, p. 44, considers, however, that the main purpose was the protections of heirs, as well as preventing the dissipation of the family heritage.

[16] Italy also resorted to insinuation of gifts as a means of protecting creditors, as indicated by Giuseppe Salvioli, *Storia del diritto italiano* (Turin, 1921), p. 601; Butera, *De l'azione pauliana*, pp. 27–8.

[17] For a late evolution of insinuation in France during the eighteenth century, see Robert Joseph Pothier, 'Costums des Duché, bailliages et prévoté d'Orléans, et ressort d'iceux', in *Oeuvres de Pothier*, vol. VII (Brussels, 1833), pp. 282 ff.; and P. A. Merlin, 'Insinuazione', in *Dizionario universale, ossia repertorio raggionato di giurisprudenza e questioni di diritto*, vol. VI (Venice, 1837), pp. 1245 ff.

[18] Joan Prince and Deputy General of Pere Terç in the *pragmatica* granted to Gerona on 18 October 1384 (Constitutions y Altres Drets de Catalunya (CYADC), II.7.4 (de alienations fetas en frau de creedors)).

[19] It is worth noting the broadness of the concept of 'disposal' in the historical Catalan law. This includes gift, sale, exchange, *datio in solutum*, pawn or establishment, among others (cf. CYADC I.4.19.2 – *usatge statuimus quod aliquis*; I.4.31.2; II.1.21.1; II.1.22.1; II.4.12.2; and Guillermo

effects are limited to the acts cited by the *pragmatica*.[20] Such presumption is coupled with the sanction of nullity of the act of alienation. Despite this, it clearly represents a step forward from Paulian action, where creditors must prove the existence of fraud, while the *pragmatica* places the burden on donors —inasmuch as they have to prove the absence of fraud. If the first step towards reinforcing the position of creditors was the presumption of fraud, the second step could not be any other than totally dispensing with the notion of fraud. And that is precisely what happened with the constitution *Per tolre fraus* (to avoid fraud) of Ferdinand II in the Court of Barcelona in 1503.[21]

M. de Brocá y Montagut and José Amell y Llopis, *Instituciones del derecho civil catalán vigente*, vol. II, 2nd edn (Barcelona, 1886), pp. 139–40).

[20] Jacobus Cancerius, *Variarum resolutionum iuris Cæsaris, pontificii et municipalis Principatus Cathaloniæ* (Tournon, 1635), pars 1, cap. 13, no. 84: 'talis contractus præsumitur simulatus, & in fraudem factus. Et sic per dicta Prag. in Cathalonia, qui talem contractum verum, & non simulatum dicere velit debet id probare, cum per d. iuris municipalis præsumptionem in ipsum sit onus probandis'. See, later, Pedro Nolasco Vives y Cebriá, *Traducción al castellano de los usages y demás derechos de Catalunya que no están derogados o no son notoriamente inútiles* (Barcelona, repr. 1989), pp. [1257–1258] and, towards the first half of the twentieth century, Antonio María Borrell y Soler, *Derecho civil vigente en Catalunya*, vol. I (Barcelona, 1944), p. 232 and n. 18, and Roca Sastre, 'L'acció pauliana', p. 127.

[21] CYADC, I.8.9.4:

Per tolre fraus que sovint se cometen en las donations ques fan, ab consentiment, e approbatio de la present Cort statuim, e ordenam, que qualsevol donations universals, o de la major part del patrimoni, o que excedissen sinc cents florins, ques faran, hajan esser scritas en las Corts dels Ordinaris, en lo cap de la Veguería hon ditas donations se faran, scrivint lo die que ditas donations se continuaran en dit Libre, qui sie intitulat *de donations, e heretaments,* ab una Rubrica continent los noms, e cognoms dels donadors, e donataris, e del Noteri qui haura testificada la donatio: e sino seran continuades tals donations deu dies ans del prestic, o contracte, no prejudiquen, ne puga prejudicar a creedors censalistas, ne altres que tingan lurs credits ab cartas, o albarans, encara que sien posteriors. Empero no sien entesas en la present, donations ques fan per contemplatio de Matrimoni, continuadas en los Capitols Matrimonials, si aquell sortira son effecte. E si las ditas donations se faran entre Vassalls de alguns Barons, o de Ecclesiastics, o de altres havents jurisdictio, e dins los termens de la jurisdictio de aquells, que aquellas hajan esser registradas, e continuadas en las Scrivanias de las Vilas, e Locs de hon era Domiciliat lo donador: e si tals donations seran fetas per los dits Barons, o altres havents jurisdictio, aquellas hajan de ser registradas, e continuadas en lo cap de la Veguería de la Ciutat, Vila o Loc ahont tendra lo donador lo principal Domicili. E las ditas donations no hajan força, ni valor en prejudici dels dits creedors censalistas, ni altres qui tingan lurs credits ab carta, o ab albara, sino del die de las continuations de aquellas en avant, e que lo Noteri per continuar la donatio no haja, ne puga haver, ne exigir sino tres sous per son salari, e en los Locs dels Ecclesiastics, e Barons sia pagat dit salari, a arbitre dels Senyors.

The constitution *Per tolre fraus* laid the foundations on which the rest of the system for the protection of creditors would be built, and is still in force in Catalan law. As with the preceding *pragmatica* of John I ('eidem [both sales and alienations] minime obsistentibus executio fieri valeat contra eos'), the constitution allows creditors to deal with the property despite the fact that this is no longer part of the debtor's assets. On the other hand, even though the constitution limited the creditor's scope – while the constitution only considered gifts, the *pragmatica* covered 'gifts, sales and alienations'– its effectiveness is further increased. The *pragmatica* declared transfers 'irritas atque nullas' since it presumed simulation ('tanquam fictas, & simulatas, ac infraudem creditorum factas'); the constitution, however, merely established the essential concept of 'non-detriment to creditors', dispensing, in addition, with the limitation to assets 'mobilibus, vel semoventibus, aut fructibus'.[22]

The non-insinuated gift

What were the legal effects of the lack of insinuation in respect of gifts? Concerning French law, Regnault stated:

> L'Ordonnance de 1539, les textes législatifs royaux qui l'ont suivie, les arrêts, la doctrine déclarent que la donation est nulle et de nulle effet faute d'avoir été régulièrement insinuée. Juridiquement, cette conception est inexacte. Car, elle tendrait à faire croire qu'une donation non insinuée ne peut produire aucune conséquence dans l'ordre du droit, alors qu'au contraire, elle est parfaitement valable dans les rapports du donateur et du donataire, mais que, du défaut d'insinuation, il résulte qu'un certain nombre de tiers ne peuvent se voir opposer la donation. D'où il faut dire que *la donation non insinuée est valable, mais qu'elle demeure inopposable à un certain nombre de personnes* qui n'y ont point été parties et qu'elle *ne peut préjudicier à leurs droits.*[23]

---

[22] See Ferran Badosa Coll, art. 58, in Anna Casanovas Mussons, Joan Egea Fernández, M. del Carmen Gete-Alonso Calera and Antoni Mirambell Abancó (coord.), *Comentari a la modificació de la Compilació en matèria de relacions patrimonials entre cònjuges* (Barcelona, 1995), p. 356.

[23] Henri Regnault, *Les ordonnances civiles du Chancelier Daguesseau: les donations et l'ordonnance de 1731* (Paris, 1929), p. 330 (italics by the author). Of special significance is art. 58 of the *Ordonnance* of Moulins, where it establishes that 'à faute de la dite insinuation, seront et demeuront lesdites donations *nulles et de nul valeur, tant en faveur du créancier* que de l'héritier du donnant' (reproduced by Regnault, ibid., p. 270, n. 4; see also p. 281). Therefore, he considers that insinuation presents a dual purpose: 'conformément à ses origines romaines et au

As for Catalonia, the constitution *Per tolre fraus* does not sanction non-insinuated gifts with nullity. In fact, it does not directly establish any sanction for not complying with the requirement of insinuation. It simply establishes that universal gifts of a major part of the debtor's assets or in excess of five hundred florins, if these are not registered, 'no prejudiquen ne puga[n] prejudicar' and 'no hajan força, ni valor en prejudici dels dits creedors'.

The Catalan doctrine of the sixteenth and seventeenth centuries clearly distinguished the effect of the Roman insinuation from that of Catalan registration. Thus Cancerius, who recognised that the lack of insinuation caused, in Roman law, the nullity of the gift, pointed out very carefully the different effect it caused in Catalonia: 'non praefigit tempus ad insinuandum [requirement to register the gift ten days in advance, established in the constitution *Per tolre fraus*] respectu donatoris, *quoad donationis validitatem*'. If at any point Cancerius indicated that a non-insinuated gift is void, he immediately added that it is void with respect to the creditors: 'donationem non insinuatam nullam, in præiudicium creditorum'.[24] Along the same lines, and after pointing out the different interests pursued by insinuation in Roman law and in Catalan law, Fontanella indicates that gifts 'non præiudicent, nec *quoad ipsos robur, & firmitatem aliquam* habeant nisi a die insinuationis', or that 'si insinuatæ nostræ donationes non fuerint, in nihilo prorsus creditoribus præiudicent'.[25]

but qui l'a fait établir, produit ses effets dans l'ordre du droit privé: elle permet à certains tiers de prétendre ignorer la donation, de ne pas se la voir opposer, lorsque la formalité n'a pas été remplie. Mais elle se présente aussi avec un caractère nettement fiscal' (p. 271). For a sample of the jurisprudence that, beyond the literal sense of his statements, responds to these ideas, see pp. 294 ff. Along the same lines Martin, *Histoire de la coutume*, pp. [486–7]: 'la donation non insinuée en leur était pas opposable [to creditors] mais n'en liait moins le donateur'.

[24] Cancerius, *Variarum resolutionum*, pars 1, cap. 8, nos. 19 and 24. This author pointed out other differences: in common law, if the gift was insinuated in a particular place, the insinuation would extend its effect to other assets located in a different place. This did not happen within Catalan law, because 'id procedit respectu validitatis donationis, secus in præiudicium creditorum' (n. 8); if the gift is insinuated only two days in advance, 'in contrahentium cum donatoribus præiudicium, non nocet insinuatio...talis insinuatio non habeat effectum in eorum præiudicium' (n. 20); or 'talis donatio iure Cathaloniæ simpliciter prohibeatur in præiudicium creditorum' (n. 24).

[25] Fontanella, *De pactis nuptialibus*, cl. IV, gl. XXIX, nn. 12 and 14. Besides, the concept of no detriment to creditors appears explicitly in n. 10, where he asserts that the expressions contained in the constitution *Per tolre fraus* 'solum disponuunt *non valere adversus creditores* donationes quæ non appareant insinuatæ decem dies ante contracto creditum'; that is, like Cancerius, when he introduces the concept of 'validity', this is mentioned in relation to creditors. In addition, Olibanus, *De actionibus*, pars 1, lib. 3, ad § rei quaedam action., n. 7, simply declares that the gift 'non noceret creditorib. donatoris, nisi continuata in libro donationum in capite vicariae'.

Finally, the different scopes of both insinuations become apparent in the arguments defended by Cancerius and Peguera when they reach the conclusion that insinuation in Catalan law cannot be replaced by oath, while the opposite was true of Roman law. Both authors concur that the interest protected by Catalan law is that of creditors not involved in the gift and that, as a result, an oath cannot replace the lack of insinuation.[26] Since the purpose of insinuation is to prevent detriment to creditors who ignore gifts made by their debtors, if a creditor has been made aware of the gift made by his or her debtor despite the lack of insinuation, then that gift will indeed result in detriment to the creditor.[27]

Thus, the effect of non-compliance with the formality of insinuation is the non-detriment to creditors, and their immunity with regard to the gift. But, how does this effect materialise? Fontanella[28] explains it with utmost clarity: creditors 'salva semper, & illesa eorum iura servabuntur, quod contractaverint ante insinuationem'. That is, for creditors, it is as though the goods disposed of had never been transferred from the debtor's assets, since they can execute them in order to recover their credit.

Therefore, if no sanction is explicitly established – as opposed to the aforementioned *pragmatica*, which qualified gifts as 'irritas, atque nullas' – if there is no mention of a hypothetical entitlement of creditors to challenge

---

[26] Cancerius, *Variarum resolutionum*, pars 1, cap. 8, nos. 5, 41; Ludovicus a Peguera, *Decisiones aureæ*, vol. I (Barcelona, 1605), dec. 150, n. 4; Fontanella, *De pactis nuptialibus*, cl. IV, gl. XXIX, nn. 5 to 9; Joannes Paulus Xammar, *Rerum iudicatarum in Sacro Regio Senato Cathaloniæ* (Barcelona, 1657), pars 1, *def.* 133, nos. 3 ff.; Josephus Comes, *Viridarium artis noteriatus* (Gerona, 1704), cap. 10, § 5, n. 50. It must be noted, however, that oath as a means of protection against fraud was introduced in CYADC, I.4.31.6 (so-called 'oath of Monzón', where Court was celebrated in 1537 by Charles I (V) and where this constitution was approved), although it is no longer a matter of 'detriment', but one of 'fraud'.

However, Hyeronimus Galí et Ramon, *Opera Artis Notariæ, theoricam simul, et practicam eruditionem complectentia* (Barcelona, 1682), p. 468, includes in his formulary the clause 'ut non opponatur insinuatio, et valebit donatio', which consists of nothing less than an apposition of oath. But it seems that the author did not trust the potentiality of the clause greatly, because he continues 'ad abundantem cauthelam', and adds: 'ipsam insinuo, &c. *Fiat clausula insinuationis*'. Gibert also maintained that the oath made up for the lack of insinuation, although Falguera corrects this in his note (Vicente Gibert, *Teórica del arte de notaría*, 3rd edn (Barcelona, 1875), p. 101, n. hh).

[27] Xammar, *Rerum iudicatarum*, *prefatio* to *def.* 133, where he summarised the doctrine of the *Real Audiencia*, illustrated in the judgment of 26 June 1603, as follows: 'is qui scivit donationem factam, non potest illam impugnare propter insinuationis deffectum, etiam si hoc scivisset ut tertis in donatione vocatus, cum insinuatio in donatione ex præfata constitutione requiratur ad occurrendum fraudibus, quæ committuntur contra ignorantes donationes'.

[28] Fontanella, *De pactis nuptialibus*, cl. IV, gl. XXIX, no. 20.

the gift and it is simply stated that such gifts cause no detriment and have no 'force', then we cannot state that we are dealing with the concept of validity. Consequently, we cannot accept that the lack of insinuation causes the gift to be void[29] or voidable. Given that all notion of fraud is dispensed with in order to focus on the concept of detriment, it is not easy to appreciate a revocatory effect. Rather, the term 'force' evokes the notion of effectiveness, and the fact that such lack of 'force' is mentioned in relation to creditors – remember the aforementioned statements from Cancerius and Fontanella – allows us to think of non-opposability,[30] as was the case with the French regulations.

It is worth noting that the same protection technique is already found in England in the statute of Edward III (1376), by which 'because divers people inheriting divers tenements, and borrowing divers goods in money or in merchandize, do give their tenements and chattels to their friends… it is ordened and asserted, that if it be found that such gifts be so made collusions, that the said *creditors shall have execution of the said tenements and chattels, as if no such gift has been made'*. Equally, the statute of Richard II (2 Richard II, St. 2, c. 3 (1379)): 'execution shall be made… in the same manner as that ought to have been, if no demise had been thereof made, notwithstanding the same demise'.[31]

The enlightened codifications

The French code civil

The code civil dedicates to the Paulian action its art. 1167, which establishes that creditors 'peuvent aussi, en leur nom personnel, attaquer les actes faits par leur débiteur en fraude de leurs droits'. This is founded on

---

[29] As much is stated by the Consejo Superior del Rosellón (this territory had been incorporated years earlier to the French crown) in their answer to the survey preceding the Ordonnance by Louis XV in 1731 (sixth question). In this, when the introduction of the requirement of insinuation in the constitution *Per tolre fraus* is referred to, it declares: 'mais les comissaires ont observé que la constitution qui a prescrit la formalité *ne prononce point la peine de la nullité'* (Regnault, *Les ordonnances civiles*, p. 442).

[30] Which has already been applied by José J. Pintó Ruiz, 'Insinuación', in *Nueva Enciclopedia Jurídica Seix*, vol. XII (Barcelona, 1977), p. 856 (and also pp. 859, 860 and 861) and 'Los bienes puestos a nombre de la mujer en el derecho civil de Catalunya', in Cátedra 'Durán y Bas', *Estudios jurídicos sobre la mujer catalana* (Barcelona, 1971), pp. 92, n. 21, 108, n. 73, 110 or 111, n. 82); and by Maximino I. Linares Gil, 'Inoponibilidad de las donaciones en el derecho civil catalán (Una propuesta de interpretación del artículo 340.3 de la Compilación de Catalunya)', (1998) *RJC* 47–9.

[31] As transcribed by Levinthal, 'The early history', pp. 11–13.

Domat's[32] work, since Pothier hardly dedicates a few lines to the study of this action in his *Traité des obligations*.[33] Domat[34] does not deflect from the already known principles about the Paulian action because he shapes it as a revocatory action whose effect is restitution, both of the transferred property and of its fruits.

Such frugal regulation in the code civil soon caused a doctrinal debate about the effects of the success of the Paulian action. On one hand, some authors defended the purely revocatory nature of the action. Duranton[35] was one of them. Others, to a greater or lesser extent, considered that there was no revocatory effect inasmuch as the contract between the debtor and a third party was and continued to be valid. Therefore, the only effect was that the creditor could pursue the alienated goods despite these being part of the third party's assets.[36] Yet others remained much more ambiguous.[37]

---

[32] Jean Domat, *Les Loix civiles dans leur ordre naturel* (Paris, 1777), book 2, title 10.

[33] Robert Joseph Pothier, *Traité des obligations*, n. 153, in *Oeuvres* de Pothier (Brussels, 1829), vol. I:

> Observez, néanmoins, que si le débiteur, lorsqu'il a fait passer à un tiers la chose qu'il s'était obligé de me donner, n'était pas solvable, je pourrais agir contre le tiers acquéreur pour faire rescinder l'aliénation qui lui a été faite en fraude de ma créance, porvu qu'il a ait été àrticipiant de la fraude, *conscius fraudis*, s'il était acquéreur à titre onéreux: s'il était acquéreur à titre gratuit, il en serait pas même nécessaire pour cela qu'il eût été participiant de la fraude.
>
> It should be noted that these brief indications are contained in art. II, *De l'effet de l'obligation par raport au créancier*, not deserving a section in their own right.

[34] *Les Loix civiles*, book 2, title 10, s I, I–VII, s II, I–III.

[35] A. Duranton, *Cours de droit civil français*, vol. VI, 4th edn (Brussels, 1841), n. 574: 'par l'annullation ou révocation des actes, les biens rentrent dans le domaine du débiteur, comme s'ils n'en étaient jamais sortis... Les biens ainsi rentrés dans son patrimoine sont donc le gage commun de tous les créanciers'.

[36] C. Demolombe, *Traité des contrats ou des obligations conventionelles*, 2nd edn (Paris, 1871), n. 245 ff., n. 247: 'cette révocation est relative, et... elle n'a lieu que dans l'intérêt du créancier demandeur, afin seulement d'empêcher que cet acte lui soit opposable'; F. Aubry and F. L. Rau, *Cours de droit civil français*, vol. IV, 5th edn (Paris, 1902), § 313, pp. 219, 234 ('l'admission de l'action paulienne contre un acte d'aliénation, tout en opérant revocation de cet acte, ne fait pas rentrer dans le patrimoine du débiteur les biens par lui aliénés: elle a seulement pour effet de rendre possible l'exercice du droit de gage établi par l'art. 2092') and n. 38; Fr. Mourlon, *Répétitions écrites sur le deuxième examen du Code Napoléon* (Paris, 1859), art. 1167: 'remaquons que cette révocation n'est pas absolue... c'est une révocation relative'.

[37] F. Laurent, *Principes de droit civil*, vol. XVI, 2nd edn (Brussels, 1876), nn. 431, 483, 484 ff. or 488, despite rejecting the opinions of Demolombe and Aubry and Rau and defending that 'le bien rentre dans le patrimoine du débiteur, et pour cela il faut que l'acte qui l'en a fait sortir soit annullé', admits that 'cet acte subsiste entre les parties contractantes', and resolves this obvious contradiction by invoking fiction.

Similarly, art. 1235 of the codice civile of 1865 stated that 'possono pure i creditori impugnare in proprio nome gli atti che il debitore abbia fatti in frode delle loro ragioni'. Authors also discussed the meaning of the verb *impugnare* with regard to the effectiveness of the *azione revocatoria*.[38] Likewise, the Spanish Civil Code incorporated with similar wording artt. 1111 and 1291.3.

The Germanic law systems

Germanic legal systems, as early as the Prussian *Allgemeiner Landrecht*, did not incorporate the Paulian action into their civil codes. Instead, this was regulated by insolvency laws. In particular, the law *Betreffend die Anfechtung von Rechtshandlungen eines Schuldners außerhalb des Konkursverfahrens* (AnfG 21 July 1879) deserves special mention, since it embodies the actio pauliana. The AnfG uses the term *Anfechtung* but does not clarify the effects of the said impugnation of the act of alienation. Despite agreeing on its restitutory effect – given the parallel with the legal consequences of nullity, according to § 142 BGB – German authors defended different positions; from relative nullity (*relative Nichtigkeit*) to real relative ineffectiveness (*relative dingliche unwirksamkeit*).[39] From there the doctrine developed towards the idea that what is really important is that the goods disposed of must continue to guarantee fulfilment of the debtor's obligations, and are subject to the creditor's power of execution, despite the use in § 7 AnfG of the term *Rückgewähr*.[40]

The Saxony Civil Code, however, gave a detailed account of the Paulian action. Paragraph 1509 starts with an indication of the creditor's entitlement to challenge gifts made by the debtor 'as required in order to satisfy the credit'. Such opposition in relation to non-remunerated gifts was not covered by the acquirer's *scientia fraudis* (§ 1513). But this subjective status had repercussions on the legal effects of the impugnation: if *scientia fraudis*

---

[38] Maierini, *Della revoca*, pp. 45 and 217 ff., for example, qualifies revocation as relative and not absolute, since it was only effective to the credit limit of the affected creditor; also Emidio Pacifici-Mazzoni, *Istituzioni di diritto civile italiano*, vol. IV (Florence, 1920), pp. 460–1 and 521; and Massimo Ferrara Santamaria, *Inefficacia e inopponibilità* (Naples, 1939), pp. 124 ff., who considered it an assumption of *inopponibilità*. Butera, *De l'azione pauliana*, pp. 94 ff, on the other hand, considered that the action implied reinstatement of the goods to the debtor's assets.

[39] See a summary of divers opinions in Möhlenbrock, *Die Gläubigeranfechtung*, pp. 50–2.

[40] Möhlenbrock, *Die Gläubigeranfechtung*, pp. 52–5.

was found, the acquirer was obliged either to restitution (*Rückerstattung*) of non-perishable goods or to restore to the creditor a *tantundem* of perishable goods (§ 1514); but if the acquirer had acted in good faith ('in redlichem Glauben'), the responsibility of the said acquirer was limited to his enrichment (§ 1517).

Codifications, recodifications and reinterpretations of civil codes in the twentieth century

The Italian codice civile of 1942

The Italian Civil Code of 1942 solves any doubts allowed by art. 1235 of the 1865 Code by establishing explicitly in art. 2.901 with the *azione revocatoria* that 'creditors, albeit their credit being subject to terms or conditions, can request that any gifts made by their debtors to the creditors' detriment, be declared void in relation to the said creditors'. Scholars considered that this article stated the relative ineffectiveness of the debtor's detrimental act. That is, the transferred property is not reinstated to the debtor's assets, but remains within the acquirer's assets subject to execution by the creditor. Creditors are thus immunised against the effects of their debtors' acts, since these are not to their detriment, despite the act remaining valid for each party.[41]

Reinterpretation of the Civil Code in France and Spain

The variety of opinions of the exegetes mentioned above has turned to unanimous thinking among French scholars in the twentieth century, who qualify the Paulian action, regulated in art. 1167,[42] as an action of *inopposabilité*. The aim of the action is believed to be no other than redressing any losses caused to the creditor as a consequence of the debtor's act of alienation. Therefore, 'il suffit que l'acte frauduleux soit privé d'effets à l'égard du ou des créanciers lésés, et dans la mesure du préjudice subi',

---

[41] Francesco Messineo, *Doctrina general del contrato*, vol. II (Buenos Aires, 1952), p. 312; Emilio Betti, *Teoría general de las obligaciones*, vol. II (Madrid, 1970), esp. pp. 407–8; Alberto Trabucchi, *Istituzione di diritto civile*, 27th edn (Padua, 1985), pp. 597–8; Pietro Rescigno, *Manuale del diritto privato italiano*, 11th edn (Naples, 1996), p. 664; Paolo Zatti and Vittorio Colussi, *Lineamenti di diritto privato*, 6th edn (Padua, 1997), p. 357; Juan Antonio Fernández Campos, 'Algunas consideraciones sobre la acción revocatoria en el derecho italiano', (1997) *ADC* 631 ff.

[42] Of essentially identical wording to the current art. 1167 of the Belgian Civil Code.

that is, 'l'*inopposabilité* de l'acte à ceux auxquels il porte préjudice'.[43] Thus, the detrimental act continues to be valid among the parties, and the remnant – after restoring any losses to the creditor – remains property of the acquirer.

In Spain, the Paulian action appears in artt. 1111 and 1291.3 of the código civil. Traditionally, it was considered to produce a revocatory effect since art. 1298, for example, refers to 'devolution' of property. Recently, however, an increasing number of authors – clearly influenced by developments in France and Italy – claim that the success of the Paulian action translates into relative ineffectiveness or non-opposability of the gift in relation to the creditor.[44]

Article 340.3 of the Compilació del dret civil *of Catalonia*

In Catalonia, art. 340.3 CDCC (enacted in 1960) includes regulation based in the aforementioned constitution *Per tolre fraus*[45] and establishes an objective system for the protection of creditors which edges around the issue

---

[43] François Terré, Philippe Simler and Yves Lequette, *Droit civil: les obligations*, 6th edn (Paris, 1996), nn. 1059–60; Christian Larroumet, *Droit civil: les obligations. Le contrat*, vol. III, 2nd edn (Paris, 1990), n. 765; Jacques Ghestin, *Traité de droit civil: les obligations* (Paris, 1992), nn. 721 ff.; Alain Bénabent, *Droit civil: les obligations*, 5th edn (Paris, 1995), n. 858; Rémy Cabrillac, *Droit des obligations*, 2nd edn (Paris, 1996), n. 494; Philippe Malaurie and Laurent Aynès, *Cours de droit civil: tome VI, Les obligations*, 7th edn (Paris, 1996), n. 1038; Jean-Pascal Chazal, 'La acción pauliana en derecho francés', in Joaquín J. Forner Delaygua (ed.), *La protección del crédito en Europa* (Barcelona, 2000), pp. 73 ff. (Spanish), pp. 177 ff. (French). Nevertheless, occasionally a statement is found which is not consistent with the shaping of the Paulian action as non-opposability; thus, Ghestin, *Les obligations*, n. 724, indicates that 'l'acte ne sera *revoqué* que jusqu'à concurrence de la somme nécessaire au paiement'; Bénabent (*Droit civil*, n. 858) considers that the third party affected by the Paulian action 'qui doit restituer le bien' need not 'être dépouillé que dans l'exacte mesure necessaire' and that, 'si le bien vaut plus que la créance de ce dernier, il peut réclamer la différence'. Likewise Malaurie and Aynès, *Les obligations*, n. 1038: 'si le tiers a été obligé de restituer au créancier l'objet frauduleusement acquis, il a donc contre son auteur un recours en garantie'.

[44] Manuel Albaladejo, *Derecho civil, II, Derecho de obligaciones*, vol. I, 9th edn (Barcelona, 1994), pp. 214, 228–9; Ángel Cristóbal Montes, *La vía pauliana* (Madrid, 1997), esp. pp. 183 ff.; Juan Antonio Fernández Campos, *El fraude de acreedores: la acción pauliana* (Bologna, 1998); Guillermo Lohmann Luca de Tena, 'Apuntes para una distinta aproximación a la acción pauliana', (1984) *RGLJ* 469 ff.; Vicente L. Montés Penadés, in M. R. Valpuesta Fernández (coord.), *Derecho de obligaciones y contratos* (Valencia, 1994), pp. 218–19, 222–3; Francisco de A. Sancho Rebullida, in José Luis Lacruz Berdejo et al., *Elementos de Derecho civil, II, Derecho de obligaciones*, vol. I, 3rd edn (Barcelona, 1994), pp. 254–6.

[45] Formally – although in practical terms it had fallen completely into disuse over a century before – insinuation was in force in Catalonia until 1960.

of fraud to concentrate exclusively on the creditor's detriment derived from the gratuitous alienation. The article establishes as the only effect that of 'no detriment' of creditors, which means that, according to the Catalan legal tradition briefly mentioned before,[46] protection is built on the non-opposability of the act of detriment to creditors.[47] Yet most authors still consider the mechanism of the said art. 340.3 an *acció revocatòria*[48] as a result of the influence of the Spanish Civil Code.

The new European Insolvency Acts

There has been a major legal reform in Germany. The old Konkurs-ordnung has been abolished and replaced by the Insolvenzordnung of 21 April 1994,[49] while a similar fate has befallen the AnfG of 1879, replaced by AnfG 1999. Thus, a distinction remains between impugnation of fraudulent transactions within and outside bankruptcy. As far as im-pugnation outside bankruptcy is concerned, in the current manifestation of the Paulian action in German law, § 11 AnfG 1999 reaffirms the line of development mentioned above, since reference is made not to norms on *Anfechtung*, but to those on unjust enrichment.[50] The obligational nature of *Anfechtungsanspruch* is confirmed: the object of the creditor's action is to achieve satisfaction of the credit allowing, if necessary, the execution of goods that are no longer within the debtor's patrimony. But without

---

[46] Basis for the interpretation and integration of current law, according to art. 1 CDCC.

[47] José J. Pintó Ruiz, 'Los bienes puestos a nombre de la mujer en el derecho civil de Catalunya', in Cátedra 'Durán y Bas', *Estudios jurídicos sobre la mujer catalana* (Barcelona, 1971), pp. 76, 92, 94, 97, 108, 110–11, 131, 135 and 141–2; Anna Casanovas Mussons, art. 19, and Ferran Badosa Coll, art. 58, in Casanovas et al. (coord.), *Comentari a la modificació*, pp. 165 and 356; Linares Gil, 'Inoponibilidad de las donaciones', *passim*; Antoni Vaquer Aloy, 'Inoponibilidad y acción pauliana (La protección de los acreedores del donante en el art. 340.3 de la Compilación del Derecho Civil de Catalunya)', (1999) *ADC* 1491 ff.

[48] Ramón M. Roca Sastre, 'La acción revocatoria de donaciones en la Compilación', (1962) *ADC* 3 ff.; Juan Egea Fernández, art. 340, in Manuel Albaladejo (ed.), *Comentarios al Código civil y Compilaciones forales*, vol. XXX (Madrid, 1985), pp. 815 ff.; Susana Navas Navarro, *El régimen de separación de bienes y la protección de terceros* (Valencia, 1996), pp. 96 and 97; Lluís Puig Ferriol and Encarna Roca Trias, *Institucions del dret civil de Catalunya*, vol. I, 5th edn (Valencia, 1998), pp. 142 ff.

[49] About the aims of the reform, Harald Hess, *Insolvenzrecht*, 4th edn (Cologne, 1996), pp. 219 ff.

[50] § 11 AnfG 1999: 'Was durch die anfechtbare Rechtshandlung aus dem Vermögen des Schuldners veräußert, weggegeben oder aufgegeben ist, muß dem Gläubiger zur Verfügung gestellt werden, soweit es zu dessen Befriedigung erfordelich ist. Die Vorschriften über die Rechtsfolgen einer ungerechtfertigten Bereicherung, bei der dem Empfänger der Mangel des rechtlichen Grundes bekannt ist, gelten entsprechend.'

resorting to their restitution – as opposed to what happens in impugnation within bankruptcy, where according to § 143 IO there is restitution of transferred property. It is enough merely to allow the creditor to execute those goods that belonged to the debtor. The main goal is to satisfy the creditor, and in order to do so it is not necessary to reinstate the transferred goods to the debtor's patrimony, if the plaintiff is entitled to satisfy his credit with the said goods regardless of their current ownership.[51]

In a similar way, § 13 of the Austrian Anfechtungsordnung grants creditors the right to claim as much as necessary to satisfy their credit – that is, the right to execute those goods that belonged to the debtor despite the fact that they are owned by a third-party recipient. This third party can avoid the said demand by satisfying the debtors' obligation which founds the action (§ 17 AnfO). Austrian case law also rules that the gift is neither void nor voidable, but that the acquirer must accept enforcement within his own patrimony.[52]

As for English law, s 423 of the Insolvency Act of 1985 takes account of a similar case to that resulting in Paulian action: transactions defrauding creditors. These are defined as: 'transactions entered into an undervalue', such as donations and transactions without consideration or 'for a consideration the value of which, in money or money's worth, is significantly less than the value, in money or money's worth, of the consideration provided by himself'. However, any similarities with the Paulian action end there. If one of the aforementioned acts is deemed executed with the intention of placing the goods out of reach of creditors or defrauding these in any way, the legal authority has the discretion to decide on a measure in accordance with provisions made by s 425 in order to repair any detriment caused to the creditor (orders requiring any property transferred to be vested in any person, requiring persons to pay money in respect of benefits received from debtor, etc.), none of which corresponds with what could be considered typical effects of the Paulian action.[53]

---

[51] Mark Zeuner, *Die Anfechtung in der Insolvenz* (Munich, 1999), pp. 242 ff.; Harald Hess and Michaela Weis, *Anfechtungsrecht* (Heidelberg, 1999), pp. 252 ff.

[52] See Franz Mohr (ed.), *Die Konkurs-, Ausgleichs- und Anfechtungsordnung*, 8th edn (Vienna, 1995), p. 739.

[53] Ian S. Grier and Richard E. Floyd, *Personal Insolvency: A Practical Guide*, 2nd edn (London, 1993), pp. 137–9; Carmen Jerez Delgado, *Los actos objetivamente fraudulentos (la acción de rescisión por fraude de acreedores)* (Madrid, 1999), pp. 94–8; Robert Stevens and Lionel Smith, 'La acción pauliana en derecho inglés', in Forner (ed.), *La protección del crédito en Europa*, pp. 95 ff. (Spanish), pp. 195 ff. (English).

The mixed legal systems

In mixed legal systems, the Paulian action is regulated by the Civil Code of Louisiana under the term 'revocatory action'. This is, apparently, the code that remains most loyal to the Roman tradition. Article 2036 states that 'an obligee has the right to annul an act ... that causes or increases the obligor's insolvency', and the result of this is that 'assets transferred must be returned' (art. 2043). However, the same article specifies that 'that act or result shall be annulled only to the extent that it affects the obligee's right', maintaining its validity in relation to third parties.[54] Therefore, it lacks a real restitutory character since, in fact, the act is valid and the acquirer maintains ownership of the object transferred, despite this being subject to the execution by the plaintiff for the satisfaction of his credit.

In Scotland, gratuitous alienations and other fraudulent transactions are subject to challenge in common law and under the provisions of the Insolvency Act (1985). In both cases, the first measure to be adopted is the reduction of the alienation or restitution of the transferred property to the debtor for the benefit of all creditors: 'The effect of the nullity is simply to restore the alienated subject to the position in which it was before the alienation. It becomes assets of the bankrupt's estate, and may be attached by the diligence of the creditor who has established the nullity, and also by other creditors whose claims are prior in time to the alienation'.[55] Equally, s 34 of the 1985 Act establishes that 'the court shall grant decree of reduction or order restoration of property to the debtor's estate or other redress as may be appropriate'. It has also been stated that 'it is in our opinion clear from the reading of s.34(4) that the general purpose is to provide that, as far as possible, any property which has been improperly alienated should be restored to the debtor's estate',[56] despite the fact that this may not be possible if a register has to be rectified.[57] The Scottish law is, therefore, the one that

---

[54] *Zuberbier v. Morse*, 1884, 36, La. Ann. 970; Albert Tate, Jr, 'The Revocatory Action in Louisiana Law', in Joseph Dainow (ed.), *Essays on the Civil Law of Obligations* (Baton Rouge, 1969), p. 134.

[55] *Cook v. Sinclair & Co.* (1896) 23 R. 925 (quoted by William W. McBryde, *Bankruptcy*, 2nd edn (Edinburgh, 1995), pp. 301–2; see also pp. 284–326). See also Grier and Floyd, *Personal Insolvency*, p. 173; Donna W. McKenzie, 'Gratuitous Alienations and Unfair Preferences in Insolvency', (1993) 38 *JLSS* 141 ff.; Donna W. McKenzie Skene, *Insolvency Law in Scotland* (Edinburgh, 1999), pp. 233 ff.

[56] *Short's Tr. v. Chung* (*in* McBryde, *Bankruptcy*, p. 311).

[57] McBryde, *Bankruptcy*, pp. 311 and 313. It should be noted, in addition, that originally the normal remedy was reduction without *restitutio in integrum*.

remains more closely related to the tradition of the *ius commune*, since the effects of challenging the gratuitous alienation are clearly revocatory.

Synthesis in the Civil Code of Quebec

A synthesis of this whole process, from revocation to non-opposability, can be found in the Civil Code of Quebec. § 3 (of ch. 6, performance of obligations, s 3, protection of the right to performance of obligations, artt. 1631 ff.) and is entitled in French 'De l'action en inopposabilité', and in English 'Paulian action'. Article 1631 establishes that 'the creditor who suffers prejudice through a juridical act made by his debtor in fraud of his rights... may obtain a declaration that the act may not be set up against him'.[58] Thus, it dispels any doubts raised by previous legislation contained in the code civil du Bas-Canada about whether the fraudulent act was null or merely non-opposable.[59] It has been pointed out that the origin of this late regulation is found in the revocatory action regulated by the French code civil.[60] Therefore, we can say that the Civil Code of Quebec synthesises the evolution experienced by the Paulian action from its formulation in Justinian times, a general development found in most legal systems containing any kind of mechanism for the protection of the rights of creditors related to any greater or lesser extent to the Roman law action.

Fraud and detriment

So far we have seen how, in Roman law, the Paulian action relied on the elementary notion of fraud; and how, from the Middle Ages, local legislators made divers efforts to separate the protection of creditors from fraud

---

[58] Consequently, as indicated by Jean-Louis Baudouin and Pierre-Gabriel Jobin, *Les Obligations*, 5th edn (Quebec, 1998), p. 553, 'le bien ne rentre pas dans le patrimoine du débiteur où il pourrait être saisi par tous les créanciers, mais, au contraire, sert les intérêts exclusifs du demandeur'. Also see Vincent Karim, *Commentaires sur les obligations*, vol. II (Cowansville, 1997), pp. 367 ff.

[59] Article 1032 stated that 'creditors may in their own name impeach the acts of their debtors', while art. 1033 involved the term 'avoid'. However, jurisprudence indicated that revocation was partial – only to the extent of the amounts of their claims – and that the act remained valid between debtor and third party. Raymond Landry, 'The Revocatory Action in the Quebec Civil Code: General Principles', in Dainow (ed.), *Essays on the Civil Law of Obligations*, pp. 115 ff. (p. 130), proposed that 'instead of declaring that the fraudulent act is void, an expression which does not indicate the true consequences of the Paulian action, the Code should simply say that the fraudulent act cannot be opposed to the creditors'.

[60] Baudouin and Jobin, *Les Obligations*, pp. 535–6.

because of the obvious evidential difficulties this posed. Modern codes have maintained the requirement of fraud, despite introducing presumption of the fraudulent nature of gratuitous alienations. So, for example, art. 643.2 of the Spanish Civil Code presumes fraudulent, *iuris et de iure*, any gifts made by those who do not keep enough property to satisfy their debts. Article 1633 of the Civil Code of Quebec (which, on the other hand, still evokes the *scientia fraudis*) considers fraudulent ('présomption irréfragable') the gratuitous transfer when the debtor becomes insolvent, thus confirming that we are dealing with a purely objective understanding of fraud.[61]

It would seem, therefore, more opportune to dispense with the notion of fraud and to focus exclusively on the prejudice caused to the creditor by the act of gratuitous alienation, as does the Catalan law. Prejudice is no more than a reduction of the debtor's assets below the level of his debts; that is, insolvency, or the inability of the debtor's estate to respond to the single or multiple creditors. We must bear in mind, however, that prejudice must be measured in relation to the debtor's solvency at the time when the debt originated. Therefore, each creditor has his or her own solvency level. So, each act of gratuitous alienation is inherently detrimental, since it causes the loss of an element of the assets without any consideration to replace it. Since most legal systems acknowledge prejudice as a requirement of the modern forms of the Paulian action,[62] this should suffice and fraud could be dispensed with as an independent requirement.

Non-opposability as a means of protection of creditors

We must nevertheless accept that *inopposabilité*, or its German relative *Unwirksamkeit*, is a figure that has not reached enough doctrinal consensus.[63] The latter, for example, carries the weight associated with dependency on relative prohibitions to dispose (§§ 135–7 BGB).[64] In general,

---

[61] Ibid., p. 550.

[62] § 1 AnfG 1999; § 2 AnfO; art. 2901 codice civile; art. 340.3 CDCC; McBryde, *Bankruptcy*, p. 293; art. 2036 Civil Code of Louisiana; art. 1631 Civil Code of Quebec.

[63] About the notion of non-opposability, Daniel Bastian, *Essai d'une théorie générale de l'inopposabilité* (Paris, 1929); Ferrara Santamaria, *Inefficacia e inopponibilità*, *passim*; Hubert Beer, *Die relative Unwirksamkeit* (Berlin, 1975); Luis-Felipe Ragel Sánchez, *Protección del tercero frente a la actuación jurídica ajena: la inoponibilidad* (Madrid, 1994); Vaquer, 'Inoponibilidad y acción pauliana', *passim*.

[64] Beer, *Relative Unwirksamkeit*, p. 94. For a summary of efforts by authors to configure these *Verfügungsverbote* see Peter Bülow, 'Grundfragen der Verfügungsverbote', (1994) 34 *JuS* 7–8;

non-opposability aims to protect creditors against legal consequences derived from certain legal acts of alienation of property by their debtors, thus
preventing detriment to their judicial position. Such legal acts are valid and
effective, but they are also ideally suited to cause detriment to the creditor, since they result in a reduction of the debtor's property and therefore
what they really pursue – without questioning the validity of the gratuitous
alienation – is to maintain that property's value for the debtor. Thus the
plaintiff is entitled to execute alienated goods found in the patrimony of the
acquirer as if these were still part of the debtor's assets, and thus recover his
or her credit. Therefore, once the creditor is satisfied, the remnant remains
the property of the acquirer.

Non-opposability constitutes a mechanism of solving the conflict created
between the third party and the owner in relation to the same asset.[65] The
donatee has acquired ownership of the object donated, in conflict with
the donor's creditor – who, alien to the donation, counted on that asset
as guarantee of his credit. The solution of this conflict involves granting
primacy to this guarantee – the creditor's – above the donatee's ownership,[66]
inasmuch as the change of ownership does not affect and is not detrimental –
is non-opposable – to the creditor. The basis, thus, of non-opposability lies
in the precedence of the credits protected. Therefore, we can say that the
precedent guarantee prevails over the subsequent ownership resulting from
the gratuitous alienation.

From this notion of non-opposability we must grant that, if the recipient
who is affected by the act of non-opposable disposal repairs any prejudice
caused – in the case that occupies us, if he or she satisfies any detriment
caused to the creditor – the said recipient can ward off the consequences
of the non-opposability, paralyse its effects, and in particular avoid the
right to execute the alienated goods. Consequently, the first limitation to
non-opposability is facilitated by the very prejudice on which it finds its
sustenance.

Jürgen Köhler, § 135, in *J. von Staudingers Kommentar zum Bürgerlichen Gesetzbuch mit
Einführungsgesetz und Nebengesetzen*, vol. I (Allgemeiner Teil, §§ 134–63), 13th edn (Berlin,
1996), pp. 137–9.

[65] Thus, Vincenzo Scalisi, 'Inefficacia (dir. Priv.)', in *Enciclopedia del diritto*, vol. XXI, pp. 355 and
359–60.

[66] The same argument was used by Lothar Holzapfel, *Ehegattenschenkungen und Gläubigerschutz*
(Bonn, 1979), pp. 22–3, to justify the faculty given to creditors to challenge donations between
spouses §§ 32.2 KO and 3.1.4 AnfG in German law.

Consequently, we can assert that non-opposability constitutes a solution of compromise or balance between the owner's right of free disposition of his property and the protection of third parties who suffer prejudice as a consequence of the act of disposal. This balance is built on the basis of indemnity, both of the validity and of the effectiveness of the act – the act remains valid and typically effective – in respect of third parties who do not suffer detrimental effects in their judicial position, or any loss or prejudice. Non-opposability represents, in short, a mechanism of protection of third parties and, in this work in particular, of the donor's creditors. This mechanism is judicially less traumatic, since the detrimental act[67] remains, from the point of view of validity and effectiveness, intact.

One last remaining issue is that of the prescription and limitation periods. There is a wide range of periods cited in the literature: one year in the Civil Code of Quebec and in that of Louisiana (art. 2041, one year from the moment where the execution of the detrimental act was known, with a maximum period of three years from the moment where the act actually took place); four years in the Spanish Civil Code (art. 1299); five in the Italian (art. 2903) and Portuguese (art. 616); twenty in Scots law.[68] In fact, the need to set a fixed period of time is questionable. If protection is based

---

[67] Authors have expressed this idea in various ways from the respective conception of this figure. Bastian, *Essai d'une théorie générale*, pp. 355–6, considers that 'l'inopposabilité constitue un principe de bonne économie juridique... destinée uniquement à la protection des tiers, elle ne frappe les actes qui leur nuissent que dans les limites strictement nécessaires'. For Ferrara Santamaria, *Inefficacia e inopponibilità*, p. 196, non-opposability 'si presenta in fine come una appropiata applicazione giuridica del principio di ragion pratica del minimo mezzo'. Gotthard Paulus, 'Schranken des Gläubigerschutzes aus relativer Unwirksamkeit', in Rolf Dietz and Heinz Hübner (eds.), *Festschrift für Hans Karl Nipperdey*, vol. I (Munich and Berlin, 1965), p. 909, states that

> Mit der Kategorie der relativen Unwirksamkeit steht der gesetzlichen Regelungstechnik ein Instrument vorbeugenden Rechtsschutzes zur Verfügung, mit dessen Hilfe das Interesse des Rechtinhabers an freier Ausübung seiner Dispositionsgewalt in besonders kunstvoller Weise auf das schon jetz beachtenswerte, aber erst später definitiv kontrollierbare Interesse eines Dritten an der Gewährleistung künftigen Erwerbs abgestimmt werden kann. Die oft als zu schroff empfundene Alternative des Alles oder Nichts ist durch eine elegante Zwischenlösung verdrängt.

Claus-Wilhelm Canaris, 'Die Rechtsfolgen rechtsgeschäftlicher Abtretungsverbote', in Ulrich Huber and Erik Jayme (eds.), *Festschrift für Rolf Serick zum 70. Geburtstag* (Heidelberg, 1992), p. 13, indicates that 'bietet das deutsche Recht durch die Konstruktion relativer Unwirksamkeit i.S. der §§ 135 f. BGB einen Ausweg, der einen Kompromiß der Interessen auf der *dinglichen* Ebene erlaubt'.

[68] McBryde, *Bankruptcy*, p. 301.

on the detriment suffered by the creditor and is built on the concept of non-opposability, it would seem more coherent to link the currency of the remedy of protection to the credit it intends to protect, so that the period during which the creditor is protected coincides with that of enforcement of the credit to which the debtor is causing detriment by his or her act of alienation.[69] On the contrary, a paradox can occur where the action to claim the right of credit prescribes before that of the Paulian action (for example, the period of expiry of the action to claim for tort in art. 1968.2 of the Spanish Civil Code is one year, while the Paulian action prescribes four years).

The fact that the Paulian action is contained, in one form or another, in the various European legal systems offers a very strong argument for its inclusion among the principles of a harmonised European contract law, on the grounds mentioned above. That is, to build the protection on the basis of non-opposability of the alienation against the creditor; thus setting aside fraud, to focus on detriment as foundation of the action in the case of gratuitous alienations, and tying its period of limitation to the currency of the credit being protected.

---

[69] And I have defended it thus in relation to Catalan law: See Vaquer Aloy, 'Inoponibilidad y acción pauliana'.

10

Epistle to Catalonia: romance and *rentabilidad* in an anglophone mixed jurisdiction

SHAEL HERMAN

Preface

Twenty years ago, two of my colleagues joined me in publishing a slender pamphlet entitled *The Louisiana Civil Code: A Humanistic Appraisal.*[1] A non-technical book aimed primarily at a readership untrained in law, it sketched the unusual history and social vision of the Louisiana Civil Code, which was first enacted by a fledgling Louisiana legislative assembly in 1808.[2] Besides sketching the philosophical and historical foundations of

---

[1] Shael Herman, David Combe and Thomas Carbonneau, *The Louisiana Civil Code: A Humanistic Appraisal* (New Orleans, 1981) (hereinafter sometimes Pamphlet). The Pamphlet formed the basis for Shael Herman, *The Louisiana Civil Code: A European Legacy for the United States* (New Orleans, 1993).

[2] The full name of the original Code was *Digest of the Civil Law Now in Force in the Territory of Orleans.* In the scholarly community, there has been debate about whether this digest was a compilation rather than a civil code along the lines of the Code Napoleon, but for present purposes the distinction is unimportant. The crucial factor is that it spoke with a decidedly Romanist or civilian voice, and historians generally regard it as the earliest Louisiana codification. The Pamphlet, p. 57, sets forth a chronology of important events in Louisiana history, including later recodifications. About the debt of the *Digest* and later codifications to French and Spanish sources, there has been vigorous debate for several decades. See R. Batiza, 'The Influence of Spanish Law in Louisiana', (1958) 33 *Tulane LR* 29; R. Batiza, 'The Louisiana Civil Code of 1808: Its Actual Sources and Present Relevance', (1971) 46 *Tulane LR* 4; R. Batiza, 'Sources of the Civil Code of 1808, Facts and Speculation: A Rejoinder', (1972) 46 *Tulane LR* 628; R. Batiza, 'The Actual Sources of the Louisiana Projet of 1823: A General Analytical Survey', (1972) 47 *Tulane LR* 1; R. Pascal, 'Sources of the Digest of 1808: To Professor Batiza', (1972) 46 *Tulane LR* 603; R. Batiza, *Domat, Pothier, and the Code Napoleon: Some Observations Concerning the Actual Sources of the French Code* (private printing, 1973); R. Batiza, *The Verbatim and Almost Verbatim Sources of the Louisiana Civil Code of 1808, 1825, and 1870: The Original Texts* (New Orleans, private printing, 1973). On the role of Roman law in early Louisiana jurisprudence, see S. Herman, 'The Contribution of Roman Law to the Jurisprudence of Antebellum Louisiana', (1995) 56 *Louisiana LR* 257; S. Herman, 'Der Einfluss des Römischen Rechts auf die Rechtswissenschaft

the Civil Code, our pamphlet sought to reply to a persistent lament from lawyers in Louisiana and other states. In Louisiana's distinctive legal tradition, the lawyers thought they confronted unacceptable complications for their business practice and a futile resistance to a United States juggernaut driving us all toward legal uniformity. Against such criticism the pamphlet's contrarian authors persevered. For us, the unusual contour cut by the Louisiana Civil Code in the legal landscape of the United States was reason for celebration rather than lament. For the state's citizens, the Louisiana Civil Code was by 1981 a permanent fixture, fully incorporated for over 170 years into the state's legal institutions and undergoing extensive modernisation to suit it to social needs and law practice in the twenty-first century. Here is the celebratory introduction of our opening section entitled 'Vive la différence':

> The Louisiana Civil Code, a one volume blueprint of society, is among the most significant landmarks in American legal history. Inspired by the continental Roman tradition rather than English law, the civil code makes Louisiana a civil law island in a common law sea. Louisiana law, because it bears the imprint of Roman, Spanish and French law, forces local lawyers to conceive legal issues differently than their counterparts do elsewhere in the United States.[3]

Fairly brimming with youthful enthusiasm and occasionally bordering upon chauvinism, the pamphlet also strayed into hyperbole and misplaced metaphor. Three examples of these venial literary sins: while we knew that our pamphlet might intrigue lawyers in jurisdictions such as Quebec, Germany and Spain, we also recognised that a great majority of United States lawyers, if asked to inventory the great landmarks of American legal history, probably would not mention the Louisiana Civil Code. Indeed, a typical United States lawyer would know too little about the Louisiana Civil Code to consider it a landmark at all. If the Louisiana Civil Code sprang to his mind, he would probably recite a disclaimer found in many United

---

Louisianas vor dem amerikanischen Bürgerkrieg', (1996) 113 *ZSS* 293; D. Snyder, 'Possession: A Brief for Louisiana's Rights of Succession to the Legacy of Roman Law', (1992) 66 *Tulane LR* 1853. For discussion of the Spanish character of the *Digest* and early Louisiana law, see generally R. Kilbourne, *A History of the Louisiana Civil Code: The Formative Years 1803–1839* (Baton Rouge, 1987), pp. 61–95.

[3] Herman, Combe and Carbonneau, *The Louisiana Civil Code*, p. 3.

States law treatises to the effect that Louisiana's civil law puts it beyond the scope of the treatise author's discussion.[4]

Itself a sort of mixed metaphor, Louisiana is more precisely characterised as a 'mixed' or hybrid jurisdiction[5] than as a civil law island in a common law sea. Within the patchwork quilt of United States private law, Louisiana's

---

[4] Professor Christopher Blakesley of the law faculty at Louisiana State University has recently confirmed this supposition:

> Anyone who attended a non-Louisiana US law school knows the frequently stated comment that: 'the law is [ ], except in Louisiana, where it is ['!'&*+%%$*]' . . . this is about the only thing about Louisiana law that many people, even law school faculty, know. They do understand that the law (and maybe everything) down here is 'different'. No doubt, Louisiana and Louisiana Law are exotic and unique. Sometimes, however, the use of the term 'unique' is a bit pejorative, based on ignorance and superficiality. The study of law in Louisiana, however unique or even exotic, for me is quite wonderful, much like our fine cuisine, music, literature, and art. (Christopher L. Blakesley, 'The Impact of a Mixed Jurisdiction on Legal Education, Scholarship and Law', in V. V. Palmer (ed.), *Louisiana: Microcosm of a Mixed Jurisdiction* (Durham, N.C. 1999), pp. 61, 66)

As a Yale property professor told me not so long ago, 'I never teach the students anything about Louisiana law, and if they think they have heard anything about the subject, then they were mistaken' (personal conversation between author and Professor John Langbein, March 1998). Alongside such disclaimers, United States scholars often provide historical information (and misinformation) about Louisiana's distinctive law:

> His majesty's colonies in North America naturally inherited the English common law system and philosophy, but here also we find remnants of Spanish (civil) law in Florida and the Southwest, and the State of Louisiana is governed by the civil law to this day. Fortunately, these two great legal systems have much in common, and the United States Supreme Court, thanks to the remarkable flexibility and adaptability of the common law, has had no great difficulty in assimilating and harmonizing such differences as exist. (P. R. Conway, *Outline of the Law of Contracts* (Brooklyn, N.Y., 1939), p. 3)

> Louisiana . . . has acquired only a smattering of common law property precepts. Louisiana held all lands allodially, and the feudal law and the accompanying common law jurisprudence as it is applicable to land has no application to land titles in Louisiana, citing *Xiques* v. *Bujac*, 7 La. Ann. 498. The other states in the Louisiana Purchase have by statute or by custom adopted the common law. (G. W. Thompson, *Commentaries on the Modern Law of Real Property*, vol. I (Indianapolis, 1980), p. 53.

> Uses and trusts were not known in the civil or Roman law . . . In the state of Louisiana trusts were originally not allowed, but were later permitted for a short period. More recently the Louisiana statutes governing trusts have been liberalized. (G. G. Bogert and G. T. Bogert, *The Law of Trusts and Trustees*, vol. I (St Paul, Minn., 1984), p. 18.

On Louisiana's reception of the trust, see generally the articles cited in n. 6 below.

[5] On this theme see generally, J. Dainow (ed.), *The Role of Judicial Decisions and Doctrine in Civil Law and in Mixed Jurisdictions* (Baton Rouge, 1974); Palmer (ed.), *Microcosm*.

private law is made unusual by the Civil Code and other specialised codes and statutes inspired by the Code's legislative techniques and nomenclature.[6] But Louisiana's public and criminal law substantively resembles public and criminal law elsewhere in the United States. Finally, we had perhaps overstated the antagonism between Roman law and English law for dramatic effect, for Roman law seems to have been studied actively in England soon after the Norman conquest. In some respects, Roman law, especially as embodied in canon law, contributed noticeably to the evolution and character of English law.[7]

For these exaggerations, *nostra culpa*. Although the pamphlet's occasional flights of hyperbole gave an impression that Louisiana law was under siege, our main goal was to appeal to lay readers who would enjoy the dramatic tension featured in a dialectic of opposites. As devotees of the civil code, we noted that:

---

[6] See esp. the Louisiana Trust Code, La. R.S. 9:1721 ff. While the Louisiana Trust Code adopted many features of the Anglo-American trust it also has civilian or 'hybrid' traits such as the usufruct in trust: La. R.S. 9:1844. On Louisiana's experience with trusts, see generally K. V. Lorio, 'Louisiana Trusts: The Experience of a Civil Law Jurisdiction with the Trust', 41 *Louisiana LR* 1721; D. Gruning, 'Reception of the Trust in Louisiana: The Case of *Reynolds* v. *Reynolds*', (1982) 57 *Tulane LR* 89; A. N. Yiannopoulos, 'Trust and the Civil Law: The Louisiana Experience', in Palmer (ed.), *Microcosm*, p. 213.

[7] The English jurist John Selden reported confidently that in the twelfth century, soon after the discovery of Justinian's texts in Italy, Lothair introduced that law into England: John Selden, *Ad Fletam Dissertation*, trans., David Ogg ([1647], Cambridge, 1925), p. 105. At the same time, William of Malmesbury (1125–42) introduced many different Roman laws including the Theodosian Code. Said Malmesbury: 'We have taken care to omit nothing regarding the rulers of Italy and Rome. It is now thought fit to add to the Roman laws . . . those of Theodosius the Younger, son of Arcadius, who collected them in sixteen books, from the time of Constantine, under the name of each emperor' (ibid., p. 107). A rich Roman literature was abroad in England before the end of the twelfth century, much of it distributed among churchmen. A brief inventory of available Roman law books appears in W. Senior, 'Roman Law MSS in England', (1931) 47 *LQR* 337. Notably, the author indicates that Pollock and Maitland, distinguished historians of English law, probably understated the quantity and breadth of Roman law materials available even at the earliest period after the Norman conquest (ibid.). On the contribution of Roman law to English legal evolution, see generally, F. W. Maitland, *Roman Canon Law in the Church of England* (London, 1898); R. H. Helmholz, *The Spirit of Classical Canon Law* (Athens, Ga., 1996); R. H. Helmholz, 'Magna Carta and the Ius Commune', 66 (1999) *Chicago LR* 297; S. Herman, 'Legacy and Legend: The Continuity of Roman and English Regulation of the Jews', (1992) 66 *Tulane LR* 1781; R. H. Helmholz, 'The Roman Law of Guardianship in England 1300–1600', (1978) 52 *Tulane LR* 223; R. H. Helmholz, 'English Common Law: Studies in the Sources: Legitim in English Legal History', (1984) *U Illinois LR* 659; Charles Donahue Jr, 'Roman Canon Law in the Medieval English Church: *Stubbs* v. *Maitland* Reexamined after 75 years in the Light of Some Records from the Church Courts', (1974) 72 *Mich. LR* 647. For several views on the contributions of Roman law to the institution of the trust, see generally R. Helmholz and R. Zimmermann (eds.), *Itinera Fiduciae: Trust and Treuhand in Historical Perspective* (Berlin, 1998).

Because [of] a national drive to uniformity in law, the worth of the civil code is constantly questioned; and one is naturally led to wonder if Louisiana's stubborn retention of the civil code is warranted. While local lawyers, in defense of the code, invoke the slogan 'vive la différence,' one may legitimately wonder if appreciating 'la différence' is worth all the trouble in a society where the intellectual spirit is intensely pragmatic, and law is an already complicated discipline.[8]

Long a powerful impulse in America, cultural diversity, we suggested, was itself a virtue in token of which a well-established national motto declared *e pluribus unum* (from many one). In areas other than law, Louisiana was known for its deviation from the cultural mainstream. If our music[9] and cuisine were justifiably world famous, perhaps diversity in law was an asset as well. Cultural diversity could also be seen as an expression of self-determination, a laudable choice in the United States as in Catalonia. For Americans had expressed their natural right of self-determination by rebelling against the English Crown and renouncing the ways of the old world. 'To thine own self be true,'[10] advised Polonius, the lord chamberlain, in *Hamlet*. Louisiana's legal difference from other states constituted a badge of cultural identity and made the civil law an exceptional patrimony to be embraced with pride.

There were pragmatic reasons as well for telling the story of the Civil Code. In an Anglophone country soon to become the only superpower in the world, our civilian experience located us at a crossroads of legal traditions. In Louisiana's jurisprudence one could find a fascinating blend of influences from both Anglo-American and civil law jurisdictions. Louisiana could be a comparative law laboratory in which, after study and comparison of many different solutions, the best approaches could be put into action through law reform. Astride an intersection of western legal traditions, Louisiana's lawyers could open windows on other great legal systems, including those of Europe, South America, Quebec, and even some Asian countries such as Japan that had embraced a civilian tradition. While the specific rules of these countries might differ, perhaps their cultural

---

[8] Herman, Combe and Carbonneau, *The Louisiana Civil Code*, p. 3.

[9] On Louisiana's distinctive jazz and Cajun music, see Jon Garelick, 'The Thrill of Discovering an Unheard of Sound', *New York Times*, 31 October 1999, p. 33, and the references therein.

[10] William Shakespeare, *The Tragedy of Hamlet, Prince of Denmark*, Act I, Scene iii, lines 78–81 (New Haven, 1947) ('This above all: to thine own self be true, /And it must follow, as the night the day/Thou canst not then be false to any man').

similarities with Louisiana would make it their close cousin. The phenomenon of civil codification, i.e. regulating civil society by means of systematically organised general principles and precepts – and some of our institutions such as forced heirship – gave us links with many of these other places. In turn, these links bore witness to an untapped reservoir[11] in the expertise of Louisiana lawyers naturally sympathetic to the problems of the other countries, and suited to interpret for other Americans the outlook of these countries: a pretty romantic, idealistic brew.

Uplifting though the romance and idealism might be, they were tempered by certain discouraging realities. Unlike New York, Texas and California, all national leaders among the states, Louisiana is a small state in terms of its land area and population.[12] Louisiana is located in the 'Deep South' of the United States, the region defeated in the war between the states (1861–5) and generally considered among the most underdeveloped in the United States. Measured by a variety of material factors, such as literacy, per capita income, effective pollution programmes, infant mortality, child poverty, teenage pregnancy and violence,[13] Louisiana deserves a negative rating. In

[11] 'The Napoleon Connection: Will Louisiana Benefit from its History?', *Newsweek*, 18 December 1989, p. 17: 'We [Louisiana lawyers] are trained to think more like European lawyers than lawyers in Texas and Florida' (Herman); 'We could produce lawyers who can speak both languages: the language of the civil law that prevails in Europe and that of the common law that prevails in the rest of the United States' (Yiannopoulos). In the same vein Professor Blakesley has noted that 'substantively and pedagogically, Louisiana has the best of both worlds for those who wish to take advantage of it': Blakesley, 'The Impact of a Mixed Jurisdiction', p. 66. But others have disagreed with the upbeat views expressed about Louisiana's legal diversity. A former governor of Louisiana, Buddy Roemer, echoing the lament described above (p. 222), said that it was important to bring Louisiana law into line with the laws elsewhere in the United States ('The Napoleon Connection').

[12] Located on Louisiana's western border, Texas dwarfs Louisiana. Louisiana covers 51,843 square miles and has 4,350,000 citizens while Texas covers 268,600 square miles and has a population of 19,128,000. E. R. Hornor (ed.), *Almanac of the 50 States* (Palto Alto, Calif., 1998), pp. 147, 347.

[13] On the state's culture of violence and poverty, see Petula Dvorak, 'Louisiana Most Lethal State for Women', *Times Picayune*, 10 October 1999, p. B-1 (by a considerable margin, Louisiana leads the US in terms of the number of women killed by men). Louisiana's financial fragility relative to other states also seems to make her law more vulnerable to the influences of other states.

La situation économique de la Louisiane est telle que sa prosperité dépend trés largement de ses relations commerciales et financières avec les autres Etats de common law. Une des conséquences juridiques de ces relations d'affaires est que de nombreux pans de droit Louisianais sont directement inspirés du droit du common law au point que plusieurs titres du code civil sont alors amendés pour refléter l'essence de la common law. (A. Levasseur, 'La Codification du droit civil en Louisiane: un langage juridique contemporain pour une cause perdue', (1986) *Revue Juridique et Politique* 587, 591)

most respects, the state is a backwater in the United States, and Louisiana politics seems historically to have been corrupt and scandal-ridden.[14] These political defects blemish our public image and constitute a real obstacle to our economic advancement. Going our own way in a national legal community inhospitable to foreign law has probably increased our isolation within the United States. This process of marginalisation has continued even as the cultural reasons for the process have brought us into contact more often than other states with nations and regions (e.g. Spain, Catalonia) travelling in civil law orbits.

The Civil Code a tool for bijural analysis

Although Louisiana suffers from these social and economic woes, the state's polychromatic legal tradition gives us methodological advantages over a more monochromatic experience anchored in the common law. The Anglo-American case method informs our legal thinking, and Louisiana cases formally resemble judicial decisions written elsewhere in the United States. But reliance upon the Civil Code permits one to have a bijural perspective not enjoyed in any other American state. The Civil Code's elegant formulations may put into sharp relief virtues and defects of another state's law that might be overlooked if the other state's law were examined in

---

[14] Accounts of Louisiana's political corruption and moral laxness are legion. Herewith a sample of accounts from local newspapers at this writing. According to Professor Wayne Flynt of Auburn University: 'Louisiana is perceived as being zany with off-the-wall politics ... and it has had pathetic political leadership. The reputations of former grand wizard [of the Ku Klux Klan] David Duke and former governor Edwin Edwards, who faces federal racketeering charges, haven't helped', *Times Picayune*, 8 August 1999, p. A-10. According to a recent editorial, New Orleans' work ethic is an 'oxymoron'; our ethic, far from stressing industriousness, is 'laissez les bons temps rouler'. Hardworking Puritans fortunately never settled here, argued the writer. Instead, Louisiana attracted the French who loved parties and debauchery. The Spaniards, whose main goals in life were leisure and red wine, brought us the siesta: Angus Lynd, 'TGIF in New Orleans [TGIF = Thank God it's Friday]: A Short History of the City shows Why the Weekend Begins Friday at Lunch', *Times Picayune*, 18 August 1999, p. E 1. The following day, the newspaper published on the front page a story about Mike Foster, current governor of the state, who committed ethical violations in his recent election campaign and paid a considerable fine to avoid a court battle: Manuel Roig-Franzia, 'Foster Pays Maximum Fines in Ethics Probe: Campaign Gifts Pay the $20,000', *Times Picayune*, 20 August 1999. A lamentable feature of the story is that the violation consisted of Foster's payment of $200,000 to David Duke, former grand wizard of the Ku Klux Klan, for Duke's contributor list. Said Foster, 'David Duke is not relevant in all this; it could have been Mickey Mouse's list.' On Louisiana's discouraging record of environmental protection and associated health issues, see Barbara Koeppel, 'Cancer Alley, Louisiana', *The Nation*, 8 November 1999, p. 16.

isolation. Knowing two systems tends to save one from assuming that the principles of either system are normative. With Hamlet we understand that 'there are more things in heaven and earth...than are dreamt of in [our] philosophy'.[15] A knowledge of both systems may aid legal harmonisation in treaty negotiations and private negotiation with lawyers from elsewhere. An understanding of the civil law's assumptions and comparative method helped a United States team of lawyers in drafting the Vienna Convention on International Sales of Goods.[16] By relying upon the ideas of the Civil Code for a harmonic counterpoint to dominant themes of United States law one may even triangulate to a third position, often more enlightened and perhaps more creative than either of the two original positions.

More concretely, how does a Louisiana lawyer exploit a bijural perspective? Assume a client has narrated facts that suggest that he was induced mistakenly to enter a lease he now realises to be extremely unfavourable to him. He would like to cut his losses by escaping the contract. To develop a diagnosis of his client's case, a lawyer can consult a popular United States treatise on contracts generally, or perhaps even a property treatise, since many other states within the union have traditionally considered leases as estates in land.[17] The treatise soon leads the lawyer to a Seurat-like *pointilliste* treatment of contractual mistake, consisting largely of footnotes heavily seasoned with citations to judicial decisions. Although the case method is stimulating and concentrates the mind on practicalities, it is made arduous by the lawyer's need to couch his analysis in terms of each opinion's vocabulary. If the judges have been scholarly and conscientious, then their judgments will lead the researcher through numerous decisions worthy of analogy or contrast. But the initial guidance gained from the cases

---

[15] Shakespeare, *Hamlet*, Act I, Scene v, lines 165–6.

[16] J. Honnold, *Uniform Law for International Sales* (Deventer and Boston, 1982). For comparative insights that assisted United States drafters, see Honnold's treatment of gap filling in national codes, with references to the experience of France, Austria, Italy and Louisiana, at pp. 96–8; good faith, pp. 93–4; specific performance pp. 192–9.

[17] American doctrinal writers traditionally refer to a tenant's interest as a leasehold estate and classify the tenant's surrender of his rights as a conveyance of real property. S. Kurtz and H. Hovenkamp, *Cases and Materials on American Property Law* (St Paul, Minn., 1987), p. 561. In a modern vein, the treatises also discuss lease as contract, speaking of mitigation of damages, and anticipatory breach. R. Boyer, S. Kurtz and H. Hovenkamp, *The Law of Property: An Introductory Survey*, 4th edn (St Paul, Minn., 1991), pp. 282–4.

sometimes may not be very helpful. Although armed with many specific case references, the lawyer realises that study of more cases may be subject to a law of diminishing returns. Despite considerable case analysis, he may still be unsure whether the law authorises a specific form of relief helpful to the client's position.

In this insecure posture, a lawyer with a bijural perspective consults the Civil Code. By studying its regulation of conventional obligations in conjunction with nominate contracts, he acquires an overview of the entire contractual landscape at a glance. Instead of reconnoitring each hill and ridge at close range, the lawyer derives from the code a more general impression of the terrain. The Civil Code concisely conveys this general impression. Systematically organised, its general contract principles may occupy fewer pages than a single decision rendered by a United States court. An excessively pragmatic lawyer trained exclusively in the law of another state within the United States may scoff that the Civil Code has not provided guidance factually concrete enough to resolve the client's issue. A general solution, the lawyer would say, does not resolve concrete cases.[18]

Au contraire. For Civil Code readers, 'generalization is the soul of codification'.[19] The Civil Code's susceptibility to analogical reasoning makes it a reservoir of solutions to unanticipated problems. In Henri Bergson's phrase, the Code embodies the *élan vital*[20] of the code reader's system. The lawyer's bijural perspective makes him wish that his sceptical counterparts elsewhere in the United States appreciated these traits of the Code, for then they might view its norms as they view those embodied in the United States constitution. Although the constitution charts public law relations rather than those among individual citizens, it is, like the Code, also a concise collection of general statements from which a great number of solutions to concrete cases may be mined. Like the constitution, the Civil Code encourages us to navigate from general propositions to specific facts, from dominant and dramatic topographic features down to a specific hill or stream of immediate concern. Perhaps generalisations do not always solve

---

[18] An often-repeated dictum by Justice Holmes in *Lochner v. New York*, 198 US 45, 76 (1905). On the role of this dictum in United States law, see generally Shael Herman, 'Historique et destinée de la codification américaine', (1995) *RIDC* 707, 716–17.

[19] C. J. Morrow, 'An Approach to the Revision of the Louisiana Civil Code', (1949) 23 *Tulane LR* 478, 487.

[20] Henri Bergson, *L'Evolution créatrice* (Paris, 1948), pp. 88–98.

particular problems. Nevertheless, generalisations, leavened by jurisprudence and doctrine, are usually handy and often crucial for reliable analysis
of particular problems.

Whenever we compare judicial cases, we try to formulate general propositions as working hypotheses. Otherwise, it would be impossible to distil
legal principles from a welter of facts emerging from the cases, and there
would be slight creative thinking beyond the specific details of the cases. Like
invisible connective tissue, general propositions link together pre-existing
cases and permit the projection of lessons from the cases to new situations.

Enhanced by case analysis, the Code's hierarchy of key concepts becomes
a potent tool for innovation. For example, while a United States treatise
teaches us that equity could relieve a contract induced by fraud or mistake,
this relief was originally discretionary, not automatically authorised by the
common law. Indeed, some states may still consider contract rescission as
discretionary relief.[21] Thanks to the Civil Code, the analytic advantages of a
case method multiply; one may evaluate the propositions distilled from the
cases in the light of the regulation on vices of consent prescribed in it. These
vices of consent are announced consecutively and lapidarily in a few titles
on error, fraud, duress and lesion.[22] An aggrieved claimant may routinely
invoke these vices of consent and locate the principles regulating his situation in a single book. Perhaps the Civil Code principles will converge with
the general observations of the common law treatise; perhaps the Code will
in some respects diverge from the treatise. With luck, the lawyer's thinking
may even ascend to a third meta-proposition that blends the essence of the
common law cases with the Civil Code.

Taking our hypothetical client a step further, let us assume that the narrated facts occurred five years ago, thus posing the question whether the
claim is time-barred. American lawbooks, of course, contain many statutes
of limitations, but for the most part they are difficult to locate because they
are strewn in no particular order throughout the various state and federal

---

[21] Discretionary rescission would inform a judicial response to a contract entered mistakenly by
a party with a bargaining position considerably weaker than that of his co-contracting party.
See, e.g., *Jackson* v. *Seymour*, 71 S. E. 2d 181 (1952). A discretionary power to rescind would
also be found in the judicial arsenal for rescission of a contract stricken by unconscionability.
See, e.g., Uniform Commercial Code s 2-302 ('Unconscionable contract or clause'). According
to Official Comment 2 explaining s 2-302, 'the court, in its discretion, may refuse to enforce the
contract as a whole if it is permeated by unconscionability'.

[22] For its regulation of error, see Louisiana Civil Code artt. 1948–52; fraud, artt. 1953–8; duress,
artt. 1959–64; lesion, artt. 1965, 2589–600.

statute books. To address the facts at hand, a few Code titles set out the basic principles of prescription from the shortest prescriptive periods to the longest ones as well as the basic principles of *liberandi* and *acquirendi causa*.

Civil Code organisation and computer operating systems

The Civil Code's allure and success may result from the fact that it is anchored in a powerful, consistently used nomenclature of verbal symbols that reinforce each other in legal analysis by regular and repeated use. Thus reinforced, these symbols channel a lawyer's thinking as musical chords and scales guide his hearing. The hierarchical nomenclature resembles a computer program activated for a user by a system of prompts or reminders. These prompts are identified by key concepts captured in buttons and icons (e.g. file, edit, view, print, delete). A skilled engineer could operate the computer without the prompts and icons, and for many years before the advent of simplified point-and-click technology, this is how the engineers functioned.

But, alas, most of us are not engineers at all. We are reassured to know that the Civil Code drafters have already performed much of the conceptual mapping for us. This cartographer's exercise is embodied in an instrumentation that reminds us of the main options in a computer menu. Thus, the user can click upon a general option (e.g. 'file'), and locate under the option a number of more specific choices (e.g. 'new', 'open', 'save', 'print', 'send', etc.). Known in 'computerese' as 'dropdown technology', this systematic architecture renders the computer more accessible and user friendly today than when it depended upon a more primitive technology. This systematic architecture has figured in a worldwide progress of computer technology. A similar architecture may have facilitated exportation of civil codes to other countries. In any case, the Civil Code's instrumentation is relatively more convenient to use than that of a case law system.

To advance the diagnosis of the lease issue described above, a Civil Code user first identifies a general category ('obligations') and then moves from conventional obligations to the elements of contract ('consent,' 'object', 'cause', 'capacity'). On 'opening' the titles on consent, he finds the vices of consent, under which there appear regulation of error and norms applicable to rescission based upon error. In contrast with the Civil Code, the more exiguous common law approach demands more guesswork, for it offers relatively fewer clues for general propositions and requires legal principles to be spotted in their case law habitat and then connected by painstaking induction.

Romance and *rentabilidad*

So much for romance in an anglophone mixed jurisdiction. Do the romance and the methodological advantage sell at Tulane Law School where students pay handsomely to study both the Civil Code and the common law? The Tulane Law School prides itself on its comparative law perspective; the faculty regularly offers a dual curriculum featuring courses back-to-back based upon both Uniform Commercial Code sales and conventional obligations, common law property and its civil law analogues, as well as common law wills and successions. Which courses do most students choose? Alas, only a handful avail themselves of the dual curriculum by studying both the common law courses and their Civil Code analogues. Like lapsed church-goers, most students steer clear of the chapel of the dual curriculum. Less than 15 per cent of our students elect to study the Code systematically, in a complement of about six or seven courses that cover its main subjects.[23] A few more students sample perhaps one or two courses in the civil law curriculum.

Attracted to the idea of comparative and international law, some students may elect a single course on the French Civil Code or comparative law. But these valuable survey courses, unlike the courses dealing systematically with the common law and the Louisiana Civil Code, do not aim to equip students to practise the law under examination. Indeed, becoming equipped in another law is beyond the reach of a great majority of students, as only a handful, other than graduate students from overseas, know a language besides English well enough to read a law text in its original language. A typical failing of United States students,[24] the language deficiency forecloses

---

[23] Conventional obligations, sale, persons, successions and donations, property, security rights, community property.

[24] 'Over the last thirty years, the portion of American college students studying a foreign language has dropped by half to 7.9 percent in 1998, according to a survey . . . by the Modern Language Association'. But there has been a 'slowing in the sharp erosion of French, which ranks second to Spanish among foreign languages taught in the US': James Brooks, 'Québec Gains as a Language Lab', *New York Times*, 16 October 1999, p. A.12. In my fall course (1999) on conventional obligations, only three of thirty-six students could read French at all, and they were not proficient enough to read French legal sources. A great majority of the courses in the Tulane curriculum

study of French law or German law from the inside, leaving most to learn whatever they can through scarce translations.[25]

Surprisingly, many students who plan to practise in Louisiana seem uninterested in studying the Civil Code. Some students fail the bar examination in Code subjects that they have avoided. Other students labour under an illusion that they can learn the Civil Code on the job, even though they are apt to make mistakes and their tuition for the training will come out of the clients' pockets. A few students report that they would like to study Louisiana Code courses, but that the choice of Louisiana for law study has provoked scepticism and puzzlement among prospective employers who wonder whether a Louisiana faculty can equip a student to practise elsewhere in the United States. According to these students, having to justify to job interviewers the curious nomenclature of civil law courses would further hinder their prospects of employment with firms outside Louisiana. We might be tempted to dismiss the students' justifications as superstition, but the superstition is held with conviction and it profoundly influences the academic climate. Rarely has a student reported to me that study of the dual curriculum helped his career prospects.

Comparative law at a crossroads

It is the rare lawyer who claims comparative law as his professional specialty, for the subject has little appeal for clients. Yet, comparative law offers both students and faculty valuable cultural insights and encourages an intellectual cross-pollination among legal systems under consideration. On the

---

have no civilian or comparative content. As in typical law faculties elsewhere in the United States, foreign language proficiency for these courses would be seen as largely irrelevant to the material. On the loss of French to the Louisiana legal community, see Roger Ward, 'The French Language in Louisiana Law and Legal Education: A Requiem', 57 *Louisiana LR* 1283; Roger Ward, 'The Death of the French Language in Louisiana Law', in Palmer (ed.), *Microcosm*, p. 41.

[25] From 1959 through about 1972, the Louisiana State Law Institute, based at the Louisiana State University Law Center, sponsored translations of French doctrine, including six volumes of Planiol, *Treatise on the Civil Law* (St Paul, Minn., 1959); F. Gény, *Methode d'interpretation et sources en droit prive positif* (St Paul, Minn., 1963), trans. J. Mayda as *Method of Interpretation and Sources of Private Positive Law* (Baton Rouge, 1963); and a few volumes of Aubry and Rau and Baudry-Lacantinerie and Tissier. Translating efforts seem to have died out around 1972. To Tulane Law School's credit, some optional language courses have been established in French and Italian, but few from the student population regularly enrol in the courses. To the credit of the Louisiana State University law faculty in Baton Rouge, visiting professors occasionally give seminars in the French language.

part of some faculty members, there have been noteworthy achievements in comparative law. The Civil Code prompts in some scholars a curiosity about solutions lying beyond the boundaries of standard United States law commentaries. I have enjoyed meeting lawyers who travel in other legal orbits. It is rewarding to open windows into other legal cultures, and to seek solutions beyond those typified in the United States curriculum. The faculty's civilians and comparative specialists are often invited to participate in colloquia and international projects (e.g. the core project in Trento). Colleagues from overseas see our hybrid law as a convenient prism for viewing curious phenomena found throughout the United States. Our evident Roman law influences make Louisiana law familiar to foreign lawyers seeking a common vocabulary and perspective for understanding United States legal conceptions.

Nevertheless, comparative and civil law courses tend to be stepchildren in a law-school curriculum that stresses a homogenised law of the dominant United States courses. Teachers of comparative law and civil law learn quickly that the school's academic climate reinforces students' views. Consciously or unconsciously, our faculty members, like their counterparts across the United States, are inclined to play down the laws of individual states and to stress a fanciful homogeneous national law that exists no one knows exactly where.[26] In the collective academic consciousness there seems to be a view that the whole is greater than the sum of its parts, and that a so-called national private law is better than and somehow different from the various laws made by the states. This assumption is reinforced in a famous adage that law schools do not teach law so much as they teach people to think like lawyers.[27] This view diminishes the Civil Code as an instrument for solving problems and makes Louisiana law a parochial state law, along with forty-nine others.[28] The impression of parochialism is reinforced by

---

[26] 'Citations of [so-called national rules] will typically be limited to cases from two or three states, and even when there are citations to more than two or three states, it is seldom if ever implied that the author of the statement warrants that every state has adopted the rule': Melvin A. Eisenberg, 'Why is American Contract Law so Uniform? – National Law in the United States 10–11' (1996; unpublished MS on file with author).

[27] Transposed to the kitchen, this reliance on process over substance would yield food processors with no food.

[28] Regrettably, Puerto Rico's legal experience, similar to that of Louisiana, hardly figures in the national landscape of United States law and legal education. Puerto Rico, both geographically and legally, is an island. Technically, it is neither a colony of the United States nor a state within the Union.

the fact that nearly all students in a civil law course come from Louisiana and are likely to remain in Louisiana after graduation to practise their profession. Having equated parochialism with Louisiana law, precisely as one would equate it with Illinois law, many colleagues then display towards this parochial law apathy and even hostility. They seem unimpressed by the argument that the Civil Code could make us less parochial by enabling us to follow the evolution of other countries' laws. Privately some colleagues confide that they would like to see the dual curriculum abolished as a distraction or an expensive luxury, but that doing so might ignite a revolt among local alumni.

Readily contracted by a great majority of students, an academic allergy to the Civil Code is symptomatic of a broad culture of the academy. In the United States, the received academic wisdom is very much 'follow the leader', and this has been increasingly the pattern since Harvard originated the case method. American law schools seem to be involved in purveying knowledge and prestige in equal parts. 'Followers' among American law schools want to distinguish themselves with a broad mix of academics from the 'leaders', i.e. the most prestigious law schools in the country, such as Yale, Chicago and Harvard. These institutions stress a supposedly homogeneous national private law to the virtual exclusion of the laws of the states where the schools are situated.

In a hybrid jurisdiction, the results of 'follow the leader' have been a bit depressing. At Tulane, relatively few colleagues (four or five among a full-time faculty of about thirty-five) teach Louisiana courses. Many of the faculty, including some who have been at Tulane for twenty-five years, have never seriously studied the Civil Code for their own benefit. Though a number of professors could offer a civil law course, or could specialise in a Code area, they seem to steer away from Louisiana law either through lack of interest or because they are drawn to the wider United States audience available if one remains in the standard curriculum. A policy of 'follow the leader' also affects a teacher's range of curricular options. I have already mentioned the limited impact and appeal of civil law courses for the students. This limitation is compounded by other factors. Even if a colleague chose to teach a civil law course, he would have to design a course for only 15 per cent of the student body at a single law school in the United States rather than for potentially thousands of law students in law schools across the country And he would face another disappointment: conscious that the course would not travel beyond Louisiana's borders, national law-book publishers are unlikely to be interested in publishing the professor's course materials.[29]

The Louisiana Civil Code as an English-language artefact

Originally drafted in French and inspired by both French and Spanish legal traditions of the early 1800s, the Civil Code has been largely modernised and renovated. Despite the legislative improvements in the Civil Code, antiquarians among us miss the quaint, now superseded formulations of the Code that they studied in law school, and chide Louisiana's law reformers for trying to fix something that was not broken. Despite its roots in French and Spanish, however, the Civil Code's official language is today English.[30] The English version of the Code has retained many elegant Latinate formulations, as well as direct translations of Spanish and French. A full comprehension of the Civil Code is impossible without a lexicon of terms such as usufruct, forced heir (*heredero forzoso*), servitude, executory process, use, habitation, redhibition, *quanti minoris*, lesion beyond moiety and naked ownership. (The Code also has many familiar Americanisms such as 'detrimental reliance'[31] and impossibility of performance.)

If before enactment of the official English version of the Code there was confusion about the meaning of a provision, the courts and lawyers regularly consulted both French and Spanish textual authorities. Consultation of these texts was a natural step because the bench and bar found it credible to illuminate an idea by reference to the doctrinal writings contemporaneous with the Code's drafting. Thus, for example, Louisiana courts in the early years of statehood routinely appealed to *Las Siete Partidas* and

---

[29] West Publishing publishes general civil law treatises and civil codes in both pamphlet and annotated form. However, Louisiana coursebooks are published either as photocopies or as products of a local press.

[30] According to Palmer, the Louisiana legislature long ago missed the boat by enshrining the Civil Code in the state constitution without doing enough to save its original languages. 'Initial casualness about the intimate relationship . . . between legal culture and linguistic identity placed at risk the viability of the mixed legal system they were attempting to find': Vernon V. Palmer, 'Two Worlds in One: The Genesis of Louisiana's Mixed Legal Systems 1803–1812', in Palmer (ed.), *Microcosm*, p. 37.

[31] On enforcement of an obligation based upon detrimental reliance, see Louisiana Civil Code art. 1967. See also generally S. Herman, 'Detrimental Reliance in Louisiana Law – Past, Present, and Future(?): The Code Drafter's Perspective', (1984) 58 *Tulane LR* 707; D. Snyder, 'Comparative Law in Action: Promissory Estoppel, the Civil Law, and the Mixed Jurisdiction', in Palmer (ed.), *Microcosm*, p. 235.

Febrero[32] for Spanish legal background, and Pothier and Domat,[33] both inspirations for French and Louisiana drafters. About 1970, when revision efforts for the Civil Code began in earnest, the drafters considered it pointless not to make English the official language of the Civil Code. After all, Louisiana lawyers from a juridical standpoint are monolingual. If many in the bar and bench resisted the Civil Code even in an English version, there was no sense in inviting more resistance by insisting on another language in which they had no interest or competence. The comments for the revised Civil Code refer to many other laws. Indeed, the Code revision has been accomplished after vigorous comparative research and exploration of a host of solutions, but these source laws would be accessible to only a handful of lawyers in Louisiana. Although some source laws have been translated into English, still there would be no reliable way for most lawyers to read the doctrine behind the sources to illuminate the intent of the new articles.[34]

---

[32] D. Combe, 'An Analysis of Civil Law Authorities in *State v. Martin*', in Palmer (ed.), *Microcosm*, pp. 298–300; R. F. Karachuk, 'A Workman's Tools: The Law Library of Henry Adams Bullard', (1998) 42 *AJLH* 160. For discussion of Spanish sources in the early Louisiana jurisprudence, see particularly Kilbourne, *A History of the Louisiana Civil Code*, pp. 61–95; J. McCaffrey, 'Febrero y la Comunidad de Gananciales en Luisiana', (1987) *RDP* 332; J. McCaffrey, 'La Controversia Candente en Louisiana Sobre La Herencia Forzosa', (1985) *RDP* 414. For discussion of links between Spanish law and Louisiana law, see the special issue of the *Louisiana LR*, 1982 (esp. J. M. Castán Vazquez, 'Reciprocal Influences between the Laws of Spain and Louisiana', 1473; R. J. Rabalais, 'The Influence of Spanish Law and Treatises on the Jurisprudence of Louisiana: 1762–1828', 1509; S. Herman, 'Louisiana's Contribution to the 1852 Projet of the Spanish Civil Code', 1509; E. Lalaguna Dominguez, 'The Interaction of Civil Law and Commercial Law', 1629; I. A. Martinez, 'Trust and the Civil Law', 1709); R. Knutel, 'Influences of the Louisiana Civil Code in Latin America', (1995) 70 *Tulane LR* 1445. For a discussion of the French and Spanish antecedents of current Louisiana procedural law, see Kent A. Lambert, 'An Abridged History of the Absorption of American Civil Procedure and Evidence in Louisiana', in Palmer (ed.), *Microcosm*, p. 105.

[33] Pothier's *Law of Obligations* and Domat's *Les Loix civiles dans leur ordre naturel* were readily available in English translations. On the availability of Pothier's and Domat's work in Louisiana, see generally Karachuk, 'A Workman's Tools', p. 32.

[34] Nombreuses sont les décisions des tribunaux Louisianais qui incluent des references à des auteurs francais; mais il ne s'agit bien souvent que de cela, des references, sans incorporation d'extraits des textes originaux. Si l'original du texte était inséré dans la décision, il est à craindre que 99% des juristes ne pourraient pas comprendre le texte en langue etrangère. Le problème majeur est en effet le défaut quasi absolu de connaissance des langues étrangères dans lesquelles sont redigés les grands traités de droit civil. (A. Levasseur and S. Herman, 'Louisiana', (1994) 44 *Journées Association Henri Capitant* 649)

The issue of which language should be authoritative in Louisiana law seems to date back to the 1820s. According to Kilbourne, the civil code revision of 1825 was prompted by the language question. Some members of the bar were proficient in Spanish and French, while others knew

In judicial proceedings, one could call upon experts to explain the law. But judges are merely local lawyers in robes, and most grow impatient with translations by experts.

The Louisiana experience a guide for foreign lawyers

If a fledgling student regards the Civil Code as a compass or a complex computer program, it is like a magnet to foreign lawyers who visit Louisiana yearly in considerable numbers to glimpse the law of our hybrid jurisdiction in action. Given the number of civil law jurisdictions in the world, it is likely that a high percentage of visitors come from jurisdictions with civil codes, and so their affinity with Louisiana is natural. For visitors, Louisiana is an oasis and a curiosity. Some visitors come to the law school to attend formal seminars on lawmaking in Louisiana. Other visitors arrive individually in the expectation of discovering how the jurisdiction functions. On the whole, they are mystified and befuddled by the idea of a mixed jurisdiction, because Louisiana's experience seems to contradict the assumptions acquired in their home systems. Among their typical questions: does the Civil Code offer us a separation-of-powers perspective like that found in, say, France or Mexico?[35] Do judges create law?[36] Does Louisiana recognise a doctrine of *stare decisis*?[37] Is doctrine a formal source of

only English and had little interest in mastering other languages. Much of the state's official business was conducted in French and Spanish and the languages were needed fully to comprehend original sources of local law. Months after cession of Louisiana to the United States, James Brown, recently arrived from Kentucky, reported that his fluency in Spanish, English and French gave him a unique advantage in law practice, and as late as 1825 Charles Watts of New York told his sister he was learning Spanish so he could read the old laws: Kilbourne, *A History of the Louisiana Civil Code*, pp. 97–8.

[35] R. David, 'Supereminent Principles in French Law', in Dainow (ed.), *The Role of Judicial Decisions*, p. 119. J. Carbonnier, 'Authorities in Civil Law France', in ibid., p. 91; W. Butte, 'Stare Decisis, Doctrine and Jurisprudence in Mexico and Elsewhere', in ibid., p. 311.

[36] See A. N. Yiannopoulos, 'Jurisprudence and Doctrine as Sources of Law in Louisiana and France', in Dainow (ed.), *The Role of Judicial Decisions*, p. 69. J. Dixon, 'Judicial Method of Interpretation of Law in Louisiana', (1982) 42 *Louisiana LR* 1661, 1662 ('La suprématie du législateur en Louisiane est plus que théorique. C'est un fait et le Code Civil est traité par le législateur et par les tribunaux et par les juristes avec beaucoup plus de respect que les autres sources écrites').

[37] Occasionally, a justice will state flatly that the doctrine of *stare decisis* should not apply in sectors regulated by the Civil Code. For example, Justice James Dennis of the Louisiana Supreme Court criticised an appellate judgment for methodological errors:

> In deciding the issue before us the lower courts did not follow the process of referring first to the code and other legislative sources but treated language from a judicial opinion

law?[38] How much does Roman law affect Louisiana's jurisprudence?[39] Do our commercial laws and practices differ from those of other states? On the whole, the visitors' questions betray a charming naiveté about United States federalism, which is quite tolerant of differences among state laws. Their questions also betray a belief that the Civil Code has a larger role for Louisiana's bench and bar than it actually has.

The Louisiana experience a guide to other codification efforts

An English-language civil code is a rather unusual artefact. In the Americas it is perhaps even unique, because other American civil codes in English translation (e.g. Quebec, Puerto Rico) also exist in another authentic

> as the primary source of law. This is an indication that the position of the decided case as an illustration of past experience and the theory of the individualization of decision have not been properly understood by our jurists in many instances. Therefore, it is important that we plainly state that, particularly in the changing field of delictual responsibility, the notion of *stare decisis*, derived as it is from the common law, should not be thought controlling in this state. The case law is invaluable as previous interpretation of the broad standard of Article 2315, but it is nevertheless secondary information. (*Ardoin* v. *Hartford Acc. & Indemnity Co.* 360 So. 2d 1331 (1978))

Despite its 'secondary status', precedent is often highly persuasive and constantly evaluated by courts and lawyers. One knowing veteran has characterised Louisiana's juristic method as 'cas par cas', thus suggesting that Louisiana lawyers are not much impressed by teleological or analogical reading of their code. 'L'attitude du juriste est encore celle d'administrer la justice au "cas par cas," de formuler une sorte de justice ponctuelle sans se préoccuper de placer cette justice dans la perspective du droit et plus particulièrement dans l'ensemble du code. Une justice au coup par coup crée des decisions judiciaires qui s'érigent en rival du code en déstabilisant la culture juridique de ce code (. . .) Ces décisions tendent à la règle normative, parfois à la dépasser sous couvert d'être mieux adaptées aux circonstances nouvelles.' Levasseur, 'La Codification du droit civil en Louisiane', 587, 589. For a judge's assessment of his role in a hybrid jurisdiction, see generally A. Tate, 'The Role of the Judge in Mixed Jurisdictions', in Dainow (ed.), *The Role of Judicial Decisions*, p. 23; A. Tate, 'Techniques of Judicial Interpretation in Louisiana', (1962) 22 *Louisiana LR* 727; A. Tate, 'Civilian Methodology in Louisiana', 44 *Tulane LR* 673 (1970); A. Tate, 'The Law-Making Function of the Judge', (1968) 28 *Louisiana LR* 211. For a collection of papers on civilian judicial method, see generally (1970) 44 *Tulane LR* 669–797. For a discussion of judicial method in Louisiana in the light of code structure, see generally S. Herman and D. Hoskins, 'Perspectives on Code Structure: Historical Experience, Modern Formats, and Policy Considerations', (1980) 54 *Tulane LR* 987.

[38] Yiannopoulos, 'Jurisprudence and Doctrine'.

[39] The answer is that Roman law is highly influential in certain traditional civilian areas. Louisiana lawyers are more conscious of their Roman heritage than counterparts elsewhere in the United States. But this is not saying much, for Roman law antecedents are practically absent from the American lawyers' education. For discussion of the Romanist tradition in Louisiana, see vol. 56 of the *Louisiana LR* entitled *The Romanist Tradition in Louisiana: Legislation, Jurisprudence and Doctrine* (1995).

language. In addition to visitors who arrive in quest of a better understanding of a hybrid jurisdiction, other groups of interested legislators come from nations in the throes of codification or recodification. Our English-language Civil Code and our ongoing experiences of revision seem to attract these lawmakers to Louisiana. These new code drafters would like to break with the ideas of the past that prevailed in their countries. Many seek closer ties with the United States. For them Louisiana seems a convenient entry point into United States law precisely because our law is in English and is thought to reflect a progressive American vision of law. At least, the Civil Code is thought to be a well-reasoned blend of American ideas and civilian ones.

Since the end of the Second World War the United States has routinely advanced its political vision by exporting its public law and constitutional law. For example, both Germany and Japan, after the Second World War, were targeted for 're-education' in the so-called rule of law. Taiwan's stability is credited to the fact that its political and financial systems are heavily influenced by American legal ideas and political values. To promote American public law ideas and political views, the State Department regularly invites foreign lawyers and judges to the United States. Such visits are likely to produce goodwill among foreign lawyers who are particularly eager to learn about judicial administration in the United States.

Less well known, but equally important for the present discussion, is that some private United States laws are exported if they are in exportable form. Such laws include corporation statutes and banking regulations. The Louisiana Civil Code fits into this group of exportable private laws. Upon the fall of the Berlin Wall in 1989,[40] many former Soviet satellites wanted to defrost their civil codes, which had been in a deep freeze for decades. For example, the Baltic states, resentful of Russia's influence, embarked promptly on a programme to modernise their Codes. As Russian hegemony waned at the end of the 1980s, Estonia sought assistance in modernising its rather antiquated Code. One of our best drafters, Professor A. N. Yiannopoulos, assisted the Estonians in their new code revision.[41] This technical assistance

---

[40] The collapse of the Soviet Union led in central and eastern Europe to liberation of twenty-seven countries called 'post Cold War transition countries': H. E. Hartnell, 'Subregional Coalescence in European Regional Integration', (1997) 16 *Wisconsin ILJ* 115, 118.

[41] For a discussion of this drafting programme, to which Professor A. N. Yiannopoulos of Tulane Law School contributed, see P. Varul and H. Pisuke, 'Louisiana Contribution to the Estonian Civil Code', (1999) 73 *Tulane LR* 1027. According to Varul and Pisuke, Soviet occupation of Estonia in 1940 prevented enactment of a draft code prepared in 1940. Even before Estonia regained its independence, the main principles underlying the socialist theory of ownership and enterprise were being undermined and new legislation was being enacted beginning in 1989. Initially the

was organised by a technical group within the American Bar Association called the Committee on East European Legal Initiatives (CEELI).[42]

Suggestions for Catalonia

A caveat is in order here. The suggestions and observations offered below may appeal to Catalonians who find similarities between Catalonia's situation and that of Louisiana. Like Louisiana, Catalonia has carved out a considerable role for specialised regional laws. But there are also historical and economic differences between Louisiana and Catalonia.

To appreciate these differences, let us reflect upon Louisiana's earliest years at the dawn of the nineteenth century. Although Thomas Jefferson welcomed the purchase of Louisiana in 1803 as a stroke of good fortune, he already had plans to substitute the common law for the civil law. Jefferson evidently preferred an entire northern continent speaking a single language and governed by one law. He believed that the 'cement of the union would not harden if it contained mixed legal systems'.[43] Recognising the threat posed to the civil law by Jefferson's policy, the first legislature of the territory of Orleans resolved in 1806 to give the civil law a solid foundation in Louisiana. The legislature passed an Act providing that Louisiana was to be governed by Roman and Spanish laws in effect at the time of the Louisiana

---

Justice Ministry, led by P. Varul, favoured piecemeal enactment of the 1940 Civil Code along the pattern followed by Latvia in re-enacting its 1937 Civil Code. But Estonia's decision was modified to provide for a completely new and modern code. The Louisiana Civil Code was considered a helpful model because it was one of the best contemporary codifications of civil law. A variety of influences helped shape the new Estonian Civil Code, and the Louisiana Civil Code affected decisions about the civil relations to be regulated as well as the content and logical structure of the Estonian project. For a more general essay on the potential for collaboration between Louisiana scholars and European code drafters, see generally M. Reimann, 'Towards a European Civil Code: Why Continental Jurists Should Consult their Transatlantic Colleagues', (1999) 73 *Tulane LR* 1337.

[42] For general background on this initiative, see *CEELI Update*, published by the American Bar Association and available at www.abanet.org/ceeli/publications. The *Update* describes CEELI as 'a project of the ABA designed to support law reform underway in Central and Eastern Europe and the new independent states of the former Soviet Union'. The states now receiving technical assistance from CEELI are Albania, Bosnia and Herzegovina, Bulgaria, Croatia, Hungary, Lithuania, Macedonia, Poland, Romania, Serbia and Montenegro, Slovakia, Armenia, Belarus, Georgia, Kazakhstan, Kyrgyzstan, Russia, Tajikistan, Ukraine and Uzbekistan. Evidently, Estonia's law reforms have progressed far enough for Estonia no longer to meet the criteria for assistance from CEELI. The CEELI-assisted countries overlap considerably with the group of twenty-seven, identified in n. 40 above as 'post Cold War transition countries'.

[43] G. Dargo, *Jefferson's Louisiana: Politics and the Clash of Legal Traditions* (Cambridge, Mass., 1975), p. 107.

Purchase. On 26 May 1806, Jefferson's appointed representative, Governor
W. C. C. Claiborne, vetoed the Act, and the legislature resigned in protest
at his veto. Shortly afterwards, a local journal, *Le Télégraphe*, published a
manifesto signed by Sauvé, the president of the legislative council,[44] and
eventually Claiborne capitulated to local pressures.

We will probably never know precisely what factors provoked in Jefferson
and his lieutenants, including his governor and the highest judicial officer, a
distrust of civil law and mixed legal systems. Jefferson's personal views could
not have resulted from ignorance, for he was as enlightened about French
history and civil law as he was about many other subjects. His great library
included many books on civil law[45] and his valuable collection became
a cornerstone of the collection of the Library of Congress.[46] According

---

[44] The manifesto declared in part:

> Now since we have the power to keep our old laws in so far as they do not conflict with the
> Constitution of the United States... no one can deny the advantage to us of remaining
> under a system to which we are accustomed ... We certainly do not attempt to draw any
> parallel between the civil law and the common law, but... the wisdom of the civil law
> is recognized by all Europe; and this law is the one which nineteen twentieths of the
> population of Louisiana know and are accustomed to from childhood, of which they
> would not see themselves deprived without falling into despair... It is a question here
> of overthrowing received and generally known usages and the uncertainty with which
> they would be replaced would be as unjust as disheartening... Overthrow this system
> all at once, Substitute new laws for the old laws; what a tremendous upset you cause.
> (*Le Télégraphe*, 3 June 1806; reprinted in C. E. Carter (ed.), *The Territorial Papers of the
> United States* (Washington, D.C., 1940), pp. 643–57.)

[45] Combe, 'An Analysis of Civil Law Authorities', pp. 295, 301. For examples of civil law works in
Jefferson's library, see n. 46 below.

[46] When the invading British army burned the Congressional Library in Washington in 1814,
Jefferson promptly offered his personal library in replacement. Congress approved the purchase
of Jefferson's collection in 1815. For further discussion of Jefferson's library as the foundation
for the collection of the Library of Congress, see James Gilreath and Douglas L. Wilson, *Thomas
Jefferson's Library: A Catalogue with the Entries in his Own Order* (Washington, D.C. 1989),
pp. 1–10. An avid book collector, Jefferson had the following works in inventory: *Projet de code
civil par portalis: code civil des François* (1804); *Code penal et d'instruction criminelle* (1810); *Code
de commerce* (1807); *Code Napoleon civil, procedure civile, criminelle, commerce: les ordonnances
concernant la marine* (1786); Domat, *The Civil Laws in their Natural Order*, six volumes of
Justinian and several volumes on Roman law (Gilreath and Wilson, *Thomas Jefferson's Library*,
pp. 77–8). Jefferson's collection on the law of nature and nations numbered over sixty works,
the majority in French, including Grotius, Pufendorf, Vattel and Barbeyrac as well as several
works on Spain and France. A number of works betray Jefferson's political interests: *Mémoires
de la France contre l'Angleterre* (1756); *Mémoires sur les droits de la France et de l'Angleterre en
Amèrique* (1756); *Paralléles des rois d'Angleterre et de la France* (see Gilreath and Wilson, *Thomas
Jefferson's Library*, pp. 57–8).

to Palmer, Jefferson was the most 'francophile of American presidents'.[47] Yet, according to Billings, 'francophile though Jefferson was, he harbored a residual distrust of the inhabitants of Louisiana and believed that their rearing in the papist and monarchist cultures of France and Spain rendered them suspect as did their lack of experience with self government and understanding of republicanism'.[48] As United States minister in France in the 1780s, Jefferson had witnessed the last years of the *ancien régime* and the turbulent prelude of the French Revolution. Like the people of Louisiana, the French, in Jefferson's estimation, were unprepared for a representative government of the American type, and he stated his views to the French King in a proposed charter of rights urging moderation. On the eve of the French Revolution, as Jefferson was leaving his post to return to the United States, his fears of turmoil and bloodshed in France were realised. In his first inaugural address in 1801 he thanked Providence for having generously separated his country from the old world by placing an ocean between the new republic and the 'exterminating havoc of Europe'.[49] The spectre of this 'exterminating havoc' seems to have awakened in Jefferson an ambivalence about establishing the French language and French law in the fledgling United States at a moment when English and English law were already in ascendancy. Though Jefferson seems to have admired the civil law more than the common law, his was perhaps an admiration of the law in the abstract. His own statements betrayed a view that blending the two systems would be inimical to the infant republic's stability: 'For however I admit the superiority of the civil law over the common law code... yet an incorporation of the two would be like Nebuchadnezzar's image of metal and clay, a thing without cohesion of parts.'[50]

Besides Jefferson's diplomatic career in France, other factors perhaps weighed on his thinking. To appreciate these factors, however, we would have to travel back two centuries and recognise that the United States, though today a superpower, saw itself in a precarious state vis-à-vis venerable and enduring European powers such as Spain and France. Fortified by a population of Frenchmen and Spaniards living in the new Louisiana enclave,

[47] Palmer, 'Two Worlds in One', p. 26.
[48] Warren Billings, 'From this Seed: The Constitution of 1812', in W. Billings and E. F. Haas, *In Search of Fundamental Law: Louisiana's Constitutions 1812–1974* (Lafayette, La. 1993), p. 7.
[49] Thomas Jefferson, 'First Inaugural Address', in M. D. Peterson (ed.), *The Portable Thomas Jefferson* (New York, 1975), p. 292.
[50] Quoted in Palmer, 'Two Worlds in One', p. 23.

France and Spain enjoyed still other strongholds in North America.[51] At New Orleans the newly purchased Louisiana territory itself surrounded the largest port in the south and the second-largest port in the nation. We know that Jefferson's goal was to consolidate his hold upon a vast new territory and especially the large port of New Orleans.[52] Consolidating an American grip over a vast new territory and the port probably seemed easier to achieve along with suppression of local laws. Perhaps consolidation by suppression of civil law was seen as a way of breaking the collective will of the Latins, and cutting down their natural cultural and linguistic impulses.

Jefferson seems also to have favoured a single language for the North American continent, and he may have seen suppression of Louisiana law as a means of reducing local inhabitants' affinity for the Spanish and French languages. There is some indirect evidence for the proposition that the Spanish and French languages themselves were undesirable badges of alien cultures in the new republic. In the mid-1850s, California lawyers displayed considerable hostility towards French and Spanish as well as civil law when they confronted a proposal to enact civil law in California. The California legislature reacted to the proposal with rhetoric evidently calculated to inflame the passions of local inhabitants:

---

[51] It is a truism that the strongholds would soon be toppled. For the present discussion, however, we should be familiar with the conditions that prevailed around 1810. Settled by Spain, a vast south-west territory included the area today occupied by Texas, New Mexico, Arizona, California, Colorado, Utah and Wyoming. On Spain's loss of this territory in 1848, see n. 54 below. For an account of the American colonisation of Texas under Stephen Austin and the other *empresarios*, see L. Newton and H. Gambrell, *Social and Political History of Texas* (Dallas, 1932), pp. 96–7. On Arkansas' situation, see Morris S. Arnold, *Unequal Laws Unto a Savage Race: European Legal Tradition in Arkansas 1686–1836* (Fayetteville, Ark, 1985), pp. 203–8. Quebec was the best example of a North American French stronghold that has endured culturally and juridically. At the time of Canada's cession to Great Britain in 1763, the Quebec population counted about 60,000–65,000 people, all francophone: Palmer, 'Two Worlds in One', p. 26. According to Palmer, the social and cultural situation in Louisiana around 1800 resembled that of Quebec in the late 1700s.

[52] The importance of the port and navigation cannot be overestimated.

> By the terms of the treaty between France and Great Britain in [1763], the Mississippi river became an international waterway 'equally free' in its whole length and breadth from its source to the sea. Open navigation was the key by which the Americans forced their way down the river and gradually usurped the incoming and outgoing trade. American trade with New Orleans expanded rapidly and northern merchants established commercial houses in New Orleans. (Palmer, 'Two Worlds in One', p. 30)

For a discussion of New Orleans as a commercial hub in the new nation, see generally Shael Herman, 'The Contribution of Roman Law to the Jurisprudence of Antebellum Louisiana', (1995) 56 *Louisiana LR* 257, 262; and generally R. H. Kilbourne, *Louisiana Commercial Law: The Antebellum Period* (Baton Rouge, 1980).

Substitute the civil for the common law, and it will be with great delay and expense, and in strange tongues, that books can be procured which will be found absolutely necessary for the lawyer and the judge in the intelligent administration of the system. The Louisiana reports, a few copies of translations of the institutes, and perhaps of the Pandects and of the works of Pothier and Domat may perhaps be procured by diligent search. Beyond this you will for the most part be obliged to resort to the original works upon the civil law, written in Spanish, Italian, French, German and Latin languages which if they can be found at all in the United States, will have to be ferreted out amongst the dusty volumes of some antiquarian bookseller, and can be purchased only at an exorbitant price; and in order to clear up a disputed point, to elucidate a novel question or to deduce new corollaries from old principles, it will become necessary to refer back to works existing only in a foreign language, to names strange to the American ear, to Escriche and Febrero, to the Nueva and Novissima Recopilaciones, to the Partidas, to the Fuero Real of Alonzo [sic] the Wise, and perhaps even to the Fuero Juzgo of his Gothic predecessors.[53]

Though 150 years separate us from the California rejection of civil law, we may still imagine the allergic reaction of California gold miners at the height of the gold rush upon hearing of a proposal to regulate their rights by the laws of Hispanic people whom they had just conquered in the Mexican war.[54]

Contrasts and comparisons between Louisiana and Catalonia

Economically there are also differences between Catalonia and Louisiana. Catalonia counts more for Spain's future than Louisiana does for the future of the United States. Many Americans can imagine the United States without Louisiana, but can the same be said for Catalonia? It is a bridge between the Iberian peninsula and the rest of the world. While Louisiana has a large port, its role as a bridge between the United States and the rest of the world is more limited than that of Catalonia.

---

[53] 1 California Appendix 588, 603 (1851) quoted in Combe, 'An Analysis of Civil Law Authorities', p. 297.

[54] The Mexican war was settled by the Treaty of Guadalupe Hidalgo. Under the treaty, signed in February 1848, Mexico transferred to the United States the territory that is now California, Nevada and Utah; most of Arizona; and parts of Colorado, New Mexico and Wyoming. Mexico also recognised Texas, down to the Rio Grande, as part of the United States.

Whether or not Catalonian legal institutions provoke a great tension with other regions of Spain, certain suggestions can be made on the assumption that Catalonians feel somehow different from their countrymen elsewhere, and that their own traditions need to be bolstered. Here follow some observations premised upon the idea that while Catalonians are Spaniards, they still wish to assure that their own language and legal heritage thrive.

(1) For preserving your own heritage and language, there can be no apologies. Catalonian differences should not result in marginalisation or a stigma of inferiority. Cultural and juridical differences require Catalonian lawyers to be professionally above reproach or criticism. Embracing a Catalonian heritage may be a significant advantage, provided Catalonian lawyers outperform counterparts from elsewhere on their own terms. No defect in one's Spanish law competence can be attributed to his Catalonian expertise. A Catalonian lawyer cannot allow people to flatter his Catalonian expertise to his face and behind his back complain that he cannot compete with Spanish law experts in Madrid or elsewhere. You master two laws, as you master two languages. In my opinion, Louisiana lawyers lost their competitive edge very early when they failed to protect the French and Spanish languages. Now, no matter how much we protest our differentness, a language deficiency handicaps us in understanding civilian ideas. Unable to absorb intellectual nourishment through study of original sources, Louisiana lawyers cannot readily convince others of useful or elegant ideas embodied in French and Spanish sources.

(2) To assure high prestige and respect for Catalonian laws among the public, Catalonians must assure high competence among lawyers, notaries and judges. Do Catalonian citizens take their regional laws seriously? Can a judge trained in Valencia serve as a judge in Catalonia even if he lacks expertise in Catalonian law and language? If he is not obliged to be competent in these laws, then like some judges in Louisiana, the judge may be tempted to apply the law he learned elsewhere to problems arising in Catalonia and deserving local solutions. Judges are professional exemplars. When judges without expertise in Catalonian law constitute a majority in Catalonia, they set the norm of competence. Their ignorance of the local law might imply that Catalonian law is less important than the law they happen to know. If the judges are not experts in

Catalonian law, sooner or later everyone will lose interest in Catalonian law and it will become a relic or a fossil.

(3) Questions may also be asked about the expertise of Catalonian practitioners. According to European Community policy, lawyers from elsewhere in Spain or even other member states enjoy the right of establishment in any nation of the European Community. One might assume that these lawyers from elsewhere can set up their offices in Barcelona and that competition will weed them out. Meanwhile, however, there is a risk of chaos in the law, and prejudice to the clients and the legal profession. What happens if both lawyers in a dispute are poorly qualified in Catalonian law? Can they simply agree to disregard it? One lawyer's incompetence will then cancel out the other's and they may never find each other out on the score of incompetence. Does the *colegio* allow lawyers to practise locally without a special authorisation in Catalonian law?[55] Does the bar specially designate lawyers who are experts in Catalonian law in addition to the national law? Is a lawyer able to advertise his Catalonian specialty on his professional letterhead?

(4) Do the universities honour Catalonian specialties? It is not enough to offer Catalonian law courses, as is already the case in the various Catalonian universities.[56] The courses must have prestige. They should be foundational blocks of the curriculum, so that students from elsewhere know that when they study in Catalonia something extra is demanded of them. Do the most distinguished faculty members offer the courses? Are there special seminars and theses in Catalonian subjects? Does the university grant special recognition of expertise in Catalonian law if one has taken a prescribed curriculum? Are awards given to the best students in the courses? Are there sufficient publications about Catalonian law and language? Do any universities in Madrid offer courses in Spain's regional laws such as those of Catalonia? Can a professor from elsewhere in Spain be appointed to a Catalonian institution without showing his expertise in the Catalonian language and law? If he can, then he may become isolated from the professors who know both Spanish and Catalonian law and he may never acquire Catalonian expertise.

---

[55] The answer seems to be yes, provided their dues are current.

[56] The law faculty of Lleida, for example, offers courses in the Family Code, the Succession Code and other institutions (mainly real rights, but also *laesio ultra dimidium*), and other Catalan faculties teach these subjects to a greater or lesser degree.

(5) Assuming a lawyer is competent in Catalonian law, there is the further
     issue of whether Catalonian law will be applied when it is in competition
     for recognition against, say, Spanish law. For immoveables and matters
     of personal status in Catalonia, a regime of Catalonian law should
     apply. In other types of transactions or legal instruments, however, can
     Catalonian law be stipulated as applicable? Without such a stipulation,
     we risk displacing Catalonian law by any other law more convenient to
     the parties. For lawyers in a hurry, the law they already know is more
     convenient than a law they must learn. For example, a British lawyer and
     a French lawyer may stipulate for arbitration in Paris or London without
     regard to Catalonian law. In other words, parties may agree to ignore
     Catalonian law and apply whatever law they wish. Can parties stipulate
     for Catalonian jurisdiction over disputes having a close relationship
     to the region? Assuming this stipulation can be made, then the parties
     ensure that knowledgeable Catalonian judges will resolve their disputes.
     In Louisiana, we routinely have a problem stipulating Louisiana law as
     applicable in many transactions because the non-Louisiana party often
     is the more powerful bargainer. New York enterprises rarely agree to
     displace New York law by any other law, including Louisiana law. So tied
     to financial power is the United States juggernaut of conformity that
     the question of which law offers the more rational or elegant solution
     to a problem is practically irrelevant in commercial negotiations.
(6) Catalonians should also ensure that their judges and lawyers are experts
     in the resolution of interregional conflicts of law.[57] Otherwise, they will
     not know when to apply Catalan law. There will always be close cases in
     which Catalan law may or may not be applicable; and the applicable law
     will depend upon the judge's discretion. But it is as dangerous to apply
     Catalan law inappropriately as to displace it when it is appropriate.

So much for Catalonia's current status on which I have already specu-
lated too much. Let us end our excursion as we began it: with Louisiana's
dual heritage. Since before Louisiana's statehood in 1812, its mixed legal
heritage has made juridical amphibians of Louisiana lawyers, who are well

---

[57] Louisiana has tried to reinforce the state judicial power over interstate conflicts of law by
integrating a short fourth book on the subject into the Louisiana Civil Code. The first regulation
of its kind enacted by a state in the United States, the fourth book of the Louisiana Civil Code
has been adopted too recently for an evaluation of its success. This fourth book of the Louisiana
Civil Code may correspond roughly to artt. 6–13 of the Spanish Civil Code.

adapted to navigating on both land and sea. Aficionados of the state's civil law might be tempted to depict the Civil Code as locked in a mortal struggle with a great adversary, the common law, but this depiction would be largely an optical illusion. In this 'struggle' there will be no winners or losers. The federal system of the United States allows Louisiana to exist as we are, and to evolve autonomously an unusual private law subject to occasional federal scrutiny for constitutionality. In fact, Louisiana lawyers, obliged to act pragmatically on behalf of clients in the United States and abroad, have reached an accommodation between the two traditions. To a considerable degree, common law and civil law methods have become fused in the collective imagination of the Louisiana bench and the bar. We have also witnessed a considerable convergence of civil law and common law ideas.

Firmly stitched into the fabric of the Union, Louisiana will not secede from the United States. For the foreseeable future, our improbable legal amalgam will evolve, occasionally tilting towards common law solutions and occasionally towards civil law solutions. Louisiana's story may fascinate foreign colleagues and may even be a source of consolation for lawyers seeking to understand their own heritages, but it has been largely misunderstood at home. This misunderstanding, rather than Louisiana's exceptional heritage, is fitting cause for lament, for a deeper understanding of Louisiana's situation could have propelled the United States legal community toward a comprehension of the other great western legal system. I trust that the Catalonian heritage will be better understood than ours. Such an understanding would work to the enduring advantage of Catalonia, the rest of Spain and the world beyond Iberia.

11

Estonia and the new civil law

MARTIN KAËRDI

Introduction

Estonian experiences in reforming its civil law – or, more precisely, in developing a new civil law system – are not widely known outside the Baltic region. Obviously this is the fate of smaller nations. It will, however, not change the fact that Estonian experiences in the legislative area deserve interest as a unique experiment in the development of a totally new legal order on a comparative basis, importing foreign experience and legal concepts. This is the story of the general processes – and, indeed, somewhat unconventional practices – used in the development of Estonian civil law. As this is also a story about the rediscovery of Estonian civil law traditions and of its lost legal culture, a short excursion into its history is necessary.

Historical notes: Estonian civil law tradition

Estonian civil law tradition goes way back in history. It has largely Germanic roots, mainly through the historical influence of that country in the Baltic. Though Estonia has, down the centuries, constantly changed hands between German, Swedish, Danish and Russian rulers, the upper class of the society remained dominated by Germans, at least up to the beginning of the twentieth century. The same applies to the legal tradition and laws that survived changes of power largely intact, preserving their Germanic and Roman origins. Estonian civil law is therefore a Germanic civil law.

These traditions were finally anchored in the so-called Baltic Civil Code (BCC), which dates back to 1865, and can be viewed as a result of the nineteenth-century Continental codification ideas in the areas of Estonia and Latvia. As a whole the BCC was a mixture of Germanic and Roman sources, largely a pandectist law. Though probably one of the most casuistic and unsystematic civil law codifications in the world, the BCC has played a vital role in determining Estonian legal traditions.

During the first Estonian independence period, 1918–40, the BCC retained its position as a primary source of civil law in Estonia. It was not without problems, though. Antiquated even in the nineteenth century when it originated, the BCC was always viewed as a temporary solution for the then newly independent Estonian civil law. From the early 1920s preparation of a new Estonian civil code began. The draft was never finalised though, as Soviet troops marched in in 1940.

The situation at the beginning of the 1990s

As Estonia regained its independence through the turbulence of 1992, the Civil Code of the then Soviet Socialist Republic of Estonia (from 1965) remained in force. It was clearly not a legal base a free-market economy could live with. Estonia needed a new civil legislation.

Early choices

Estonia did not aspire to produce a new draft civil code at once. Instead, the decision was to adopt the classical parts of a civil code (general part, obligations, property law, family and inheritance law) through a series of separate enactments that would gradually render obsolete the 1965 Civil Code of Soviet Estonia. The decision for gradual reform had a strong practical argument on its side. The time factor was important, so the acute problems had to be dealt with first.

These were decisions concerning formal methods or legislative techniques. Apart from an apparent need for the reformation of civil law, nobody at that time (in 1992) had an answer for the conceptual question – what should these future laws look like? Or even, more generally, what kind of a society would they initially govern?

At least the starting point was clear: the Parliament adopted the principle of legislative continuity to the first independence period of 1918–40.[1] Politically it was always of the utmost importance to view the first republic as the legal predecessor of our re-established independence. Basically the

---

[1] Declaration of Riigikogu (the Estonian Parliament) on legislative continuity, of 1 December 1992.

historical argument was used as an identification factor. A logical step for the civil law reform was to seek out the civil code draft of 1940. As the draft was discovered by one of the MPs, merely by accident, it came close to being passed into law without detailed examination. More thorough research indicated its deep-seated weaknesses. Since major changes would have been needed to adopt it as a law, the whole idea was dropped and the door was opened for other concepts.

First results

The first product of the civil law reform was the Property Law Act, containing a concept a German lawyer would call *Sachenrecht* (law of things). This order of priority might seem peculiar, but there was good reason to begin with property law. Property law as such was largely non-existent in Soviet law. Firstly the land, which to the state was not in civil circulation (which meant the total absence of such provisions). And what is probably even more important, the key issue in property law, at least for the economy – securities *in rem* – was a practically non-existent notion for the Soviet lawyers. As land reform and the restitution of ownership to those whose property had been expropriated after 1940 was one of the first decisions of the independent Estonian Parliament,[2] the new property law regulation to support it was needed immediately.

This practical need was basically the starting point of the whole civil law reform. And where to start can be a challenging question if one is starting from scratch. Of course there was a parliamentary conception of legal continuity, which was also reflected in the Estonian constitution of 1992.[3] It meant building up a legal system on the basis of that of the first republic. The problem was that the choice in civil law would have been between the mid-nineteenth-century feudal codification and the 1940 draft civil code. As mentioned, the first more thorough inspections of the 1940 draft had showed that it could only serve as a fairly general base for the new property law. Therefore the search for the new legislative models began. Basically, two approaches were possible:[4]

---

[2] Land Reform Act of 17 October 1991.
[3] Preamble to the constitution of the Republic of Estonia, 28 June 1992.
[4] A similar argument is brought by H. Mikk, 'Über die Zivilrechtsreform in Estland', in Justizministerium der Republik Estland, *Referate der grundbuch- und Notartage 1999* (Tallinn, 2000), p. 286 (almost the only comprehensive publication on the Estonian civil law reform).

– dropping the idea of the 1940 draft altogether and trying to modify the Soviet civil legislation still in force; or

– using the conception of the 1940 draft and amending it with modern comparative sources of the same pedigree, thus creating an entirely new civil legislation.

The first alternative was largely supported by the practising lawyers, and also by the university professors, and more generally by the older generation of legal professionals with a Soviet background. After a heated debate the second alternative, which was supported by the Ministry of Justice, prevailed, mostly because of its political advantages for Parliament.[5]

As a consequence, most of the inspiration for the property law draft, though it was largely presented as an amendment of the 1940 draft, came from the German BGB. The choice of the BGB as the main comparative source is not so surprising, bearing in mind the local civil law traditions, especially the origins of the draft – it was a development of the BCC, which itself was a codification of Roman law rules with strong influences from Germanic law.

The result of the work – the Property Law Act – was passed by the Parliament in 1993. It shows, both in its basic conceptions and in detail, a strong resemblance to its German 'big brother'. It has a strong Germanic-type land-register system, run by the courts; we even know the principle of the abstract nature of rights *in rem*. It is not all German law, though, as influences from the Swiss Civil Code and even, peculiarly enough, from Quebec and Louisiana are visible.[6]

The importance of the Property Law Act does not lie in its detail, however. The property law determined the conception of the whole future Estonian civil law. The discussion over the different conceptions of the development of Estonian civil law was actually a discussion over the conceptions of the property law regulation. Its outcome showed that the Estonian legislators are willing to make a fresh start with a legal culture governed by western standards and are therefore not afraid of using comparative law arguments in the drafting process. Of course in the case of property law one can

---

[5] Those 'political advantages' can be traced back to the coalition treaty of the first coalition in the first post-independence parliament.

[6] For example, the general provisions on 'property'/'things' in the Estonian Property Law Act contain a number of influences from Louisiana and Quebec; in later amendments they seem to be gradually disappearing, however.

talk about comparative research only conditionally, as much of the work on the draft was incidental in its methods, sources and conclusions. The comparative argument has, however, grown significantly in importance for the latter drafts.

Since the Property Law Act the Ministry of Justice, which has directed and controlled the preparation of civil legislation, has used basically the same drafting methods for the whole of civil law. We have usually had the so-called main text or a general model. In the case of the Property Law Act it was the *Sachenrecht* of the BGB (together with the historical concept in the 1940 draft); it remains to be seen how that pattern changes for later civil law drafts. This main text or model supplied the main concepts and principles for the draft, which could then be built up in detail, also using other comparative materials.

This is of course usually not a 'standard operating procedure' in drafting national legislation, resembling rather the work of the comparative law lawyer. The use of strong comparative arguments had, in the case of Estonia, however, some obvious advantages. The two main factors that have determined the early stages of Estonian efforts in civil law are the already mentioned 'time factor' and the 'personal factor'.

As far as time is concerned, we had a situation where new legislative solutions were needed immediately; on many occasions they were needed out of nowhere. Moreover, these solutions had to work out in practice, and a glance into foreign legal orders could offer an ideal medium for domestic solutions. Though never admitted publicly, the Estonian effort in civil law has largely been a pragmatic one. The law has not been viewed as an object of national pride or distinction, but rather as a mere instrument for achieving certain goals.

The 'people factor' has played an even more important role; it has been a major problem for the reform process. The Soviet system did terrible things to lawyers and legal education. It had, seemingly, a special tendency to produce bad civil lawyers. When asked to identify the key issue of the civil law reform in Estonia, one can only reply that it was most certainly to find the right people. This has mostly been due to the efforts of our Secretary of State in the Ministry of Justice, who, at the beginning of the 1990s, changed most of the staff in the department. He put his faith in the young lawyers coming directly from the university, especially in the law-drafting areas. The Property Law Act was largely a result of a fight between generations of Estonian lawyers. Different drafts were presented; the two basic alternative conceptions are mentioned above. It has been mainly the enthusiasm and enterprise of these young people that has carried the reforms, which were strongly supported by the foreign experts we have engaged. From the Property Law Act, cooperation with the German Foundation of International Legal Cooperation[7] started, which has been most successfully continued for the latter drafts also. That this cooperation has worked out so well is mainly to the credit of these young people, who were prepared to change their way of thinking, away from the predetermined patterns usually characteristic of Soviet lawyers.

The property law draft from the Ministry at first received heavy criticism from the 'old lawyers'. It only went through thanks to the political will of the Parliament. Most of the criticism of the new legislation has, however, remained destructive. The usual argument is that 'practice and reality have nothing to do with the wishes of the drafters; this cannot be applied anyway, or is just a paranoiac fear of anything new'. It has mostly been their natural incapacity to produce any viable alternatives to the ministerial drafts that has taken the older generation out of the reform process. Many of their criticisms have also proved to be wrong. In its acceptance by legal practitioners, we are happy to note the positive effect that a strong land register system has had in regulating and organising the market.

In the years following the Property Law Act, the Family Law Act and the law on the general part of the Civil Code (both of them in 1994) as well as the Inheritance Act were adopted by Parliament. They were mostly based on the 1940 draft civil code and casually amended by other comparative materials. This also marked the end of the early stage in Estonian civil law reform, a stage that drew mainly on historical precedent. This had resulted in rather mechanical methods of legal drafting, as many of the legal concepts and solutions were directly copied from historical or comparative sources, the latter usually confined to the provisions of the BGB.

Comparative approach in law drafting

From early 1995 a new wave in Estonian civil law drafting appeared. It can be described as a comparative approach. Elements of this approach were already visible in the work done on the new property law, although the draft was elaborated under substantial time pressure and in somewhat chaotic

---

[7] Deutsche Stiftung für die Internationale Rechtliche Zusammenarbeit.

circumstances. It was clearly not based on thorough research, being rather
a simple adaptation of the BGB property law for Estonian needs. In recent
years, a more refined approach has been adopted.

The first of these 'new' drafts was the Commercial Code, which, despite
its name, contained almost only company law provisions (as Estonia does
not have the dualistic 'commercial law' for commercial entities). Notable
comparative work was done on the draft. The starting point had again been
the relevant provisions in German law (the HGB or the German Commercial
Code, Aktiengesetz and GmbH-Gesetz). While most research and effort had
stopped here in the case of the property law, a substantive step forward was
made with the Commercial Code, as the relevant company law provisions of
most European countries were worked through thoroughly (mainly those
of Sweden, Denmark and Holland, even including Spanish legislation; not
to mention the EU company law directives). Even materials on Japanese
and US company law provisions were examined.

The biggest difference with the elaboration of property law lies not, however, in the number of comparative sources but in a methodical approach
to them, which has became more and more evaluative and critical of its
sources. Much of this progress is due to foreign expertise. The cooperation
with German experts that had started with the preparatory work on the
Property Law Act was most successfully carried on. We were especially fortunate in having Professor Dr Carsten Schmidt as one of the main advisers
on the draft; his sketch of modern company law codification provided a
base for the Estonian legislation.

Altogether the originally much-criticised Commercial Code has so far
been the success story of our legal reforms. It is hard to measure the effects of
the legislation in practice, but probably a fair amount of Estonian economic
success is owed to the regulative effects of the new company law and the
strong commercial register run by the courts.

The most challenging part of the Estonian civil law reform yet has been
the drafting of the Law of Obligations Act.[8]

When the Ministry of Justice started working on the law of obligations
the main goal was not only to carry out thorough comparative research but
also to create a draft that would outlive – or at least easily cope with – the
inevitable unification process in Europe in that area.

---

[8] Together with the law of obligations the new version of the law on the general part of the Civil
Code was also elaborated, the two drafts following mainly the same models.

As a general consequence of that directive, a significant change away from the early German model in Estonian civil law can be established. What makes the law of obligations, especially contract law, so interesting for the drafter is of course its unification perspectives. From the comparative works of Ernst Rabel in the 1920s to the Vienna CISG convention, the Unidroit Principles of International Commercial Contracts and the Principles of European Contract Law from the Lando Commission, not forgetting the works of the German commission on the reform of the law of obligations and the new Dutch Civil Code, all these works point in the same direction and use similar structures. This manifests the unification of the foundations of European contract law.

As the idea of a European contract law has grown significantly in acceptance and found elaboration even in its detail through the above-mentioned works, the Estonian drafters could not have overlooked these developments when determining the ideology of the new law of obligations. Estonia has indeed been in a unique position as far as unification tendencies are concerned. The main impediments to the drive towards a European civil code, or – less ambitiously – towards a European contract law, are of course the traditions and prejudices of national laws (not, of course, in a negative sense). The fact that Estonia was cut off from the roots of its own legal traditions had in that sense also some positive effects. As the new contract law was basically initiated with a blank slate, with no predetermined authorities, we were indeed offered a unique opportunity to realise all those unification and harmonisation ideas that most of Europe itself can only dream of.[9]

The comparative approach to legal drafting is the key here. This was not only the idea of having a really modern civil legislation: in the Estonian case, the approach was a pragmatic one. Firstly, one has to consider Estonian ambitions towards the European Union, as we are one of the 'first wave accession candidates' from eastern Europe. This of course brings the necessity of adopting the *aquis*, the relevant EC directives and proposals. At least in the private law area we have not seen it as a mere technical task. We have tried to integrate the private law directives into the very system of private law, mainly into the law of obligations. This can be a creative challenge, as the directives are going more and more into the deep essence of contract law

---

[9] See, e.g., the two declarations of the European Parliament from 1989 and 1994 (OJ C158/400-401; EUCP 95, 669), containing an appeal for a European civil code.

itself, affecting – as now for the case of Consumer Sales Directive 99/44 of 1999 – the whole system of legal remedies in contractual relations. For the national legislator it obviously means that the whole contract law system has to be compatible with the possible European regulations. Anticipating what this European system might look like from the different, detailed regulations issued so far is indeed a difficult task; especially as the regulative interests in Brussels are only starting to move from isolated specific areas into the more general, systematically challenging fields of civil law. On a more general level, therefore, the Estonian decision to base its law of obligations on the PECL and Unidroit principles has paid off; this also applies to the EC regulations. Directive 99/44 is a good example of it: we only had to make a few minor changes to the law of obligations draft after the regulation came out. More such directives will follow, but at least in the Estonian case they will not be viewed as an unpleasant burden, destroying the local private law system. In that connection the general Estonian experience arising from the law of obligations has been one of surprise at how much more sense this whole chaotic and incoherent picture of Community civil law makes when put into a private law system that supports it. It is this lack of a system at the European level that seems to call for a more systematic approach in the national legislation. That would mean not treating private law directives as alien concepts, but rather trying to integrate them into the system of private law itself. It is probably the first of such national law solutions; the 'European contract law' will emerge. The Estonian idea here has been not to follow that process, but to create a regulation that could systematically cope with possible future trends in European private law.

The law of obligations draft itself is currently in the parliament. It contains some 1,200 paragraphs, which is unconventionally large for the law of obligations, yet most of this unusual quantity derives from the special part, mainly from the special contracts, and the Community law-based provisions.[10] There was a long period of preparatory work, of almost four years (from late 1995) – a long time, that is, in Estonian terms. The Ministry of Justice organised a fairly small working group, with up to four or five active members, mostly lawyers of the younger generation. The main features of the draft are clear from the above. It has been built up on the basis of PECL and Unidroit principles, adopting especially their distinctive system of legal remedies for the contract law. The other important

---

[10] As a matter of fact, twenty-one different EC directives have been harmonised into the draft.

comparative sources used are of course the new Dutch Civil Code and the German projects for the reform of the law of obligations of the BGB.[11] Again a number of foreign experts were engaged. Special thanks go here to Professor Dr Peter Schlechtriem, also an active member of the Unidroit group and the above-mentioned German *Schuldrechtskommission*, who has been the main architect of the Estonian law of obligations. The Estonian drafters were also fortunate in having such distinguished lawyers as Professors Hein Kötz and Schmidt-Räntsch from Germany and Professor Gras from Holland as our experts. Altogether a draft of considerable quality has been achieved, even at the European level.

The law of obligations will finalise the structure of Estonian civil law. It will, however, mark only the conclusion of the first phase in the process of Estonian civil law reform. The second and perhaps an even more challenging task – and nobody in Estonia has any illusions here – will be converting these achievements into practice. The construction of a functioning and effective legal order as a basis of civil society will clearly take considerable time and effort from the participants. The re-education programmes for lawyers, already started, will be the first step. Anchoring the new rules in the consciousness of the society is the ultimate challenge and will take years. Our problem has of course been these lost fifty years, which have largely predetermined the unconventional nature of the legal reforms. We clearly did not have the time to wait for new laws to grow out of the changing structure of the society; this process, normal elsewhere, was reversed in the Estonian case. The law was, rather, an instrument to help the society to grow into these new structures. The new laws in Estonia have in that sense played a rather peculiar – even an abnormal – role. They represented a legislative ideal, a directive for the future developments.[12] Therefore the practical outcome and the effects of the reforms have to be evaluated in a different way. At the present moment it is not so much the 'result' that matters but rather the 'direction'. It is a gamble, of course, as far as the long-term effects are concerned, but we are positive about the outcome.

[11] Mainly contained in Bundesminister der Justiz, *Abschlußbericht der Kommission zur Überarbeitung des Schuldrechts* (Bonn, 1992).
[12] The same idea occurs in Mikk, 'Über die Zivilrechtsreform in Estland', p. 305, when describing the local legislative efforts as 'retrospective'.

12

The positive experience of the Civil Code of Quebec in the North American common law environment

CLAUDE MASSE

Presentation

The Civil Code of Quebec occupies a special place on the North American continent. Quebec is virtually the only state in North America[1] to be endowed with a civil code in a juridical environment almost wholly dedicated to Common Law. In our opinion, Quebec's historical development and dynamic current show that a small state's civil code is capable of developing itself and becoming the prime source of inspiration in the private law of the citizens of a community, even though such a community represents a minority within a broader setting.

Moreover, far from being a cause of legal acculturation and cultural alienation conflicting with Quebec's civilist culture, the coexistence of Common Law and Civil Law in Canada has been, from the very beginning of Quebec's history, a unique opportunity to benefit from a good number of innovations and unique institutions drawn from one or the other legal tradition. Very few countries have the good fortune of being at the bridge of two great juridical traditions as rich as the French-inspired Civil Code and the British-inspired Common Law. However, in the very near future, the globalisation of economic markets, as well as the move towards legal harmonisation, namely in the context of the North American Free Trade Agreement (NAFTA) and the Canadian Agreement on Internal Trade, will have to be monitored closely to ensure the continuity of our most fundamental legal institutions, especially the Civil Code of Quebec.

---

[1] Along with Mexico and the American state of Louisiana with whom trade and juridical relations are currently rather insignificant quantitatively speaking.

Before we look into the contents and implementation of our Civil Code, a brief historical overview appears imperative.

A bit of history

Formerly a French colony, Quebec was conquered by Britain and its American colonies in 1759. The 1774 Quebec Act recognised Quebec's right to maintain its civil code (property and civil rights). From then on, French law would apply in civil law cases, whereas British law would apply in both public and criminal law cases. At that time, the Civil Law of Quebec was not codified and it drew its sources mostly from the *Coutume de Paris* which was supplemented by Roman law, canon law and the French royal legislation in force prior to 1759. As a British colony, Quebec evaded the 1789 French Revolution and the power of Emperor Napoleon who, as we know, implemented the French Civil Code in 1804.

At first, the 1804 French Civil Code had almost no direct impact on Quebec's Civil Law system. It was only in 1866, on the eve of its entry into the Canadian federation to be created in 1867, that Quebec adopted its very first civil code – the Civil Code of Lower Canada – which was inspired by the French Civil Code. It seems worth mentioning that the French model had been adapted to fit the reality of a Quebec which, at the time, was entering into an era of extreme economic liberalism.

The adoption of the Civil Code of Lower Canada in 1866 obviously created a renewed interest in the civilist model on the part of Quebec jurists. However, the Civilian foundations of our private law were more often than not challenged in the nineteenth century. In fact, Quebec's Civil Law system was then submitted to powerful phenomena of legal acculturation favouring the Common Law system. This could be explained partly by the fact that the business sector was solely in the hands of an English-speaking élite, and also because many jurists and judges were only trained in the Common Law school. During the twentieth century, that trend was totally reversed, which helped preserve the integrity and application of our Civil Code.

Lastly, in terms of our legal history, we may point out that Quebec adopted in 1991, and implemented in 1994, a wholly new comprehensive and modern Civil Code to which were added, in specific domains, civil laws of a general order.[2]

---

[2] Such as the Charter of Human Rights and Freedoms, the Consumer Protection Act and the Automobile Insurance Act.

An overview of the contents of the Civil Code of Quebec

The Quebec legislature has been clear in its intent to make the Civil Code the fundamental law and *ius commune* of Quebec's legal system. The Civil Code even applies, unless the public law provides expressly otherwise, to the government of Quebec, as well as its institutions and representative bodies, namely in terms of contract law and civil liability.[3] The Civil Code's preliminary provision states to that effect:

> The Civil Code of Quebec, in harmony with the Charter of human rights and freedoms and the general principles of law, governs persons, relations between persons, and property.
>
> The Civil Code comprises a body of rules which, in all matters within the letter, spirit or object of its provisions, lays down the jus commune, expressly or by implication. In these matters, the Code is the foundation of all other laws, although other laws may complement the Code or make exceptions to it.

Just like any modern civil code, the Civil Code of Quebec, which contains 3,168 articles, covers all aspects of private law. It comprises ten books presented in a manner that differs somewhat from the French model. Moreover, it is interesting to see the number of nominate contracts included in this code which is structured as follows:

Book One: Persons
Book Two: The family
Book Three: Successions
Book Four: Property
Book Five: Obligations
   Title One – Obligations in general
   Title Two – Nominate contracts
      1– Sale
      2– Gifts
      3– Leasing
      4– Lease
      5– Affreightment
      6– Carriage

---

[3] According to art. 1376 CCQ.

7– Contract of employment
8– Contracts of enterprise and contracts for services
9– Mandate
10– Partnership and association contracts
11– Deposit
12– Loan
13– Suretyship
14– Annuity
15– Insurance
16– Gaming and wagering
17– Transaction
18– Arbitration agreement
Book Six: Prior claims and hypothecs
Book Seven: Evidence
Book Eight: Prescription
Book Nine: Publication of rights
Book Ten: Private international law

The sphere of application of the Civil Code of Quebec is therefore wide-ranging. However, it does not *a priori* and directly apply to Canadian governmental institutions because we are living in a federal system where the government of Canada is responsible for its applicable law. According to our constitution, the government of Canada exercises jurisdictions that, in certain cases, are closely linked to the civil law of Quebec. For example, we can quote the Bills of Exchange Act, the Bank Act, the Bankruptcy and Insolvency Act and the Divorce Act. It is therefore not surprising that the government of Canada, after having formally recorded the adoption of the new Civil Code of Quebec, launched an ambitious programme to harmonise federal legislation with the Civil Code of the Province of Quebec. This initiative, which was taken within Canada's bijuridical system (common law–civil law), has been very successful up to now.

In addition, the Civil Code of Quebec is supplemented and implemented by the Code of Civil Procedure of Quebec which includes more than a thousand articles, and is currently in the process of being reviewed.

But this is not exclusively founded on the theory of law and general principles. For Quebeckers, the Civil Code has indeed a real life of its own and an immense social importance.

The concrete implementation of the Civil Code of Quebec

At first, the current balance of power would seem to lead to a complete marginalisation of the Civil Code, even on the territory of the Province of Quebec. In fact, Quebec, which is the only one among the ten Canadian provinces to possess a civil code, represents less than 25 per cent of the total population of Canada. Furthermore, Quebec accounts for 2 per cent of the entire population of North America (not including Mexico) and is, along with Louisiana, the only North American state to possess a Civilian tradition. Of the sixty states or provinces in North America (not including Mexico), only two thus possess a civil code, the others being governed by Common Law.[4] In this context wholly dominated by Common Law, we could be led to believe that the Civil Code of Quebec is merely a folkloric remnant of the past, devoid of any practical significance. This is not the truth. The Civil Code of Quebec is of the utmost importance and its influence is felt in every domain of our social and economic life. Here are a few examples.

In the last ten years, 160,000–210,000 new judicial files have been yearly opened in Quebec in first-level proceedings,[5] such cases involving civil law matters.[6] Each year, almost 50,000 court orders are issued concerning Civil Law matters, including more than 15,000 comprehensive written judgments. Moreover, we find in Quebec more than 18,000 lawyers who are members of the Quebec Bar. Among those, 12,000 are private practice lawyers, and 70 per cent of this private practice concerns civil law and commercial law, the latter being a direct extension of the former. The Civil Code is so important in Quebec that its implementation in 1994 compelled all Quebec lawyers to take 36 to 60 hours of classes in 1992 and 1993 to help them get better acquainted with the contents of the new Code.

The Civil Code of Quebec is not only surviving; it possesses a full and rich social life that we take pride in. This continental coexistence with Common Law could become more problematic for our Civil Code in the

---

[4] With the exception of Puerto Rico, which is endowed with a very distinctive legal status within the USA.

[5] Cour du Quebec (civil appeals division), Cour du Quebec (small-claims court), Superior Court (civil appeals division), Superior Court (family appeals division), Superior Court (divorce).

[6] Sources: Report on activities of the Direction générale des services de justice, quoted in *La Révision de la procédure civile*, Comité de révision de la procédure civile, Government of Quebec, February 2000.

years to come, primarily because of the opening of economic markets and the necessary harmonisation of our commercial laws, namely in terms of contracts.

The trend towards legal harmonisation in the North American context

Quebec's economy is greatly open to the world, especially to the United States. As is the case in Europe, the globalisation of trade is an extremely important issue in North America. However, when we address this issue from the point of view of Quebec, one crucial fact must be acknowledged: the globalisation of trade has become a clear-cut and pervasive reality in Quebec, where 55 per cent of all the goods produced and manufactured are sold abroad, mostly on North American markets. This trend is becoming fast moving in the service sector where we are exporting our knowledge more and more, especially in engineering and computer-related industries. No economic systems are so intertwined and interdependent as the American and Canadian economies; and in this case, Quebec ranks number one in Canada.[7]

The harmonisation of a certain number of commercial rules on a Canadian or continental scale is not only unavoidable but, in many cases, it appears commercially sound for Quebec, whose economy largely rests on the export of goods and services. Unavoidable and desirable it certainly is, but according to certain conditions. This market continentalisation, characterised by the adoption of NAFTA in 1993[8] and the signing of the Canadian Agreement on Internal Trade in 1995, is aimed at harmonising rights. And it obviously gives precedence to American and Canadian commercial rights that rest on Common Law. Since this law varies from one state or province to another, we can ask ourselves if it would not be desirable to adopt for the whole of North America a law on trading that could largely be inspired by the proposals submitted within the setting of Unidroit, which draws, to my knowledge, the best from Common Law and Civil Law experiences.[9]

---

[7] Louis Balthazar and Alfred O. Hero, *Le Quebec dans l'espace américain* (Montreal, 1999).

[8] The signatories of this agreement are the United States, Mexico and Canada.

[9] E. Charpentier and P.-A. Crépeau, *Les principes d'Unidroit et le Code civil du Quebec: valeurs partagées* (Scarborough, Ontario, 1998).

Some lessons to be drawn from the existence of Common Law in Canada and Civil Law in Quebec

The Civil Law of Quebec has not remained closed to Common Law experience. In fact, Quebec has benefited from the example of Common Law to integrate into its law system some institutions or orientations that were foreign to Civil Law. This phenomenon became noticeable from the codification of 1866 concerning, for example, commercial law, testamentary freedom and, in law of evidence, the rule of the best evidence.[10] Moreover, the Civil Code of Quebec, which came into force in 1994, makes room for institutions such as the foundation (created by trust) and moveable hypothecs. It is also worth mentioning that our civil procedure has for a long time been marked by the use of class actions and the appeal to the small-claims court. The lesson has been learned so well that, in certain cases, these institutions have become more efficient in Quebec law than they are in Common Law provinces in Canada.[11]

In conclusion

Private law reflects the fundamental values of a people, as well as its history and true aspirations. Our Civil Code is undoubtedly the mainspring of our private law. The Civil Code of Quebec is embedded in our most cherished values and remains one of the true-born expressions of our distinct culture within Canada. The vitality of our civil codes is proof of the dynamism of small communities, whether we refer to Catalonia, Scotland, Estonia or Quebec. From this standpoint, I sincerely believe that the experience of the Civil Code of Quebec on a North American continent strongly influenced by Common Law has overall been extremely positive and noteworthy.

[10] J. E. C. Brierley and R. A. Macdonald, *Quebec Civil Law: An Introduction to Quebec Private Law* (Toronto, 1993), paras. 33–5, pp. 34–7.
[11] This is the case particularly for class actions in certain Canadian provinces such as Ontario.

13

From the code civil du bas Canada (1866) to the code civil Quebecois (1991), or from the consolidation to the reform of the law: a reflection for Catalonia

ESTHER ARROYO I AMAYUELAS

Introduction

The following pages explain why private law was codified in the territory which we know today as Quebec, and how and why the task of recodification was approached over one hundred years later. Quebec's experience is interesting because, on the one hand, it was successful and it is contemporary, and, on the other hand, because the political and social situation of Quebec is similar to that of Catalonia, and therefore it can serve us as a model of comparative law. Both nations have acknowledged competence in civil law matters, but neither of them has full competence (artt. 92.12 and 13 of the British North American Act, and art. 149.1.8 of the Spanish constitution (CE)).[1]

This chapter is part of the DGES PB 98-1173 project, directed by Professor Ferran Badosa Coll, and is included in the *II Pla de Recerca de Catalunya* funded by the Comissionat per a Universitats i Recerca of the Autonomous Government of Catalonia (1999SGR 00394).

[1] Quebec has general competence for legislating in civil law matters (property and civil rights), except in relation to the conditions and requirements for marriage (the province can only regulate issues relating to the formalisation of the agreement) and divorce, which falls under federal domain (art. 91.26 BNA). In this respect, see André Tremblay, *Les compétences législatives au Canada et les pouvoirs provinciaux en matière de proprieté et de droits civils* (Ottawa, 1967). The competence of Catalonia is more restricted: the regulation of rules of application and effectiveness of legal norms, forms of matrimony, public registries, the grounds for contractual obligations, rules for resolving conflicts of law and the determination of sources of law (although in the latter case fully abiding by the rules of regional laws) always corresponds to the state. In relation to this issue: Encarna Roca Trias, 'L'estructura de l'ordenament juridic espanyol', (1983) *RJC* 125; Esther Arroyo i Amayuelas, 'Le pluralisme juridico-civil en Espagne et l'ordonnancement civil de la Catalogne', (1998) 29 *RGD* 411.

An analysis should allow one to discuss the feasibility of the codification technique, which Catalonia has also chosen recently, and debate how a modern codification should be approached. Basically, should the law that we now have and know be consolidated? Or should we break with the previous law? But before answering these questions, it may perhaps be convenient to ask ourselves about the suitability of civil codes as instruments for modernising law.

In Quebec, codification was successfully handled on two separate occasions, the last in 1994. The code symbolises a different culture and society in North America, dominated for the most part by Common Law which, historically, has tended to phagocytise the *droit civil*.[2] However, to the extent that 'civilian tradition' and 'codification of law' are not indissolubly linked concepts,[3] it would not be out of place to wonder what made Quebec choose recodification – that is, a new code – now that it seems as though the prestige of this instrument has diminished considerably, as a result of the incessant impact of special statutes that create microsystems of regulations, and, to no lesser degree, in Europe, due to the growing number of EU regulations and directives. Codes are today a questioned tool, and in this context, Quebec and the Netherlands, which have adopted 'classic codes', are notable representatives of an exception that confirms the rule.[4]

We are referring to a model of a code that aspires to fully regulate all civil law, which is an instrument for the rationalisation and systematisation

---

[2] Regarding the phenomenon known as bijuralism, John E. C. Brierley, 'Bijuralism in Canada', in H. P. Glenn (ed.), *Contemporary Law/Droit Contemporain* (Cowansville, 1992), p. 22; George A. Bermann and Meinhard Hilf, 'Bijuralism in Federal Systems and in Systems of Local Autonomy', in Académie Internationale de Droit Comparé (ed.), *Rapports généraux XIIIe congrès International Montréal 1990/XIIIth* (Cowansville, 1992), p. 21.

[3] Indeed, the correlation that is often made between 'code' and 'civilian systems' does not always work. For example, Scotland and South Africa are civilian systems that have not codified their law, whereas, on the other hand, California and Montana are 'codified' common law jurisdictions. In any case, it is convenient to clearly understand what type of code is being spoken of in each case. For example, the American Uniform Commercial Code leaves the law in each state to subsist. Regarding American codification, see Shael Herman, 'Historique et destinée de la codification américaine', (1995) 3 *RIDC* 715; Jean-Louis Bergel, 'Principal Features of Codification', (1988) 48 *Louisiana LR* 1076, 1090–3; John Henry Merryman, *La tradición jurídica romano-canónica*, trans. Eduardo L. Suàrez ([1969], Mexico, 1998), pp. 60–1, 70. See further n. 8 below.

[4] Cf. Académie internationale de droit comparé, *La Codification, forme dépassé de législation* (XIe et XIIe Congrès) (Caracas, 1982); *Codification: Valeurs et langage* (Actes du colloque international du droit civil comparé) (Montreal, 1985); Mirjan Damaska, 'On Circumstances Favoring Codification', (1983) *Revista Jurídica de Puerto Rico* 355; Bergel, 'Principal Features', 1077–8, 1081 ff.

of law, and which, moreover, is a legal body whose rules and regulations are drafted on the basis of generality and abstraction thanks to the use of 'valve' concepts allowing judges to adapt them to the specific case in hand. It is a code, in effect, that is common law with respect to special legislation which, undoubtedly, the civil code can never fully replace.[5] This is the model chosen by Quebec. The other is the French model, namely that of codification 'à droit constant', where there is no will to reform and where law is contemplated 'as is'.[6] This type of codification does not solve the problem of adapting rules to a changing society, and only solves the problems of law practitioners (judges, lawyers, etc.), although it facilitates the task of knowing laws because it orders, systemises and groups pre-existing statutes. But it doesn't change them.[7] Technical – and above all ideological – elements come into play in choosing one or the other option.[8]

It was deemed appropriate to divide this exposé into two parts. The first, as we have already mentioned, will try to explain very briefly what law is being codified in Quebec and why. The second part will be a general reflection on codification in Catalonia, after having seen the results in the country that serves as a model. Finally, it must also be said that this approach is of a general nature. Therefore it is unimportant that the process of codification of Catalan civil law is currently being carried out on a sector-by-sector basis, by themes, because sooner or later the consolidation of the codes that we already have will have to take place.[9] So then we will enter a new process of codification of law, for which some of the arguments set out here are not

---

[5] Regarding the Quebec Civil Code, John E. C. Brierley, 'The Civil Law in Canada', (1992) 84 *The Law Library Journal* 163; John E. C. Brierley, 'Quebec's "Comon Laws" (droits communs): How Many Are There?', in Ernest Caparros et al. (eds.), *Mélanges Louis-Philippe Pigeon* (Montreal, 1989), pp. 122–3; Alain Bisson, 'Dualité de systèmes et codification civiliste', in *Conférences sur le nouveau Code civil du Quebec: Actes des journées louisianaises de l'Institut canadien d'études juridiques supérieures 1991* (Quebec, 1992), pp. 46–7.

[6] Guy Braibant, 'El modelo francés de la nueva codificación', in *Seguridad jurídica y codificación* (Madrid, 1999), p. 91; Guy Braibant, 'Utilité et difficultés de la codification', (1997) 24 *Droits* 61; Marc Suel, 'Les Premières codifications à droit constant', (1997) 26 *Droits* 19; Pierre-Yves Gautier, 'De l'art d'être furtif le "droit constant" des codes de la propriété intellectuelle et de la consommation', in Bernard Beignier (ed.), *La Codification* (Paris, 1996), p. 107; Antonio Pau Pedrón, 'La segunda codificación', in *Seguridad jurídica y codificación*, p. 80–3.

[7] But cf. Gérard Timsit, 'La Codification, transcription ou transgression de la loi?', (1996) 24 *Droits* 83.

[8] As for the diversity of meanings of the concept of 'code', Jacques Vanderlinden, *Le Concept de code en Europe occidentale du XIIIe au XIXe siècle* (Brussels, 1967).

[9] Agustí Bassols Parés, 'Vers la codificació del dret civil català: La reforma prèvia de 1984' (1993) *RJC* 397; Preamble I, 9, Act 9/1998, Family Code (CF).

unfamiliar, especially because the culmination of the codification process in Catalonia cannot consist merely of a simple compilation of existing law.[10]

The tradition of civil law in Quebec: the (double) codification of law

While the Canadian provinces in general have been ruled by common law from the outset, given the English prevalence during the colonisation, in Quebec the French colonisation was followed by a British conquest that, naturally, conditioned the evolution of law.[11] The interference of British elements in a legal culture with a French base makes law in Quebec a mixed law.[12]

Codification: the 1866 code civil du bas Canada

The first French colonisers to settle Canada (1608) followed the law that was in effect in the country where they came from: either customary or written law.[13] The so-called *Coutume de Paris*[14] (customary common law in northern France)[15] went into effect in the colony starting in 1628, but this did not prevent recourse to other sources of law that were also in force (especially Roman and canon law).[16] After the British conquest, a new

---

[10] On 30 December 2002 the Catalan Parliament passed Act 29/2002, *Primera Llei del Codi Civil de Catalunya* (First Act of the Civil Code of Catalonia, DOGC 3798, 13 January 2003). This Act contains several provisions dealing with the efficacy of norms, the exercise of rights, and the prescription and lapse of rights.

[11] Frederick Parker Walton, *Le Domaine et l'interpretation du Code du Bas-Canada*, introduction by Maurice Tancelin (Toronto, 1980), p. 47; André Morel, *Cours d'histoire du droit (1991–92)*, 11th edn (Ottawa, 1991), pp. 47–8.

[12] Brierley, 'The Civil Law', p. 167. Tancelin, in Walton, *Le Domaine*, p. 23, defines mixticity based on the fact that, since the Quebec Act (1774), public law pertains to common law and private law follows the tradition of Roman and canon law (*droit civil*). Mixticity is also qualified based on the receiving skill of foreign law sources; thus, Patrick H. Glenn, 'Le Droit comparé et l'interprétation du Code civil du Quebec', in *Le Nouveau Code civil interprétation et application: Les journées Maximilien-Caron 1992* (Montreal, 1993), p. 180.

[13] Morel, *Cours*, pp. 39, 47.

[14] Ibid., p. 50; Louis Baudoin, *Le Droit civil de la Province de Quebec: Modèle vivant de droit comparé* (Montreal, 1953), p. 62.

[15] Roderick A. Macdonald and J. E. C. Brierley (eds.), *Quebec Civil Law: An Introduction to Quebec Private Law* (Toronto, 1993), p. 8. On the contents of customs, see John A. Dickinson, 'New France: Law, Courts and the Coutume de Paris, 1608–1760', (1995) 23 *Manitoba LJ* 39–42.

[16] Morel, *Cours*, pp. 54–63; Walton, *Le Domaine*, pp. 36–8; Macdonald and Brierley (eds.), *Quebec Civil Law*, pp. 10–14; John E. C. Brierley, 'Quebec's Civil Law Codification: Viewed and Reviewed', (1968) 14 *McGill LJ* 547–54; Brian Young, *The Politics of the Codification: The Lower Canadian Civil Code of 1866* (Montreal, London and Buffalo, 1994), pp. 18–21.

model of judicial organisation made it possible to serve justice according to English law and equity.[17] French Canadian law was not restored until 1774, with the Quebec Act (art. 8), although it was not applied to the legal regime concerning land which, thereafter, was granted by the king (art. 9).[18] In addition, it introduced the freedom of disposing of the estate by will in the province (art. 10) and provided for the future creation of a *Conseil legislatif* (art. 12) with powers to enact statutes in relation to the establishment of courts of justice. This meant that existing legislation would necessarily have to be adapted to the structure of this new organisation of the courts. The changes would particularly affect procedural and commercial law.[19]

With the Constitutional Act of 1791, the territory was divided into two colonies – Lower Canada (modern-day Quebec) and Upper Canada (modern-day Ontario) – with their respective francophone and anglophone majority populations which would be governed, respectively, by French Canadian and by English law.[20] The latter already dominated commercial transactions throughout the entire continent, whereas French Canadian law became increasingly outmoded and anachronistic, which explains why neither the civil governors nor the courts applied it. Judges were not trained in the *droit civil* system, and Canadian law was lacking in systematic order and was written in a language that was not accessible to all. Naturally, this did not make lawyers' work easy either.[21] Under these circumstances, a codification 'à droit constant' was necessary, but, as we will see, it was also necessary to bring the laws up to date. Along these lines, under the union of the two provinces (1840), statutes were enacted to abolish the right of 'retrait lignager' (1855), the abolition of the onerous

---

[17] Citizens boycotted the courts through frequent recourse to arbitration. See André Morel, 'La Réaction des Canadiens devant l'administration de la justice de 1764 à 1774', (1960) 20 *R. du B.* 53; Michel Morin, 'Les Changements des régimes juridiques consécutifs à la conquête de 1760', (1997) 57 *R. du B.* 695–8; Macdonald and Brierley (eds.), *Quebec Civil Law*, p. 15.

[18] John E. C. Brierley, 'The Coexistence of Legal Systems in Quebec: "Free and Common Socage" in Canada's "pays de droit civil"', (1979) 20 *C. de D.* 277.

[19] Macdonald and Brierley (eds.), *Quebec Civil Law*, pp. 16–18; Murray Greenwood, 'Lower Canada (Quebec): Transformation of Civil Law, Higher Morality to Autonomous Will, 1774–1866', (1995) 23 *Manitoba LJ* 137–42; Michel Morin, 'La Perception de l'ancien droit et du nouveau droit français au Bas Canada, 1774–1866', in Patrick Glenn (ed.), *Droit québécois et droit français: communauté, autonomie, concordance* (Quebec, 1993), pp. 13–19. On procedural law, Jean Maurice Brisson, *La Formation d'un droit mixte: l'évolution de la procedure civile de 1774 à 1867* (Montreal, 1986).

[20] Morel, *Cours*, pp. 81–2; Walton, *Le Domaine*, p. 46; Paul-André Linteau, *Histoire du Canada* (Paris, 1994), pp. 35–6.

[21] Morel, *Cours*, pp. 152, 162–7; Brierley, 'Quebec's Civil Law Codification', pp. 533–42; Morin, 'La Perception', pp. 19–22.

aspects of the French seigneurial system (1854) and the liberalisation of usury (1858). But above all, the most important law enacted was the one that repealed the feudal system, because it represented the first step towards codification.[22]

The approach to codification (1866)

Codification was reached because of the need to impose order on the multiplicity of juridical sources existing in Lower Canada: the *Coutumes*, Roman and canon law, French royal provisions, edicts, local British provisions, British Parliament statutes, provincial assembly legislation, etc. Strictly technical motivations led to the rationalisation and systemisation of law.[23] The project later known as confederation between the various provinces, which was adopted only one year later (1858), had a notable impact on the subsequent meaning of the Code, which came to be considered as an instrument for the affirmation and defence of Lower Canada's identity as a nation, in order to avoid the danger of being assimilated by the other British provinces governed by common law and likewise interested in striking an agreement.[24] This would lead to the civil code being presented as a *iuris continuatio* with *l'ancien droit* and to minimisation of the changes, which were indeed significant to keep in step with the demands of economic liberalism. Once the code civil du bas Canada was in force, the tendency was to distort things by exalting it as a symbol of the Québécois' loyalty to their roots.[25]

How was the Civil Code viewed during this period? First of all, the anglophones contemplated it with a certain scepticism. They argued that

---

[22] Macdonald and Brierley (eds.), *Quebec Civil Law*, pp. 19–24; Greenwood, 'Lower Canada', pp. 159–67; Sylvio Normand, 'La Codification de 1866: context et impact', in Glenn (ed.), *Droit québécois et droit français*, pp. 44–51; Brierley, 'The Coexistence', p. 286.

[23] As for the reasons, purposes and method of codification, in addition to the Acte pour pourvoir à la codification des lois du Bas Canada qui se rapportent aux matières civiles et à la procédure (1857), see C. de Lorimier and A. Vilbon, *La Bibliothèque du Code civil de la Province de Quebec (ci devant Bas-Canada) [ou recueil comprenant entre autres matières...]* (Montreal, 1871–90); also *Civil Code of Lower Canada. Reports of the Commissioners for the Codification of the Law of Lower Canada Relating to Civil Matters: First, Second and Third Reports; Fourth and Fifth Reports; Sixth and Seventh Reports and Supplementary Report* (Quebec, 1865).

[24] Brierley, 'Quebec's Civil Law Codification', pp. 527–33; David Howes, 'From Polyjurality to Monojurality: The Transformation of Quebec Law', (1987) 32 *McGill LJ* 528–9; Robert Yalden, 'Unité et Différence: The Structure of Legal Thought in Late Nineteenth-Century Quebec', (1988) 46 *U Toronto FLR* 370.

[25] Normand, 'La Codification', p. 60.

the continuous expansion of Canadian society demanded constant changes that were entirely incompatible with the immobilism that characterised the setting of law by means of a code.[26] For the francophones, on the other hand, the advantage was that law was written down in organised fashion, and that it was able to be interpreted systematically and logically, while at the same time allowing for general principles to be adapted to specific cases. This is a task that enormously complicated the fragmentary and casuistic nature of the sector-based legislation that is inherent to countries ruled by common law.[27]

The task of codification fell to three judges, two of French and one of English origin, who relied on their respective bilingual secretaries, all of them attorneys.[28] This make-up of the commission indicated that a code for the practical, not for the learned, jurists was desired.[29] In general, the models to be followed in the work were the French and Louisiana Codes, although the purpose was to incorporate the provisions in force in Lower Canada. In this sense, it should be noted that very few of the articles of the *Coutume de Paris* remained unchanged by this time, and that there were elements of British common law that were well rooted in the province, including the testamentary forms and the principle of freedom of disposing of the estate by will, which had been in force since 1774.

The Code had to serve to sum up, order and systematise law, not as much to innovate; hence the fact that law prior to 1866 was not expressly repealed (see art. 2613 original) and the customs and the old doctrine (basically, French law and its commentators) continued to be valid for interpreting what might not be clear in the new Code.[30] At any rate, the statement that codification was not intended to innovate should be qualified: indeed, the traditional, pre-revolutionary family principles (male prevalence,

---

[26] W. D. Ardagh, 'Codification and Consolidation', (1980) 6 *Upper Canada LJ* 220–1; Greenwood, 'Lower Canada', pp. 168–9.

[27] Bergel, 'Principal Features', p. 1089; Roderick A. Macdonald, 'Civil Law – Quebec, New Draft Code in Perspective', (1980) 58 *R. du B.* 187–90. As regards the difference between the two types of legislation, see Louis-Philippe Pigeon, *Rédaction et interprétation des lois*, 3rd edn (Quebec, 1986), pp. 19–25; Alain Bisson, 'A Comparison between Statutory Law and a Civil Code', in Raymond A. Landry and Ernest Caparros (eds.), *Essays on the Civil Codes of Quebec and St Lucia* (Ottawa, 1984), p. 225.

[28] Young, *The Politics*, pp. 68–81, 84–98.   [29] Morin, 'La Perception', p. 35.

[30] Pierre Basil Mignault, 'Le Code civil de la province de Quebec et son interprétation', (1935–6) 1 *U Toronto LJ*, 104–14; Brierley, 'Quebec's Civil Law', pp. 542 ff.; Greenwood, 'Lower Canada', pp. 174–81.

Catholicism) were preserved, but regulation of property was adapted to the new situation, and, in keeping with the new times, the freedom of contract and the private property cult were also proclaimed.[31]

Recodification

At first, the code civil du Bas Canada was very positively valued because it allowed judges and jurists to attain a precise knowledge of the law, thus stimulating the teaching of law and promoting the uniformity of jurisprudence.[32] But the Code slowly became obsolete because it consecrated principles that were not in keeping with the times to which they had to be applied. Their shortcomings were compensated at times by means of legal reforms of the Code itself, and other times through statutes that ran contrary to the Code's principles, often leaving jurisprudence to solve any problems arising from such conflicts, with the added risk that a case might be decided by judges who had no civilian training.[33]

But finally, Quebec took on the task of drafting a new civil code.[34] Recodification involved a general review of the code and not a simple 'update' of the old regulations. This meant a change of principles, adapting law to the Quebecois society of the time, as well as the task of harmonising pre-existing legislation. In addition, it was convenient to regulate certain matters *ex novo*.

---

[31] For the ideology and principles of the 1866 Civil Code, see Louis Baudoin, *Les Aspects généraux du droit privé dans la province de Quebec* (Paris, 1967), pp. 22–30; Macdonald, 'Civil law', pp. 192–3; Macdonald and Brierley (eds.), *Quebec Civil Law*, pp. 41–5; Greenwood, 'Lower Canada', pp. 178–81; Louis Perret, 'L'Evolution du *code civil du Bas-Canada* ou d'une codification à l'autre: Réflexion sur le Code Civil et son effet de codification', (1989) 20 *RGD* 723–4.

[32] André Morel, 'La Codification devant l'opinion publique de l'époque', in Jacques Boucher and André Morel (eds.), *Le Droit dans la vie familiale: Livre du centenaire du Code Civil*, vol. I (Montreal, 1970), p. 27; J. E. C. Brierley, 'Quebec Legal Education since 1945: Cultural Paradoxes and Traditional Ambiguities', (1986) 10 *The Dalhousie LJ* 20–2.

[33] As for the ageing of the code and the decodification effect, see Louis Baudoin, 'De Certaines réformes nécessaires du droit québécois', (1967–8) 2 *Ottawa LR* 363; Louis Baudoin, 'Le Code civil québécois: Crise de croissance ou crise de vieillesse', (1966) 44 *R. du B.* 391; as for its modifications, see Ernest Caparros, 'Overview of an Uncompleted Journey: From the Civil Code of Lower Canada to the Civil Code of Quebec', in Raymond Landry and Ernest Caparros (eds.), *Essays on the Civil Codes of Quebec and St Lucia* (Ottawa, 1984), pp. 18–27; Perret, 'L'Evolution', pp. 726–32.

[34] Jean-Louis Baudoin, 'Réflexions sur le processus de recodification du Code Civil', (1989) 30 *C. de D.* 819.

A civil code project was already prepared in 1978, with 3,288 precepts and their corresponding motives and comments.[35] However, the government not only did not approve it, but it decided to parcel out the codification effort, making it necessary to start work again from scratch.[36] At first it was considered convenient to reform only family law, which entered into force in 1981.[37] This was not a reform of the existing civil code; rather, it would become the first book of the new Civil Code of Quebec. The corresponding part of the old Civil Code was repealed, although the remaining books continued to subsist. Other sections were the object of drafts and reform projects between 1982 and 1990, but not all of them came into force. Finally, on 18 December 1991, the code civil du Quebec[38] Bill was passed.

The new Civil Code, which replaced the 1866 and 1981 versions, came into force on 1 June 1994 in its bilingual version.[39] It declared itself as 'the ius commune' (preliminary provision)[40] and has 3,168 articles, spread out in 10 books, 1 preliminary provision and several final provisions. Certain parts are strongly influenced by comparative law, including EC law and international treaties. It 'imports' from common law the family patrimony,[41] moveable hypothec (art. 2660 CCQ) and also, given its influence and,

---

[35] For a description of the objectives and methodology of the reform, as well as the project's contents, see Paul-André Crépeau, 'Les Enjeux de la révision du Code civil', in André Poupart (ed.), Les Enjeux de la révision du Code Civil: Colloque sur la révision du code civil ([1979], Montreal, 1980), pp. 11–36; Paul-André Crépeau, preface to the Projet de l'Office de revision du Code Civil: Rapport sur le Code Civil (Quebec, 1977), p. XXV; Paul-André Crépeau, 'Civil Code Revision in Quebec', (1974) 34 Louisiana LR 930; Paul-André Crépeau, 'La Révision du Code civil', (1977) 2 CP du N 339; Paul-André Crépeau, 'La Réforme du Code civil du Quebec', (1979) 2 RIDC 269. Also Jacques Beaulne, 'Les Point sur la réforme du Code civil', (1987) CP du N 395–437; Macdonald, 'Civil Law', 194–205.

[36] Critical, Paul-André Crépeau, 'Les Lendemains de la réforme du code civil', (1981) 59 R. du B. 625. For the official explanations, see Marie-Josée Longtin, 'Une Expérience de révision générale du droit privé: le code civil du Quebec', (1986) 40 RJPIC 541–4.

[37] Jean-Louis Baudoin, 'Code civil. Droit de la famille. Projet de loi núm. 89', (1981) 79 RTDC 488.

[38] Gil Rémillard, 'Présentation du projet de Code civil du Quebec', (1991) 22 RGD 5.

[39] Pierre-Gabriel Jobin, 'Le Droit transitoire et le Code civil du Quebec: chronique de droit civil québécois', (1995) 1 RTDC 207.

[40] For the value of this clause, Brierley, 'Quebec's "Comon Laws"', pp. 116–18; Rémy Cabrillac, 'Le Nouveau code civil du Quebec', (1993) Dalloz 267 at 269; Bisson, 'Dualité de systèmes', in Actes journées louisianaises, p. 46.

[41] Highly critical in this respect, Ernest Caparros, 'Le Patrimonie familial: une qualification difficile', (1994) 25 RGD 251; Ernest Caparros, 'Le Patrimonie familial québécois: comme un oeuf de coucou dans le nid du Code civil du Quebec', in J. Beaulne and M. Verwilghen (eds.), Points de droit familial/Rencontres universitaires notariales belgo-québécoises (Montreal, 1997), p. 147.

specifically, the influence of the trust, it is affirmed that it accretes the role of the patrimonies by appropriation (art. 1256 ff. CCQ). Other changes make reference to the establishment of a number of general principles on the administration of the patrimony of others or computerised records, etc. In reference to persons, it recognises that every person is the holder of civil rights and that he exercises his civil rights, although depending on the circumstances has to exercise them through representation or assistance (artt. 4, 153 ff. CCQ); and, especially, the personality rights (art. 3 CCQ). Articles 2166–74 CCQ admit the mandate given in anticipation of the mandator's incapacity, that is, the appointment of a mandatary to take care of himself in case of a future lack of discernment.

However, despite the in-depth reform, the new Code is not viewed as breaking with the past, as most of the principles are a continuation of the prior doctrinal and jurisprudential stock of knowledge.[42]

The Code as a means of law reform

National codification in the context of internationalisation and Europeanisation of law

Does codification make sense when we are now moving closer and closer to the internationalisation of jurisprudence?[43] We have seen that, in Quebec, the answer is yes.

Catalonia has a more restricted competence in civil matters than Quebec, to the point that it could never have its own regulations affecting the bases of contractual obligations because these are common to all of Spain (art. 149.1.8a CE) and, indeed, they should be common to all of Europe. This makes one think that the next Catalan code, which is already known as the 'patrimonial code', should strive for a more modest title, such as the 'code of real rights' or 'code of contracts and property law', as presented by the *Consellera* of Justice in this book.[44]

---

[42] In general, see Cabrillac, 'Le Nouveau'; Pierre-Gabriel Jobin, 'Le Nouveau code civil: chronique de droit civil québécois', (1993) 4 *RTDC* 911; Jean Pineau, 'La Philosophie générale du Code civil', in *Journées Maximilien-Caron*, p. 271; J. E. C. Brierley, 'The Renewal of Quebec's Distinct Legal Culture: The New *Civil Code* of Quebec', (1992) 42 *U Toronto LJ* 495; Marie-Michéle Blouin, 'Le Nouveau Code Civil du Québec de 1994', in Beignier (ed.), *La Codification*, p. 167. See also nn. 61 and 78 below.

[43] Sceptical, Bruno Oppetit, 'L'Avenir de la codification', (1997) 24 *Droits* 78.

[44] Above, pp. 164–71. The policy of the Catalan Ministry of Justice has since changed. The aim is no longer the enactment of an independent code of patrimonial law, but a complete civil

European unification or harmonisation does not prevent the codification of national laws – in this case, Catalan civil law – from making sense, because the process can hardly affect all areas of law.[45] Certainly, contract law is the least likely to remain unchanged. Or, in other words, it appears obvious that the future code should exclude *ab initio* such matters as have already been regulated by economic practice or international treaties – and that regardless of the fact that competence may not exist if they fall within the scope of mercantile law (art. 149.1.6 CE) – and, in general, all those that can be subject to rapid technical evolution. In relation to property law, it is possible that the system of transfer of property (need of *traditio* or not) or credit guarantees (in the sense of allowing or prohibiting fiduciary transfers as a form of surety, or establishing a uniform guarantee type that would facilitate commercial practices) may be affected by the impact of unification. But in the remainder of matters, it is to be assumed that the states will be given leeway to set up a *numerus apertus* of real rights. In any case, we start with the assumption that harmonisation will not entail the disappearance of national law, whether codified or not;[46] and if it is codified, nothing prevents the modification of the code, the generic formulations of which should enable the addition of new assumptions.[47] This adaptation will have to be one of the tasks of the Private Law Legal Observatory of Catalonia, recently created by the autonomous government of Catalonia.

The function of the civil code in modern societies

In Catalonia, the purpose of codification is not to restore the lost hegemony of a civil code, as occurs in the other countries that have engaged in a recodification process, but to achieve a civil code for the very first time. Therefore, it should be well done and in accordance with the most contemporary experiences. In this sense, the characteristics of such a code in Catalonia should

---

code for Catalonia, book V of which will be devoted to patrimonial law (acquisition and loss of property, possession and detention, administration of the property of another, community, usufruct, rights of pledge and hypothecation and other real rights, such as ownership, servitude, emphyteusis, apartment rights etc.).

[45] Antonio Padoa-Schioppa, 'Il diritto comune in Europa: riflessioni sul declino e sulla rinascita di un modello', (1997) *ZEUP* 707.

[46] In reference to this, see Santiago Espiau Espiau above, pp. 199–220.

[47] As noted by Damaska, 'On Circumstances', p. 357, when drafting a code it is necessary to think about principles with a level of abstraction that allows potential problems to be taken into account.

be those that are set forth in modern-day second-generation codes: that is, adapted to the new social structures, using a language that reflects the modernisation of law and permeable to the influences of comparative law. And, above all, it should be the result of a collective effort, involving the collaboration of large sectors of society in the formulation of proposals. All of these are notes that today define the code civil du Quebec.[48]

Catalonia has never had a civil code because the Spanish civil war, which laid to rest the so-called Second Republic, broke off the codifying initiative that had been launched several years earlier by the autonomous government. But, in general, with the exception of this parenthesis, the movement towards codification in Spain in the nineteenth century was characterised by its conception of a sole civil code for the whole of Spain, and therefore it imposed the overcoming of legal particularities.[49] Regional civil laws subsisted, but they were condemned to be structured by means of a system of appendices, and, after 1946, through a system of compilations, which did not allow things to be contemplated differently, since in no case did a system of sources of law exist to serve as a basis. The Compilation, which was the technique by which Catalan civil law at the time (1960) was finally articulated, had to be done by adapting to the systematic nature of the Spanish Civil Code and avoiding coincidences and repetitions with this body of law. Nonetheless, the ultimate goal was to arrive at a new general civil code for all of Spain.[50] Therefore, the Compilation included only those genuinely Catalan institutions that it was considered convenient to preserve. The proclamation of the Spanish constitution (1978) meant the recognition of legislative authority and the ability to take on competence in civil law. This facilitated the evolution of Catalan law, and little by little, steps have been taken towards codification.[51] It is necessary to note the thrust that the project has acquired since, in a relatively short period of time, Catalonia now has two sector-based codifications in place: law of succession and family law. The third, relative to patrimonial law, is near

---

[48] Pineau, 'La Philosophie', pp. 272–3; Patrick Glenn, 'Le Droit comparé et l'interprétation du Code civil du Quebec', in *Journées Maximilien Caron*, pp. 187–90; Pierre-Gabriel Jobin, 'Le Droit comparé dans la réforme du Code Civil du Quebec et sa première interprétation', (1997) 38 *C. de D.* 488–93.

[49] Mancomunitat de Catalunya (ed.), *El dret català i la codificació* (Barcelona, 1919), pp. 11–12.

[50] Antoni Mirambell and Pau Salvador, *Projecte d'Apèndix i materials precompilatoris del Dret Civil de Catalunya* (Barcelona, 1995), p. XXVII.

[51] Bassols, 'Vers la codificació', p. 395, situates the beginning at around 1986.

completion.[52] Very few of the precepts dating from the 1960 Compilation (which was reformed in 1984 in order to adapt it to the constitutional principles, and which has been the object of successive modifications) remain in force today.

Nowadays, modern codification makes sense from the perspective from which Quebec has carried it out (or other European countries such as the Netherlands) for the second time. This is the same as saying that, at least in theory, codification should not be viewed simply as a way of presenting the law. Codification must above all be a process of reform. This affirmation ties in with a more general theme, namely the function of codes in modern-day society. On the other hand, it is an affirmation that attempts to set itself apart from the French codification movement, the so-called codification 'à droit constant', where the purpose is to take 'le droit tel qu'il est, sans volonté de reforme'.[53] It is, therefore, an approach that entails the risk of inflating partial codes, since the reduction, simplification and reformulation of law is strange to this type of codification.[54] It should be noted that, unlike any of the countries mentioned earlier, civil legislation in Catalonia has not been as abundant, firstly because the competence in private law is not as broad, and secondly because the vacillating decisions handed down by the Constitutional Court with regard to the extent of competence have generated an excessive prudence on the part of legislators. This means that the main purpose of codification is not to provide order in a setting of legal chaos, because – at least until now – such chaos does not exist. In Catalonia, codification has always been guided by another consideration, namely to avoid the invasion of the Spanish Civil Code (at present, see Preamble I, 3 Act 40/1991, *Codi de Successions per causa de mort en el dret civil de Catalunya* (CS)), in the same way that in Quebec, the goal was to avoid the application of English common law.

Codification: a political option

Codification is a political option. Traditionally, in Catalonia, the proposal to codify law has been, to a large extent, a manifestation of the rejection felt

---

[52] See *Diari de Sessions del Parlament de Catalunya*, 30 June 1998, Series P., no. 85, 5887 in which the Justice Chancellery announced a completion date of 2001. A few years later, the councillor herself provided another, more realistic date: 2003. However, as mentioned above, the idea of partial codification has been rejected, and now a general civil code for Catalonia is planned, although no schedule has yet been set.

[53] See nn. 6 and 7 above.   [54] Oppetit, 'L'Avenir', pp. 78–9, 81.

by the Catalans towards the imposition, from the Madrid government, of a Catalan appendix to the Spanish Civil Code, considered to be a common law.[55] In addition, the code has always been viewed as a useful tool to halt the expansion of the unifying jurisprudence of the *Tribunal Supremo*. Indeed, the indiscriminate application of the Spanish Civil Code in matters where it was not applicable even as subsidiary law completely undermined Catalan law.[56]

The latter conception subsists to this day (Preamble CS, I, 2). Now if the purpose is to allay the application of the Spanish Civil Code in Catalonia, the exercising of competence seems rather more important than the technique used. The aspiration of having a civil code has been a far-reaching claim in a context in which the subsistence of local laws was a mere concession of the (sole) political power. But after achieving autonomy – and therefore, at a time when it is possible to choose between one formula and another – one must ask oneself what has prompted legislators to opt for a code rather than a compilation. Even further, the question of why the line of special reform and development Acts is not maintained should be asked. Indeed, what makes one think that codification is the best system available? Is not the codification ideology a thing of the past?

It can be argued against compilation that it is a consolidation of the past, and is therefore an attack on the evolution of law.[57] Moreover, compilation was an imposition from the central government, and in any case, the law being compiled is nothing more than a catalogue of isolated institutions. A compilation, like an appendix, represents the denial of Catalan civil law as a whole and of its systematic nature, because it is drafted with one eye on a general civil code that is applicable to all of Spain.

The debate should thus focus on the benefits and drawbacks of special statutes or a code. Both techniques look forward – that is, they allow for the

[55] Joan Maluquer Viladot, 'El procés del nostre dret des del congrés català de jurisconsults del 1881 fins a l'Estatut i la Comissió Jurídica Assesora', in *Conferències sobre l'Estatut de Catalunya* (Barcelona, 1933), p. 272. The system of appendices only permitted the subsistence of specific institutions, and not that of the whole system of law.

[56] Antoni M. Borrell i Soler, *El Còdic civil a Catalunya* (Barcelona, 1904). The problem of the imposition of Castilian law and its general principles over Catalan law is prior to the effect of the CC. See Esther Arroyo i Amayuelas, 'Vigència i aplicació del dret a Catalunya: la fixació del dret supletori per la jurisprudència del Tribunal Suprem en el període 1875–1889', (1998) 79 *Boletín del Centro de Estudios Hipotecarios de Catalunya* 360.

[57] Pau Salvador Coderch, 'El futur del Dret Civil Català', in *Simposi Dret Civil de Catalunya: XXV anys de la Compilació* (Barcelona, 1989), p. 124; Martin Vranken, *Fundamentals of European Civil Law* (Sydney, 1997), p. 36.

development of a new law. Which of the two should we choose? The argument against development through statutes is the danger that confusion and disorder could be generated by a multiplicity of regulations, perhaps with different and even contradictory principles (Preamble CS, I, 3). Furthermore, statutes, like the Compilation, only regulate specific institutions.

The choice in favour of the code – which is a law where the whole is more important than the parts that make it up[58] – leads us to ask ourselves first of all what law the legislators wish to codify, and second what the effect of codification is. Answering the last point implies considering codification as a technique for the planning of law, and, to a lesser extent, it also implies referring to the ideology that underlies the use of such a technique.

Consolidation or breaking off?

The question that we posed at first can also be formulated in another way, namely: how does codification affect the evolution of law?[59] Is it necessary to codify only what practice and case law have already consolidated? We have already seen that this is the solution chosen by Quebec in 1866.[60] Or perhaps it is necessary to go beyond this view and adopt new formulas? The new model followed in recodifying law in Quebec has resulted in a new Civil Code, and not simply in a renewed Civil Code.[61] In essence, these are the same terms of the discussion that confronted Thibaut (1772–1840) and Savigny (1779–1861).[62] Savigny only conceived the possibility of codifying law that had already been crystallised, once it had been interpreted by doctrine and the courts. This is tantamount to saying that codification is possible only when a strong corpus of doctrine and reiterated case law exists, and that in the meantime the solution is to cultivate the technique of statutes and leave the interpretation of law up to courts, which,

---

[58] Denis de Béchillon, 'L'Imaginaire d'un Code', (1998) *Droits* 178.

[59] In this respect, Gérard Cornu, 'Codification: valeurs et langages', in *Codification, valeurs et langages*, p. 34; Pio Caroni, 'Saggi sulla storia della codificacione', (1998), 51 *Quaderni fiorentini: Per la storia del pensiero giuridico moderno* 189–99; Timsit, 'La Codification', p. 83.

[60] Cornu, 'Codification: valeurs et langages', pp. 34–5.

[61] Jean-François Niort, 'Le Nouveau Code Civil du Quebec et la théorie de la codification: une perspective française', (1996) 24 *Droits* 137, although to some the reform was not as far-reaching as needed. For one view of the matter, see Jean-François Niort, 'Le Code civil face aux défix de la société moderne: une perspective comparative entre la révision française de 1904 et le nouveau *Code civil du Quebec* de 1994', (1994) 39 *McGill LJ* 868–9; brief, Blouin, 'Le Nouveau Code Civil', p. 169.

[62] Alfred Dufour, 'L'Idée de codification et sa critique dans la pensée juridique allemande des XVIIIe–XIXe siècles', (1996) 24 *Droits* 50–7.

in turn, would require having judges who did not mechanically apply law in a standardised fashion. The time for codification would arrive only when juridical praxis was sufficiently consolidated, so that behind the code one could read the legal history of the country. It is a line of thought followed by most codifications in the nineteenth century, with the exception of the French,[63] and which was also followed by Catalan legislators in the Second Republic, where codification was advisable only 'when the new definitions of Catalan law have been consecrated by experience'.[64]

In the task of accommodating legislation to the social reality of Catalonia, which began immediately following the reform of the Compilation in 1984, the philosophy behind the legislative work of the Catalan Parliament is to vindicate the role that Catalan civil law has played in the past through the updating and modernisation of its classic principles (Preamble CS I, 5 b and II, 1; Preamble CF, II, 2 and III, 28). This is highly reminiscent of the declaration that, following the same general outline, constituted one of the conclusions of the second Section of the *First Catalan Legal Congress*.[65] The section advised that civil law should be reformed by maintaining a prudent coordination and balance between two tendencies: the preservation of the spirit that had informed Catalan law throughout history, and its renovation or reform, done according to the current needs and convenience of all Catalans and adjusted to their habits and customs.[66] This meant the preservation of the regulation of the family patrimony, and the modernisation of certain aspects of the law of succession.[67]

Just as during the republican period,[68] today the path towards codification also requires the gradual enactment of statutes as a means of offering new technical means to solve the problems of society, with a view to their consolidation before proceeding to undertake definitive codification

---

[63] Merryman, *La tradición*, pp. 61–70.

[64] Words of one of the Ministers of Justice of the time, Pere Coromines. See *Diaris i Records, III: La República i la guerra civil* (Barcelona, 1975), p. 117.

[65] 'Orientació general sobre la reforma del dret civil català i conveniència o no d'una codificació immediata' (General orientation on the reform of Catalan civil law and the convenience – or not – of an immediate codification), *I Congrès Jurídic Català* (Barcelona, 1936).

[66] Encarna Roca Trias, 'La modernització del dret català: reflexions en torn a la reforma de la Compilació', (1985) *RJC* 589 and, referring to parliamentary discussions on the same issue, pp. 592 ff.

[67] Report of the second section, base 6, 14.

[68] Ramon Coll i Rodés, 'El dret civil a Catalunya. El problema de la codificació del dret català', in *Conferències sobre l'Estatut de Catalunya*, pp. 72, 74; Ramon Coll i Rodés, Bases 8 and 9, in *I Congrès Jurídic Català*, report of the second section, pp. 15–16.

(Preamble I, Act 10/1996, *d'Aliments entre parents* (of support between relatives) (LAEP); Preamble I, Act 12/1996, *de la Potestat del pare i de la mare* (of the parental authority) (LPPM); Preamble I, 8, Act 9/1998, *Codi de Família* (Family Code) (CF)). But, do we use the code to remake law, i.e. to modernise it and, above all, to simplify it? Or do we simply consolidate one or more parts of the law in the form of a code?[69] Unfortunately, despite the declaration of innovation (Preamble CF, II, 2 and 10 and III, 28; but only partial, Preamble CS, II, 1), the tendency is to do only the latter (Preamble CF I, 9 and 13; II, 1, 10, 12). The explanation lies in the fact that codification nurtures itself from statutes that have been approved very recently. Currently, Catalan legislation is developing practically at the same pace as the codification work[70] and, therefore, it is obvious that few changes can be expected, as it is not convenient to subject the citizens to very sudden legislative reforms. But if this is so, then technically perfect laws should be demanded. It is impossible to attribute to the code the mission of establishing a new civil order if the object of the consolidation is casuistic, poorly drafted regulations[71] which, in addition, are often incomplete at birth.[72]

The next patrimonial law code – and, at length, the general civil code of Catalonia, should be sensitive to all these issues. The modernisation of law implies the work of creating general parts, not only regulating specific institutions. As for the latter, it would be proper to eliminate those that are of no service (because maintaining them contributes to a loss of prestige) and, above all, to seek new applications for the others that can already be considered to be classics. In this sense, the example provided by Quebec law is paradigmatic, since it 'incorporates' the common law trust by promoting the notion of patrimonies by appropriation. Therefore, there is no need to force juridical concepts that are inherent to the civilian tradition, which

---

[69] They are different questions, as noted by Braibant, 'El modelo francés', p. 96.

[70] Paradigmatic examples include the LAEP and the LPPM, both passed only two years before the CF.

[71] In relation to the planned recodification in France, Philippe Rémy, 'La Recodification civile', (1997) 26 *Droits* 16.

[72] Act 39/1991, of Guardianship and Guardianship Institutions (LTIT) did not contemplate self-guardianship, although the institution was already recognised in Catalan legal tradition (art. 19 of the Draft Guardianship and Curatorship Bill, dating from the republican period, 18 July 1934). Significantly, it is introduced in the reform that took place by virtue of Act 11/1996 (art. 5 LTIT) and, being an incomplete reform (because it did not provide for the possibility that a person in anticipation of his incapacity could determine how care of himself was to be provided), the provision would be modified once again in its final draft (art. 172 CF).

means not having to resort to the theory of divided property, which serves as a basis for the trust (art. 1260 ff. CCQ).[73]

The effect of codification

Codification has a two-pronged effect: ideological and technical.

As for ideology, codification causes an effect of national reaffirmation.[74] In fact, this effect would result more from being a nation with its own civil law (although, in fact, most of Catalan law was European *ius commune*) than from the fact of having one's own civil code. But the code provides prestige.[75]

It is necessary to point out two aspects of the issues that have just been presented.

The vindication of Catalonia as a nation, and therefore the vindication of its legal tradition – that which indicates a certain way of being, of approaching and thinking law – is something that must remain entirely disconnected from the legitimacy provided by history (as a tool justifying law, according to Savigny's theory), since it no longer makes sense at a time when full legislative competence and legislature exist. History does not always serve to find answers to the problems posed by modern Catalan society. It is not incompatible to advance down the path towards codification and, at the same time, give up the 'essences' of Catalan law.[76] This does not necessarily mean that preservation, development or modification of law should always presuppose the abandonment of principles or classic institutions. There would be nothing wrong with keeping them alive if they continued to provide solutions that are fitting for today's problems. But their force would then arise from their ratification by the legislative power.

---

[73] Article 1260: 'La fiducie résulte d'un acte par lequel une personne, le constituant, transfère de son patrimoine à un autre patrimoine qu'il constitue, des biens qu'il affecte à une fin particulière et qu'un fiduciaire s'oblige, par le fait de son acceptation, à détenir et à administrer'. Jacques Beaulne, *Droit des fiducies* (Montreal, 1998); Madeleine Cantin Cumyn, 'La Fiducie en droit Quebecois, dans une perspective nord-américaine', in J. Herbots and D. Philippe (eds.), *Le Trust et la fiducie: Implications pratiques* (Brussels, 1997), p. 71; J. E. C. Brierley, 'Regards sur le droit des biens dans le nouveau Code civil du Quebec', (1995) 1 *RIDC* 42–9; Roderick A. Macdonald, 'Reconceiving the Symbols of Property: Universalities, Interests and other Heresies', (1994) 39 *McGill LJ* 769–60, 773–4, 781–3.

[74] Brierley, 'The Renewal', p. 496.

[75] Joan Egea Fernández, 'El Codi de Família: de la codificació sectorial al futur Codi Civil de Catalunya', (1998) *La Notaria* 18–19; Béchillon, 'L'Imaginaire', p. 178; Niort, 'Le Nouveau', p. 142.

[76] In this respect, Roca Trias, 'La modernització', pp. 585 ff.

The continuistic nature of our legislation is clearly manifest in the fact that codes do not repeal but simply 'replace' prior Catalan civil law (Preamble CS I, 3 and First Final Provision CS; Preamble CF, II, 1 and III, 28 and First Final Provision CS).[77] In Quebec, the CCQ final provision also refuses to break with the past. It is a desired effect, since many court decisions and opinions of doctrine have now found a definitive place in the articles of the Code.[78] But this is not the case in Catalonia. Here, the same *iuris continuatio* formula used in the Compilation (Second Final Provision), imposing interpretation according to Catalan legal tradition (art. 1.2 Compilation), is followed, as this was the incarnation of law that would later be reflected by the articles of the code. It was, thus, an outdated, fossilised law, since Philip IV deprived Catalonia of all regulatory powers in 1716.[79] The application of this same formula to the modern-day codes[80] fosters an interpretation of the new law in accordance with the old law and leaves aside the interpretation resulting from the new structure of the code. In addition, it is scarcely compatible with the purpose of completion of the codes (Preamble CS I, 3 and 5 *a*; Preamble CF, III, 27) because it implies that prior law subsists in all cases not regulated by the new codes.

The second issue refers to the prestige of the codes and their central role in the legal system of Catalonia. For the effect not to be merely psychological, it must be reinforced by the use made thereof by doctrine and courts.[81] Such use, hence, must break with the inertia of solving current litigation according to prior legal rules and not according to the internal logic of the code. Above all, such use must dispense with the systematic recourse to the precepts of the Spanish Civil Code when this is not applicable.[82] It is clear that this tendency, which breaks with unity and detracts from the systematic nature of the code, is propitiated by the fact that many of the new precepts

---

[77] According to Egea, 'El Codi', pp. 46–7, the terms are synonymous.

[78] Madeleine Cantin Cumyn, 'Le Recours à l'ancien Code pour interpréter le nouveau', in *Journées Maximilien-Caron*, p. 163; Jean-Louis Baudoin, 'Quelques perspectives historiques et politiques sur le processus de codification', in *Journées Maximilien-Caron*, pp. 18–19.

[79] Pablo Salvador Coderch, 'El derecho civil de Catalunya: Comentario al nuevo art. 1 de la Compilación catalana', in Pablo Salvador Coderch, *La Compilación y su historia* (Barcelona, 1985), pp. 370–8.

[80] As for its adoption due to political reasons, see Agustí M. Bassols Parés, *La col·lació en el Dret Civil de Catalunya* (Barcelona, 1997), p. 71. This provision is now repeated in art. 111–2.1 of Act 29/2002, with the same content.

[81] In this respect, Damaska, 'On circumstances', pp. 362–6.

[82] See Albert Lamarca Marquès, 'La prescripció de les accions que no tenen assenyalat un termini especial en el dret civil de Catalunya: la seva inaplicació', (1999) *RJC* 957.

are virtually word-for-word reproductions of the precepts contained in the Spanish Civil Code. This is obviously an attack on the proclaimed principle of a 'different society' which we are so fond of proclaiming (see Preamble 3 of the Act 13/1984 reforming the Compilation).

Technically, codification causes an effect of rationalisation, arrangement, simplification and stability of law, which naturally facilitates its application. The code provides an internal consistency that is not granted by statutes.[83] Nevertheless, the current codification by sectors and by stages hinders this consistency. Indeed, between one code and another (or between these and statutes) there are terminological and/or content-based maladjustments that pose enormous difficulties for the task of interpretation.[84] Reforms become incomplete as they lack a global view of the problems. Quebecois doctrine also denounced the lack of consistency of a policy based on legislating by stages.[85]

Codification requires the formulation of cases using open formulas that make it possible to advance solutions to future problems, that are permeable to the passage of time, and that allow the application of the abstract rule of law to specific cases.[86] In the Quebec Civil Code, title VII, *De l'administration du bien d'autrui* (artt. 1299–1370) is a good example of the expansive force of its precepts.[87]

It is not necessary to include everything in a code. Questions of detail, or which regulate problems that tend towards a rapid disappearance, should be regulated separately, in a separate statute. From this point of view, the code cannot entirely suppress legal particularities; if it did, then it could not consecrate general principles, or, in any case, these would be devoid of their immutable nature. But if special legislation does not pivot around the central idea of the code, and instead is constructed disregarding the code, then this would open up the way to a process of decodification. This is what has occurred, for instance, in the area of consumer law in most European legislations as well as in Quebec's. The solutions that are now being proposed are: either the removal from the civil code, whereupon

---

[83] Jean-Louis Baudoin, 'La Codification, mode dépassé de legislation?', in Association québécoise pour l'étude du droit (ed.), *XIe. Congress international de droit comparé* (29 August–4 September 1982; Caracas, 1982), pp. 4–9; Cornu, 'Codification', pp. 39–40.

[84] Egea, 'El Codi', p. 18.   [85] Crépeau, 'Les Lendemains'.

[86] Alain Bisson, 'Effet de codification et interprétation en droit civil québécois', (1986) 40 *RJPIC* 528; Bergel, 'Principal Features', p. 1083; Bassols, 'Vers la codificació', p. 396.

[87] Bisson, 'Dualité de systèmes', p. 48. For an in-depth study, Madeleine Cantin Cumyn, *De l'Administration des biens d'autrui* (Cowansville, 2002).

the code would be limited to standardising the contract leaving specific to statute, or the inclusion in the general part of contracts (which is still lacking a doctrinal construction in Catalan civil law) of the principles that regulate this matter. Not without great controversy, the Quebec Civil Code chose the former possibility (art. 1384).[88]

Conclusion

Codification of law in one of the federated provinces of Canada – Quebec – and codification of law in one of the autonomous communities of Spain – Catalonia – sheds light on the existence of a process of assessing national legal traditions, in relation to which the role of the codes, as symbolic instruments of different societies, doubtless helps to enhance the value of the realities that they represent. But it also shows that the codification process is not an anachronistic project, even though modern rules of law are more complex and society advances at a faster pace than a century ago. The process has not yet been completed in Catalonia, although the drive and political will to do so is not lacking. But it would be convenient not to hasten things. The code requires social consensus, and it must have the collaboration of those who are responsible for applying it. Clear guidelines must be set and followed, and the issues to be dealt with must also be clear. It is necessary to create expert committees so that everyone can be apprised of the work being done by others. And the results must be made public. Quebec's experience can serve as a model of comparative law and can help to establish the conditions needed to ensure the success of the endeavour.

[88] Critical, Pierre-Gabriel Jobin, 'Legislation: chronique de droit civil québécois', (1989) 4 *RTDC* 845.

14

The evolution of the Greek civil law: from its Roman–Byzantine origins to its contemporary European orientation

Brief presentation of the Greek civil law before the introduction of the Greek Civil Code (GCC) (in force since 23 February 1946)

The Greek revolution of 1821 against the Turks, after which the modern Greek state[1] was founded,[2] marks the beginning of a new era in the history of Greek law. On 1 January 1822, in Epidaurus (Peloponnese) the first revolutionary assembly adopted a liberal and democratic constitution modelled on the French Declaration of Human Rights.[3] This constitution as well as the second revolutionary constitution, adopted in Astros (Peloponnese) in 1823, designated 'the law of our ever-memorable Byzantine Emperors' as the main source of Greek civil law. In the third constitution, however, adopted in Troizena (Peloponnese) in 1827, a wish was expressed that all future codes should be based on French models. The influence of French doctrine and legislation in Greece may actually be traced to the years preceding the revolution, at a time when parts of the French commercial code of 1804 had been translated into Greek and were in use among Greek merchants, and to a Greek criminal code of 1823 based on that of France. In spite of the constitutional wish, the adoption of French models was confined to these two codes, and the Code Napoleon, though seriously considered, did not become a Greek civil code. Governor Capodistrias, the first governor

---

[1] For a summary general background of the country see Michael Stathopoulos, *Contract Law in Hellas* (The Hague, 1995), pp. 19, 20.

[2] Before this revolution, the Greek people had lived under Ottoman occupation for almost four centuries.

[3] Athanassios Yiannopoulos, 'Historical Development', in K. D. Kerameus and P. J. Kozyris (Eds.), *Introduction to Greek Law*, 2nd edn (Deventer, 1993), p. 7.

of the newly established Greek state, clearly disregarding the constitutional directive, designated the Byzantine laws[4] as the source of Greek civil law and in 1830 announced his plan for collecting and classifying them in an orderly fashion. This work was never accomplished.[5]

After Capodistrias' assassination in 1831, a period of anarchy and chaos followed and order was not re-established till the arrival of young King Otho in 1833.[6] Under King Otho four major codes (on civil procedure, on the organisation of justice, a penal code and a code of criminal procedure), based on French and Bavarian models, were drafted by the Bavarian lawyer G. L. Maurer, a member of the Regency Council. Maurer did not draft a civil code. An adherent of the historical school of jurisprudence, he believed that native institutions and ideas of law should prevail at least with regard to civil law, and, accordingly, started collecting local customs and current interpretations of Byzantine laws that were regarded as manifesting the spirit of the people. This project was interrupted by his dismissal from the Regency Council in 1835. Subsequently, a Royal Decree of 1835 declared that 'the civil laws of the Byzantine emperors contained in the *Hexabiblos* of Harmenopoulos[7] shall remain in force till the promulgation of the civil code whose drafting we have already ordered' and that 'customs, sanctioned by long and uninterrupted use or by judicial decisions, shall have the force of law wherever they prevail'. This Decree became the cornerstone in the edifice of civil law in Greece and profoundly influenced the path of the law during the next hundred years.[8] Perhaps because of inadequacies in Harmenopoulos' compilation, the scarcity of copies of the *Hexabiblos* and the increasing elaboration of Roman law by the Pandectists in Germany, the Greek courts adopted a broad interpretation of the decree. Thus the entire Byzantine legislation from Justinian's time up to the dissolution of the empire, contained not only in the *Hexabiblos* but in any collection, was reintroduced in modern Greece. For this purpose, the work of the German Pandectists was not only useful but almost necessary. And Greek

---

[4] Byzantine law, representing a fusion of Roman tradition, Christian ethics and Greek legal thought, exercised a deep influence on the legal system of most eastern European and Balkan countries (Yiannopoulos, 'Historical Development', p. 6, among others). For a bibliography on Byzantine and post-Byzantine law see ibid., p. 11.

[5] Ibid., p. 9.   [6] Ibid., p. 8.

[7] The *Hexabiblos* of Harmenopoulos, compiled by a local judge in Thessaloniki in 1345, was one of the last Byzantine collections.

[8] For a bibliography (in Greek) on the history of the law of the modern Greek state see Yiannopoulos, 'Historical Development', pp. 11, 12.

legal thought, which had been oriented almost exclusively towards France, became increasingly oriented towards Germany. Indeed, by the end of the nineteenth century the redaction of the German Civil Code (hereafter BGB) seemed to set a pattern for future codification. But at the same time the Greek jurists developed a more critical attitude and proceeded to new legislative efforts by evaluating achievements in western Continental countries.[9]

Pursuant to the decree of 1835, a committee was appointed to draft a new civil code. Although the final objective of the committee was not realised, its preparatory work resulted in important legislation in the field of civil law, including a comprehensive statute entitled Civil Law in 1856. A draft civil code of 1874, based on French, Italian and Saxon models, was not adopted. In the meanwhile, Greek legislation had been introduced in 1866 into the Ionian islands; later, in 1882, into the newly liberated provinces of Thessaly and Epirus; and in 1914, into the islands of the Aegean, Crete and Macedonia. However, special provision was made regarding the Ionian Civil Code of 1841, the Civil Code of Samos of 1899, the Civil Code of Crete of 1904 and the Code of Civil Procedure of Crete of 1880, which were allowed to remain in force. This situation gave rise to a conflict of local laws and increased the urge for a new civil code that would apply throughout the state.[10]

After another attempt at codification failed in 1922, a new five-member committee was appointed to the task in 1930. This committee published a series of drafts up to 1937, and in the following year professor G. Balis of Athens University was appointed to coordinate these. His project was successful and resulted in the passage of the Civil Code of 1940.[11] The backbone of this code was Byzantine law, the national Greek tradition dressed in modern clothes. Far from being a revolutionary codification, it reproduced to a large extent law that was already in force, developed by judicial decisions and scholarly elaboration. The comparative method was also widely used, and an attempt was made to modernise and systematise the law by employing legislative techniques tested in other modern Continental codes.[12] The 1940 Code was scheduled to become effective on 1 July 1941. By that time,

---

[9] Ibid., p. 9.   [10] Ibid., pp. 9, 10.

[11] For a detailed report on the drafting of the GCC, its contribution and its application see A. Gasis, 'The Drafting of the Civil Code' (in Greek), (1996) KritE 111–21.

[12] See A. Litzeropoulos, 'The First Ten Years of the Civil Code' (in Greek), (1956) 4 NoV 238, 239; G. Daskarolis, 'The First Ten Years of Application of the Civil Code' (in Greek), (1996) KritE 206.

however, Greece had been overrun by the Axis forces. After the liberation of the country a new committee was appointed to make a final revision of the Code, and a revised version was put into effect in 1945. Subsequently, this revision was repealed and the original 1940 Code given the force of law retroactively from 23 February 1946. By the introductory law of the Code, all local pre-existing codes and customs were abrogated. The Civil Code of 1940 (hereinafter GCC), along with other legislation, was introduced in the Dodekanese islands after their liberation in 1948.[13]

The Greek Civil Code, its inspiration from the other civil codes of western Europe, its main differences from the German Civil Code of 1901 and the innovations it brought

The GCC is divided into five books (General Principles, Law of Obligations, Property Law, Family Law and Law of Succession) and comprises 2,035 articles. In its first article, the GCC defines the sources of law; these are legislation and customs. The latter are today of extremely limited extent. As a third source of law, recognition is accorded by art. 28§1 of the Greek constitution of 1975 to 'the generally accepted rules of international law' and, of course, to those rules of Community law that have force directly in member states. By way of contrast, international treaties do not constitute a separate source, since these have force in the interior of the country by virtue of their ratification by a law. Nor does jurisprudence qualify as a source of law, according to the Greek legal system.[14] Nevertheless, judicial decisions together with legal writing (doctrine) are largely taken into consideration when 'interpreting' legislation or deciding a case.[15]

---

[13] Yiannopoulos, 'Historical Development', p. 10. For the civil law in Greece before the introduction of the GCC, the works that led to the GCC and its main features see, among the rich relevant bibliography (in Greek), P. Doris, *Introduction to the Civil Law* (Athens and Komotini, 1991), pp. 202–19; P. Doris, 'Historical Review – Contents – Basic Characteristics' (in Greek), in M. Stathopoulos and M. Avgoustianakis, *Introduction to the Civil Law* (Athens, 1992), pp. 109–25; A. Gasis, *General Principles of the Civil Law* (in Greek) (Athens, 1970), Introduction, pp. 9–45, A. Georgiadis, *General Principles of Civil Law*, 3rd edn (Athens and Komotini, 2002), pp. 69–81; N. Papantoniou, *General Principles of the Civil Law* (in Greek), 3rd edn (Athens, 1983), pp. 67–77; K. Simantiras, *General Principles of Civil Law* (in Greek), 4th edn (Athens and Komotini, 1988), § 2.

[14] See, among others, Stathopoulos, *Contract Law in Hellas*, p. 23.

[15] See, in English, Anastassia Grammatikaki-Alexiou, 'Sources and Materials', in Kerameus and Kozyris (eds.), *Introduction to Greek Law*, pp. 13–15, and in Greek, among others, M. Stathopoulos, 'The Application of the Civil Code during the First Fifty Years of its Force', (1996) *KritE* 135–45.

In the part of the GCC dealing with pecuniary relations, the model was primarily the BGB,[16] though the national (chiefly Byzantine, as previously mentioned) legal tradition was not ignored. The critique of the provisions of the BGB was also taken into account to some extent. A typical example of the national legal tradition in this part of civil law is the introduction on a wide scale of general clauses into the GCC, such as good faith, good morals etc., which are based on the principle of equity; they give the judge broader authorities when specifying their content using objective criteria,[17] and permit its modernisation.[18] Such general rules had long been a feature of Greek customs and they characterise the spirit of the GCC, as being basically *ius aequum* and not *ius strictum*.[19] Thus, in the GCC there exist explicit provisions on the civil protection of the personality (art. 57), on the prohibition of the abuse of a right (art. 281), on the possibility of dissolution or adjustment of a contract by reason of an unforeseen change in circumstances (art. 388) etc., provisions[20] which are not encountered in the BGB and which have been recognised in Germany subsequently only through court rulings.

A brief presentation of the said articles follows:

Protection of the personality (artt. 57–60)

After the Swiss Civil Code, the GCC was the first Continental civil code to recognise an all-inclusive, comprehensive right of personality of natural persons, and to accord it the protection of the civil law. This protection overlaps with, but also goes beyond, the protection of the criminal law, since it encompasses compensation for the victim. It also goes beyond the protection of constitutional law, which, strictly speaking, protects the person from the state rather than from private intrusion. The GCC deliberately does not define the exact perimeters of the concept of personality, thus

[16] For the influence of the BGB on the GCC see A. Georgiadis, 'Der Einfluss des deutschen BGB auf das griechische Zivilrecht', (2002) *AcP* 493.

[17] A. Georgiadis, 'The Contribution of the Civil Code to the Renewal of the Law' (in Greek), (1996) *KritE* 131.

[18] P. Zepos, 'Twenty Years of Civil Code: Achievements and Tendencies' (in Greek), (1966) *EEN* 319; Roi Pantelidou, 'Trivial and Notorious Provisions in our Civil Code' (in Greek), (1996) *KritE* 222.

[19] Stathopoulos, 'The Application of the Civil Code', p. 135; A. Georgiadis, 'The Civil Code Jubilee' (in Greek), (1996) *KritE* 161.

[20] A detailed analysis of these provisions can be found in the rich relevant literature (in Greek); a presentation of this literature, however, is not within the scope of the present chapter.

allowing expansion of the concept as the fabric and mores of society change. It is generally said that personality encompasses all the tangible and intangible elements that constitute one's physical, emotional, intellectual, moral and social existence.

The GCC grants a general action for the protection of one's personality against any 'unlawful' intrusion, invasion or infringement. The action is available even against a defendant who is not, or is incapable of being, at fault, and may result in a prohibitory or mandatory injunction. If at fault, the defendant may be forced to pay monetary compensation or make other reparation for moral damage (art. 59) and may be sued under general tort law for patrimonial damage. A similar action is available for the protection of the memory of a deceased person. Special protection is provided for a person's name by art. 58, which is interpreted to extend to juridical persons as well. Article 60 grants a general action for the protection of the products of one's intellect. This action has the same conditions and contents as the action for the protection of one's name. It is to be mentioned here, however, that, in addition to the GCC, rights of intellectual and industrial property are protected by a dense network of special statutes and international conventions signed and ratified by Greece.[21]

Prohibition of the abuse of right (art. 281)

Unlike the French, and like the German, Austrian and Swiss Civil Codes, the GCC has expressly codified the doctrine of abuse of rights, originally developed by the French courts in the middle of the nineteenth century. Article 281 provides that 'the exercise of a right is prohibited when it manifestly exceeds the limits dictated by good faith, or good morals, or the social or economic purpose of the right'. This formulation of the doctrine is broader than that of § 226 BGB (already expanded by German jurisprudence), which considers unlawful the exercise of a right when 'its purpose can only be to cause damage to another', and is more concrete and categorical than that of art. 2 of the Swiss Civil Code, which merely 'does not sanction the manifest abuse of rights'. A provision parallel to art. 281 of the GCC is now found in art. 25§3 of the Greek constitution of 1975, applicable apparently to matters of public law.

---

[21] Symeon Symeonides, 'The General Principles of the Civil Law', in Kerameus and Kozyris (eds.), *Introduction to Greek Law*, pp. 56, 57.

In order to be abusive, and thus prohibited under art. 281, the exercise of the right must 'manifestly' exceed the limits dictated by the deliberately vague concepts of good faith, good morals, or the social or economic purpose for which the right was granted in the first place. These limits are determined judicially on the basis of objective considerations. The personal motives of the obligee, although material, are not determinative. According to established jurisprudence, all private rights – patrimonial, extrapatrimonial or facultative – are subject to the limitations of art. 281, including rights derived from juridical acts or from rules of public order, and extending into areas outside the civil law. Article 281 is itself a rule of public order that cannot be derogated from by contrary agreement. It is disputed whether the abusive exercise of a right may be taken into account *ex officio* by the court, but it may be raised by the affected party at any stage of the proceedings, provided the supporting facts were pleaded timeously. The abusive exercise of a right is not merely 'not sanctioned', but is 'prohibited'. This means that if the abusive exercise of the right took the form of a juridical act, the act will be void. Otherwise, it may give rise to an action for injunction and potentially to a claim for compensation.[22]

Unforeseen change of circumstances (art. 388)

A contract, from the moment that it is concluded, is binding upon the contracting parties. The binding nature of contracts (*pacta sunt servanda*) is a basic principle of the GCC. Nevertheless, in certain cases this commitment may prove onerous and harsh for one of the parties, particularly if the circumstances that existed at the time of the conclusion of the contract have changed in such a way as to destroy the balance of the contract to the detriment of one of the parties. The GCC deals with this problem by an express provision – that of art. 388, which is one of the most basic and most forward-looking of those contained in the GCC. Starting out from the principle of the inviolability of contracts, the provision provides, on strict conditions, for the concession of this principle in recognising the possibility of a judicial dissolution or of revision of a reciprocal contract in the event of an unforeseen change in circumstances and of the upsetting of the balance between performance and counter-performance. The provision of art. 388 of the GCC is none other than a special expression of the principle

---

[22] Ibid., p. 60.

of good faith which is formulated generally as to the law of obligations in art. 288, which lays down that 'the debtor is obliged to effect the performance as good faith requires, after consideration also of common usage'. Without the introduction of art. 388, art. 288 could lead basically to similar solutions. Thus in Germany, where in absence of a provision corresponding to that of art. 388 of the GCC, para. 242 of the BGB (corresponding to art. 288 of the GCC) is invoked. Nevertheless, in practical terms, the adoption in the GCC of the special provision is useful, because it gives clearer and more particular expression to the will of the legislator in this connection. However, it has been accepted that when the conditions of art. 388 of the GCC are not met, the possibility of resort to art. 288 remains as an 'ultimum refugium'.[23]

In art. 388 of the GCC we have a combination of views and criteria drawn both from classic theories on the need for an equilibrium between performance and counter-performance (here of course in order to deal with the *ex post facto* upsetting of any initial balance) or on the *clausula rebus sic stantibus* (but on strict terms today), and more modern doctrines which have been developed internationally in the twentieth century, particularly the German doctrine of the collapse of the underlying basis of the transaction ('Wegfall der Geschaeftsgrundlage') and the French theory of the unforeseen circumstances ('théorie de l'imprévision'). The basic idea, however, which permeates the institution is that of *bona fides*.[24]

In the field of torts or unlawful acts we find a successful combination of the German model with its detailed enumeration of torts and of the French and Swiss model having only a general clause. The GCC, in the relevant chapter (artt. 914 ff.), has introduced two general clauses (art. 914: 'Whoever unlawfully and culpably provokes damages to somebody else is obliged to pay damages'; and art. 919: 'Whoever intentionally in a manner that violates the commands of good morals provokes damages to somebody else is obliged to pay damages') as well as an enumeration of unlawful acts. This system was familiar to the Greek jurists, as similar general clauses existed in the three above-mentioned regional codes (the Ionian Code, the Code of Samos and the Code of Crete). Also, the jurisprudence already existing before the introduction of the GCC was so vast that it was considered to have the function of a general clause.[25]

---

[23] Stathopoulos, *Contract Law in Hellas*, p. 192.   [24] Ibid., p. 193.

[25] Georgiadis, 'The Contribution of the Civil Code' pp. 126, 127.

As already mentioned, the GCC was also influenced by the Swiss Code of Obligations and (to a somewhat lesser extent) by the French Civil Code.[26] The substance of the artt. 947–1345 of the GCC, consisting of book III of the Civil Code dealing with property law, has been derived from the Romanist tradition – indigenous Greek variations developed in the nineteenth century, and from the modern (at the time) civil codes; the influence of the French, German and Swiss Civil Codes is particularly noticeable here.[27] In the part devoted to family law the decisive role was played by Greek traditions and the attitude of the Orthodox Church.[28] Until recently, the law prescribed different roles for each spouse and considered the husband as the head and main supporter of the family. But gradually traditional ideas changed and the role of the wife became important as well.[29] The Greek law of succession has its roots in ancient times, and several of its basic concepts, such as testate and intestate succession, legacy or the office of the executor of a will, are found in the Attic law of inheritance. Later developments mainly followed the destiny of Roman–Byzantine law in Greece. The GCC, with its arts. 1710–2035 of book V, improved the law of succession and modernised it considerably, introducing new institutions and concepts. Undoubtedly, it is the product of a comparative study of the then existing Greek law and other Continental laws of inheritance. Law 1329/1983, which has widely amended the family law, has brought a number of changes to the law of succession, which became necessary for the preservation of the systematic unity of the codified civil law. The task of the legislator in formulating the rules on succession is not easy. The continuation of economic life must not be interrupted by someone's death and the family must be protected. This calls for the reconciliation of various and frequently opposed interests: those of the deceased, his family and other relatives, the state and the creditors. These factors, combined with the pandectist influence, made the Greek law of succession highly technical, formal and detailed.[30]

---

[26] Stathopoulos, *Contract Law in Hellas*, p. 22.

[27] See P. Zepos, 'The New Greek Civil Code of 1946' (in Greek), in P. Zepos, *Greek Law* (Athens, 1949), p. 104. A. Yiannopoulos, 'Property', in Kerameus and Kozyris (eds.), *Introduction to Greek Law*, p. 121, in which also (in n. 1) there is a list of the standard works (in Greek) on the law of property.

[28] Stathopoulos, *Contract Law in Hellas*, p. 22.

[29] A. Grammatikaki-Alexiou, 'Family Law', in Kerameus and Kozyris (eds.), *Introduction to Greek Law*, p. 143.

[30] A. Grammatikaki-Alexiou, 'The Law of Succession', in Kerameus and Kozyris (eds.), *Introduction to Greek Law*, p. 161.

Amendments to the Greek Civil Code

The provisions on family law, contained in book IV of the GCC, have been largely amended and modernised with laws 1250/1982, which introduced civil marriage, and 1329/1983,[31] which amended or repealed most of the articles of family law in the light of our constitution of 1975. The latter explicitly declares (art. 4§2) that 'Greek men and women have equal rights and obligations'. In order to abide by this provision of the constitution our entire legislation had to be amended accordingly. In the area of family law a major reform took place and equal rights for the two sexes were introduced; the dowry was abolished; the husband ceased to be the head of the family, deciding on every matter arising in everyday life; the wife ceased changing her surname after marriage, and women now keep their maiden names; the spouses, before the marriage, can choose their children's surname, which can be either the father's or the mother's or both; paternal authority has been replaced by parental care[32] etc.

The revision of the family law has thus been extensive. The transformation reflects the impact of the changed social context on the law. Of the 364 articles in the book, 264 have been amended or repealed. After these changes, Greek family law presents certain basic characteristics which clearly show its constant progress, balanced between tradition and change. The mandatory character of most rules is an indication of the interests of society, represented by the state, in marriage and family. At the same time family law is liberal, marked by a considerable individualism. Consistent with the contemporary social trends is a tendency of radical renewal. This tendency is hard to reconcile with another characteristic, which has always dominated Greek family law: the strong influence of the Greek Orthodox Church, dating back to Byzantine times. Marriage impediments, the compulsory religious wedding service until 1982 and certain grounds for divorce are some of the most striking examples of the influence of the Church on the law. Today this influence has subsided considerably, but it still exists. It

---

[31] For a general bibliography, in Greek, on Greek family law, both after and before its reform see A. C. Papachristos, *A Manual of Family Law* (in Greek) (Athens and Komotini, 1998), pp. XIII, XIV.

[32] For a brief illustration (in English) of Greek family law before and after the 1982 and 1983 amendments see Eugenia Dacoronia, 'The Greek Family Law and the Principle of the Equality of the Two Sexes', in G. Levi (ed.), *The Marriage*, M. Rotondi: Inchieste di Diritto Comparato, no. 11, (Milan, 1998), pp. 231–9.

produced the main opposition to the establishment of civil marriage as the only legal form of contracting a marriage.[33]

The reform of Greek family law was continued with law 2447/1996[34] on the adoption of minors. According to the said law, the adoption of adults is an exception and applies only when the adopted adult is a child of the spouse of the person undertaking the adoption. The law also contains sections on guardianship of minors, when the parental authority does not exist or is inert; on foster families – that is, the undertaking of the actual care of a minor by third persons (foster parents); and on judicial assistance for persons of full age (not minors) when these persons are incapable of taking care of their personal or pecuniary affairs due to physical disability, mental or psychological disorders, or because they expose themselves or their close relatives to the danger of living in privation due to spendthriftiness, habitual drunkenness or chemical dependency. With the subsequent law 2521/1997 (art. 19) two important amendments to Greek family law took place. The first refers to the introduction of the possibility of contesting paternity by a third person, the man with whom the mother, separated from her husband, had a permanent relationship with sexual intercourse at the time of the child's conception; the second deals with adoption by spouses. In the case of adoption by spouses, only one of the spouses, not both, has to meet the requirements for the adoption to take place.

The reform of Greek family law was completed with law 3089/2002[35] on medically assisted human reproduction (artificial insemination), which has replaced artt. 1455–60 of the GCC. Apart from artificial insemination, this law also deals with issues of personal relationships and inheritance, as well as with some procedural issues related to the above. The main innovations of these new articles of the GCC are the following:

(1) Artificial insemination is permitted only during the reproductive years of the assisted person, and only in order to treat fertility problems naturally or to avoid the transmission of a severe genetic disease to the child; cloning and sex selection are prohibited (art. 1455).

---

[33] Grammatikaki-Alexiou, 'Family Law', pp. 143, 144.

[34] For an analysis (in Greek) of the provisions of Greek family law after law 2447/1996 see E. Kounougeri-Manoledaki, *Family Law* (in Greek), 2nd edn (Thessaloniki, 1998), and Papachristos, *A Manual of Family Law*.

[35] For an analysis of the new law 3089/2002 see E. Kounougeri-Manoledaki, *Artificial Insemination and Family Law* (in Greek) (Athens and Thessaloniki, 2003); and I. Spyridakis, *The New Regulation of Artificial Insemination and Personal Relationships* (in Greek) (Athens, 2003).

(2) Artificial insemination is available to non-married couples and to single women as well as to married couples (art. 1456 §1).

(3) The identity of the donor of the reproductive material is not disclosed to the persons wishing to have a child, and the identity of the child and its parents is not disclosed to the donor (art. 1460).

(4) *Post mortem* assisted reproduction and the transfer of fertilised ova from one woman to another are subject to strict conditions (artt. 1457, 1458).

The latest amendment of the GCC is law 3043/2002, on the liability of the seller for inherent defects of, or the lack of agreed qualities in, goods sold; it changes certain provisions of the Civil Procedure Code and other related provisions (in force since August 2002), and incorporates Directive 1999/44/EC of the European Parliament and of the Council on certain aspects of the sale of consumer goods and associated guarantees.[36] The Greek legislature considered[37] that the provisions of the said Directive on certain aspects of the sale of consumer goods could be generalised and, therefore, made applicable to the sale of any property, moveable and immoveable; so, instead of amending law 2251/1994 on consumer protection in the relevant matters, or introducing a new law, they chose to amend the GCC, in particular certain provisions of the chapter of sale, and also some articles related to the contract of lease and the contract for work. As to whether the reforms should be extensive, as in Germany, or limited, the Greek legislature opted[38] for minor reform, touching mainly on the provisions of the law of sale and in particular those on the liability of the seller for inherent defects and lack of agreed quality in the goods. The provisions of the general part of the law of obligations of the GCC on non-performance have not been touched. This is because it was thought that the Greek legal world would need time to accept radical changes to the Civil Code, and the short deadline for the incorporation of the Directive did not allow for such radical amendments. The only amendments to the general part of the law of obligations are those of artt. 332 and 334 §2, which have been replaced. In the new art. 332, which, as a rule, repeats the old wording of the article,

---

[36] For this reform see P. Filios, *Law of Obligations, Special Part* (in Greek), vol. I/I, 5th edn (Athens and Komotini, 2002), p. 36; P. Kornilakis, *Law of Obligations, Special Part*, vol. I (Athens and Thessaloniki, 2002), pp. 94–103, 218–319.

[37] See the Explanatory Note on the draft of law 3043/2002, ch. A, 3.

[38] See the Explanatory Note on the draft of law 3043/2002, ch. A, 4.

two more prohibitions of exemption clauses for slight negligence have been added, in order to increase protection of the weaker contracting party. For the same reason, under the new art. 334 §2 all exemption clauses, which are prohibited when the debtor acts in person, are also prohibited in the case of vicarious liability.

As mentioned above, law 3043/2002 mainly modifies the chapter of the GCC that regulates the contract of sale: artt. 534–7 and 540–61 regulating the liability of the seller for inherent defects and lack of agreed quality have been replaced and artt. 518 and 538 abolished, in a manner that reflects the philosophy of the incorporated directive. The new art. 554 has extended the prescription period for actions against the seller in such cases to two years for moveables and five years for immoveables.

This law has also amended artt. 689 and 690 in the chapter on the contract for work regulating the rights of the employer, so that the term *anastrofi* (cancellation of the contract) is replaced by the term *ypanachorissi* (rescission of the contract), which has also been used in the new art. 540, when describing one of the rights of the buyer. According to the Greek legislature,[39] *anastrofi* and *ypanachorissi* are synonymous; hence, 'cancellation of the contract' will in future be 'rescission of the contract', and where there is no contrary provision in artt. 540 ff., the general provisions of the law of rescission will additionally apply.

In the chapter regulating the contract of lease, art. 582 has been abolished.[40] This article prohibited the preclusion or limitation of the liability of the lessor for defects in the thing leased or lack of agreed qualities only where there was intentional (wilful) conduct on his part. The abolition of art. 582 brings the law of lease into conformity with the law of sale, where also the provisions of artt. 518 and 538, which prohibited an exemption clause for legal defects and defects of the thing, respectively, only when the vendor intentionally (wilfully) omitted mention of the defect, have been abolished. The said special provisions did not speak of gross negligence, as the general provision of art. 332 does. According to art. 332 exemption clauses are void when they preclude liability not only for intentional (wilful) conduct but also for gross negligence. This disharmony in the wording between the special provisions and the general provision had led to disputes,[41] which

---

[39] See the Explanatory Note on the draft of law 3043/2002, ch. A, 10.
[40] Consequently, in art. 583, the reference to art. 582 is deleted.
[41] For which see Stathopoulos, *Contract Law in Hellas*, p. 346.

will cease to exist, as now in both contracts, of sale of goods and of lease, the general provision of art. 332 will apply.

The Greek civil law at the beginning of the twenty-first century

At the beginning of the twenty-first century, the Greek civil law presents the following characteristics:

1. There is an increasing tendency to interpret the provisions of the GCC, the 'applied constitutional law in the field of regulation of private relations',[42] according to:
   a) the Greek constitution of 1975; and
   b) the provisions of Community law.
2. In parallel to the GCC a body of laws has been enacted:
   a) introducing new forms of modern contracts such as franchising, leasing, forfeiting, factoring etc.;[43] and
   b) incorporating European Union directives,[44] such as those for protection of the consumer, for the protection of the human being from the processing of personal data, for the protection of the environment, for the mass media[45] etc.

The role of the Greek constitution and of Community law in the interpretation of the GCC

The role of the Greek constitution

The respect and protection of the values that form the existence of the human being constitute the primary obligation of the Greek state

---

[42] As characteristically mentioned by P. Kargados, 'Fifty Years of Civil Code' (in Greek), (1996) *KritE* 179.

[43] See A. Georgiadis, *New Contractual Forms of Modern Economy* (in Greek) (Athens and Komotini, 1998).

[44] For the Greek civil laws that incorporate Community directives and the influence of European law on Greek civil law see Stathopoulos et al., *Community Civil Law I*; I. Karakostas, *Community Rules and National Civil Law* (in Greek) (Athens, 1997); Kalliopi Christakakou-Fotiadi, 'Der Einfluss des europaeischen Rechts auf das griechische Zivilrecht', (2000) 53 1 *RHDI* 277.

[45] For the mass media law in Greece see I. Karakostas, *Media Law* (Athens and Komotini, 1998) (in Greek). For the protection of the personality from radio and television commercials see A. Chiotellis, 'The Protection of Personality from Radio and Television Commercials' (in Greek), in M. Stathopoulos, A. Chiotellis and M. Avgoustianakis, *Community Civil Law I* (in Greek) (Athens and Komotini, 1995), pp. 20–38 (in Greek).

(art. 2§ 1 of the constitution), and the right for general and personal freedom is considered the 'main general fundamental right' (art. 5§ 1).[46] Another obligation of the Greek state is the protection of the natural and cultural environment (art. 24). Personality and environment form a unity, which means that every offence to the environment entails an offence to the value and the personality of the human being, the latter having the right to a healthy and viable environment. To the above three articles of the constitution corresponds the right of personality established by artt. 57–60 of the GCC.[47] These provisions of the GCC, as well as others thereof (such as artt. 281 on the abuse of rights, 914 and 919 on torts, 1003–5, 1027 and 1108 on ownership etc.), are interpreted in the light of the above articles of the constitution[48] – that is, they are interpreted in such a way that the personality of the human being and the environment are both respected as primary values.

This is an example of how the provisions of the constitution have an indirect effect on private law and apply to it through general clauses and provisions of the civil legislation.[49] This so-called 'interpretation of the law in conformity to or in harmony with the Constitution'[50] is a method of interpretation first developed in German law with a series of decisions of the Federal Constitutional Court, adopted by the French *Conseil Constitutionel*, and applied at a continuously increasing rate in Greece.[51]

---

[46] I. Karakostas, *Environmental Law* (in Greek) (Athens and Komotini, 2000), pp. 169, 170, in which also (nn. 80 and 81) there are more references regarding personality.
[47] I. Karakostas *Environment and Civil Law* (in Greek) (Athens and Komotini, 1986), p. 42.
[48] Ibid., p. 39.   [49] Ibid., pp. 38, 39.
[50] The term used by P. Dagtoglou, when translating the German term 'verfassungskonforme Gesetzesauslegung': see relatively his treatise *General Administrative Law* (in Greek), 4th rev. edn (Athens and Komotini, 1997), nos. 291–8, pp. 135–9. For this kind of systematic interpretation of the law see, among others, in the German literature, Karl Larenz, *Methodenlehre der Rechtswissenschaft*, 6th edn (Berlin, 1991), pp. 339–43; Friedrich Mueller, *Juristische Methodik*, 7th edn (Berlin, 1997), nos. 100–4, pp. 90–3; and in the Greek literature, apart from the Dagtoglou treatise already mentioned above, G. Kassimatis, 'Constitution and Ordinary Law' (in Greek), in *The Influence of the 1975 Constitution on the Private and Public Law*, Publications of the Greek Institute of International and Foreign Law No. 9 (Athens, 1976), pp. 130, 131; A. Gerontas, 'The Interpretation of the Law in Conformity to the Constitution and the Control of the Constitutionality of the Laws in Western Germany' (in Greek), (1982) 8 *Syntagma* 1; P. Doris, note under the decision of the Athens Court of Appeal (= EfAth) no. 6761/1984 (in Greek), (1984) *NoV* 1557–9; A. K. Papachristou, 'The Protection of the Personality and Article 299 of the Civil Code' (in Greek), (1981) 7 *Syntagma* 57; M. Stathopoulos, *Law of Obligations, General Part* (in Greek), 3rd edn (Athens and Komotini, 1998), pp. 9, 10.
[51] Georgiadis, *General Principles of Civil Law*, p. 69, with reference (n. 19) to the Greek jurisprudence that applies to the above method.

The provisions of Community law

As previously mentioned, the existence of a wide range of general clauses into the GCC, which are based on the principle of equity, is considered one of its main features. For the interpretation of these general clauses it is necessary to take into consideration the social, moral and economic notions and values of the society. Since joining the European Community, the social, moral and economic notions and values of Greek society have been influenced, at a constantly growing rate, by its notions and values, as they are expressed in Community law, even when the latter does not have immediate force in the internal law of Greece. For example, the notions of good faith, of public order, of good morals, of conventional mores, of the social or economic purpose of rights cannot be specified today without the principles of Community law,[52] as these are specified mainly by the European Court. Article 86 of the European Convention and other analogous provisions and principles of Community law give crucial criteria for the interpretation of artt. 178,[53] 281, 288 etc. of the GCC. That means that Community law has an indirect effect on Greek internal law.[54]

Incorporation of European Union directives

The directives for harmonisation issued up till now by the European Union do not seem to have a direct impact on the general principles of the civil laws of the member states, despite the fact that many directives regulate matters belonging to the law of obligations (contract law), such as for example the responsibility of the producer of defective products, doorstep sales, or contracts on organised travel. In general, it is to be noted that the European Union did not opt for the entire harmonisation of the civil laws of member states, not even for the entire harmonisation of their contract laws, but was content with a case-by-case handling of certain types of contracts belonging mainly to the area of specific contracts (a special part of the law of obligations),[55] avoiding the harmonisation of rules in the general part of the law of obligations.[56] Also, the interest of the European Union in the

---

[52] See also, from recent literature, ibid., pp. 65–7, 91, 92; A. Georgiadis, *Law of Obligations, General Part* (in Greek) (Athens, 1999), p. 8.

[53] Stating that 'juridical acts that are contrary to good morals (*boni mores*) are void'.

[54] M. Stathopoulos, 'Introduction' (in Greek), in Stathopoulos et al., *Community Civil Law I*, 11, 12; Karakostas, *Community Rules and National Civil Law*, p. 48.

[55] Cf. O. Remien, 'Illusion und Realität eines europäischen Privatrechts', (1992) *JZ* 278 ff.

[56] A. Georgiadis, 'The Harmonisation of Private Law in Europe' (in Greek), (1994) *NoV* 336.

harmonisation of property law – with the exception, perhaps, of the law of real securities of claims – of family law and of the law of succession is, justifiably, very limited to non-existent, as the corresponding provisions are not directly linked to the aims of the European Union (common market and free competition).[57]

As far as Greece is concerned, most of the directives regulating matters of civil law have become internal law.[58] Among the Greek laws that regulate civil matters and have a European origin can be specially mentioned – because of their importance – law 2251/1994 (regulating the responsibility for defective products,[59] protection against abusive clauses[60] and the protection of consumers in the case of door-to-door sales[61]) and law 2472/1997 (on the protection of the human being from the processing of data having a personal character). This European origin of regulations within the national law obliges the judge, when interpreting those regulations, to take into consideration the principles of European law according to which national laws of European origin are interpreted so that the aim of the Community regulations can be accomplished.[62]

Conclusion

It is known that different tendencies have developed regarding the need for and the extent of the harmonisation of private laws of the member states of the Community, ranging from the proposal for the creation of a codified common European private law[63] to acceptance of the attempts at harmonisation of certain provisions of the national private laws – and

---

[57] Ibid., p. 335.

[58] For a detailed list of these Community rules and the relative Greek Acts, by which they have been incorporated into the national law, see Karakostas, *Community Rules and National Civil Law*, pp. 26–34.

[59] For which see I. Karakostas, *The Responsibility of the Producer for Defective Products* (Athens and Komotini, 1995) (in Greek); I. Karakostas, *Consumer Protection* (in Greek) (Athens and Komotini, 1997).

[60] For which see M. Avgoustianakis, 'Contents of the Contract: Protection from Abusive Terms and Secondary Obligations' (in Greek), in Stathopoulos et al. *Community Civil Law I*, pp. 79–123.

[61] For which see Xeni Skorini-Paparrigopoulou, *The Protection of the Consumer in the Doorstep Sales Contract* (in Greek) (Athens, 1999).

[62] P. Dagtoglou, *European Community Law I* (in Greek) (Athens, 1985), pp. 94 ff.; Karakostas, *Community Rules and National Civil Law*, p. 37 and n. 23 therein for the relevant German literature.

[63] See *Official Journal of the European Communities* (1989), no. C 158, p. 400.

only to the extent that such harmonisation is obviously necessary for the operation of the European Union.[64] We are of the opinion that even after the much-desired unification of Europe, the existence of regional laws, which have long been known by the lawyers and courts of the region in which they are in force, is useful and contributes to the security of the law. Even more, if the said laws are interpreted under the scope of Community law, the need for unification will appear less urgent. In some fields especially, such as in the field of property law, family law and the law of inheritance, the different historical and legal tradition of each country belonging to the European Union has dictated a diversified legal status, which does not have to disappear for the sake of uniformity. After all, the unification of Europe does not mean changing the identity of the nations that form it.

In any case, as Apostolos Georgiades, Professor of Civil Law and member of the Greek Academy, states:

> unification of the private laws of the European countries, even if it seems attractive as a vision, is not easily attainable. It presupposes a long and titanic attempt at compromise of national concepts on different problems of private law. It also presupposes that the jurists of each European country manage to go beyond the guidelines of the jurisprudence of each member state, which is the result of processing legal notions and provisions of private law for decades.[65] What is plausible, however, and also inevitable, is the gradual and continuous convergence of the private laws of Europe towards each other.[66]

In this regard, we share the opinion of Michael Stathopoulos, Professor of Civil Law at the University of Athens and ex-Minister of Justice, that a European code of contract law, which would unify the basic rules of this branch of the law, is worth promoting and seems easy to realise.

---

[64] See mainly Christoph Hauschka, 'Grundprobleme der Privatrechtsfortbildung durch die Europaeische Wirtschaftsgemeinschaft', (1990) JZ 521 ff.; Bodo Boerner, 'Rechtsangleichung als Interessenangleichung – Die Wirtschafts- und Waehrungsunion', in Festschrift für Kegel, pp. 381 ff.; Rittner, 'Die wirtschaftliche Ordnung der EG und das Privatrecht', (1990) JZ 842; Georgiadis, 'The Harmonisation', p. 326.

[65] Georgiadis, 'The Harmonisation', p. 343.

[66] Ibid., p. 344; A. Georgiadis, General Principles of Civil Law, p. 93. See also Stathopoulos, 'Introduction', p. 26. From the most recent articles on the prospects of the civil law in the European Union see Ewoud Hondius, 'Finding the Law in a New Millennium: Prospects for the Development of Civil Law in the European Union', in Mélanges en l'honneur de Denis Tallon (Paris, 1999).

INDEX